STRANGE
Punks and Drunks and Flicks and Kicks
The Memoirs of **Richard Strange**

André Deutsch

This book is for Charlotte,
who has saved my life so many times.

First published in Great Britain in 2002 by
Andre Deutsch Limited
20 Mortimer Street
London W1T 3JW

ISBN 0 233 999 91 4

Cover design by Alison Tutton

Contents

Acknowledgements

Thanks to Charlotte,
Rene,
Geno,
Tom,
Louisa,
Brian Harding,
Vicki and Nona,
Brian Clarke,
Marek Pytel,
Jane Withers,
T.V. Smith,
Dominic Berning,
James Birch,
and Rose Dempsey,
for helping me to remember.

And to Betsy de Lotbiniere,
Cristina Zilkha,
Jane Withers,
Philip Gumuchdjian,
Ilaria Benucci,
Howell James,
David Coulter,
Bev Woodroffe,
Clare Conville,
Jonathan Goodman,
Lorna Russell
and Rosalind Beckman
for just helping.

The Fifties and Sixties

PRE-HISTORY

While there was no cast-iron genetic inevitability that I should end up scratching out a living from words and music, two names in my ancestry may have rattled a heavy hint down the hereditary chain to indicate the road my life might take. The first, and arguably the more celebrated of the two guilty forbears, was my great-great-uncle on my father's side, the improbably named Sir Arthur Quiller Couch.

Born in Bodmin in Cornwall in 1863, Quiller Couch is best known for compiling what was, for many years, the definitive English language poetry anthology, *The Oxford Book of English Verse*, the set book reviled by acned adolescent youths in bored classrooms the length and breadth of the Kingdom, indeed the Empire, as then was. In the preface he wrote: "The lyrical spirit is volatile and notoriously hard to bind with definitions; and seems to grow wilder with the years", and with the passing of time I have discovered the wisdom of those words. In addition to his academic work, Sir Arthur wrote a great deal of sprightly historical fiction, especially romantic adventure yarns with titles such as *The Splendid Spur, Dead Man's Rock* and *The Ship of Stars*. He also produced a staggering amount of journalism. He was deeply depressed by the death of his only son, Bevil, who had died of pneumonia shortly after the end of the First World War, and by the twenties he had all but finished with fiction. He lived out his days in Fowey, dying there in 1944 as the American army were preparing to embark from the harbour for the Normandy landings.

At exactly that same time, Stan Emeny, my mother's brother, was combining a war spent in the RAF with the career that he had followed before 1939: that of a musical entertainer. Uncle Stan was the only one of my direct forbears whom I am aware of who had dipped his toe into the muddy water of show business and decided to take a swim.

My uncle Stan was a quarter of the four-man, close-harmony singing group The Radio Revellers, whose popularity reached its height in the forties and fifties. Like the other group members, Art Reed, Al Fearnhead and Freddie Holmes, Stan had developed his musical talent by working through those quintessential English institutions, variety and music hall. The music was lightweight and innocent, but just a little bit *risqué*. The Radio Revellers toured the United Kingdom non-stop before and after the war, appearing at all the great concert halls along the way. Typically, they would appear on huge variety bills with the stalwart superstars of the day, including Arthur Askey, Tommy Trinder, The Crazy Gang and Tessie O'Shea. These travelling entertainment extravaganzas would play one-nighters at venues such as The London Palladium and The Glasgow Empire. They also starred in several musical films. They enjoyed a few hit records in those days of radio, and were never without a gig.

Their by-line was "Four Men, One Song" (or, as Stan rather cryptically paraphrased it for our childhood amusement, "Four Forks, One Prong") and they sang in a skilful, four-part harmony style, with the emphasis on comic songs and on-stage tomfoolery. In a review in the *Sunday Mirror* of a show they did at The Victoria Palace in April 1947, the reviewer gushed, "In the same way that Hollywood cashed in on The Inkspots, I'd like to see one of our film companies groom The Radio Revellers. As close-harmony comedians, they are slick, smart and as polished as a mahogany table." The *Musical Express* (before it was "*New*") were even more lavish in their praise: "The Radio Revellers, that brilliant vocal team which has risen to such phenomenal heights since its inception, actually stop the show. This act is on a par with any American product." In the early fifties, The Radio Revellers travelled to the US and performed at New York's Radio City Music Hall. Of the four, Stan was the most gifted at light comedy and, with his conventional good looks and an added talent for harmony whistling, he was something of a matinee idol.

By the early sixties, The Radio Revellers' innocent style of light entertainment was about to be rendered all but obsolete by the crashing waves of teenage hysteria, which greeted the arrival of the beat music boom. They had weathered both the skiffle storm and the rumblings of rock and roll coming from the other side of the Atlantic through the late fifties, but against Beatlemania they, like most of their generation, were completely lost. For the first time in history, the post-war British teenagers had spending power, and they were going to spend their pounds, shillings and pence on the music that belonged exclusively to them. And of course, the more that music made their parents howl in horror, disgust and disbelief, the better that music sounded.

The two guitars, bass and drums format sounded the clamorous death knell for close harmony whistling. I have an amusing cassette recording, however, which suggests that it was a close-run thing. It was given to me by my Auntie Else, Stan's wife, a ravishing German redhead, a sort of local Leni Riefenstahl, who never lost her caricature North German accent despite living in England for 50 years. She came across the tape while going through Stan's personal effects after he died. It contains a recording of a radio broadcast from the BBC Light Programme, the forerunner to wonderful Radio One. In this recording, a middle-aged English presenter pronounces himself sceptical about whether this phenomenon called Beatlemania really is sweeping the country as everyone says, or whether the whole thing is a myth. To get to the truth, a reporter is sent out to a number of provincial towns, microphone in hand, and presumably wearing the BBC uniform of the day – a belted gabardine mackintosh and trilby hat – to "ask the people". The highlight of the tape is when a middle-aged couple from Barnsley are asked, "Excuse Sir, I am from the BBC. Tell me, do the names John, George, Paul and Ringo mean anything to you?" They murmur apologetically, "Er, no, sorry". Then comes the follow-up: "And what about the names Stan, Art, Al and Freddie?" Without hesitation comes the reply, "Oh, aye. They're The Radio Revellers."

By the time I really got to know Stan, in my teens and early 20s, that whole world had changed. He was a genuinely amusing, genial, clubby sort of man, a 24-carat uncle, in fact. He had moved into business and enjoyed playing golf during his leisure time. He derived enormous pleasure from his memories and his moment of fame without bitterness, regret or neurosis. It was a lesson I should have learned.

GROWING UP IN SOUTH LONDON

Throughout the fifties and early sixties, my brother Brian (who was two and-a-half years older than me) and I did all the usual kid stuff together: fishing, train-spotting, stamp-collecting, apple-scrumping and knocking on neighbours' doors and running away. Although we were warned by our parents not to, we often played in bomb sites, those precarious, half-demolished houses that had taken a Second World War hit from the Luftwaffe, but hadn't yet been cleared. There were bomb sites all over South London and they made wonderful playgrounds for kids with imaginations, despite, or perhaps because of, the inherent dangers. Later, when we were older, Monopoly, Cluedo or Scrabble marathons at home would occupy us through the wettest, windiest and foggiest afternoons.

Our father, Robert, was a man whose life had no discernible joy. He was a conformist to the point of insanity. A product of the lower middle class, he was cursed with all the stifling small-mindedness and misplaced snobbery that characterises them. He was, however, only modestly aspirational, believing that forelock-tugging and arse-licking would ensure him the quiet life he craved. But he lacked the social graces even to be a competent arse-licker.

Mum had to put up with so much from that unreasonable, moody, ill-tempered man and, like many women of her generation, for whom divorce was never really an option, she gritted her teeth and bore it for the sake of the three children. She was working class. Her father had been a gilder until the war, and then washed up in a restaurant for the rest of his working life. Her mother, my favourite grandmother, who called everyone "mate" except her husband, whom she called "Pa", took in washing. Mum was not an educated woman, having left school in 1932 at the age of 14 to start work as a telephonist for the GEC (General Electric Company) in London's Kingsway. It was there that she met my father, a statistician in those days before calculators, computers and business modelling, and they were married for nearly 40 years. Although they bought the family house as a joint purchase, my Dad somehow managed to dupe her into having it registered solely in his name. As a consequence, she was totally reliant on him financially.

As well as a housewife and the mother of three children, Mum was also a skilled dressmaker, who worked every evening at her sewing machine at home to earn a few extra pounds for the family. She could make anything from loose upholstery covers to wedding dresses, and often worked well into the night to get something finished. Occasionally her patience would snap and she would dramatically fling a difficult skirt or jacket across the room, shouting, "bugger it!", only to retrieve it minutes later and persevere. She was an exceptionally placid, loving mother, who saw the funny side of all our scrapes and adventures, and bore her hardships with an exemplary stoicism and equilibrium. She was fiercely protective of her three sons and once, when Brian was being bullied by a school-gang, she pursued them over Tooting Bec Common and slapped the ringleader's face. She ended up in court for a breach of the peace but that boy never bullied Brian again.

Her singing often wafted in from the kitchen or while she was doing the housework, and her choice of songs always betrayed a wanderlust that she never really indulged. *AroundThe World* and *A Gypsy Am I* were favourites, as was the song with the lines "Lonely as a desert breeze, I may wander where I please." Hearing her sing those songs always sent me off into a reverie. Her greatest passion, though, was for the Hollywood movies of the thirties and forties, and she could always be relied upon to put the right name to the most half-remembered face.

Dad had suffered from mental illness all through my life, and had one of the first lobotomies in the UK. He was prone to epileptic-type fits and deep black depressions. Sometimes I would arrive home from school with a friend, expecting Dad to still be at work, only to find him perched high on top of one of the cupboards in the living room, his tie askew, a finger pressed to his lips and a look of terror in his eye, like some dumbstruck, demented, cornered bird. In all my life I probably only exchanged a thousand words of conversation with him. Years later, when I asked my eldest brother, John, what he remembered about the lobotomy, he told me that he remembered a man coming from the GEC to explain to Mum and him what the operation entailed. John, who was about eight at the time, asked the man, "What will it do to Dad?" and the man had replied, "It might make your dad a little bit kinder, John." In truth, it didn't. But it is difficult to imagine, in today's profit-obsessed times, any multinational corporation extending such patrician, pastoral care to the family of one of its more menial employees.

My father's operation was not one of the great success stories of pioneering surgery. The rows that flared between my father and mother, triggered by the most insignificant event, would sometimes rage into the night, long after we had gone to bed, and the sound of raised, angry voices and the occasional male hand slapping a female face, was often the only soundtrack in an otherwise silent house. My father would sulk for days, sometimes weeks, after one of these confrontations, and would apply reprisals when he felt aggrieved. For example, he would withhold Mum's housekeeping money for a week, forcing her to get by on what little she could earn from dressmaking to buy food for us. On another occasion, ranting like a wild beast after some perceived sleight, he removed every light bulb from its fitting and hid them, obliging us to sit in darkness for days as he seethed until his madness passed. There were many times when, if Mum had asked the three of us kids, "Shall we make a dash for it?" we would have unhesitatingly have said "yes". Now, in adulthood, I understand much better that Dad was sick but I find it hard to revise my opinion of him as a man.

We grew up in the South London backwater of Tooting Bec. On Saturdays, Brian and I would go to the Mayfair cinema for Saturday morning pictures. Two hours of *Don Winslow of the Navy* and *Captain Marvel*(Like *Superman*, but with a dodgy tailor), plus The Three Stooges, Laurel and Hardy and The Marx Brothers, and we would career out into

Tooting High Street, blinking into the daylight, on tenterhooks from excitement or literally aching from laughter.

We were by no means a religious family but, nonetheless, Brian and I were sent to the drab local Sunday School, but only in a desultory way, since neither of our parents were church-goers. It soon became clear that we had no real calling and the pre-Sunday lunch routine was allowed to lapse. Of much more interest were our weekly raids on the sweet shop, buying fruit salad and blackjack chews (four for a penny), flying saucers – which melted exquisitely on the tongue – liquorice bootlaces and pipes, sherbet fountains, sweet prawns, sweet tobacco, coconut ice, pineapple chunks and jamboree bags ("A bloody waste of money" was Dad's verdict, as we rummaged in the threepenny bags for a penny toy or a metal puzzle.)

For Christmas we received football boots and torches, scarves, comic book annuals and toy soldiers. Sometimes an Airfix model kit of an aeroplane (plastic for me, balsa wood for my more accomplished model-making older brothers). We gave socks, handkerchiefs, talcum powder, slippers and Wills Whiffs cigars, indiscriminately. The VP wine put in its annual appearance on the sideboard, alongside the sherry and a soda siphon, and a few small bottles of Watneys brown ale, but as my parents had no friends, only relations, and never touched a drop themselves from one Christmas to the next, it remained largely undrunk until the following year.

Occasionally, a much-loved uncle – either Stan or mum's other brother, Peter – would accompany the grandparents to our house for Christmas dinner, which was invariably the turkey distributed by the GEC to every married male employee. Dad would arrive home from work early on Christmas Eve, after the office party, the only day of the year when we ever saw him slightly the worse for wear, and ceremoniously divest himself of the 20-pound carcass. On Christmas Day, roast potatoes, Brussels sprouts and parsnips would accompany the bird, so enormous that we imagined it had spent the whole of its short life with its head in the sand. It would be followed by the pitch-black Christmas pudding, the colour of asphalt, which we had helped Mum to make back in the autumn, blanching almonds, de-stalking raisins and stirring, stirring, stirring. Dinner on Boxing Day would be a repeat performance with cold turkey, and would feature jacket potatoes, salad and onions pickled by Dad, his eyes stream-ing like Niagara, on a cold wet October evening.

Uncle Stan or Uncle Peter would tell a joke, wear a jaunty paper hat or play with us on the floor for half an hour, beneath the tree. We lived for the moments when these uncles would come and bring a touch of humour and levity into the fractious house. The toys, so gratefully received yesterday, would already be in need of repair or, worse, surreptitious disposal. It was the only time of the year we used "the other room", which was at the back of the house. The high-ceilinged room was on the rear corner of the Edwardian building that had suffered damage from a falling bomb in 1942, while my parents sheltered in the cellar during a daytime Luftwaffe air raid. The coal fire would smoke and grudgingly choke forth some warmth into that so-draughty room, but usually it required constant cajoling by Dad in the form of red-faced blowing at the embers, which would inevitably precipitate a coughing fit. It was also the only day of the year on which we were allowed to use the indoor lavatory, rather than brave the elements and slippery stairs that led down to the outdoor one. A true cause for celebration.

Mum and Grandma would always give the best presents, indulgent, impractical and fun, while Dad's typically tended toward the functional. Occasionally a pack of cards would be produced and an uncle would organise a game of Newmarket, with walnuts as the stake as Dad disapproved as much of gambling as he did of everything else. As the evening drew in we would read *The Beano* and *The Dandy* annuals for Dennis the Menace, The Bash Street Kids and Desperate Dan. When we were older, we read *The Lion* or *The Tiger* for Roy of the Rovers and Battler Brittan, or *The Guinness Book of Records* for no particular reason whatsoever. Sometimes, as a special treat, Mum would take us to a panto in the West End, or a seasonal film such as *A Christmas Carol*, and afterwards, excited beyond words in our short trousers, gabardine macs and scarves, she would walk us down to see the Christmas tree in Trafalgar Square and the lights in Regent Street, and we would be transported by the magical power of Christmas.

Left to our own devices in the school summer holidays, on a hot day Brian and I would pack sandwiches and head for the *faux* Mediterranean turquoise exoticism of The Tooting Bec Lido on the far side of the Common, and spend the whole day there. Sometimes we would pay the threepence entry fee, but it was always more fun to climb over the fence of the rear, grassed sunbathing enclosure and spend the threepence on a drink. Changing in the wooden cubicles that lined either side of the hundred-yard pool, we would hope to catch a glimpse, through a crack in the wall, of a naked woman changing in an adjacent cubicle. In the winter, we played football on the Common, with the other local kids. We would put two sweaters on the ground to make a goal, and play endless games of three-goals-and-in. We even thought about forming a team and playing in a league. The increasingly frequent arrival of the silver-haired Mr White, in his smart mackintosh, telling us about some boys clubs that he worked with in Surrey who would maybe agree to a fixture, increased our enthusiasm. As he stood next to me, nine years old or so, I had no idea that his behaviour was untoward when he slipped his hand down inside my football shorts and played with my cock – I imagined it was some sort of physiotherapy that they used in the higher echelons of the game. The fixtures never materialized and Mr White was seen off by some older, savvier boys, and I felt stupid for being so gullible.

Summer family holidays were usually spent in claustrophobic proximity in a caravan or chalet on the south coast and, later, in a small bed and breakfast establishment in Ilfracombe in North Devon. Every day, in good or bad weather, Dad would take us on a hike to some or other beauty spot where we would have a picnic, and swim or fish in the rock-pools if we were by the sea. The walks would sometimes be completely killing, up and down apparently vertical gradients in seemingly tropical heat. These walks were often partaken in mortifying, teeth-gritting, arse-clenching silence, particularly if Mum and Dad had had a row the night before. It was like taking a walk with death. On rare occasions we would be allowed the luxury of a bus for the return leg of the journey but, as often as not, we would complete the whole excursion on foot. I still remember every step of some of those route marches, with Dad striding off at the helm, windswept and oblivious, and the rest of us struggling to keep up.

Strangely, I remember those holidays with great affection, despite those awful atmospheres that built up like bad-weather fronts between my parents, with all their predictable and depressing frequency. The idea of the family going to a holiday camp, such as Butlin's, was never discussed, despite its economy. In a holiday camp we might have been forced to socialise with other people, a prospect that Dad could never have entertained. There was also a feeling that people who went to Butlin's were somehow beneath us. God knows why, or how.

At home we drank tea, not coffee. Lunch was referred to as "dinner", and dinner was "tea". Throughout my entire childhood we never once ate in a restaurant. We never once gave a dinner party and we never ate foreign food. My older brother John was the first of our family ever to set foot on foreign soil, on a school trip to France. Later, in the early sixties, he started work in the travel business and went to Spain and returned with such exotic souvenirs as a bullfight poster and a bottle of sherry. Neither of my parents had ever been out of the country. We lived, worked and holidayed in the post-war Britain of the fifties, and wondered why we could hardly breathe.

That same big beat boom that killed off The Radio Revellers, which to all intents and purposes actually started in January 1963 with the exhilarating, chiming opening bars of The Beatles' *Please Please Me*, and finished in 1967 with the ominous acid-drenched, foreboding piano chord of their *A Day in the Life*, provided the four-beat soundtrack to my adolescence. The Beatles, The Rolling Stones, The Kinks and The Who were my personal favourites from the British contingent, while the latest offerings from one of the black American sonic magicians of Tamla Motown or Stax, or from the crazed, stoned genius, Phil Spector, were awaited with an almost maniacal religious fervour. The Supremes, The Four Tops, The Miracles, Otis Redding, James Brown, The Ronettes and The Crystals were all held in the highest regard, and their records possessed an iconic power over me. Six shillings and eightpence would buy you a shiny new, seven-inch, 45rpm two-and-a-half minute masterpiece in those days. That's 33p in today's money. The only agony was the long deliberation on a Saturday morning in Tooting market over which one to buy. Whether to spend the pocket money on the Kinks' *You Really Got Me* or on The Who's *I Can't Explain*. Fortunately the obliging record shop owner would spin both, as we crammed ourselves into the honeycomb perforated listening booth and were transported, as if in a sound-proofed rocket ship, to ecstasy.

In 1963, I became aware of the irresistible attraction of sex. From the age of eight or nine I had always been able to get an erection at will. I remember the thrill of masturbation long before the drenching, proud surprise of my first pin-up-assisted orgasm, around the age of 12. It wasn't only Uncle Peter's airbrushed black and white dirty mags with enigmatic titles such as *Spick and Span* that got me going. Talk of death or religious ecstasy would provoke exactly the same physical reaction. In all the time that has elapsed since, sex has never, for one single day, lost its fascination, nor diminished in the daily demands it makes on me.

Like most kids of my age, my information about the act itself came piecemeal, and from an unlikely source – a court case involving John Profumo, a minister in Harold Macmillan's Conservative government who was accused of spying, and a couple of call-girls with whom he was associated. Their names, Christine Keeler and Mandy Rice-Davies, became synonymous with forbidden pleasures. The case had everything – men in power, espionage, the secret service, the Cold War connection, a half-comprehended conspiracy theory and sex, sex, sex. We devoured the salacious Sunday newspapers avidly to find details that we barely understood, but which sounded so illicit we thought they must be fantastic. It was the first time I had ever heard the term "sexual intercourse" – it certainly wasn't a phrase that cropped up at our breakfast table with any regularity. I remember the squirming embarrassment both of my parents and my brothers and I as we listened to the news together on the radio, and details of the case were coyly reported. It seems that I was not the only one to become aware of sex at that time. The British poet Philip Larkin wrote:

Sexual intercourse began
in nineteen sixty-three
(Which was rather late for me) –
Between the end of the Chatterley ban
And the Beatles' first LP.

Just as our brother John had done before us, Brian and I used the cellar of our family house for parties whenever our puritanical father would allow (or, slightly more risky, on those sadly rare occasions when we thought he was away for a couple of nights at a cricket umpires' conference). A burgundy-coloured Dansette record player would endlessly spin those recent vinyl purchases as we furtively drank cider by candlelight, struggled to look comfortable with cigarettes and hoped to get a snog or even a feel from one of the bee-hived girls we had somehow persuaded to join us. Fervent discussions would last way into the small hours (or what seemed to us to be the small hours – probably 10.30 or so) as to who wore the better jacket: Ray Davies or Brian Jones, or whether the pyrotechnic Keith Moon was a better drummer than the rock-steady Charlie Watts. When the cliché question, "Where were you when John F Kennedy was assassinated?" is asked, I remember vividly that we were in that cellar, furtively drinking cider and listening to the Ronettes and the Dave Clark Five's newest records. I remember, too, finding the assassination and the subsequent events that the media covered packed an enormously erotic charge, which was unleashed on my hormonally riotous psyche. The whole tragedy, and especially the role played by Jacqueline Kennedy, triggered in me a distinctly sexual thrill in the midst of the global mourning.

Early in 1964, The Beatles made their debut appearance on the hugely influential US prime-time TV programme, *The Ed Sullivan Show*, for CBS. They performed five songs live, and won over their host and the nation with their in-joking, surreal interview style. Prior to the Beatles there had been no real rebellious white pop stars – Elvis Presley had joined the Army, for God's sake! The Beatles were iconoclastic, witty and irreverent, and we loved them. On the back of *The Ed Sullivan Show* they became an overnight sensation in the USA. Not everyone was enthusiastic, however. The cantankerous American critic and lecturer William F Buckley Jnr wrote of the new phenomenon, "The Beatles are not merely awful . . . They are so unbelievably horrible, so appallingly unmusical, so dogmatically insensitive to the magic of the art, that they qualify as crowned heads of antimusic".

The only drawback to The Beatles' American popularity was that they consequently spent less time in the UK and, when they did play, the tickets for their concerts were made of "unobtainium". Occasionally, though, we would get to see our other idols playing live at a local dance hall or some other venue. The very first live rock gig I ever saw was The Kinks playing at the Streatham Ice Rink. We were given free tickets by a neighbour from the next street, the manager of the support band, James Fenda and the Vulcans, who played insipid cover versions of chart hits. It was the week that *You Really Got Me* went to number one (I guess that must have been in September 1964) and the place was jam-packed. A small stage had been set up on the ice and those who weren't skating watched from the galleries.

The excitement was overwhelming, the music louder and rawer than anything I had ever imagined, as Ray and Dave Davies waged all-out war for position on the stage, a fabulously physical battle of wills. The entire band was dressed in what had become their trademark hunting pink jackets, and they thrashed their way through great R'n'B classics, Chuck Berry tunes and Ray Davies' own compositions. It was impossible to pick out a single lyric from the aural onslaught. The volume increased with every number, and the primitive amplification equipment was at the point of meltdown. The atmosphere was like Jonestown. It was the first time in my 13 years that I had experienced hysteria, and it was how I had always imagined religious ecstasy to manifest itself. It was venal, erotic and primeval. We were transported. We would have died for that band that night. The subsequent development of all heavy rock stems, to my ear, from the majestic, distorted cacophony that The Kinks produced that night. The combination of the physical, the visual and the aural, and the relentless build-up of overhanging harmonics were irresistible. It was an unforgettable night.

Around that time I also remember seeing The Rolling Stones on a bill with the great American R'n'B legend, Bo Diddley, at the Tooting Granada, an extravagantly ornate 1930s rococo homage to the golden age of cinema. Bo Diddley was a magnificent, burly, black showman with square horn-rimmed spectacles, who played a square-shaped, cherry-red, Gibson electric guitar and patented one of the classic rock rhythms, "dum da-dum-dum, dum dum", which was eventually stolen by everyone from the Rolling Stones on *Not Fade Away* to George Michael on *Faith*. He was supported, as always, by his two faithful sidekicks – The Duchess and Jerome. They produced a thunderous, churning noise, driven by Diddley's guitar and the incessant rhythmic rattle of The Duchess's maracas. In those days of the package tour, it was possible to see three or four of our favourite groups on stage on the same bill at a local theatre or cinema.

There were a couple of smaller local venues where we would sometimes go to watch a live band. St Boniface Hall in Tooting Broadway was one attended toward cover bands playing the latest pop hits. The other, and the more sophisticated, was the Trinity Jazz Club near Wandsworth Common, where we regularly saw a blues band called The Downliners Sect. They were distinguished by a chap who wore a natty deerstalker cap onstage, and they played a furious version of Howlin' Wolf's *Smokestack Lightnin'* with a couple of frenzied instrumental crescendoes punctuating the vocals. We always knew there would be two of these crescendos but to amuse ourselves, after the first one we would ask our friend, the blues fanatic, Paul Ludlow, "Have they finished, Lud?" to which he would invariably reply, with his face fixed in concentration on the stage, and his spectacles slipping down his sweating nose, "No! They're going up again!" For some reason the weekly repetition of this exchange caused Brian and I unbounded amusement.

In the early sixties there were still a large number of cinemas all over South London. My first proper "date" with a girl was in 1964, when I arranged to meet Jill Watson, a junior school sweetheart, outside the bakery at the end of my road one evening at five o'clock. We walked to Balham, where the Ritz was showing *GI Blues,* Elvis Presley's first film since being de-mobbed, which featured classic songs like *Wooden Heart* and *Blue Suede Shoes.* Although the film was made in 1960, for some reason it didn't get to Balham until 1964. I remember how, pole-axed by shyness, I didn't exchange a single word with my date that entire evening, despite walking her all the way home to Streatham with a throbbing erection after the film. To avoid embarrassment I told my family I was going out with a school friend. Of course, they found out the truth before I was even home and I was ribbed mercilessly by my brothers. If I hadn't fancied the Elvis film, I could have sat in stony silence with the demure Miss Watson in one of eight other cinemas within a walk of my home: in Tooting there was the Mayfair, the Classic, the Vogue (which tended to specialise in a rather more *risqué* repertoire, featuring plunging décolletés and Hammer Horror) and the Granada. In Streatham there was the Astoria, the ABC and the Odeon, and in Balham one could luxuriate at the Ritz or the Rialto. Today not one of those palaces of dreams still functions as a cinema.

In retrospect, I cannot imagine that, in all history, there was ever a better time for a white, lower middle-class London kid to grow up than at exactly the early sixties. Perhaps we all think that about our youth, but I would take a lot of persuading that any other time was as golden and full of such promise. We hardly were aware, as 13 and 15 year-olds, of what was going on in the world outside. It barely registered, for example, that in July 1964, the US government agreed to send 5000 "military advisors" to a south-east Asian country we had barely heard of, called Vietnam. Or that in November 1964, Martin Luther King was jailed for civil rights actions in Florida. Or that in that same week Nelson Mandela was jailed for life for treason in South Africa by the heinous apartheid government.

Closer to home, we were aware of London's more eccentric political figures, from local no-hoper candidates such as the Communist, Joe Bent, to the steadfast Commander Bill Boakes of the Road Safety Party, who stood in every election I can remember in those early days, and always took a drubbing. Another figure of fun was Stanley Green, the passion protein man, who walked along Oxford Street in fair weather or foul, with his hand-written placard condemning the undesirable effect of "seven passion proteins" – fish, meat, bird, cheese, eggs, peas and beans, and nuts – and sitting on the male libido. In his peaked cap, National Health glasses, stiff-legged walk and monotone delivery, he was the butt of a thousand insults a day.

Since we didn't have a TV in our house, all our information came from the radio. It was permanently switched on in the corner of the room – a comforting, voluble presence in an otherwise silent house. To this day radio is my favourite broadcast medium, and it is the very first thing I put into a suitcase wherever I am travelling in the world. We used to love the popular radio comedies of the day: *Round the Horne*, *The Navy Lark* and *Hancock's Half Hour*. Sunday lunch was always roast meat and vegetables, the smell of the cooking emanating from the tiny kitchen for hours before the resulting meal was served. Dad carved the overcooked joint with a shaky hand and the meal was demolished to the sound of *Two-Way Family Favourites*, with its mysterious code of BFPOs and messages of "It won't be long till Christmas", and the raucous, but corny, accompaniment of *The Billy Cotton Bandshow*.

Sunday Night was our weekly bath night. As young children we had climbed into a galvanised zinc bath in front of the fire. The water was always either too hot or too cold, and the sound of the bath scraping against the cinders in the hearth never failed to set our teeth on edge. Later, when we had a bathroom installed upstairs, we would put three pennies in the gas meter slot for a bath and the same water would be used by all three of us. After the bath we would get a taste of how death must be, in the form of the anodyne, syrupy melancholy of *Sing Something Simple*, possibly the most depressing programme ever broadcast on radio. Just hearing the very first notes of the introductory music would plunge me into a feeling of deepest suicidal gloom.

Much more enjoyable were the radio plays, which would allow me to enter the strangest worlds and revel in my own imagination. As they say, only half-jokingly, the pictures are better on radio. When we did eventually get a television, it was a small black-and-white set that was prone to breaking down just prior to a favourite programme, and no amount of judicious thumping would bring it back to life. Alternatively, we would be obliged to watch while holding the aerial at an awkward, arm-numbing angle, presumably turned in the general direction of the Crystal Palace transmitter. Brian and I loved English cop series such as *Murder Bag* and *No Hiding Place*; later American imports *The Fugitive* and *Perry Mason*; or comedies like *I Love Lucy* and *Sgt. Bilko*. But mostly it is the innocent jingles from the early commercials that I remember, for instance "Murray Mints, Murray Mints, The too-good-to-hurry mints". If only I had remembered Tennyson and Catullus as well.

My eldest brother, John, was a war baby, older than Brian and I by some years, so while we were still pre-teens he had already commandeered the mahogany-stained family gramophone and filled the house with his music. The first wave was trad-jazz and New Orleans jazz on 78-rpm recordings – artists such as Louis Armstrong and Kid Ory, and then, a little later, came Elvis Presley, Bobby Darin, Johnny Ray, and Bill Haley on the new 45-rpm vinyl singles.

John followed the trad-jazz road that led, every Easter, to a Ban The Bomb march to or from the government research facility at Aldermaston in Berkshire, where white-haired stalwarts of protest such as Bertrand Russell, Michael Foot and Canon Collins would brave the English spring in mufflers and duffle coats and denounce the government of the day, while a gale blew their grey hair inside out. These same men were routinely pilloried by the press for being the "loony left" of the day, but the marches were always good-humoured affairs with the protesters accompanied by a handful of bobbies exchanging idle chit-chat with the cream of the British left-wing intelligentsia. A trad-jazz band always accompanied the marchers as they trudged into the, and I think that was what attracted John to these events, rather than any great political zeal. He, too, had a duffle coat, on the back of which he had daubed the Ban-the-Bomb logo (although we never used the word "logo" in our house, or any other word ending in a vowel for that matter. We mistrusted words that ended in vowels – they smacked too much of Johnny Foreigner in our little part of Little England).

However hard he tried to love the new artists who were beginning to break, John just couldn't find it in himself to surrender to their music, because it was *ours* – Brian's and mine. But, for the same reason, the bond that our music forged between Brian and I meant that we were close to inseparable for the whole of the sixties. He introduced the caught-in-the-throat poignancy of Dusty Springfield and the introspective existentialism of Scott Walker into the mix. And, perhaps most significantly of all, he turned me on to Bob Dylan, and the power of the pop-song lyric.

While I was soaking up all the fabulous music of the time, I was clocking on for school every morning at nine o'clock, making the two bus journeys it required getting from Tooting to Tulse Hill. Even though I had passed my 11-plus exam, and was entitled to go to the local grammar school, Battersea Grammar, which John had attended, I opted instead for Tulse Hill because Brian was already there. It could be seen as the earliest of countless instances throughout my life where my lack of judgement has ended up working to my advantage.

Tulse Hill School was a flagship comprehensive school, which opened in the late fifties. It was a massive, full-square, eight-storey, glass built structure, set in a couple of acres of green, more like the headquarters of a multinational corporation than a state school. It had four huge, well-equipped gymnasiums, a large outbuilding for woodwork and metalwork on site, and used sports pitches in Ewell, near Epsom, for games. We would be transported from the school in fleets of coaches for an afternoon of rugby, soccer or hockey in the winter, or cricket or athletics in the summer. Once a year, always in the middle of winter, in driving rain or blizzard, the entire school would participate in an eight-mile cross-country run in the Surrey countryside. That was the low-point of the entire sporting calendar, dreaded by all but the most committed masochist. It was the sponsor of a hundred sick-notes.

The headmaster had been deputy head at the nearby public school, Dulwich College, and consequently the school took many other features from the British public school system and transported them, with mixed success, to this inner-city, multicultural, single-sex, 2000-pupil Lambeth slum academy. We were taught Latin, for example, as 11-year-old first years. There was an army cadet corps, which we always thought of as a bit of a joke; mercifully, participation was not compulsory. Sport was highly competitive, and fixtures against other schools were played on Saturdays and occasionally midweek, too. Sporting tours to other counties and sometimes to other countries were arranged, as well as skiing trips, sailing courses and shooting competitions at the army ranges at Bisley. There was a school orchestra, which gave annual Christmas concerts at the Royal Festival Hall, and with 2000 or so sets of parents to dragoon into buying tickets, the concerts were always full. There was a drama group that put on modern and classic plays to an extraordinarily high standard. I joined up and loved every moment. We did productions of Pinter, Bond and Jarry.

Looking back now, I remember the school was pretty good, with some highly committed and motivated members of staff who really believed in the comprehensive system of mixed ability teaching. The philosophy was rather undermined by the streaming that started from the first year, but those of us who were lucky enough to be in the top sets were able to go as far as we wanted academically. The fact that two of the school's more celebrated old boys are Ken Livingstone, the left-wing firebrand who, in May 2000, became the first Mayor of London, and Linton Kwesi Johnson, the highly-regarded Caribbean writer, may give the misleading impression that it was a little like a Maoist training camp. That was not really the case, but it is true that the teachers who were on the political left fought a constant battle with the forces of conservatism and retrospection, with occasional but infrequent success. Exchanging reminiscences about the school with Ken Livingstone recently, I was genuinely surprised how different our memories of Tulse Hill School were. While I feel that my days there were generally enjoyable and at worst bearable, he found his whole time there insufferable. He truanted often and immersed himself in reading and writing to get himself through. He left in 1962, the year I started, so many of the teachers overlapped, but he was hard-pressed to find a single good word to say about it except "Good that it has now been demolished".

One of the greatest influences on my life from the age of about 14 to 18 was my English teacher and form tutor, Bev Woodroffe, a genuinely decent and inspired man who was both smart and sensitive. He was a man who loved his subject, and introduced me, when I was feeling the first piquant stirrings of a love of the arts, to so many ideas that were thrilling and new. His love and understanding of literature was such that he enthused me with the most unlikely mix of writing: not only to Chaucer and Shakespeare, for the purposes of the examination syllabus, but also to Pinter, Joyce, Beckett and Kerouac; not only to Wordsworth's *Prelude*, but also to the poetry of Dylan Thomas, R S Thomas, T S Eliot and Allen Ginsberg. Every time I showed an interest in a poet or a writer, he would fuel that interest with footnotes, anecdotes and suggestions for further reading and discovery.

Without question it was Mr. Woodroffe who first made me believe that one day I would either write or act, and then gave me the technical building blocks to do so. He bought tickets for the whole class to go and see the Harold Pinter play *The Homecoming* at The Aldwych Theatre just because one afternoon we had a good English lesson chatting about Pinter's *The Birthday Party*. It was the first time I had ever been to a West End theatre and I loved it. Michael Bryant starred with Pinter's wife, Vivien Merchant, and it was sublime. The next time he took us to the premiere of Tom Stoppard's *Rosencrantz and Guildenstern are Dead* but it bored me rigid because I didn't know *Hamlet*. (I now know *Hamlet* rather well, but *Rosencrantz and Guildenstern are Dead* still bores me —I have slept through two different stage versions and the filmed version.) Most memorably, in 1966, he arranged a trip to see Peter Brook's coruscating production of the Marat/Sade by Peter Weiss, or to give the play it its full title: *The Persecution and Assassination of Marat As Performed by The Inmates of The Asylum of Charenton Under the Direction of The Marquis de Sade*, which he warned us was unlike anything we had ever seen. The thrill of seeing that production was like catching a virus which has been with me for the rest of my life.

I didn't know as I walked into the theatre that night that I would walk out a lifelong devotee of the Theatre of Cruelty, but I do know that everyone I have ever met who has gone on to do something creative in their lives can point to an inspirational figure, a mentor, at school who showed them the way, or who lit the fire within them. Bev Woodroffe and all those like you – We salute you!

Between the years 1965 and 1967, my best friend and confidant was Joe Gilbert, a Tooting mod from the local grammar school. Joe was very sharp, very bright and very cool. We were both incredibly precocious, me at 14–15, Joe at 16–17, and we shared a common delight in discovering great writers, artists and films. In addition, we were both committed Francophiles, and we were on fire with a love of Camus and Sartre, Rimbaud and Apollinaire, Eluard, Bardot, Belmondo, Jean-Luc Godard and Françoise Hardy. In the school summer holidays of 1966 we travelled to Paris together, a sort of pilgrimage, and were totally inebriated as we drank up both the atmosphere of the city and the cheap red wine. Everything was new, exciting and sexy.

On a stroll along the Left Bank after visiting Notre Dame, we stumbled by chance on the legendary bohemian bookshop Shakespeare and Co. For us it was like Aladdin's Cave, The Library at Alexandria and the Ark of the Covenant rolled into one. Once over the unprepossessing threshold we were transported into another world. The interior defied all the rules of physics, containing infinitely more books on its precarious, rickety shelves than science would suggest possible. One tiny room led into another dusty alcove. We were in boho heaven as we devoured the stuff from those shelves that we had previously only vaguely heard of, or read about in obscure American literary magazines. We scoured the poetry section for Allen Ginsberg, Gregory Corso and Lawrence Ferlinghetti, and found them in vast quantities. The black-and-white covers of the City Lights imprint from San Francisco displayed the titles which became our prayer books such as Ginsberg's *Howl*, *Kaddish* and *Reality Sandwiches*. Its opening line – "I saw the best minds of my generation destroyed by madness" – grabbed me like a claw and I sat on one of the shop's battered old sofas and read the entire poem through for the first time. When I was I finished, I felt like someone had just passed a thousand volts through me.

We found to our delight that they had books with the distinctive olive green jackets of the Olympia Press whose cool black lettering always promised forbidden pleasures. We discovered John Dos Passos. Our excitement was unbridled as we found rare Henry Miller, Alex Trocchi, RD Laing and our personal Holy Grail – William Burroughs. They had *Junkie* and *The Naked Lunch* in the original versions.

I can honestly and unashamedly say that these books changed every idea I had ever had about literature, about politics and about the nature of authority and control. Joe and I became obsessed. We spoke to each other in Burroughsian sentences for the next two years: What's the Green Deal? What's with you – you wig already? Storm the Reality Studio, Retake the Universe! Word Falling . . . Image falling. . . . We were there, living at the very centre of those books, just as surely as if we had been named characters within them. We expanded our fantasies. To each other we became Rameses II and The High Priest of Ptah. We both had French girlfriends and fell hopelessly, dizzily in love.

The first great love of my life was a Parisian girl called Jacqueline. She was two years older than me, blonde, pouting, rebellious in a thrilling, dangerous way I had never known English girls to be, and sexy in a way that was beyond my wildest imaginings. When I was with her I felt that I had inherited all the worst aspects of my dad's personality. I felt lower middle class, uninformed, narrow-minded and boring. But she showed me the door marked "escape". Why she spent her time with me is, to this day, a mystery, for she was a goddess and I was a gauche 15-year-old. She didn't love me back, but it didn't really matter. I was just so thrilled and beguiled by her. I hung on to every word that dropped from her unutterably kissable lips as if it were from the Oracle. She had this accent, you see, and this look and this way, and at 15 I would honestly have died for her if she had asked it. She introduced me to jazz. To desire. And to drugs. I had my first puff on a joint with her and quite liked the sensation, but most of all I think I liked the *frisson* of excitement that I was actually "taking drugs". It seemed glamorous and exotic and interesting.

When it was time to return home, I swore undying love for her and promised I would be back as soon as I possibly could. She smiled indulgently, kissed me tenderly and said, "*oui*". But I knew it was already over for her. It wasn't until I was on the train that the tears, which I had so far held in check, started to fall uncontrollably, and between the sobs I was thinking that I had never felt so wounded – nor had I ever felt so alive. Every nerve in my body tingled, because I knew I had gone to Paris as one person and returned to London as another. And that the "me" I had left in Paris was now gone forever. My anticipation of what my new life might hold mingled with my love-sickness in a way that was overwhelmingly erotic. I ached in my groin from the taut excitement of the whole experience.

Fortunately, by late summer and autumn 1966 there was so much great music being made that the pain was soothed and gradually healed by the wonders of records of sublime and enduring quality. Records such as the blissful perfection of *Good Vibrations* by The Beach Boys; the dizzy raga-rock of *Eight Miles High* by The Byrds; the gender confusion of *I'm A Boy* by The Who; the quintessential English, gently satirical side-swipes of *Dedicated Follower Of Fashion* and *Sunny Afternoon* by The Kinks; the proto-psychedelia of *Shapes Of Things* by The Yardbirds; the majestic swagger of *Reach Out, I'll Be There* by The Four Tops; the organ-propelled, four-to-the floor *Gimme Some Lovin'* by The Spencer Davis Group; and The Rolling Stones' mutant masterpiece, *Have You Seen Your Mother, Baby, Standing In The Shadows?* were an unforgettable soundtrack to the latter half of 1966. These were in addition to essential albums like the Beatles best album by far – *Revolver*; The Beach Boys' *Pet Sounds* and Bob Dylan's greatest-ever recording – *Blonde On Blonde*. Records like those can help to get you through anything.

Oh, and the England soccer team won the World Cup final at Wembley, beating West Germany 4–2 in extra time.

I returned to Paris the following Easter, at the age of 16. A school friend had told me that his uncle had a petrol station in Paris where I would be able to work through the vacation to improve my French, and like a fool I believed him. When I arrived, I found that the address did not even exist. There was no uncle and there was no filling station. I called Jacqueline but she was rather cool on the telephone and I got the message. Eight months is an eternity in the life of a teenager and emotionally you move very quickly.

I had sort of prepared myself for the trip, so I decided to make the most of my stay and turn it into an adventure. I slipped myself into Parisian lowlife like it was a comfortable shoe. I slept under bridges and in disused cellars with beatniks, smoked inordinate amounts of dope, stole bread from bakers' delivery vans, and milk from outside shops. I would make a cup of coffee on the terrace of a café last three hours, and bum Gauloise cigarettes from young girls or appalled first-arrondisement dowagers. Then, at an opportune moment, I would race off, like a caffeine-fuelled whippet, into the warren of back streets without paying, scooping up and pocketing the tips left on an adjacent table for good measure. This was a high-risk strategy, as Parisian waiters, often so lethargic in their service, would be galvanised into becoming Olympic sprint champions in pursuit of a tip thief. Many times I received the hard slap around the face from such an escapade, but the danger only served to increase the thrill and the risk. When the weather changed for the worse, I went in search of a modicum of comfort and checked into the cheapest room in a grubby little hotel just behind Notre Dame.

One afternoon I met an American girl with a sort of Jean Seberg haircut, stumpy legs and full breasts. She was reading a book at a table in the café on the Gare St Lazare when I met her. I was on a Monet trip and wanted to see the station that he had painted so memorably. We got talking and she told me that her name was Karen, that she was 19, came from Minnesota and that she was studying art at the Ecole des Beaux Arts in Caen. She had a rucksack with her and when I asked her where she was going, she said "south". At first I thought she was catching a train, but then she said that she had just seen a friend off from the station, and was actually planning to hitchhike to Marseilles, down the RN7 which, after Route 66, was probably the most romantically-charged highway in the world. If things went to plan, she intended to then follow the coast eastwards, maybe as far as Genoa, over the Italian border. We talked a while longer and, since we got on pretty well, she invited me to join her. It was all I needed, so I agreed, hurried back to my hotel room to pick up my bag and checked out. Within two hours of meeting her we were on the road together, heading south.

For the first couple of days the journey was great, the lifts were coming and we got on pretty well. I was sexually totally inexperienced and couldn't believe my luck, travelling with this girl and fucking each night in a different hotel bed. I was not a particularly good-looking or charismatic kid, in fact, my too-big nose and crooked teeth were a real liability, so on-tap fucking seemed like the best thing in the world to me, and I was much more interested in seeing how often we could come in a day, than how far we could go. She started to resent my constant pawing, quite understandably in retrospect, and whined, "Cut it out. All you ever wanna do is make out." This was not far from the truth, but we came to an arrangement that we would only fuck at night, in bed, but then as often as I wanted until morning. I thought that on balance it was a pretty good deal and I agreed. It rather amused me to think that all the while my parents thought I was pumping gas at a schoolfriend's uncle's garage in Paris.

The rides started to dry up after four or five days, and I began to realise that it was unlikely that we would get as far as Marseilles, let alone further, before it was time to turn back and head for home. In Toulouse, after a long hot day without a single ride, and with funds dwindling, we decided to call a halt, to jump a train to Paris and hide in the lavatory for the duration of the journey so as to save the expense of a ticket.

The idea was good, but the reality was a disastrous farce. Since the cubicles were so small and so hot, and stank like a tiger's cage, we decided to hide in separate toilets and to meet up after the ticket inspectors had gone through the train. After the first stop at a station, the ticket inspectors boarded and started to check tickets. I heard them knock on the door to the toilet I was inside and, as I had not locked it, they half-heartedly pushed the door open while I held my breath inside, hugging the wall behind the door until I thought I heard their footsteps fade down the corridor. After a couple of minutes, sure that the coast was clear, I emerged from the fetid claustrophobia of my hiding-place and tapped on the door of the cubicle opposite, where I had left Karen. I hissed "Karen, come out. It's all clear. They've gone. We've done it!"

I heard the sound of the lavatory flush, the door opened and there, to my horror, stood a uniformed ticket inspector with a clipboard and leather shoulder bag. He eyed me suspiciously and, sensing my fear like a predator, demanded to see my ticket as he zipped up his fly. I fumbled around rather unconvincingly in my pocket, then admitted I didn't have one. He was delighted, his officious moustache bristled as he radioed a colleague and marched me off to the guard's van, clutching my sleeve with nicotine-stained fingers. He asked how much money I had; when I told him £23 he did some calculations and wrote me a ticket to the next station, Brive, which left me with about £15 to last me back to Paris. Minutes later Karen was frogmarched into the guard's van and I watched her suffer the same fate. As we were escorted off the train at Brive she was seething with rage, and I knew that our night-time sexual arrangement was over. It was the first time I'd ever heard the expression "You stoopid motherfucker".

Most of the long, hitchhiked journey back to Paris was undertaken in a sullen, taciturn sulk. Hours would pass without a single lift and we would scream insults at the drivers as the cars sped north with empty seats while we roasted under the midday sun. We slept in derelict farmhouses and once, because the night was so cold, we lit a small fire, which got out of control, and we had to evacuate the building as it filled with smoke. It took two-and-a-half days to get back to Paris, and we eventually arrived at about three in the morning, exhausted. Desperate to sleep, we found an apartment block with the entrance hallway door open. We entered, got into our sleeping bags and fell immediately into a deep sleep on the marble floor. What seemed like seconds later we were awoken by a ferocious, ranting concierge who threw a bucket of cold water over us and told us in no uncertain terms to make ourselves scarce. Dazed and soaked and bemused we made our way into the street like two bedraggled refugees and, as dawn was breaking in Paris, we parted forever.

Returning to London, I was immediately struck by the fact that there was something weird happening with the music charts. There were two very different and distinct audiences buying pop records. At the same time as the unmitigated pap of Engelbert Humperdinck's *Release Me*, Sandie Shaw's *Puppet On A String* and Frank and Nancy Sinatra's *Something Stupid* was tying up the top spots, a new music, an "underground" music, was starting to nibble into the charts, with records like Jimi Hendrix's *Purple Haze*, The Move's acid-fuelled *I Can Hear The Grass Grow* and the first record by Pink Floyd, the paean to the transvestite, *Arnold Layne*, all making their presence felt. That April the underground counter culture showed out in force for the first major London happening of the new alternative, the graphically-titled *14-hour Technicolor Dream* at the Alexander Palace in North London. It featured music, performance art (known at the time as "happenings") and film projections. Like the first raves of the eighties, it was a coming-together of a subculture that most adults hadn't known existed. And like rave culture, the media focused in on the drugs.

It was at this time that Mick Jagger and Keith Richards appeared in court following their *News of the World*-engineered bust; a few days later fellow Rolling Stone, Brian Jones, was arrested on drugs charges. Jagger, Richards, Jones, plus their acolytes, art dealer Robert Fraser and the singer Marianne Faithfull, were soon monopolising the front pages of the more salacious tabloids for weeks on end with prurient reports of naked girls in fur rugs. On 29 June, Jagger, Richards and Fraser were jailed, (later released on appeal) and on 1 July, newspaper editor William Rees-Mogg wrote himself into sixties cultural history when his famous Alexander Pope-inspired leader, "Who breaks a butterfly on a wheel", which protested at the heavy-handedness of the Establishment's response, appeared in *The Times*. The Establishment was rattled and angry by these perceived threats to the old order, and followed up their drug purges with the draconian closure of all the so-called "pirate" radio stations. The most influential were Radio London and Radio Caroline, which broadcast 24-hour pop music into Britain from offshore, in direct competition with the non-commercial BBC. The Establishment didn't quite seem to know what the youth of the country were up to – but they knew they didn't like it.

BEATS, BOHOS AND PSYCHEDELIA

The summer of 1967 was, for me, an epiphany. Those of us who had worshipped at the feet of The Beats, Kerouac, Ginsberg and Burroughs, were easy converts for the new breed of free-living, anti-establishment bohos, the hippies. The news of these rebellious, longhaired, drug-taking, apolitical kids in San Francisco, practising free love and pacifism and wearing flowers in their hair, travelled fast on the bush telegraph of TV, magazines and pop culture. Their greatest appeal for me was their avowed adherence to Gandhian principles of non-violence and their laid-back attitude to personal conduct. So long as you didn't hurt anyone else it was OK to "do your own thing, man". I was a pushover.

The new drug *de choix* was LSD, lysergic acid diethylamide, known to all with an assumed familiarity as "acid". We quickly heard about its unique characteristics, its ability to induce a six- to eight-hour long hallucinatory experience, full of insights, visions and personal revelation, where the sensual information was scrambled and re-routed so that you could smell sounds and taste colours – "the trip". As soon as we heard about it, we knew we wanted to try it. Of course our pop superstars were able to get their hands on the stuff long before we were, but the effect that it had on them was, to us, irresistible.

We watched our local heroes metamorphose before our eyes. The British bands who had been making the most interesting music in 1966, The Beatles, The Stones, The Who, The Yardbirds and The Small Faces, were transformed in 1967. The Beatles, who according to rock'n'roll legend may have dropped acid as early as 1965, shed their stiff, uptight, chrysalid suits, grew their hair much longer and became butterflies. The Stones, following the lead of their resident dandy and fashion leader, Brian Jones, started to wear silks, satins and velvets (with the notable exception of Charlie Watts, who always looked more comfortable in a sensible cardigan). The new buzzword was "psychedelic", which, we were told by those in the know, meant "mind-expanding". Originally used to describe drugs, its use was expanded first to describe a style of music, and then a style of dress. Thereafter it rapidly became a catch-all word to mean anything that was colourful, dissonant, dreamlike, surreal or in many instances just plain pretentious.

Great new music started to arrive on records imported from the USA at shops like One Stop in South Molton Street. For the first time, fabulously exotic sleeve art became *de rigeur* for all new albums, whereas hitherto a suitably moody group-shot would suffice. Groups were now called "bands", and outfits with ludicrous names such as Iron Butterfly, The Strawberry Alarm Clock and Fever Tree jockeyed for position in shop window displays with the first great albums of the psychedelic genre: Jimi Hendrix's debut album *Are You Experienced*; The Doors' first album, which contained both the exuberantly sexy *Light My Fire* and the dark, brooding, Oedipal *The End*; and Jefferson Airplane's *Surrealistic Pillow*, which featured the original acid-anthem, *White Rabbit*.

One of my greatest favourites was the less well-known Los Angeles band called Love, led by the enigmatic Arthur Lee. With the 1967 release of their third album, *Forever Changes*, they metamorphosed from being a jingle-jangle, Byrds-soundalike, with the sweetest harmonies, to being an audacious meltdown of Johnny Mathis, Mariachi and Methedrine. They sang songs with complex structures, original melodies and edgy, paranoid lyrics which sustained the promise of titles such as *A House Is Not A Motel*, *Alone Again Or* and *The Good-Humour Man – He Sees Everything Like This*. Rumours abounded about the band's extravagant drug habits, claiming that they were dangerous psychedelic psychopaths who had hung their roadie in a drug-fuelled ritualistic slaying, but no one was ever able to verify the story. Certainly after *Forever Changes* the band disintegrated and sadly their enormous promise was never fully realised.

The Brits answered back with some startlingly original new bands. The atmospheric, spaced-out freeform of Pink Floyd, featuring the dippy young genius Syd Barrett. The demented gothic theatricality of The Crazy World of Arthur Brown, with their use of fire, exotic costumes and an integral light show took pop somewhere it hadn't been before, as though someone had spiked Screamin' Jay Hawkins's joo-joo juice with acid. The William Burroughs-inspired Soft Machine made music that borrowed both from be-bop jazz and Edith Sitwell's lyrics for *Façade*, and mutated the result into something both cerebrally and physically stirring. On one occasion, like a distant echo of Erik Satie, they drove a motorbike onstage and miked up the engine noise as part of their set.

Every pop star whose career needed a boost jumped on to the psychedelic bandwagon. Old blues rockers such as Eric Burdon, (whose bizarre predilection for cracking eggs on to the bodies of the women he made love to allegedly inspired John Lennon's line, "I am the Eggman") Zoot Money and John Mayall all put on Indian kaftans and strings of beads, and started to use light shows and sing about dippy spirituality. Even those hoary old bruisers from Shepherds Bush, The Who, got in on the love-and-peace act.

Pop began calling itself "rock", and respectable arts journalists who should have known better started analysing every new record release as though it were Mozart. This only served to encourage the bands to ever-greater excess and self-indulgence. The Beatles released their epoch-defining concept album, *Sergeant Pepper's Lonely Hearts Club Band*, and the floodgates were open for every other band with a recording budget, a sitar and a string quartet to follow suit. Its sleeve art, featuring a rogue's gallery of the icons of the age – from Oscar Wilde to William Burroughs – was the first to employ a *real* artist (the British pop-artist Peter Blake) to create a record cover. Subsequently, everyone from Andy Warhol (The Rolling Stones' *Sticky Fingers*) to Julian Opie (Blur's *Greatest Hits*) has been pressed into service. The Rolling Stones, always the Beatles' rivals, tried to make their own *Sergeant Pepper* – the bizarre, murky *Their Satanic Majesties Request*. But despite its 3-D holographic sleeve and swampy musical doodlings, the drugs didn't work and the album became the first British acid casualty.

In my school holidays, excited by the hippy thing and wanting to be part of the scene, I started selling the London-based hippy newspapers, *Oz* and *International Times* on the street. I got to keep a few pence from each copy I sold but, more importantly, I got to hang out with cool people and had a perfect excuse for going up to the prettiest girls and starting a conversation. My favourite spot for selling the papers was Carnaby Street, which was at that point well past its mod sell-by date, but was re-inventing itself, along with Portobello Road and King's Road, as the grooviest street in London. Every shop got on the hippy trip, with florid, baroque clothes, posters of Hendrix, Dylan, Ginsberg and The Doors, and the incense and the music pulled in the punters from all over the world. It was as tacky as hell, but it had a gruesome charm similar to that of the British seaside. It was a commercial Gomorrah but for a while it became Mecca. Although selling the newspapers was only a holiday job, I was already starting to develop an independence and an entrepreneurial free spirit which only served to confirm my own suspicions that I would probably end up living my life on the edge of the mainstream, and that the alternative and the maverick would always seem to me more attractive than the orthodox and the journeyman.

London's psychedelic clubs in 1967 were stupendous palaces of sensory excess. UFO, a former Irish ballroom in Tottenham Court Road, was the best of the lot, the most psychedelic, with its black and day-glo decor, UV lighting and the all pervasive smell of incense and furtive dope-smoking, but the more whimsical Middle Earth in Covent Garden also had a beautiful vibe. The music in both places was more or less interchangeable – top live underground acts such as Pink Floyd, Tomorrow and Tyrannosaurus Rex, which featured another Tooting boy, Marc Bolan, plus the latest records imported from the USA. Entering one of these clubs was like entering a forbidden world. Each time I crossed the threshold of UFO, it felt as if I had left my parents' generation's values and cynicism behind. Of course, that feeling waned in time and I realised that the club scene was just another money-spinner. But for a while, for this 16-year old, the London club scene was pretty damned close to Nirvana.

August 2 1967 was our parents' silver wedding anniversary, and they went away to New York for a month to celebrate. Given my father's surly demeanour I can't imagine that the trip was an especially festive affair, although to this day my mother still rhapsodises about the night they spent in Greenwich Village. Left alone for the first time, Brian and I had the most fabulous August in London. It was hot, exciting and beautiful. We met Pete and Al, a couple of American draft dodgers on the run in Europe, and they came and stayed with us for the whole month. They were like the John the Baptist and the Jesus Christ of acid. These were the guys we had been waiting for. They turned us on for the first time with some acid they had brought with them from California and we had the most fantastic trip. It was funny, mellow and full of the most wonderful hallucinations. We did the usual stuff that everyone did on acid, listening to music, looking at paintings or just goofing around. It had none of the paranoia or the edginess that some later trips had. I could understand perfectly why people were speaking of it as a deeply spiritual drug and realised what a powerful tool it was for increasing self-awareness. I became an instant apostle.

A subsequent acid trip came to an abrupt and extremely disagreeable conclusion. One Sunday we were tripping at our friend John Skinner's house. Skinner was very groovy, a sort of Captain Trips figure who said the word "nice" a lot, which was a prerequisite in those days. He had a goatee beard and wire glasses, and had an ultra-violet light in his bedroom, that made the Hendrix posters on his walls look fabulously other-worldly. He *loved* to take drugs. Around midday his friend Dave Rivett dropped by and, seeing we were all out of our heads, offered to cook us Sunday lunch. Dave Rivett worked as an undertaker and was a bluff, thick-set fellow who would have been more impressive if his voice had not sounded like he had ingested an overdose of helium. He dressed in the morbid attire of his profession and had the appropriate lugubriousness, but Rivett was a major drug taker and prankster.

While we got deeper and deeper into our trips, Rivett beavered away in the kitchen, and after what must have been a couple of hours preparation he beat the gong and summoned us to the lunch table. He had set the table as if for a formal luncheon, with glassware and silverware gleaming, and white china plates decked with linen napkins. In the middle of the table sat a huge platter topped with a silver dome. Once we were seated, he poured wine into our glasses and with great ceremony whipped off the silver dome to reveal a contorted human hand, which he had roasted with potatoes and parsnips, sitting in the centre of the platter. It was cooked to a shrivelled, golden brown perfection, the skin like pork crackling or those wind-dried ducks you see hanging in restaurant windows in Chinatown. The fingers had curled up into a desperate grasp in the heat and it was surrounded on the plate by Brussels sprouts and the roasted root vegetables. We gazed in mute horror for an instant, thinking that we must be hallucinating. Then we all simultaneously recoiled as Rivett entreated us with his helium voice to "tuck in, boys." It was a monstrous prank, and it freaked us out completely. In retrospect I think I find it was the premeditation of the act that was the most gruesome aspect of the whole thing – the fact that he had arrived at Skinner's with the hand in his briefcase, the outrage already planned.

Many of my friends at this time gloried in extremely picaresque names. The role call was like the dramatis personae of a long-lost play by Damon Runyon. In addition to John Skinner and Dave Rivett, the Tooting contingent of fellow druggies comprised Snakey Morrison, Worm, Boring Jeff, Idle Jack, Dollar-Deal Dave, Little Fred and, for ease of identification, Big Fred, Richard The Cunt, Ugly Trevor, Tony (double-eff) Ffrench, Eamonn Burton, John Berry and The Red Brown. The girls included Christine The Man and Alsatian Annie, Vonny and T. Our main interests were drugs and rock and roll, with sex a long way down the list. Cannabis had become a staple and conversation was often replaced by extended bouts of giggling or introspection.

In addition to the hippy newspapers that I was selling in the daytime, in the evenings I started selling pen and ink cartoons of "Swinging London" from shop doorways around Leicester Square with a school friend, Keith Surridge. The cartoons were grotesquely exaggerated caricatures of typical London characters that were very popular with tourists. We didn't do the drawings ourselves, but bought xeroxed copies from the guy who did, a Scottish alcoholic called Bob. We bought them for a shilling (5p) each and sold them for five shillings. We quickly realised that if we xeroxed them ourselves, without him knowing, we could increase our profits even further. That is exactly what we did. We seemed to be making a fortune and we laughed ourselves senseless every night at the absurdity of what we were doing. Bob never could understand why the demand for his work tailed off so dramatically while our lifestyle seemed to be on a meteoric upward curve. Travelling home from one of these evenings I met the lovely Birgitte, a sulky Danish schoolgirl of the most exquisite frosted beauty, and for her entire two-week stay in London I wooed her with a potentially lethal mix of scrawny charm and hippy nonsense. To no avail. When she returned to Copenhagen I was heartbroken but swore that I would one day hunt her down and find her again.

In September 1967, my friend Joe Gilbert, who was a gifted painter, went up to Newcastle University to study fine art with Richard Hamilton. We wrote to each other two or three times a week, 20-page letters, covered with drawings, and raving about this or that new film, or poem or painter. We had discovered the artist, Francis Bacon, and made pilgrimages to the Tate to gaze at the great 1944 triptych, *Three Studies for Figures at the Base of a Crucifixion*. We also got hooked on pop art, particularly Warhol, Rauschenberg and Jasper Johns. We were especially mad for Andy Warhol and the films he made with Paul Morrissey – *Lonesome Cowboys* and *Chelsea Girls* were our favourites. During Joe's vacations, when he returned to London, we would hunt them down at all-night cinema clubs and smoke cigarettes throughout to stay awake.

When we heard that Warhol was working with a rock band called The Velvet Underground, and that Nico, our favourite actress in *Chelsea Girls,* was singing with them, we just *knew* that we were going to love them, but I really didn't know I would love them *quite* that much. Their masterful first album, *The Velvet Underground and Nico,* was released in the USA in March 1967 and in the UK in the following November, and from the gentle musical box introduction to *Sunday Morning* to the apocalyptic maelstrom of *European Son (to Delmore Schwarz)*, we were blown away. There is not a single bad track on the entire album, and the diversity of its stylistic and formal approach is still breathtaking even today. The fusion of the mainstream and the avant-garde has never been more seamless on a rock record, and Lou Reed's lyrics on that album were more influential than any song lyrics since Dylan. From the opiate rush of *Heroin* to the aching desolate beauty of *Femme Fatale*, it never once puts a foot wrong. Neither Lou Reed nor John Cale ever bettered it in 30 years of trying. Hearing it in 1967 was like having a red-hot poker inserted into one ear and then having it hammered into your cerebral cortex. It was a coruscating epiphany. Brian Eno once said, "Everyone who ever bought that album went out and started their own band," and it's probably true.

I have never absorbed so much information or so many influences, never been so stimulated or so inspired in my life as I was through those few years. Like many other kids I started writing poetry, angst-driven self-righteous rants against authority and hypocrisy, imbued with an indeterminate spirituality. I was trying on the words and the ideas for size, and the result was the usual confused and unfocused raw material of a kid my age.

Throughout the whole of 1968, I was studying for my A levels, in English, French and Art. School was pretty relaxed by now, and as long as you were working the teachers didn't harass you too much if you turned up with beads around your neck, or long hair, or shades. Brian and I developed a Friday night ritual whereby he would pick me up from school on his Lambretta motor scooter, we would buy a couple of bottles of a cough mixture called Dimaryl from the local pharmacy, drink one each and ride home. An hour later, after we had finished dinner, the effects of the morphine in the cough mixture would start to take hold, and we would spend the next five or six hours enjoying a mild hallucinatory state, giggling wildly as we listened to the Beatles' *White Album*, The Doors' *Strange Days* or Pink Floyd's *Saucerful of Secrets*. I fancied myself as a teenage Thomas de Quincey and started to dress as a fop. We followed that regime for about six months until no chemist in the whole of south London would sell us the fabulous linctus. The other drug of choice was Mandrax, a sleeping tablet which, if you fought the soporific effects, would make you feel very horny and very tactile, and make you talk the most appalling nonsense. It was a great drug to take, but a shocker to be on the receiving end of.

Hashish was still taboo in those days and I got into a lot of trouble at school when I stupidly gave a little bit of hash the size of a pea to a girlfriend in exchange for a blowjob. The next day the silly cow took it to school to show it off and promptly got busted. She told them the whole story and the next thing I knew was the rozzers were knocking at my front door and arresting me for supplying. It caused all manner of upsets at home, with my dad, totally out of character for a man who was in such thrall to figures of authority, attempting to bribe the rozzer who was nicking me. As he offered money in the hallway, in a very indiscreet way, the embarrassed copper said, "I think you had better put that away, sir, or I will have to arrest you, too." In the end I had to go to Croydon Court and was given a one-year conditional discharge. It shook me up quite a bit, I must admit, but didn't stop me smoking. It just made me more careful. Dad, curiously, never mentioned the incident again.

The teachers at school were great about my little spot of local difficulty. Those to whom I was closest were, for the most part, good liberals who thought it was only a matter of months before cannabis would be legalised. A couple of the teachers whom we knew to be gay, or "homo" as we then referred to them in those unenlightened times, said that it was just like the homophobic witch hunts of the late fifties. Thirty-three years later most good liberals I know are still saying it's only a matter of time before cannabis is legalised.

Through the summer holidays Brian and I were street trading again, this time with our own business, selling jewellery and badges and those cartoons of swinging London. For work, Brian wore what can only be described as a patchwork suit, which he fashioned himself from scraps of fabric. It was ridiculous but eye-catching. Brian was by now a tall, skinny, handsome kid with great cheek bones and a cool haircut, and I loved him. We were making what seemed to us like a fortune. Every morning we would load our display stands into a black cab and arrive at Carnaby Street by ten o'clock to start work. Earning money was not without risk. If we had been arrested the day before, we would go to Marlborough Street Magistrates Court first to face Mr St John Harmsworth or one of his colleagues on a charge of "Obstructing Her Majesty's Highway, contrary to section 121 of The Highways Act 1959". We always pleaded guilty and were fined a fiver and went straight out to work.

Working on Carnaby Street was fantastic for a 17-year old with a few quid in his pocket. We could afford to be ludicrously extravagant and wantonly wasteful. My confidence started to grow by the hour. We would meet new girls more or less every day and would lavish them with attention and gifts. Sometimes we would pop a few amphetamine pills and just talk the day away, and not even notice that we'd taken a couple of hundred quid. Picking up girls was the easiest thing in the world then, and we enjoyed it to the full.

The other great joy of the summer of 1968 was a series of free concerts in Hyde Park, featuring many of the bands whose music we most enjoyed. The concerts were blissful affairs, staged down by the Serpentine Lake. The sun always shone and the vibes were always great. The same team who organised the Hyde Park Concerts, Blackhill Enterprises, also organised some all-night concerts on Parliament Hill Fields, near Hampstead Heath.

One warm summer night there was a Pink Floyd all-nighter, and a bottle of acid-spiked lemonade was passed around the audience, and after an hour or so I started to get a bit edgy and wanted to leave. Brian was very protective towards me, his younger brother, and suggested we walk home to Tooting, through the middle of town, even though we were totally off our heads. It was the most bizarre walk I have ever had. Somewhere around Tottenham Court Road we got disorientated, and couldn't remember the way home. It seemed the most logical thing in the world to approach the shop window of Burton's, the tailors, and consult the dummies in the window for directions. In our hallucinatory state their arms started to whirr like helicopter rotor blades, finally coming to rest pointing us down Charing Cross Road. This was, indeed, the right direction. We thanked them and continued our journey.

In those days you could walk unchallenged right up to the door of 10, Downing Street, which we did on that occasion, at about three in the morning, and laughed at the symbolic lunacy of tripping while standing on the threshold of the nominal seat of political power that had forbidden us to get into that state. A bemused bobby stood guard as we giggled and staggered off. It was a strange sensation. As dawn broke, we were crossing Vauxhall Bridge, and all the street lighting was extinguished as we took our first step across the river. It seemed very meaningful. We kept saying to each other, "This is it! This is the trip!", as if the walk home from Hampstead was a great sort of personal odyssey for the two of us. We arrived in Tooting to catch Mum going off to work. We hit the sack for a couple of hours, got up, had breakfast and started a new day. The things you can do when you are young.

It was a strange time, because the world was really changing in a big way while we watched these bands. The Utopian ideal of the hippies, an egalitarian, anarchic world where everyone loved one another – referred to in the press as "flower power" – gave way to a more pragmatic political realism. The American involvement in the Vietnam War was a focus for the protest of kids all over the world. We marched on the US Embassy in Grosvenor Square and down Whitehall to Trafalgar Square, for huge demonstrations addressed by hippies who had already become politicised. People like Tariq Ali and Vanessa Redgrave gave rousing speeches for us to rally to. We became familiar for the first time with Alberto Korda's heroic photograph of the freedom fighter Che Guevara, the first rock star revolutionary, who had been murdered in the Bolivian jungle in October of the previous year, and was now revered as a saint-like martyr to the liberation struggle. The notion of feminism, or Women's Lib as the tabloids called it, was also starting to seep into the public consciousness. We felt like we were inventing everything anew. The protest movement, environmentalism, feminism, drugs, sex, The Media – my generation invented the lot. Or so we believed.

In May 1968, there was rioting in Paris, which came very close to revolution, with French workers, students and intellectuals forming a startlingly powerful alliance until, on 21 May, with Paris at a complete standstill, the full force of an angry French state was turned upon them with all the ferocity of a cornered animal. Since that glorious day the French Left has slipped into gradual but irreversible decline. French art has gone into a similar free-fall. No more Godard, Camus, Sartre or Truffaut, and since so art little of any substance comes out of Paris these days, it is no wonder that the Culture Minister's budget is spent elsewhere, to build fabulous museums, libraries and opera houses like magnificent, extravagant tombstones in a cultural graveyard.

At the end of the summer holidays we decided to drive to Copenhagen on Brian's scooter. We drove to Dover and crossed on the ferry to Ostend, then up through Belgium, Holland and Germany. It was a hellishly uncomfortable journey, sitting astride this snarling piece of metal, like some infernal mythological hornet crossing the Underworld, for the best part of three days, teeth gritted into the wind, sleeping rough and stopping only to eat or use a public toilet. The wretched scooter finally gave up the ghost about 10 miles outside Copenhagen. We had thrashed it so hard it had gone lame like a loyal but ageing cart-horse. We wheeled it to a ditch by the side of the road, pissed on it in a ceremonial valediction and travelled the last leg of the journey by bus. It was a less-than-glorious entry into the city. We spent our time in Copenhagen fooling around and dating girls. We loved it there and the living was easy.

Back in London it seemed to me that the gains in civil liberties that we had made in 1967 were lost again in 1968, as the British government cracked down hard on the protest movement. There was a massive police response to anti-Vietnam war demonstrations. This culminated in the bloodbath in Grosvenor Square on 17 March, when 100,000 protesters were involved in a pitched battle with the police using horses, dogs and tear gas. This episode, the likes of which had not been seen in London in my lifetime, inspired not just one, but two great rock songs: The Rolling Stones' *Street Fighting Man* and The Beatles' *Revolution*.

I took my A levels and left school in June 1969, having applied to university without telling my parents. I guess I knew what their reaction would be but I thought I would try it on anyway. I wrote to Brian, who was still in Copenhagen, three or four times a week, crazy letters ranting, fantasising and enthusing about new music or films or girls. In July 1969, I met an Anglo-Irish girl named Rene in Carnaby Street. She was street-selling a magazine called *Student*, which a pushy young guy called Richard Branson had just launched. We got chatting and we hit it off straight away. She was only 16 and still at school. She had long straight brunette hair, wore short straight skirts and National Health specs. I fell totally in love with her on the spot. I wrote to Brian that same night saying, rather presumptuously, "I have just met the girl I am going to marry." We didn't actually ever get round to marrying, but for the next 20 years Rene Eyre was my lover, my soul mate, my best friend, my supporter, my confidant, the mother of my son and my occasional emotional punch-bag.

We were devastated to hear on the radio news, one July morning, that Brian Jones, the most flamboyant, the most bohemian and by far the most glamorous of the Rolling Stones, had drowned in his own swimming pool in Gloucestershire. A few weeks previously, Jones had been unceremoniously dumped by the band because of his increasingly serious drug problems. Aside from the drugs sapping Jones's creative zest, his two earlier drug busts meant that his US visa had been revoked, and that consequently he would not be able to perform with the band in the USA in the foreseeable future. It struck me as an incredibly sad and lonely death at the time. It may be a cliché, but if ever anyone was a victim of his own success, it was Jones. He had had everything – success, wealth, admiration, talent and good looks, but none of those things were enough to save him from his own self-destructive streak. Before he died he had already written his own epitaph, "Please don't judge me too harshly."

Two days later, the Rolling Stones played a free concert (again promoted by Blackhill) in Hyde Park, and a massive crowd, 350,000 by some estimates, turned up. Rene and I got there at sunrise to stake out a good vantage point, and there were already over 50,000 kids milling around. We found a pretty good spot and just sat back and waited for the afternoon. We'd taken some speed the night before and were on a bit of a comedown, but the time passed agreeably enough as we lolled in the warm sunshine watching the endless parade of London's freaks arriving, like pilgrims to a shrine. For many there I think the event was as much a fan's way of paying their respects to Brian Jones as it was a live concert, and that impression was reinforced when Mick Jagger, in his white Ossie Clark dress, read a stanza from *Adonais*, the poem that Percy Bysshe Shelley wrote on the death of his dear friend, John Keats, as an elegy to Brian:

Peace, peace! he is not dead, he doth not sleep –
He hath awakened from the dream of life –
'Tis we, who lost in stormy visions, keep
With phantoms an unprofitable strife.

At its end he released thousands of butterflies, though the intended poetry of the moment was slightly lost in the indecorous shaking of the brown cardboard boxes in which the creatures had been stored.

The performance that followed was a ramshackle, somewhat lacklustre affair musically, as if the emotion and the ritual had sapped both the band and the audience of their desire to party. Even the addition of an African percussion band in appropriately ethnic dress for a roughed-up rendition of *Sympathy For The Devil* failed to ignite the audience, and slowly the audience started to drift away, content that we had done the right thing by Brian. It was not a great week for Jagger, all in all. On the 8 July, his girlfriend, the singer and actress Marianne Faithfull, took a drugs overdose in Australia and fell into a coma. She survived.

While my brother Brian was away in Copenhagen I decided to try to expand our business, so that when the hippy thing had finally burned itself out we would still have an income. It was on a trip to Amsterdam that summer that a possible business opportunity caught my eye. In the sprawling flea market on Waterlooplein, I saw a guy selling German leather greatcoats from the Second World War. They were massive, rigid garments, more like wood than leather, with belts and leather buttons, like the Gestapo used to wear in the movies. They came in brown, green, navy blue and black, weighed the best part of 20 pounds each, and were as stiff as boards. They could almost stand up by themselves. I decided that these would sell well in Portobello Road, which was just starting to attract London's trendsetters. I negotiated a bulk price of about £4 each with the guy and took about 25 coats.

I was travelling with two friends from Brixton, Bill Gibson and Keith Surridge (with whom I had sold cartoons with in 1967). Both Bill and Keith could drive. We loaded the coats into the back of the van we had travelled in and, having fulfilled my business commitments, we headed for the Dutch coast at Zaandvoort. Jubilant at having arrived safely and with relative ease, we drove the van down on to the beach for a lap of honour and immediately got stuck in the sand. The more the wheels spun, the deeper we got embedded, and within minutes the wheels were buried up to the chassis. Initially we thought this rather amusing, and only a slight inconvenience. It was when the tide turned an hour and a half later, and we were still stuck fast with the sea only 30 yards or so away, that we started to get truly anxious and considered abandoning not only the van but also its precious cargo of coats. Fortunately Zaandvoort is very a popular resort with German bodybuilders and, just as we were realising the seriousness of our predicament, and it was dawning on us that we were *in extremis*, a group of about ten of them came sprinting over to where the sea was just starting to lap around the front tyres. They dug the sand away from the wheels with their bare hands, worked the vehicle out of its hole and manhandled it out of danger. Once on dry sand we put one of the massive leather coats under each wheel and inched our way to the road and safety.

We thanked our Teutonic rescuers profusely and offered to buy them drinks but, like a testosterone-fuelled apparition, they were gone.

We decided to celebrate our rescue and seeming invincibility by sampling some of the fine Dutch gins on offer at a local beach bar, then after a few glasses we moved on to beer. After a few beers it was dark and it started to rain. We decided, none too soberly, to try to drive to the Hook of Holland and catch the night ferry to Harwich. It was a stupid idea, but 18-year olds can be quite stupid, so we went for it. An hour or so into our drive, Keith, who was driving, misjudged a bend in the road and went into a skid. He tried to regain control, but his violent turn of the steering wheel only exacerbated the situation, and the van went into an uncontrollable spin, and as it left the road it hit a tree stump and suddenly we were airborne. We did two somersaults and the back doors flew open. The coats went flying out, like angels ascending to the heavens, and we landed upside down in a field with the wheels still spinning and the engine still running. As always in those sort of accidents, the whole action seemed to happen in slow motion. By the time we had realised what had happened, we also realised that we were all, miraculously, unscathed. Switching off the engine, we climbed out of the open doors and started to gather up the coats in the dark. Just then we heard a put-put-putting sound in the distance, and we saw two farmers were coming along the road on a tractor. We flagged them down and they towed the van back on to the road and helped us get it into an upright position. Apart from a few scratches and dents, the van had survived the incident as well as we had, and we managed to resume our journey once more, albeit at a rather more sedate pace. It was a truly remarkable piece of luck that we weren't seriously injured or killed, but luck was with us on that trip.

Arriving at the Hook of Holland with plenty of time to make the ferry, we discovered to our horror that the wallet, which contained our return tickets and all our cash, had been lost, either in the incident on the beach at Zaandvoort, or during the accident. We had about £5 between us, and needed about £60 to get the van and ourselves across to Harwich. We were in deep despair and were considering driving to Rotterdam or The Hague to borrow money from the British Consul. In this gloom Bill Gibson put a cap on his head that for some reason had been with us since we left London. It was a white Express Dairyman's cap, vaguely nautical in appearance, with a large letter "E" badge on the front and a small "Express" written underneath. It gave me an idea. "Why don't we take it in turns to pretend to be railway porters and meet the passengers coming in from Harwich on the boat train?" I asked no one in particular. "We can carry their bags and cases to the train and raise the money that way. It's worth a try. The hat looks official enough." "As long as we don't try it on a milkmen's Awayday excursion," said Bill sardonically, suspicious of the whole idea.

As it was my idea, I was deputed to try out the plan when the first boatload arrived. To my astonishment it worked like a charm, and soon all three of us were at it, taking it in turns to wear the talismanic cap. We greeted the English passengers with a cheesy grin and an enthusiastic, if none-too-convincing "Velcome in Holland", and asked them where they were travelling on to. Most were heading for Amsterdam. We knew which platform that train stood at and hauled their luggage across the forecourt, into a carriage and waited for our reward. As the British are notoriously bad at understanding foreign currency, we often were extravagantly and handsomely rewarded. Those who proffered too little were prevailed upon to increase their donation. Those passengers who were travelling further afield, heading for Germany or Belgium or Poland, for example, fared less well. I am afraid and ashamed to say we took pot luck with their trains and loaded them in to any waiting carriage we could find, with a cheery wave. I am sure some poor unfortunate travellers, expecting a quiet weekend strolling around the churches of Bruges, ended up in the coalfields of Katowice. Financially we did incredibly well out of the enterprise, and we raised enough cash not only to get the van and our cargo home, but also to sleep in first class cabins after a superb dinner in the restaurant. It was a great trip.

There was a terrible rumpus from Dad when I stored these coats in the cellar for a few days without him knowing. As he was the sort of man who would go into the cellar occasionally to count the number of logs he had, or to weigh the coal, like some Dickensian miser, it was inevitable that sooner or later he would discover our precious stash. An unholy row ensued as he manhandled the coats upstairs and deposited them on to the street, while I in turn brought them back into the house through the front door like a scene from a surreal farce. Mum, as ever, was on my side, the side of sanity and reason, while Dad huffed and puffed in apoplexy at his authority and power of veto being undermined. Eventually he marched me to the local police station to have me hear an embarrassed and disinterested station sergeant agree that, yes, technically he was within his rights to throw any merchandise off his property that he didn't want on it, so long as he did not commit a littering or public order offence in so doing. I just laughed at the stupidity of the whole situation.

That August my A level results arrived and I was astonished and delighted to have passed all three with pretty good grades. I hadn't realised quite how much passing them meant to me throughout my two years of hedonism, but I had really wanted to do well for the sake of the teachers who had inspired me and stuck by me through those pain-in-the-ass years. Also I wanted to spite my dad. I fixed my mind on doing Scandinavian Studies at the University of East Anglia. The course appealed to me because students got to spend a year in a Scandinavian country of their choice, and by this time I was very fond of Copenhagen. After an interview at the college, just outside Norwich, on a God-forsaken windy day, they offered me a place. It was a bit of a hell-hole, but summoning up my courage I broached the subject with the old man.

Three good A level passes, and the offer of a place at East Anglia University, and he still said "No, you're not going." The reason he gave was that he wasn't prepared to disclose his income on the grant assessment form and no form meant no grant. No grant meant no university. End of story. "You've got to pull your weight, get a job and pay your way. No member of our family has ever been to university. Why should you be any different?"

"Well", I thought to myself (not brave enough to say it), "fuck you, Dad. I just *am* different. It's not a choice, it's a curse. Long before you had used your favourite "N" word, I knew I would never be a number-cruncher like you, even though I have absolutely no idea what direction my life is going to take." But I was already planning my escape. Yet as I travelled to

Copenhagen to visit Brian, who had moved there, at the start of that beautiful hot summer of 1969, 18-years old and clueless, I had no inkling that this trip would affect the rest of my life.

My new life began when I brought my first guitar, a Levin acoustic six-string. I haggled with the pimply, long-haired blond boy in the coffee shop just off the Strøget, Copenhagen's main pedestrian thoroughfare, for 15 or 20 minutes. His English was as good as mine, but my negotiating skills were better than his, honed by my three summers "in trade"; and, since I was the only person vaguely interested in what he had to sell, eventually I just wore him down until we agreed on a price – about £19. It didn't have a carrying case, it needed new strings, and the strap looked like a dressing-gown cord, but the body was sound and the neck was straight. I knew it would leave me short of money for the rest of my stay, but I didn't care – I felt I was investing in my destiny.

I had already seen every legendary rock gig there had ever been in this country: I'd seen Dylan at the Albert Hall in 1966, The Doors at the Roundhouse and The Rolling Stones in Hyde Park. Remember the impromptu valedictory concert The Beatles gave on the roof at Apple on 30 January 1969? I was in the West End that chilly day, bunking off school and hoping to pull some pretty tourist girl in Carnaby Street. I decided to wander down to the Apple Offices in Savile Row to see if I could catch a sight of one of the Fab Four as I had many times before, and as I turned off Regent Street I heard their music. It was a miracle. (I'd once accosted John Lennon outside Apple while he waited with Yoko for a cab. I said, "John, I'm 17. I'm a poet and I want to get my poetry published. Can you help me?" He must have been bugged a hundred times a day by no-hopers like me. He looked at me down that thin, aquiline nose, peering through his glasses and said, "I help them as helps themselves", and it somehow struck me as incredibly profound. For some reason I didn't take it as a brush-off, but as words of infinite wisdom from the lips of a sage.)

The John Lennon and the Plastic Ono Band gig at the Lyceum? Yep, that's me in the rimless glasses and long hair, dressed all in white, looking for all the world like a young Lennon, with Rene trying her best to look shy and Japanese as we blagged our way in through the artist's entrance at four o'clock in the afternoon. To our amazement it worked. Then all we had to do was stay hidden in a broom cupboard for six hours, fucking and sleeping, till the doors opened. A piece of cake. Once onstage the band, which included Eric Clapton, played a killer version of *Cold Turkey*, then Yoko got into a bag and screeched, squawked and howled for 25 minutes. It was probably awful but it was Lennon so we loved it. Afterwards Rene got the tube home to Acton and I headed south for Tooting Bec. Another time we saw a white-faced David Bowie support T. Rex, with a piece of narrative mime detailing, if I remember correctly, the plight of a young Tibetan monk. That was at the Queen Elizabeth Hall in 1969.

Scroll forward to 7 June 1977. The Sex Pistols "God Save the Queen" Jubilee event on the boat on the Thames? Check out Don Letts' definitive photos. That's me and Rene about to board from Charing Cross pier. Somehow, like Zelig, I always happened to be there. Sometimes it happened by accident, sometimes by design and sometimes simply because I was a fan whose antennae for music were extraordinarily finely attuned. I even took my mum to see Jimi Hendrix on a bill with Englebert Humperdinck, Cat Stephens and The Walker

Brothers in the baroque splendour of the Tooting Granada. She was appalled. The only major gigs in the entire history of rock that I didn't get to see were Elvis in Las Vegas and Johnny Cash at San Quentin.

Oh, and Altamont. The name of that speedway track outside San Francisco became synonymous with all that had gone bad in pop culture that year. One December day in 1969, The Rolling Stones were playing a free concert, and after a few numbers a black kid in the audience called Meredith Hunter, high on something or other, stood up and started to wave a gun in the air. He was set upon by the Hell's Angels whom the Stones had entrusted with the show's security, and was stabbed to death. The Stones played on for another hour. With the death of Brian Jones, the attempted suicide of Marianne Faithfull and the murder of a member of their audience all happening within six months, the flirtation with elemental evil, which was always part of the Stones image, was casting a long and sinister shadow over our lives. It was as if they had done some catastrophic Faustian deal when they wrote and recorded *Sympathy For The Devil*.

Although the Stones were in their hedonistic pomp at that time, there were some great new bands coming out of the USA who were also getting my juices flowing. Two of my favourites, The MC5 and The Stooges, both came out of the Detroit suburb of Ann Arbor. The MC5 were a highly politicised heavy rock band who described themselves as White Panthers. They were neither the first nor the last rock band to identify something in popular culture and mistake it for a potential political force. Their best known song, *Kick Out The Jams*, was a furious, teeth-gnashing, high-octane precursor to what became known as punk rock, while the Stooges lead singer, Iggy Pop, né Stooge, had his provocative, self-abusive stage show appropriated by everyone from David Bowie to Johnny Rotten; his songs, such as I *Wanna be Your Dog* and *No Fun* became blue-chip punk staples for the next generation.

The sixties began when I was eight and finished when I was 18, but the amount and the speed with which the world changed in those 10 years can never be exaggerated. It is tempting to see that decade as the great coming-together of radical alternatives; in fact the process, which started in the sixties, is a long and arduous one that is for the most part still going on. The nature of social change always seems to be very much of the two steps forward, one step back variety. Feminism, black activism, environmentalism and the whole protest movement all had their genesis in that giddy decade, but how closely the different interest groups were aligned can be gleaned from a single quote from Black Panther Eldridge Cleaver. When asked by a female interviewer, "What is the position of women in the revolution?" his glib, one-word reply was "Prone". Right on, brother!

The Seventies

MUSIC IS THE BRANDY OF THE DAMNED

By 1970, having spent some part of every day with my guitar, I was smart enough to know I was never going to be a great musician since I had started playing far too late in life, when my hands were already fully formed and clumsy. I knew that instead I would either have to become an artist or go into show business, where musical virtuosity can be an advantage but is not a pre-requisite. My dad was constantly on my back to get a job. His lobotomy and subsequent course of medication, which he was on for the rest of his life, rendered him by turns taciturn and aggressive, obstinate and uncommunicative. I stalled him with a succession of casual fill-ins, working in record shops and in a bread factory. I already instinctively knew, at the age of 19, that my life would be lived out in public, not in an office, and I needed to get cracking without him always breathing disapprovingly down my neck.

I bought a tape recorder and almost before I could play a chord on the guitar I started writing songs. The earliest attempts were fairly typical for anyone my age: ham-fisted playing and an uncertain voice trying out overwrought lyrics, sung in a bedroom to an indulgent and encouraging girlfriend, Rene. My ambition and imagination, as always, far outstripped my talent. I was soon writing 20-minute long songs of deconstructed angst, based around the chord of E minor (I still like this key, incidentally). They were excruciating, but, as the cliché goes, even the longest journey begins with the first short step.

A lot of my earliest song-writing influences originated in what was loosely known as the "protest movement". These included people such as Bob Dylan, Paul Simon and Roy Harper, who wrote songs about social and political injustice. In 1970, at the Kent State University in Ohio, USA, there was a horrifying incident when four young students were killed by National Guardsmen in an anti-war demonstration on the campus. The singer-songwriter, Neil Young wrote and recorded a furious, rage-filled diatribe entitled *Ohio* with his band Crosby, Stills, Nash and Young just after the incident, which I found both moving and inspiring.

When President Nixon announced that the US would invade Cambodia, a deliberate and cynical escalation of the Vietnam War, it triggered a wave of student demonstrations and unrest on campuses across the entire country. On 2 May, the US Army hut on the campus at Kent State University was burnt down during one of these protests, and the following day the national guard was sent to the campus to deal with it. On 4 May, four students were killed and nine were wounded when the Guard suddenly opened fire on a peaceful noonday demonstration. The students who died were more or less the same age as me and, like many others at that time, I was stunned and outraged by the killings and the subsequent judicial cover-up that followed.

The Neil Young song, which laid the blame for the deaths firmly at the door of Nixon's White House, reminded me once again of the raw power of pop music, and how it could address issues as well as emotions. Astonishingly, it even achieved a top twenty chart position. Not that Nixon would have noticed that – he was busy awarding Elvis Presley a Drug Enforcement Agency badge in a highly-publicised White House ceremony, thinking that Presley still held some sway over "the kids". Apparently, Presley's advice to Nixon on drugs was "Kick John Lennon out of the country".

In music, as in sport, you should always try to play with people better than you. That way you learn stuff and improve. Peter di Lemma was a school friend of several years standing. He had a drum kit and he had already been playing for some time. He always wanted to be a jazz drummer, but I somehow persuaded him to give rock music a try. I had already written a handful of songs, and it was so exciting to go down into the cellar of his house in Brixton where he kept his drum kit, plug the guitar into an old Selmer 30 amp which I had recently bought, crank it up and play.

Peter and I started our first band, The Great White Idiot, in 1971. Standing about five feet seven, Peter wasn't exactly fat, but he was what you would call powerfully built. He was one of those guys who, while never truly creatively inspired, was always enthusiastic, whole-hearted and optimistic, and fulfilled the important role of a great facilitator. He was not a pretentious smart-ass like me, and was often at a loss for words, but he was an invaluable collaborator. He always saw the prospective up-side or fun of a situation, rather than focusing in on its potential for disaster. I never saw him really fazed by anything and on those rare occasions when he lost his temper, he always did so in a slightly embarrassed and half-hearted way, as if he couldn't really be bothered to upset anyone. He was stoical and loyal, and always prepared to put in the hard work. He never felt that anything was beneath him. He was, all in all, a 24-carat good bloke. Outside of music, Pete's greatest love was surfing, and he surfed every spare day that he had. Any time of the year, in hail or heat wave, he would somehow get down to the nearest coast, put on his wetsuit, wax his board and disappear into breaker heaven.

Bill Gibson, another Brixton kid who had been on the fateful Holland adventure, sat in on an old Hohner Clavinet electric keyboard. It had a electrical fault which meant that 10 times a night it would splutter, crackle and eventually fall silent until it was turned off, allowed to cool down, and then restarted. It did this once too often for Bill one night and he smashed it to pieces in exasperation, reducing it to crude electronic matchwood with an axe that was lying around in the Pete's cellar for the purpose of chopping firewood. He was a pretty good player, but *so* temperamental. He left the band on several occasions but always returned, usually with an instrument he had borrowed from a friend or stolen from an enemy. He was terrified of making any sort of commitment to the group, and started drinking pretty heavily. Alarmingly, at the height of his drinking he was a railway guard on British Rail Intercity high-speed trains between London and Scotland. Sadly his career as a guard was brought to an abrupt and embarrassing end when he was discovered by an inspector, who found him wearing mascara, lipstick and rouge, passed out in his guard's van in an alcoholic coma, with an open copy of Dostoevsky's *Crime and Punishment* still in his hand. A couple of years later I wrote a song about him, called *Billy, Watch Out!* which eventually appeared on The Doctors of Madness's first album, *Late Night Movies, All Night Brainstorms*.

Gradually we worked out enough songs to play a 40-minute set, and started to beg a few support gigs at pubs and colleges. We looked forward to these rare public outings enormously, and invited all our mates along, but to be honest these gigs were always disappointing. Either they were plagued by technical deficiencies, which dramatically highlighted our own musical shortcomings, or they were flat affairs played to the wrong audience or, worse, to no audience. Rene's sister had a friend who was a pornographer in Shepherd's Market, in Mayfair, and he offered to try to help by passing our demo tapes on to those of his customers who worked in the music business, including two BBC Radio One DJs, both household names at the time, a Radio Luxembourg DJ and the manager of a top band of the day, but nothing materialised. A south London agent called Reg heard a demo tape that we did and paid for us to go into a better studio. We recorded a slushy song I had written called *Don't Do It Now*, but without consulting us he went on to swamp it with an orchestra and French horns and we lost any affection for the song that we might have had. I started to feel that our whole approach was too conventional, too orthodox, too "old school". I realised that since I would never have the technical expertise to cut it purely as a musician, I would have to compensate for my musical shortcomings with sheer force of personality and an element of visual spectacle and drama.

I wrote long and regular letters to Brian, who was now living permanently in Copenhagen, trying to keep him abreast of my life. I didn't want us to grow apart just because we no longer lived under the same roof. He replied in kind. Coming across some of those letters recently, I am amused at my precocity, my scattergun take on reality and by the rambling nature of the letters. One reads:

You Old Cunt,

Among my interests now is "being hard". I have dyed my hair blue-black, but it's nearer purple. I wear a big straw hat that I ripped off [Roy] Harper, and occasionally smoke king-sized filters, swear a lot and scowl at my bass-player. We make the early Great White Idiot look like a bunch of incompetent fairies. I hope to spend close to £1million on clothes this summer. I wanna be the smartest cunt in London. I ain't the kinda person who thinks too much, but you really couldn't call me a jerk. You would do well to get over here soon to hear our new improved version of Waiting For The Man. Thursday we got a mix of that fucking single of ours. It's OK but we've had to hang around so long. Reg told us that a bloke at the BBC (Boring, Bigoted Cunts) reckons it's a good song, but I can't relate to it anymore, cos it's taken so long.

Between 1971 and 1973 I must have seen at least a dozen David Bowie gigs. I was a great fan of both his music and his image in that golden period between *The Man Who Sold The World* and *Ziggy Stardust*. I saw Bowie and Roxy Music, the two most influential acts of the early seventies, gigging together at the Greyhound Pub in Croydon in 1973, and the cost of admission was less than a pound. I wasn't into glitter or glam as such, but I liked Bowie because he liked what I liked. He liked the Velvets and Dylan and Warhol and Burroughs and Iggy and Scott Walker and Jacques Brel, and his influences were plastered over every song he sang. His theft of other people's ideas was shameless, and because it was never furtive I always thought it was 100 per cent legitimate. He never claimed to be an original, merely a repackaging and re-branding colossus. I loved his sense of theatre and his respect of tradition. He knew where things came from and where you could take them. For me the glam/bisexual thing was just an added bonus, which struck a long-suppressed chord.

It goes without saying that image is critically important in rock and roll, and Bowie had image in spades. An audience has an instinct for authenticity and can immediately tell the bogus from the real thing. Sometimes they don't care if you're bogus, so long as you're good and you don't pretend that you're real. That is why there are always a multitude of imitators of any successful band, one or two of whom will make a decent living by simply being dragged along on the coat tails of their more illustrious role model. Take Lenny Kravitz as an example, an imitator who is twice removed from the real deal. He wasn't hip enough to go to the source and rip off Hendrix direct; he went for Prince, the "lite" version, who'd ripped off Hendrix and mixed it with a bit of James Brown and cleaned up. That's why, to my ear, Kravitz always comes over as insipid and ersatz, and as fake as a Gucci handbag in a Singapore market. All the bits are there in the right places, but you know it's a Sexton Blake. That's why he will grow old in the second division.

It's no good trying to sell a band as weird, mutant low-life if half the guys aren't switched on to the idea, and if their one concession to stagewear is simply to loosen the tie they normally wear to work, or to put on a zany T-shirt. It is nigh on impossible to make a convincing show if they look embarrassed and uncomfortable, as if they would rather be at home in front of the TV with a takeaway. Roxy Music managed it despite the fact their drummer looked like a welterweight wrestler, because they made a virtue of that fact by dressing him as a welterweight wrestler, complete with leopard skin leotard and wrestling boots, but they were an exception, not least because they had glamour and brains to spare with their two front men, Bryan Ferry and Brian Eno.

In 1973, Rene and I moved in to our first flat together, in north-west London. I was working at Cheapo Cheapo Records in Soho, and the flat was rented to us for a nominal rent by Phil, the guy I worked for. It was a four-room apartment on the second floor of a thirties block in Brooklands Rise, in the deceptively-named Hampstead Garden Suburb. He wanted to keep one of the rooms to store records in, but the rest of the flat was ours. It was a long way from anyone we knew, and since we relied on public transport we felt a bit isolated, but we were both excited about leaving home for the first time. I continued to work for Phil at the Soho shop and slowly we furnished the flat with second-hand furniture. Rene, who was studying art at Twickenham, had a workroom and I set up some recording equipment. Despite the intrusive curiosity of some of our neighbours, life was good.

In December 1973, The Great White Idiot played a gig at the 100 Club, in London's Oxford Street. It was a college Christmas party and the social secretary of the college was David Bidmead, an old school friend of mine, and we negotiated the massive fee of £90 for a two-hour set. It was a reckless arrangement as we knew we didn't have anything like two hours of material rehearsed. Indeed, we could only play my angst-ridden dirges, delivered with a lot of highly confrontational attitude, but with only a modicum of proficiency, while the students quite understandably wanted to dance to cover versions of the latest Tamla Motown and Soul hits. I remember a thick-set youth sidling up to the stage and warning me, "Play *In The Midnight Hour* or *Mustang Sally* or we'll smash your gear up." I said, "Sorry, we don't do requests." Despite the fact that I had grown up with that music and loved it all, I had never learned to play it. I was, and remain, very "white", musically.

To this day my ability to sing other people's songs is woefully limited. I believe this has prevented me from being the hit of every party. The audience at the 100 Club that night were very insistent, and their dissatisfaction with us grew in direct proportion to the length of time we played and the amount of cheap booze they consumed. We actually only played for 20 minutes before abandoning the stage to the DJ, but it seemed like a very long, lingering death that we died that night. I think David Bidmead was lynched but not before the cheque had cleared. I know the Great White Idiot disbanded soon afterwards.

THE DOCTORS OF MADNESS

Throughout 1974, Peter and I must have auditioned 20 or 30 musicians in his small Brixton cellar. While it was impossible to be specific about what we were looking for, we knew we would recognise it when we heard it. We were after a vibe, an understanding of atmosphere and a freedom of style. My songs were getting darker, and we needed a couple of musicians who could make them really work dramatically and dynamically. We listened to guitarists so devoid of talent that it was all we could do not to laugh before we sent them packing after a diplomatic interval, promising to get in touch. We listened to guys who had played with bands like Cockney Rebel, or Mott the Hoople, but none were right. They were conventional old musos looking for any old gig. Sure, they could play okay, but they would never be able to get inside my head and translate these noises I was hearing. We listened to synthesiser players, but they all seemed to come out of that horrible Yes–Genesis school that we despised. They all wanted to wear capes decorated with stars and crescent moons, and to play too many notes. They would look at me blankly if I said, "Could you just get it to rumble for five minutes, like bubbling mud?" Eventually we took a side step, and I called Stoner, a bass guitarist who I had known for some time, and invited him to come down to play. He was good, with a style that was both melodic and rocking, and the three of us immediately started to develop a rapport.

After a single audition, we offered the exotically named Urban Blitz a job. We had found him in the time-honoured way, in the *Melody Maker* classifieds, and he joined on electric violin and guitar. I found him a bit tense and edgy, but I really liked the noise he made. It pressed all the old Velvet Underground buttons that I had in my head, and I knew he could both play music and make noise. That was crucial. We had fixed our line-up at last. I sang and played guitar, Stoner was on bass and backing vocals, Urban Blitz played various electric violins and guitar, and Peter di Lemma stayed on drums and backing vocals.

We changed our name to The Doctors of Madness. I'm not sure why. I think now that it's actually not a very good name. It's *almost* funny, like The Mothers of Invention is *almost* funny. I think I had William Burroughs's medical maniac Dr. Benway in mind. I liked that contradiction between the notion of the trusted Doctor and the reality of the psychopath. Typographically "The Doctors of Madness" is too long to make an impact on a poster or in a headline, but to sub-editors and photographers who wanted a "theme" or costume picture, it was a gift: "Mad, these new Doctors of Rock ", that sort of thing. Within a couple of years we had lost count of how many photographic stylists had arrived at a photo session weighed down with white coats, stethoscopes and hypodermic syringes, saying "I've had this great idea for the shoot . . ." Fortunately we soon learned how to tell these lame-brains "no thanks".

Rene was extravagantly supportive, and used her art school grant to buy us a small second-hand PA system, which meant for the first time our sound could be heard with a modicum of clarity. We rehearsed in Peter di Lemma's cellar three nights a week. It was freezing in the winter, and we played in coats and scarves and took nips from a bottle of whisky to keep alive. In the summer it was sweltering, and we stripped down to our underwear.

All through this period I was writing furiously. I was into The Velvets, Burroughs, Bowie and Wagner. The music was the focus for the four of us. We had no choice but to make the music that turned *us* on. Who could try to follow the market in a year that saw *Billy, Don't Be A Hero*, and Barry White's *Can't Get Enough Of Your Love, Babe* setting the charts alight? Socially we didn't see a great deal of each other. Urban Blitz always made me feel uneasy. He reminded me too much of my dad, with his mood swings between painfully forced good humour and a violent temper that threatened to explode with the least provocation. He always seemed to be on the edge. But there was no mistaking the fact that he could play, and that was all we needed. After all, this was a rock band not a marriage. Or so I thought.

By the end of the year we were ready to break out of the cellar and start doing some gigs. The music was still rough and ready, but it had started to develop its own identity, and we were beginning to play with the confidence that that brings. The new songs were comparatively complex structurally, often going outside the straight verse/chorus pattern, and going off into a weird angularity. I sent Brian a cassette with a note, which read: "The tape is not as good as I would like you to have, but your impatience knows no bounds. 'Pigface' is my favourite. Urban, the violinist, and Peter are superb on this. I'm pretty hot on 'Doctors', and Stoner is the best bloke I have ever had in the band. He *knows* what it is about. And you should see him on stage. Weird!"

We spent whatever money we earned on making sure that our show looked and sounded as professional as possible. Bowie had set a new standard in the production values of a rock concert. He had raised the bar. We would arrive at a venue with a lighting rig, a soundman and some rudimentary idea of staging the show. We made sure that local press were mailed and primed, and sometimes even paid for posters, which Rene or Stoner's wife, Elaine, would design and print at college. All this organisation and expense fell principally on the shoulders of Peter and myself. We all still had day jobs, of some sort or another. Pete was working with a building firm, Stoner in a clothes shop, Urban Blitz was a draughtsman and I was still working at Cheapo Cheapo Records. With no one managing the band, the logistics of making sure that personnel and equipment arrived at the venue at the right time and functioned correctly were both time-consuming and exhausting. Why anyone chooses to manage an unknown band is a great mystery to me. It is the arse-end of the business.

Early in 1975, we were offered a gig at The Speakeasy, which at that time was a hugely prestigious club in Margaret Street, London, for which we received £20, less £2 agent's commission. In truth, we would have done The Speakeasy for nothing as it was such a cool place. Everyone had played there, Hendrix, The Who and any number of visiting US acts, and the entire music biz hung out there. Playing The Speakeasy was, for us, like playing at Lord's would be for a young cricketer. It felt to us like our first really legitimate gig. We were playing with the Big Boys when we played there. We weren't especially good that night, and the small audience's response was lukewarm, but I had been bitten by the performance bug and its effects were lethal.

Meanwhile, back in the real world, the final humiliation of the US military machine was nearly complete in Vietnam, as the Vietcong surged south and eventually took Saigon. On 29 April 1975, the last Americans were evacuated, under fire, from the roof of the US Embassy in Saigon, with 70 people crammed on to a helicopter designed to hold 50. As the helicopter slowly rose and teetered above the battle-strewn capital, it marked one of the most extraordinary military defeats in history. The following day, the South Vietnamese forces surrendered unconditionally to the victorious Vietcong army. I felt euphoric that it was over and Goliath had lost.

It had been a disastrous campaign from start to finish, and had left an entire generation of Vietnamese and Americans totally traumatised. The failed campaign had cost the US treasury an estimated $200 billion, and totally derailed both President Johnson's domestic programme and that of his successor, Richard Nixon. More than 47,000 Americans were killed in action, nearly 11,000 died of other causes, and more than 303,000 were wounded in the war. The North Vietnamese and Vietcong suffered about 900,000 troops killed and an unknown (but huge) number of wounded. In addition, more than 1,000,000 North and South Vietnamese civilians were killed during the war. Large parts of the countryside were scarred by bombs and mutilated by chemical defoliation, and many of the cities and towns were reduced to just rubble and scrap.

By spring 1975, having attained a certain degree of competence and the confidence that goes with it, we started to promote our own gigs in the back room of a pub that Rene had found near to the art college in Twickenham, where she was studying. It was called the Cabbage Patch and we played there every Saturday night for about six weeks. A combination of flyers, free listings in *Time Out* magazine, posters, friends, college students and word of mouth provided us with an audience that doubled in size each week, and by the fourth week there was a healthy crowd.

We had already started to introduce a rather crude, low budget theatricality into our stage show, using strobe lights, smoke, slide and super-8 film projections and dramatic up-lighting. The music was being played with more attack and less caution, and one Saturday evening in May we did a show of frightening intensity and fire, a show which transcended all of our technical and musical shortcomings, and which culminated in a spontaneous audience invasion of the stage, as feedback howled and the drum kit was demolished. It sometimes happens that a rock band makes a virtue of all the frustration and aggravation that having neither manager nor agent, neither record company nor budget brings. The set we played that night was a seething rant against our own inadequacies and the audience had roared back their approval. They had screamed, unmistakeably, "Yes – we like this". This was our greatest moment to date. Our coming of age. You only do this job for approval and acclaim, and when you get them for the first time, it is honey-sweet. Afterwards, in the pokey little anteroom, no more than a cupboard really, which served as our dressing-room, we were euphoric and already longing to play next week's show and to build upon that night's success.

After that show, while winding down with a beer before performing the deflating and embarrassing ritual of dismantling our own stage equipment in front of the audience we had just rocked into a frenzy, we had two visitors to our dressing room. The first one through the door looked sort of familiar, and introduced himself as Jonathan King, who we knew was managing the successful but po-faced, prog-rock band, Genesis, at that time. I was not and am not a fan. He had had a couple of minor hits in the sixties with his own songs. His marketing angle back then was that he was that rarity, an educated pop singer. He was a Cambridge undergraduate. In those days pop singers didn't get university degrees. They didn't need to. They were gods. But King was different. He had education. My God, never did a man wear so little learning so heavily. Unfortunately, the lyrics to his songs were so brain-numbingly banal that if a seven-year old from an inner-city slum school came up with something similar today, the school inspectors would be sent in and the establishment would be closed down pronto for falling standards. But Jonathan King had education.

Like King, Genesis, the band he now managed, was also being hyped on their public school–university pedigree, like prissy little poodles at Cruft's. Jonathan King is that uniquely middle-class English sort of a man who mistakes smarm for charm. Until recently he was still wheeled out sporadically to pontificate on some or other new pop phenomenon on soft-core entertainment TV, and he strained oh-so-hard to be witty, or even mildly controversial, like a constipated stand-up comic trying to shit out a decent punch line. Then a spot of bother with underage boys saw him locked up, and that was that. Ah, education.

Our other visitor that night was Bryan "Morry" Morrison, who had managed Pink Floyd, but had made his substantial fortune from music publishing, with the Floyd, T. Rex, and The Bee Gees among his acts. While visually conforming to the most crudely-drawn caricature of a cigar-chomping, East End Jewish wide-boy, the complete social antithesis of King Wasp, he was in fact a self-educated man of astonishing flair and instinct, charismatic and confident to

the point of arrogance, who could be relied upon to turn the most unpromising set of circumstances to his advantage. He had a big, fit, robust physique, and a cannonball head, a
close-trimmed beard and expensive teeth. He had already lost much of its hair but with
Morrison it didn't matter. He was polo-playing testosterone on legs, nervously hyperactive
and overwhelmingly macho. He filled any room he walked into. I cannot imagine that in his
entire life he has once uttered those deathless, late twentieth-century words "I'm trying to get
in touch with my feminine side."

I told Bryan I was a big fan of Syd Barrett, the founder member of Pink Floyd, who had
fried his brains with acid and been ousted by the band when he no longer knew that his guitar
wasn't even plugged in onstage. Bryan's mood blackened. "Don't talk to me about fucking Syd
Barrett. He's doing my head in at the moment." I asked Morrison why.

> He comes into the office for publishing royalties. I say, 'Syd, you're not owed any-
> thing till the next quarter. You were in here two months ago and I gave you a cheque
> for everything we owed you.' Syd says, 'No I wasn't. I don't recognise this room. I've
> never been here before.' Fortunately, I took the precaution of getting him to sign a
> receipt for the cheque, 'cos I knew he was out of his tree. I show him the receipt.
> Look Syd. You took a cheque two months ago. He goes quiet for minute, and then
> he says, 'You cheating bastard!' I say, 'What?!' and he says 'That's signed in red ink.
> I never use red ink. I *hate* red!' and storms out of the office calling me a cunt.

Morrison had a vengeful, brutal streak, which meant that somehow or other he would get
even with anyone who crossed him, however long it took and however much it cost him. Years
after I met him, I heard the story that he had tried to join the local real tennis club near his
home in Wraysbury, near Windsor. The club membership secretary was rather sniffy about
letting this parvenue, this cockney with a Hockney, join their exclusive club, and kept him on
hold for months. Bryan, by now enormously wealthy, bided his time, made the right contacts,
and eventually bought the tennis club and sacked the secretary. Few things in his life had ever
given him so much pleasure.

Bryan Morrison had started managing rock bands in the early sixties, when rock was
still called pop, while he was an art-student at St Martin's College of Art, in the Charing
Cross Road. It was at this time that rock bands, following the Beatles' lead, started for the
first time to write their own songs rather than to have them provided by song-writing
hacks from Tin Pan Alley. Morrison realised very quickly that there was potentially a
lot of money to be made from music publishing and set up his first company, Lupus
Music. To Lupus Music Morry promptly signed the band that he was managing at the
time, The Pretty Things, who were reckoned to be the wildest bunch of long-haired
rhythm and blues mofos that London had ever seen. They made The Rolling Stones,
their direct contemporaries and rivals, seem like pussies by comparison. They had a few top
forty hits, including *Rosalyn*, *Don't Bring Me Down*, and *Honey, I Need*, before slipping out of
fashion and into semi-obscurity.

In 1964, even more than today, Charing Cross Road was full of shops selling second-hand books and records. It was a great haunt for boho intellectuals and Soho hipsters. While browsing though some second-hand vinyl one lunchtime, something caught Morrison's unerring, entrepreneurial eye. It was a 78-rpm recording of the Chinese national anthem. To most of us this would have been unremarkable, but Bryan scanned both sides of the record label and found that there was no publisher listed for the music. He bought the record and immediately took it home, had a musicologist friend transcribe the music into manuscript form and registered it with the Performing Rights Society, naming the publisher as Lupus Music. It just so happened that 1964 was the year of the Olympic Games, and every time China won a medal, as they stood on the podium receiving their medal for ping-pong or gymnastics, the national anthem was played and Bryan Morrison, via Lupus Music, received a royalty! As F Scott Fitzgerald wrote: "Let me tell you about the very rich. They are different from you and me." (Incidentally, I always liked Hemingway's laconic riposte: "Yes. They have more money.")

When the Bee Gees made their comeback in the seventies with *Saturday Night Fever*, Bryan no longer had them under a publishing contract. However, one of their old songs, to which he did still hold the publishing rights, was the B-side of the single *Night Fever*. This could only be attributed to a major administrative blunder on their part. They could have put any song on the B-side and collected 100 per cent of the publishing royalties by setting up their own publishing company for that one song. The single sold 20 million copies worldwide. Since the A-side and the B-side of a single earn the same mechanical (sales) royalty for a publisher, and as at that time a single got to number one in the UK with a sale of something like 100,000 copies, that B-side earned him total royalties equivalent to 200 consecutive UK number ones. He was recently listed as the UK's seventieth wealthiest person. Not bad for someone who is completely tone deaf, can never remember the title of a song and who dropped out of school at 15, only to learn later that he was dyslexic. So much for education.

That night at the Cabbage Patch we spoke to Morrison and King separately in our dressing room. They both admitted to being very impressed by what they had just witnessed, but something puzzled Morrison. "Why are you wasting yer fucking time playing to 80 punters in a shit-hole like this?" he asked, never one to mince his words. I told him why. "Because we want to always be top of the bill. Even if the audiences are small we know that those who are there are there to see *our* show on *our* terms."

What we were doing was different from both the music and the general approach of other bands at that time. We were passionate and uncompromising and raw. We made no pretence at being virtuoso musicians. We weren't like those big bands of the day: Yes, Genesis, Supertramp, or Jethro Tull. Our music was not about cut-price mysticism or empty-headed pomp and bombast. We didn't even come from a third generation, three-chord, 12-bar blues background. Our songs were angular, irritable and abrasive. They were downright ugly or, at best, bittersweet. They were about paranoia, control systems and Class A drugs. After a few minutes of small talk both Morrison and King had offered us management contracts on the spot. Barely able to maintain our pretence of "cool", I told them we would think about it over the weekend and call them Monday. It was no contest, really. We hated Genesis!!!

"GIVE IT PLENTY!"

We signed with Morrison and his colourfully-named partner, Justin de Villeneuve, with whom he had gone into business. They had an office in Eastbourne Mews, near Paddington Station, which they shared with seventies heartthrob David Essex, but which was in truth run by the pretty, and ruthlessly efficient Cora Jackman, Bryan's secretary. Like most people of my age, I was first aware of Justin when he managed the top model of the sixties, Twiggy. (Coincidentally, it had been my misfortune at school to be nicknamed Twiggy on account of my slender, willowy frame.) More recently, he had taken the stunning photograph of Twiggy and David Bowie for the sleeve of Bowie's latest album of sixties cover versions *Pin Ups*.

Justin was a chancer, with all the shy reserve of a fairground barker. Born Nigel Davies, he changed his name to the more exotic Justin de Villeneuve when he started to manage Twiggy. I asked him "Why de Villeneuve?" and he just shrugged and told me the concept of "the new town" was quite glamorous at the time he changed. He was a sort of Fagin character, who spoke in the rhyming-slang patois of the barrow-boy, but he could camp it up with the best of them, and socially he could mix equally well with viscounts and villains. He was a wheeler-dealer, and was totally and uniquely London. No other city in the world could have spawned a character like Justin. He was a very amusing raconteur who knew everyone remotely responsible for making the sixties swing. His close friends were people such as Paul McCartney, David Bailey, the painter Peter Blake and the designers Ossie Clark, Tommy Roberts and Mary Quant, plus the obligatory sixties sprinkling of gangsters. He had all the natural ebullient frothy charm of a hairdresser, which he once was, cutting and shampooing for Vidal Sassoon, and would promote himself as energetically as he promoted his clients. He was exactly what he aspired to be – a lovable rogue. He adored women and could never resist a beauty. He really thought the world was his own personal playpen and so naturally he wanted to play with the best toys.

Soon after signing with Morrison de Villeneuve, as their partnership was called (I can only imagine the fights between these two mammoth egos as they slogged it out for top billing like two heavyweights), I was having lunch with Justin at San Lorenzo, in Knightsbridge. Loosening up with each other after a bottle or two he said to me: "You know, one of the first things that attracted us to you was your 'Fuck You' attitude to the audience. We've never seen that in a new band before." I told him that he was only partly right. "Our 'Fuck You' attitude isn't just directed at the audience, Justin. It is two fingers to the whole fucking world."

Of our two managers, Justin was the more flamboyant, the more hands-on. He was given to wearing extravagant jewellery and frilly shirts. He was once pulled by the police for doing 120mph down Bond Street in his Lamborghini, and sweet-talked his way out of getting a ticket. Morry was the shrewder, more strategic thinker and a nerveless negotiator. They were fiercely competitive, both for our affections and their own material acquisitions. They followed each other into marriage, too, with an unsettling symmetry. They both married models, of course. Justin went for the cool, sleek, swan-necked modernism of the American beauty Jan Ward. Morry married the more classically beautiful Canadian, Greta van Rantwyk.

When the first Range Rovers came on to the market, Morry was furious that Justin had taken delivery of his a full week earlier than him. Morry, so chippy and aspirational, is able to live his entire life without a shred of self-irony or self-deprecation, whereas Justin could always tell a good joke against himself, referring to himself often as "the little fat boy".

Justin had more clothes than any man I had ever known. He had rooms full of them. He was the first man I had ever met who actually loved shopping. He would go into a clothes shop and two hours later would leave with armfuls of new purchases, many of which he would never actually wear. He just got caught up in the thrill of the purchase. He loved spending money simply because he had money to spend. Every once in a while the band would benefit from a cull in his wardrobe or a change of his sartorial style. We would gratefully harvest his cast-offs, as they were invariably either English classics or top designer labels of the day. Mr Howie and Mr Fish, Zandra Rhodes and Biba. Sadly, I did less well than the others from these impromptu rummage sales, as I was tall and skeletal. Justin, on the other hand, was neither.

Because of his connection with the fashion world, Justin was able to coerce or persuade some of the top photographers of the day to do photo sessions with The Doctors of Madness. We spent hours sweltering under the lights in the studios of Terry Donovan, one of the truly great British photographers, or John Swannell, who had been Bailey's assistant but was now becoming a big name in his own right. All the while Justin kept up a constant background banter of small-talk and scurrilous gossip, all the while exhorting us to "Give it plenty!"

The deal that Morrison de Villeneuve offered us was one-sided, greedy and excessive, but our excitement and naiveté was such that we signed with them anyway. Morrison de Villeneuve wanted us to sign not only a management deal with them, for which they took 20 per cent of all earnings from live work (concerts and broadcasts), but also a record production deal for which they would take a massive 50 per cent of all record advances and royalties *and* they insisted on a publishing deal entitling them to 40 per cent of all my future song-writing royalties. Lock, stock and every fucking barrel, smoking or non-smoking! They owned a large percentage of every conceivable means we had of earning money.

In return for our signatures at the foot of the page, we benefited from their unique combination of flair and hard-nosed professionalism. I must admit that they were without equal in the delicate art of winding up the record companies. Their reputations were such that we could have signed to any record label we chose without them even hearing a single tune. But that wasn't the way Morrison worked. His plan was to play the record companies off against each other. He wanted to work them up into such a frenzy of desire that they were bidding ludicrous amounts against each other for our signatures on a 3-album contract. To this end various ploys were used.

On 6 June 1975, Morrison de Villeneuve threw a party (which I expect the band ended up paying for!) at Ladbroke's Gaming Club, a members-only casino in Hill Street in Mayfair. I think it was the first time any of us had actually set foot inside a casino. To be honest we hadn't spent a great deal of our time in Mayfair for that matter either. The launch party was a crude but effective way of introducing us into the glossy world of show business and celebrity. More importantly, it was a way of introducing the media to us. Then, as now, the print media in particular had an insatiable appetite for the famous, the glamorous and the exotic. I had decided to make a splash by having my hair dyed cobalt blue earlier that day by a hairdresser friend of Justin's, Daniel Galvin, especially for the occasion. The evening's black tie affair was somehow curiously quaint, like a debutante's coming-out party. With their connections, Justin and Bryan were able to invite many of the A-list celebs of the day to the launch party of The Doctors of Madness. The party scene has never really changed; it's only the names on the lists that are constantly being updated. There is perhaps a nucleic list of a thousand people, maybe fewer, who will make up the bulk of any weekday London social call. Popstars, minor aristos, City people, sportsmen, models, actors and artists who can be relied on to turn up smiling to the opening of a film, a play, an exhibition, even a can of fruit, if champagne or something stronger is promised.

Surrounded by this illustrious company we were incredibly gauche and ill at ease, and in all honesty rather embarrassed to see so many stars at our party. There were the four band members, plus Rene, Elaine (Stoner's wife), Nigel Willoughby, our soundman and Bill Gibson, the guy who had the best selection of mascara on the entire British Rail network. We would have quite liked to have had all our mates along but it wasn't really that sort of party. We huddled together for support, looking a little sheepish, nipping into the lavatories to do a line of speed, then drinking too much, too quickly, for the first couple of hours, and nudging each other like embarrassed schoolkids each time the arrival of a familiar face triggered another energetic bout of air-kissing. Among the guests that night I still remember were Peter Sellers, Sophia Loren, Omar Sharif, Twiggy, Bryan Ferry and Yves St Laurent who, in that unique and inimitable way of the very famous, tended either to stick together or be spirited off into side rooms for privacy or recreation. Bill, who by now was well-oiled and had nothing to lose, tried to enter into the spirit of things by engaging Sir John Mills in conversation by the sweet trolley, but things turned distinctly frosty when Bill said, "I hope you don't mind me saying this, Sir John, but I've always thought of you as a poor man's Alec Guinness". The poor old thespian nearly choked on his sachertorte. You could have heard a meringue drop.

That night in Mayfair, surrounded by swank, we felt a mixture of excitement and foreboding in equal measure – a feeling that our lives were about to be changed and that we were about to relinquish control. These four oiks from south London, The Doctors of Madness, were eating lobster with Doctor Fucking Zhivago and Doctor Fucking Strangelove. None of the guests had a clue who we were, of course, but the champagne never ran out, the food was exceptional, and they stayed late and were photographed leaving *our* party. The next day we were in every gossip column in every national daily newspaper and the press wanted to know more and more. Who was this band that no one had heard of, no one had seen, and no record company had yet signed. How did they get all these stars to go to their party? And . . . who was this outrageous singer called Kid Strange, and why did he have blue hair!

The record company wind-up was fuelled even further by our showcase gigs. We rented a warehouse in the railway arches under Charing Cross Station, where the club, Heaven, now is, and we would rehearse there all day every day for 10 weeks, refining the songs, the moves, seeing what worked. Trying out new performance ideas, costumes and new instruments, trying to find how best to achieve a sonic brutality.

Once the rehearsal warehouse got burgled in the middle of the night, and a tape recorder and some tapes were stolen. The next day we rigged up an absolutely lethal burglar deterrent to make sure it never happened again. Our method of deterrence was essentially to connect the entrance's metal door handle to a cable from the electric mains, going through an American step-down transformer. Another cable was attached to a metallic doormat on which any unsuspecting burglar would naturally stand. Touching the door handle while standing on the doormat would send 120 volts through the uninvited guest. We giggled like maniacs as we set the trap, not really knowing whether 120 volts could kill or merely deliver an unforgettable jolt. We arrived expectantly the next morning, like poachers going to inspect their snares. The whole lobby was blackened with soot, but the door had not been breached. We howled with laughter for days as we imagined the tableau, the blackened face and torn clothes of the putative thief, his hair standing on end as he fled for his life empty-handed.

Once a week, a top record company executive from some or other label would be invited to come along and watch us play an informal short set, with Morrison and de Villeneuve schmoozing and dispensing hospitality. We got to be the masters of the 15 minutes blitz – four great songs and out you go! On one occasion I remember Clive Davis, the head of CBS records at that time, the guy who signed Springsteen, came to watch us. The show had gone well, and Morry and Justin were exchanging conspiratorial winks with us onstage. In the middle of our fourth song finale, where thunder flashes, strobes and smoke were supposed to deliver the *coup de grâce* to any sceptical mogul, a rogue electrical cable beneath Davis's chair ignited and soon his exclusive seat was in flames. Unsure whether to vacate or stay put, he stayed put. His elegant cashmere suit was ruined as Nigel Willoughby, our roadie, somewhat over-enthusiastically turned the fire extinguisher on him and he left in something of a hurry. We didn't sign to CBS.

At weekends we would host great bacchanalian parties in the warehouse, inviting everyone we knew. The parties sometimes lasted 48 hours, and we would always get up to play and to try out new songs on this captive but critical audience. My brother Brian felt a strange combination of pride and envy at my new confidence and comparative celebrity, and one evening at one of these parties, fuelled by drink, he could contain his ambivalence towards my success no longer and threw a punch at me. While the physical pain the punch caused was minimal, the emotional pain and the symbolism of the act affected us both deeply. I can truthfully say that our relationship was never quite the same after that night, despite his tearfully sincere apologies and my genuine forgiveness. I know that to this day he has never forgiven himself for the recklessness of that act and I suspect that his subsequent problems with drink owe much to that emblematic blow.

Eventually, after a great deal of brinkmanship and the seemingly endless addition and subtraction of contractual clauses, the Morrison de Villeneuve strategy paid off and we signed a three-album deal potentially worth £150,000, with Polydor Records. The deal tied us to Polydor for the whole world, excluding the USA and Canada. We retained the rights to the albums for these territories and could consequently negotiate separately with other record companies for releases in these territories. All monies paid by US or Canadian companies would be, in effect, a bonus, as the costs of recording the albums had already been absorbed. Bryan thought signing to Polydor was a good omen: Polydor was the first label the Beatles had been signed to when they were still playing in dingy cellars in Hamburg. Polydor was not a glamorous or fashionable record company. In fact, they were unspeakably boring, full of bearded, overweight company-men in bad suits, or balding, bad-breathed middle-aged schoolboys in nylon tour-jackets, for whom the new album by Status Quo or Rainbow represented a cultural highlight. They were hot for a new band that would pep up the dreary image of Polydor Records and, by extension, pep up their dreary corporate lives.

Our man at Polydor was a likeable, but seemingly none-too-bright, New Zealander who later went on to manage The Cure and become a multi-millionaire in his own right. His name was Chris Parry. Bryan and Justin could play him like a pipe, gaining instant access to the company's hitherto unheard of marketing budgets and promotional gimmicks. Some time late in 1976, Parry came to Bryan with the tapes of a new retro mod/punk band from Woking, called The Jam, that he was considering signing to Polydor. Using Parry as a conduit, Morrison got his offer for their publishing in first and signed them for a nominal advance. He then set up a new company, And Son Music, solely for the purpose of publishing The Jam, or, more specifically, frontman Paul Weller's confused, derivative, but highly commercial pop songs. Chris Parry was made a partner in And Son Music, earning performance and mechanical royalties for every single radio play and every single record sale of The Jam thereafter. All this was in addition to drawing a healthy salary as an A and R man at Polydor. To no one's astonishment, The Jam were signed to Polydor Records by Chris Parry in early 1977 on a four-year, worldwide contract. Probably not illegal, but an unusual arrangement to say the least in those days; a perfect music biz fix of "You scratch my back and I'll scratch yours".

On Morrison's suggestion, The Jam supported us for four consecutive weeks at the Marquee Club in Soho. This was at the time when young Weller was still a fresh-faced cheerleader for Margaret Thatcher, a fact he rarely seems to remember in interviews these days. At that time his music was a fairly up-and-down rip-off of The Who, right down to the Rickenbacker guitars and the Union Jack jackets. It was before he added the Curtis Mayfield/Steve Marriott/Tim Hardin/Steve Winwood songbooks to his collection. At least you always know what you'll get with Weller – you'll get someone else! That's probably why Noel Gallagher, another no-mark who would probably spontaneously combust if he ever had an original idea, rates him so highly.

As soon as our first cheque from Polydor cleared, an initial instalment advance of £20,000, Morrison de Villeneuve put the band, plus Nigel Willoughby, who was by now our soundman and our two roadies, Hobbs and José, on wages. The band members were to receive the princely sum of £25 each per week. The roadies, who never stood to get seriously rich from the project, were on rather more. It was, even then, a pittance, but somehow at that moment it didn't matter because we had all just realised one of our dreams. We were now, for better or worse, a fully professional rock and roll band, and we were determined to enjoy it.

At the same time as we signed our record deal, we signed an exclusive agency deal with the Chrysalis Agency. An agent is responsible for arranging the performance side of a rock band's career. They book the band into the live concerts, the TV appearances and the radio shows, both at home and overseas, and we were represented there principally by a fresh-faced young graduate with a name that could have come from the pages of *A Pilgrim's Progress* – Martin Hopewell.

In August 1975, Rene and I decided that now we had the prospect of a bit of money coming in, we should try to have a baby. She had finished college and was working from home as a freelance illustrator, doing children's books, record covers and anything else that came her way. We were extraordinarily lucky and we were both shocked and thrilled when she conceived almost immediately, with the prospect of a birth the following May.

In September 1975, we went into Majestic Studios, a converted cinema in Clapham in south London, with a producer who might have been named by a Bunyonesque market researcher – John Punter. Majestic didn't have a great deal going for it as a studio except that it was in south London, where we all lived; Eno had recorded his first solo album there; and it was cheap. John Punter didn't have a great deal going for him as a producer except that he lived in London, he'd worked with Roxy Music and he was cheap! He hadn't been our first choice – we'd wanted Eno, or Tony Visconti or Bowie's engineer, Ken Scott. But they were all either too busy or too expensive, so we got Punter.

Recording your first album is, by definition, a unique and unrepeatable experience, whoever your producer is. All the ideas you have had while writing and performing the songs live start to crystallise as you head towards recording the definitive version of a song. Only later do you find out that there is no definitive version, only versions that are fixed in time or medium, and which work more or less well. The possible permutations of recording a four-piece band on 24 tracks of tape are limitless. It is like a monstrous game of chicken in which, at some point, someone, producer, band member, manager or record company loses their nerve and says "Stop! We've got it!" At over £100 per hour all-in, in 1975, it could have been a very expensive game of chicken. In fact, we negotiated a lockout rate with the studio, which meant that we had 24 hour-a-day access to record, overdub and mix the album, and the whole process took about six weeks.

We went in with the idea of recording nine songs, from which we would select the best eight for release on the album. In those days, before samplers and computers became as common-place in studios as microphones and amplifiers, it would take literally hours, sometimes days, to get even a basic drum kit sound together. As this was usually the first job to be done before starting recording proper, the three non-drumming members of the band tried to maintain enthusiasm throughout the first days as Peter di Lemma's kit was dismantled, stuffed with cushions, taped up, slackened off, tightened up, compressed, limited and equalised in an attempt to move on to the next phase of the process. Microphone distances from the drums and cymbals were minutely adjusted and all the while we were chomping at the bit, just aching to get on. These first days of a recording session are typically attended by a whole retinue of band members, girlfriends, roadies, management, record company execs, hangers on and liggers, all passing through to see how you're progressing, only to leave after two excruciatingly boring hours during which the drummer tries to find out why his bass-drum pedal is squeaking.

Eventually, when a workable drum sound has been achieved, or when the boredom of the other members has reached such a pitch that not only the idea of murdering the drummer, but also a method of disposing of the body is being seriously discussed, and when another cup of tar-coloured coffee will turn the producer positively psychotic, it is the turn of the bass player to inflict his own singular torment on the others. This will normally consist of an ineptly played two- or three-note pattern that initially overloads the speaker cabinet and then starts to shake it so profoundly that the amplifier, which is sitting precariously on top of it, comes crashing to the floor and then falls suddenly and ominously silent. This is the signal for a roadie, who earns more than any single band member, and who has spent the last three days on the telephone trying to score some overpriced speed or cocaine, to spring into action with a screwdriver and a bewildered frown. He is fully competent at removing the wooden back panel of the amplifier, the bit on to which he has crudely stencilled a dyslexic Docors of Mandess [sic] in cheap emulsion, but there, sadly, his expertise ends.

It is a constant source of wonderment to me how many separate pieces, small and large, fall out of the back of a broken bass amplifier, but the sequence of events that follows is always the same: a delay of several hours while the surly roadie, distracted from his one true passion in life, the pursuit of the finest Class A drugs, goes off in search of an equipment-hire company who have a selection of bass amplifiers in stock, and a management company secretary who can find someone in the office authorised to sign a cheque for the hire. This is where the money and the time go. Another cast-iron certainty in rock and roll is that when, many hours later, the replacement amplifier is finally brought to the studio and installed by the sweating, cursing, harassed roadie with a parking ticket now showing out of his back jeans pocket, the bass player will not be happy with the new equipment. He will reprise the two- or three-note pattern ever more ineptly, curl his lip and go into a terminal sulk, becoming positively homicidal or suicidal when told by a helpful colleague or producer, "Believe me, it sounds great, and anyway, we've really got to crack on." He will then proceed to make the roadie's life hell for the next two days.

A guitarist's chosen method of irritating the hell out of his musical colleagues is not subtle, but is very effective. His preferred *modus operandi* will be to plug his guitar into a wah-wah pedal or similar effects unit, which will invariably introduce an inordinate amount of both humming and crackling into his deafening, but otherwise undistinguished, guitar sound. Each time he depresses the pedal with his snakeskin-booted foot, or even so much as touches the guitar lead, a blood chilling sound issues from the loudspeaker like a bronchial geriatric banshee clearing her throat to make way for the final death rattle. It will never occur to him to turn the amplifier volume down until the fault is found and cured, as this would be tantamount to surrender. And besides, when you have spent the best part of a week witnessing the technical and musical inadequacies of your fellow band members, your roadies and your producer, boy you've *earned* these few moments of your own.

The foregoing, briefly and with little exaggeration, describes our first week in the studio. You find out quite quickly when you turn professional which of the guys in the band you actually like and which you don't. The rest of your professional life together is spent coming to terms with that realisation and finding a way of working within it. The unique sound of the Doctors really came jointly from the musicianship of Stoner and Urban Blitz. Peter and I were just about competent and adequate musicians, but the racket that those two guys made was what made our sound. As a vocalist I knew I was no great shakes, my range is too limited, but as a performer who could put over those songs I'm pretty good. I work within my limitations, but always try to push myself to expand them.

With the early technical problems overcome, we set about our task of recording a great first album with a genuine relish and a manic intensity. I wanted to make an album that would contain, reflect and mutate everything I had ever felt, ever experienced in my 24 years. I wanted it to reflect every joy, every disappointment, every grudge and every resentment. I wanted it to be full of bitterness, desolation, alienation, bile and fury. Such tenderness as there was would be tempered with cynicism and distance. Such romance as there was would be doomed to painful breakdown. I wanted the record to be dark, cinematic and colossal. My subject matter was urban decay, neurosis and corruption. I had the anarchist's loathing for all systems of control. Lyrically, my roots were in the singer-songwriter tradition of Bob Dylan, Leonard Cohen, Jacques Brel and David Bowie, but my songs were seasoned with a sour edge and a rotten middle, courtesy of William Burroughs. Musically I loved the energy, directness and gonzo *avant gardism* of the Velvet Underground at their most uncompromising. Walls of white noise and feedback laid over speed-fuelled, dumb-ass rhythm. The harmonic equivalent of bare-knuckle fighting. Sonic porn.

We set ourselves into a circle in the studio, turned down the lights and attempted to blow each other off the face of the earth. We recorded several versions of each song, changing our performances each time. All the tracks were recorded live in the studio, with any overdubs and corrections done later. It meant that the album was hell to mix because there was so much sound spillage. For instance, the drum microphones were picking up the sounds of the guitar, the violin and the bass so it was impossible to alter the sound of the drums without also altering the sound of the other instruments. But we felt that what the songs lost in clarity and definition of sound, they gained in spirit and atmosphere.

We settled on recording nine songs in all: *Waiting, Please Don't Shoot The Pianist, B-Movie Bedtime, Afterglow, Mitzi's Cure, I Think We're Alone, The Noises Of The Evening, Billy Watch Out,* and *Mainlines.* The first three tracks were out-and-out rockers, and the other six were mutated wide-screen ballads. *Waiting* and *Please Don't Shoot The Pianist* were recorded straight to tape with no breaks in between, with a basic drums, bass guitar, rhythm guitar and violin line-up. That's how we played those two songs live and so it seemed natural when recording them to run one into the other. More guitars were added to *Waiting*, almost a punk song in its clattering four-to-the-bar simplicity, and the lead vocal was patched up where required. When deciding whether to repair or redo things, we always opted for feel over precision. If something *felt* right, it didn't matter if it didn't quite *sound* right, it stayed in.

Stoner and Peter added backing vocals, and a tambourine was added to *Please Don't Shoot The Pianist*. That was about it.

B-Movie Bedtime was another of the earliest recordings in those sessions, and it benefited from the addition of a frantic harmonica solo which I put on the last half-verse instrumental section. Urban Blitz played the second electric guitar on that track. He had a very unconventional approach to guitar playing, and his solo and counterpoint guitar lines always had a very angular quality to them. Lyrically, it was a stream of consciousness type of song, which owed quite a debt to William Burroughs:

I had written *Mitzi's Cure, I Think We're Alone* and *The Noises Of The Evening* as a trilogy of songs, almost as a mini-soap-operetta, and that's how we played them, both live and in these recording sessions. They chart the breakdown of a friend of mine at the time (whose name *wasn't* Mitzi). The first song lists unrelated everyday events, like headlines from a newspaper, combining the dramatic with the banal, the sensational with the humdrum, against a slow, simple melody. It used the cut-up method of writing, discovered by the surrealist Tristan Tzara, and championed by William Burroughs and Brion Gysin; letting random and chance dictate a narrative and descriptive flow.

The music for the verses is hypnotic and repetitive – bass, acoustic guitar and drums all washed over by Urban's restrained, modulating droning violin, which was fed through a variety of effects to warp the sound still further. On the refrain the drones clear, and the clarity of simple guitar arpeggios and guitar harmonics comes as a relief as the voices of Peter and Stoner act as the Greek chorus in a two-part, understated harmony. When the song reaches its climax, another acoustic guitar slides out from underneath and leads the song into *I Think We're Alone,* which I performed solo with just the acoustic guitar. The song finds Mitzi in hospital, traumatised and sedated, trying to co-operate with the doctors, but feeling frustrated by their lack of understanding.

The third and final song of the sequence, *The Noises Of The Evening*, is brought in by a mutated funk riff on Stoner's fuzzed-up bass, a choppy rhythm guitar, a honking alto sax which I found lying around in the studio, ambulance sirens, then a dirty guitar solo and finally Urban's violin takes up the same riff as the bass guitar and sees the frenzy home to the second section. A totally contrasting atmospheric soundscape, with acoustic guitars, violin and assorted sound effects acts as the musical platform for a phased lead vocal. A blistering instrumental section follows the vocal verses which, when I hear it now, sounds like a Dervish vortex. The music spirals with an ever increasing intensity, led by Blitz's jazz-fired violin solo, while di Lemma adds timbales to punctuate the rhythm of his kit and Stoner plays one of the finest bass lines he ever devised, a bursting, bubbling loop. When the music can get no higher or more intense a final vocal coda intervenes, to close the song.

These three songs, jointly and separately represent the gloomiest and darkest music I have ever written.

Billy Watch Out! was another song with a multi-part arrangement structure. I wrote the song about several friends of mine who were all going through some very weird scenes at the time.

"Billy" was Bill Gibson, the guy who had once been in the band but had become an alcoholic and was on the skids. Tony was a guy at Rene's college who wanted so desperately to have an affair with her that he ended up in one of the many mental hospitals around the London-Surrey borders. He had also played bass guitar with us for a couple of the earliest gigs. He was actually a very nice guy who just smoked too much dope and got into that downward spiral. Nancy was an olive-skinned, Jewish-American beauty, the mother of a child whose father was Roy Harper, the English singer-songwriter and veteran of all the 1968 Hyde Park free concerts. He was a friend and a major song-writing inspiration to me at one time.

He turned me on to Friedrich Nietzsche and Bertrand Russell. I loved the anger and the passionate intensity of his songs such as *I Hate The White Man* and *She's The One*, and I liked the commitment and fire he showed in live performance, and his ability to involve an audience in a dialectic. Or, at least, make the audience feel like they were involved in a dialectic – in fact for the most part his rants were just stoned monologues, but usually they were no less enjoyable or memorable for that.

Nancy came to live with Rene and me when her baby was born and her relationship with Harper was becoming increasingly destructive and antagonistic.

Eventually Nancy and the baby moved out, and Harper subsequently became consumed by self-pity and staged a melodramatic, but none-too-convincing, suicide attempt. He turned up on our doorstep wrapped in a blanket, saying he had tried to kill himself and needed a place to stay. Rene was fantastic with him, calming him down and chilling him out, and listening as he raved into the night. When he found another girlfriend a few weeks later he was gone, the interlude was excised from his memory and typically he never showed Rene any gratitude for what she did for him that night.

Harper is an egotistical, emotional bully. But he is much more besides, which is why so many women love him. For a while in the early seventies he was Led Zeppelin's constant companion and jester. The famously hedonistic lifestyle enjoyed by Zeppelin on the road nearly killed him physically and artistically. He bought into the whole trip, wanted that sort of success more than anything in the world, and was nearly destroyed by it.

I wrote *Billy, Watch Out!* at a time when I felt bullshitting was an enjoyable and instructive way of passing time, and four or five of us would routinely spend a whole night just shooting the breeze and expounding ill-conceived theories or poorly reasoned arguments.

Afterglow was a big, squelchy, amorous ballad about post-coital bliss. It was essentially an acoustic guitar sort of song, but on the recording the bass guitar really becomes the lead instrument. Stoner plays a beautiful aching, yearning line, full of melody and yet somehow very controlled and restrained. At his best he was a bass player with sublime taste and touch. Phil McNeill of the *New Musical Express* got it dead right when he said, "[Stoner] is a superbly fluent bassist whose every note, whether guiding the music or soloing against it, is totally in accord with the meaning of the song."

Drums and violin completed the instrumental line-up, with Peter adding some congas on the middle-eight. The song featured a lot of vocal harmonies from Stoner and Peter, and a certain amount of flanging on the guitars and violin, which made the whole thing swirl and sound very pretty. On reflection I think now that the song starts and stops too often, but that aside, it is one of the best tracks on the album.

The standout track on the album was a song that became a show-stopper for us in live performance. It was a 15-minute plus wide-screen audio movie about lowlife and the urban underbelly. It was called *Mainlines*. It began with a sort of prologue, sung against a electric baritone viola, electric guitar, a massive fuzz bass and huge symphonic drums:

> *This is the place the rats come to die*
> *This is the crossroads for you and I*
> *To the left is a wilderness of animal fun*
> *To the right is the vacuum of life in the sun*
> *Behind is the dirt-track that was our survival*
> *Ahead the fear-factories await our arrival*

An instrumental bridge follows, which leads into the second section of the song, a sparse, urgent off-beat verse-chorus structure.

A four-minute long coruscating violin solo ensues, which Urban drives to hell and back, displaying all the fabulous warped dynamics of his playing, from hoarse-whisperer to banshee wail. The impressive thing about Blitz's violin playing is that, unusually for a rock violinist, he never tries to sound cod-classical. When there is nowhere left for him to go, the last verse hammers in, and the songs finishes on a repeated coda, "Mainline trains could never find drivers to run a service out to here", sung over and over, with more and more voices joining the refrain, and the whole band slugging it out. Urban Blitz and Stoner trade riffs like prize-fighters, and samples from all the other songs on the album are spun into the maelstrom of noise, until it is all like so much white noise. It was a glorious session, with the rawness of the dynamics and performance being perfectly in sync with the subject matter. We listened back to it once in the control room and said, "Yep. That's it."

Mid-recording I wrote to my brother Brian to give him an update:

> Things are so wonderful for us at the moment. We are three-quarters through the LP, which is going to be incredible. Really brain-damage time when that is out. We have just completed the first two gigs of a 40-date tour that reads like Division Four of the Football League. Reading, which was dire, and St Alban's, which was phenomenal. They really loved us there, especially Urban Blitz, crawling round on his knees playing mind-warp solos.
>
> PS The lovely Rene is having a baby in May and if it hasn't got blue hair there will be some questions asked.

The mixing stage of the recording process is where the most fights occur. Mixing is the part of the process after recording when the 24 separate instrumental and vocal tracks that you have recorded are balanced against each other to create the most effective and sonorous whole. Or at least that's what it should be. In reality it is an opportunity for all the grudges and resentments that have been built up through the recording stage to be wheeled out once again, and for old scores to be settled. The trouble is this: we all hear music differently. To some, the power of the music should come from the very depths, the almost subliminal interplay between bass and drums, a dark primeval rumble. This is most obvious in music such as reggae and hip-hop, music that is driven more by rhythm than by melody. To others, the "wall of sound" is the desirable end result, where no individual instrument really takes precedent over any other, but the whole "sound" is what matters. The Rolling Stones and just about every other rock band would fall into this category. And to others still, it is essential that the lyrics of the songs sit atop everything, for the listener to hear. This is heard most typically in folk music and with singer-songwriters.

Now it is inevitable that, just as an actor really only watches his own performance on screen, a musician naturally attunes his ear to what *he* is playing on a song, and to him it becomes the most important part of the song. If a bass player says, "Could you turn the bass guitar up a little in the mix?" it means something else will immediately sound quieter, as "turning up" and "turning down" are only relative to the levels of the other instruments. This is where the trouble starts. A perfectly serviceable mix of a song will be sabotaged by a simple request such as "Could you turn the bass guitar up a little?" as it will provoke the drummer to ask, "Can you just push the bass drum a bit?" to maintain it's parity with the bass guitar. With bass guitar and bass drum now louder than they were, the overall balance of a song can start to sound a bit wonky, or a bit muddy. This is where the guitarist now wants *his* instruments level increased as "It's getting a bit lost against the bottom end". Suddenly, you can no longer hear the vocals, because everything behind them has been increased in volume.

Next, a record company executive will drop by to listen to what you are doing, will share his drugs with you and tell you that he feels the song sounds a little slow. You get the picture. That is why mixing is so fraught with pitfalls and why a strong producer at the controls is a must if all-out internecine war between the band members is to be avoided. Sadly, Punter was not an especially strong producer, and we ran riot over the mixing stage, to the detriment of the record. We eventually finished at the end of November.

In all we had recorded about 55 minutes of music, which in the days of vinyl was still considered too long, as sound quality starts to deteriorate on vinyl after about 45 minutes. The grooves on the record get forced too close together, and a loss of volume and frequency range results. With modern compact discs you can squeeze a lot more music on to an album, but in those days of vinyl and analogue, an hour of music on an LP was out of the question.

We hadn't really thought a great deal about the cover of the album, but since Rene had put in so much unpaid work on our behalf over the years I thought the least we could do would be to commission her to design the sleeve. We agreed that the front cover image would be an illustration rather than a photograph, and, since the album title was *Late Night Movies, All Night Brainstorms*, we had the idea of the band sitting in a cinema – a rather obvious and literal idea in retrospect. Justin took reference photographs of us from which Rene worked, and eventually she produced a cover that was a slightly weird and unsettling image of the band watching themselves on a cinema screen. The reverse was a sort of burnt-out version, as if we had just spontaneously combusted. I think she was paid £200 for the finished artwork. Along with the normal playing and writing credits on the back, I insisted that the album cover should offer the following advice to the listener: "This record to be played with the gas full on".

Although neither I, nor anyone else except a handful of fans who were actually there knew it, on 6 November 1975 a band called the Sex Pistols played their first ever gig. They supported a pub-rock band, Bazooka Joe, who featured a guy calling himself Adam Ant on vocals, at St Martin's Art College in London. While no one remarked on it at the time, it seems to me now that in the six months between the evacuation of the last Americans from Vietnam and that first Sex Pistols gig, my "younger generation" had been replaced by the next one.

In the autumn of 1975, Justin had managed to pull a few strings so that on the 12 December we got a spot on *The Twiggy Show* on BBC2. Twiggy had already found her way out of mod-elling via the catch-all world of the Light Entertainment TV show, and the format of these shows was always the same. Fronted by a celebrity (Cilla Black, Dusty Springfield, Lulu, etc.), these heavily scripted shows would feature a few songs by the hostess, a mercifully short, lame comic sketch which showcased the hostess's acting skills (or not), and a couple of guests. On one such show we were her guests. We sang two songs (we played *Doctors Of Madness* alone and *Perfect Past* as a cheesy duet with Twiggy). It must be said that, with the exception of the memorable appearance by Jimi Hendrix on *The Lulu Show* in 1967, no band like us had ever crossed over into that world before; without Justin we would not have got past the front door of Television Centre.

We milked our allotted six or seven minutes for all they were worth. I wore the white suit, and with the blue hair and contact lenses I looked like one of the Undead. I can only imagine the disgust of Middle England, sitting down with their tea on their laps hoping for a cosy night with Twiggy, only to have their evening calm shattered by the brutal sonic assault of *Doctors Of Madness*. We went berserk and the studio technicians were horrified, not knowing whether to run for cover or pull the plugs. All the while Justin and Morry, beaming at the spectacle from the wings, were cajoling us with cries of "Go on, my sons. Stick it up 'em!" The ballad, *Perfect Past*, which eventually appeared on our second album, sounded positively sac-charine by comparison, with Twiggy and myself exchanging verses and cuddling up. Yuck, it must have looked revolting.

With our first television appearance, we started to get an inordinate amount of music press coverage, even though we hadn't yet toured or released a record. Jonh Ingham of *Sounds* was the first to write about us. He came to the management office and we chatted nervously for an hour or so. In December 1975 he wrote: "Their music, especially Urban Blitz's violin, is commanding, and there is no doubt that Kid Strange's stage presence is developing into a *tour de force*". He also interviewed Bryan and Justin, which may have been a bit of a mistake. You don't want your managers at an interview any more than you want your parents at your first date. Bryan bragged, "We've got something lined up for America that is the biggest thing ever.

No other British band has done it except the Beatles before they arrived." The "something" to which Bryan was referring was indeed a masterstroke. He had persuaded the giant US TV network NBC to do a whole programme about the Doctors of Madness for their prime time *Weekend* slot. The 40-minute show would be shot in the UK and would follow the band into every aspect of their lives. It was agreed that they would have unlimited access to all the band members, plus interviews with Morry and Justin, the roadies, the Chrysalis Agency, Polydor, the fans and Uncle Tom Cobley and all.

Soon after the agreement was reached a small TV crew arrived from the States and started to follow us round, with a preppy, podgy guy called Greg as director-anchor man. We found a big municipal concert hall in Bishop's Stortford, an hour and a half drive from London, which we booked for three weeks to rehearse our stage show. Every day we would drive up from London in a flotilla of vehicles, rehearse for eight hours and drive back. It was punishing but essential if we were to make the transition from the intimacy of the back room of a pub to the comparative vastness of the seated concert halls that we knew Martin Hopewell at Chrysalis was booking us into for the winter.

The television crew filmed everything, the journeys, the rehearsals, the out-of-tune vocal harmonies, the fights, the sulking, the dope-smoking, with an easy-going conspiratorial friendliness. We soon were hardly aware of their presence. For the band interviews they came to our houses and interviewed us separately. For mine they came to our flat and we shot it in the sitting room. We had no central heating, just a three-bar electric fire to warm the room. For the interview they asked me to switch two of the bars off as it would look more poignant – the Artist freezing in his garret. We spoke for an hour or so and they left happy. They did something similar with all of the other band members and the roadies. When they interviewed Bryan and Justin they did so at their homes, or in smart restaurants, or at a polo match in the country. This whole process went on for about a month.

On New Year's Eve 1975, Martin Hopewell had booked us on to a massive indoor music festival at Olympia, in West London. It was called something ludicrous like *The Best of British Rock*. We were the absolute bottom of the bill of about 10 acts, most of whom were either soft rock or heavy metal. Top of the bill were 12-bar boogie merchants, Status Quo. As it was an all-day affair, we arrived in good time, as we knew we would be opening the show. We filed past the hierarchy of the changing-room trailers, from the massive Winnebagos, which were like mobile chateaux for the headline bands, past the Mercedes top-of-the-range, long wheel-based campers for the middle order until eventually we found ours, a tiny caravan parked next to the lavatories.

We tried to be upbeat but it was depressing. The stage-manager told us we were due onstage at 11am sharp. We thought that he meant for our sound check, but in this we were sorely mistaken and we ushered towards the stage at 11am and told to play. When the last gig you played was to about 100 people in the back room of the Cabbage Patch pub in Twickenham, the terror you feel stepping on to the stage in the cavernous Olympia is enough to cause instant and dramatic incontinence.

We used to open our show with a tape recording of Marlene Dietrich singing *Falling in Love Again* to set an appropriately louche atmosphere, and we saw no reason to change that for this show. Things got off to a bad start as the tape got mangled in the machine after 30 seconds and we were still a good minute's walk from the stage. We quickened our step, but by the time we arrived at the stage there had already been 30 seconds of a tape that sounded like a German chanteuse being eaten alive by a hump-backed whale. The audience warmed to the sport and decided that we must be a comedy act. We gazed out at 8000 people and began our first number, an extreme, Burroughsian piece of grotesque entitled *Pigface And The Shiny Gang*. It was a slow, funereal dirge enlivened by some nifty lyrics, some over ambitious time-signature changes and a ham-fistful of crunching power chords. Since we had had no sound check, the monitor balance on stage made it impossible to hear each other. We huddled together in an attempt to pick up visual cues from each other, but to little avail. The sound was sucked into the aircraft hanger of a building and bounced back off the far wall five seconds later. We were shambolic. The audience had come to boogie and to rock, and the song went down like a lead balloon.

The next few numbers fared little better but gradually Nigel, our soundman, started to make sense of the mixing desk, which he was using for the first time in his life. We started to get some grudging applause from a small band of enthusiasts at the front of the stage, and we began to pick up some energy from them. In an attempt to leave the audience with a favourable impression of us, for the last number we slammed into *Waiting*, the nearest thing we had to an out-and-out rocker. On one of the instrumental passages, under the intermit-tent flashing of a temperamental strobe light, I threw handfuls of Doctors of Madness badges and silver promotional flexidiscs out into the audience. It was a dramatic moment, watching them hang in the strobe-lit air as if they were suspended in space. It was unspeakably dispir-iting when the audience started picking them up and hurling them back at the band onstage, along with mince pies, coins and beer cans. We left the stage with catcalls and boos ringing in our ears. It had not been a good gig.

Back at the caravanette, Justin was furious. "I told you not start with that fucking song! *Pigface* is instant death. It was like throwing a bucket of cold water all over the audience before you'd even fucking started." Bryan was similarly unimpressed. "You blew that one, my sons," he said encouragingly, sucking on his cigar, "What did you start with that fucking song for? It's a bleedin' dog!" The atmosphere in the caravanette was dire. The guys from the agency and from the record company filed by, like mourners paying their last respects to a little-loved friend. Oh, and of course Greg and our friends from NBC were there to record the whole unhappy scene. We knew we had made a mistake doing the show at all, but there was no way to undo it. "We got a lot of work to do, my sons," said Morrison as he headed for his Range Rover. "Happy New Year," and with that he and Justin left Olympia. It seemed that they didn't like our "fuck you" attitude quite so much any more.

Nineteen seventy-six got off to a terrible start, with Justin telephoning me and saying that he couldn't work with Bryan anymore, that he was a pig and that the band had to choose whether we wanted Bryan or himself to manage us from now on. We couldn't have both. I called a meeting at my home with the other guys in the band, plus the inner sanctum of intimates: Nigel and Hobbsy, Rene and Stoner's wife, Elaine (both now conspicuously pregnant). We discussed the two options open to us for a couple of hours, weighing up the pros and cons of each of our two managers, and finally came down on the side of staying with Bryan. Although he wasn't as flamboyant or hands-on as Justin, or even as much fun to be with, we reckoned that he was more of a heavyweight and had more clout in the business. It was horrible having to telephone Justin and tell him our decision but he was extremely gracious and forgiving. He wished me well, and said he would leave the door open. I think the Olympia show had shaken his faith in the band or at least brought home to him that it might be a long haul to the success we all craved, and he decided to withdraw. The rivalry between Bryan and him had only served as the catalyst for his withdrawal.

Bryan decided that the best way for us to get over the disappointment of Olympia was to get back out on the road as quickly as possible, to play to audiences and to improve our stagecraft, so immediately afterwards we did our first European dates, in Holland and France, and started to get some good reactions. We were getting better with every gig that we did. It is the most appalling cliché, but there really is no substitute for experience for any sort of live performer. One of the best shows we did was at the renowned Parisian venue, Le Bataclan. We played a fantastic set there and brought the house down. The audience went wild, Bryan Morrison was ecstatic and bought everybody champagne, and the critics were rapturous: "To see them evokes the first Roxy Music gig at The Bataclan," gushed the taste-making *Rock and Folk* magazine. "The same sensation this night in '76 that the Martians have landed. They are violently modernist. Urban Blitz played the most incredible violin we have heard since John Cale wielded his bow at the Mont de Piétié. Their record comes out in March, but please, someone bring them back before then."

We returned to the UK with our confidence sky-high, a French record company who couldn't wait for the record to come out and, most importantly, with Bryan Morrison believing in his boys again.

While we had been recording the album, back in October and November, Martin Hopewell had been looking into various possibilities for live appearances. The options are pretty limited for an unknown band, even for one with a record contract. The choice was either to play tiny toilets the length and breadth of the country, and try to build up a following and get some press coverage in time for the release of the record, or to support a bigger band who already had a following of their own, and whose audience might be supposed to be receptive to the music of the support band. That way you get to play to much larger audiences from the start. Bryan and Martin had already decided that a supporting role was the way forward for the Doctors, and a tour supporting the band BeBop Deluxe was arranged.

We were not particularly happy about playing a support slot to a headlining act. It sort of went against what we had always tried to do – to make every show our own. I guess in a way this was our first big compromise, our first sell-out. Pragmatism ensured that it would not be our last. The record company and agency convinced us this would be the short cut to a large following.

Running through January and February 1976, it was a 27-date UK tour, playing some of the biggest rock venues in the country, like the Manchester Free Trade Hall and Leeds University. We were paid a flat fee of £50 a night, and out of that we had to pay all our own expenses.

The shows were fraught with the soundcheck and equipment problems that are customary on these tours. The headline band arrives at a venue at six o'clock, fools around on stage for an hour-and-a-half while their sound man gets a sound together, then shambles off to leave the support band (us) to get their equipment on to that part of the stage that is not yet occupied by a drum riser or a bank of keyboards. The support band then also tries to get some semblance of a sound balance whilst all the time being admonished by the headline band's sound crew. "Don't touch that microphone, it's set for Bill" etc. Invariably at some point during this humiliation the doors of the auditorium will be thrown open by an over-zealous steward, and the great unwashed will surge forward to grab the best viewing positions and you will flee the stage in embarrassment and frustration. Twenty minutes later, when you are due to start your set, your first three songs will disappear in a howl of feedback while your soundman tries to ascertain which microphone is on which piece of equipment. Fortunately the audience cannot see your blushes as your lighting man has not yet found the master fader for the lighting desk, and you are playing in pitch darkness.

Sometimes this state of affairs could be positively dangerous. One night we played at the Malvern Winter Gardens where we had to go on without even the most basic sort of sound check. On taking the stage I plugged in my guitar, played the introduction to a song, and as soon as my lips touched the microphone I received a massive electric shock, which sent me literally flying headlong over the orchestra pit and into the second row of the stalls. Miraculously I wasn't hurt and, with a little help from the audience, I was manhandled back on stage, and when the fault was fixed we carried on. The rest of the band were totally unaware that I had got an electric shock, and thought that I was just working on another way to pull focus. Despite all this we managed to pull off some great shows, and started, on that first tour, to build a following around the country. We also began to make friends and enemies in the press. Reviewing one of those early gigs, Phil McNeil of the *New Musical Express* said, "The Doctors of Madness provided an entertaining and edifying opener. Kid Strange appears to write good songs, Urban Blitz is a good, brain-damaging violinist and Stoner, one of the best-looking people in rock, is a surprisingly lyrical bassist. The whole band understands what's happening."

As for BeBop Deluxe, we kinda liked them, but they were a bit paranoid and a bit straight. They were very ambitious, and their record company, EMI, sank a lot of money into them in the form of tour support. Tour support, put simply, means financial assistance towards the huge cost of touring, helping out with such things as the hire of a PA system and lighting rig, transport, hotels and wages. Before videos and TV became the main marketing tools for record companies, the only viable way for a band to build up a major following was literally to take to the road, so the companies treated tour-support as part of the marketing or promotional budget.

The opening to their show was a ludicrously overblown affair, typical of the excesses of rock at that time. The four band members stood moodily in a seven-foot high glass tube in the middle of a dimly-lit stage, looking a little gormless and embarrassed, while dry ice swirled all around and the song *When You Wish Upon A Star* from Disney's film, *Pinocchio*, played over the PA. At an appropriately dramatic moment the tube was supposed to be hydraulically lifted clear of the band, leaving them free to grab their instruments and crash into their first number. It was woefully ill-conceived as a piece of drama, because any impact that may have been made by the initial image was dissipated by the undignified and hazardous rush across a cluttered stage in half-darkness to their instruments. There were just too many potential pitfalls built in.

On one hilarious occasion, the hydraulic lift failed and the four increasingly restive-looking members were marooned in their glass tube, which was filling up alarmingly with noxious fumes. Only the quick-witted action of their roadie saved their lives. He set about the structure with a six-pound hammer and reduced it to smithereens. How we laughed from the wings. That tube was never seen again after that night. There is a scene in the painfully accurate Rob Reiner "rockumentary", *This Is Spinal Tap*, in which an almost identical piece of misfortune befalls the band. That is just one reason why that film has an almost macabre fascination for me. Every single scene in the film happened to me, either exactly or in a variation, at some point in my rock career, (except, regrettably, the number five hit in Japan).

Despite the rivalries and petty jealousies of being on tour, I enjoyed the company of Bill Nelson, BeBop Deluxe's Yorkshire-born frontman. He was, and as far as I know remains, a fine, subtle and original guitar player who was never really cut out for the rough and tumble of rock and roll excess. In spite of receiving the hefty support of EMI, and being handled by a very ambitious and ruthless management company, his band never really crossed the Rubicon from being popular to being big. I suspect his heart was never really in it. He certainly always seemed happiest when we were in a dressing room or a bar after a show, chatting about the films of Jean Cocteau or the plays of Jean-Paul Sartre. On our second album I dedicated a song to him called *In Camera*, after the Sartre play.

Our accounts for the year ending 31 December 1975 showed that we had earned a total of £1624.16 from playing gigs, but that our expenses from the day we had signed with Morrison de Villeneuve were in excess of £11,000. Because our income from this tour was negligible, Bryan decided that we should make savings wherever possible. He hit on the idea that since our greatest expenses would be transport and hotel accommodation for the seven members of the band and crew, why not combine the two and hire a mobile home for the duration of the tour? In theory it didn't sound a bad idea, but in practice it was purgatory. Living and working 24-hours a day with this extended family, with no means of escape and no privacy was my idea of hell. Add to this the fact that it was mid-winter and that sometimes in Scotland the temperature outside was minus 10 degrees, and that most nights we were sleeping in a motorway lay-by or car park, with juggernauts thundering by and threatening to upend us, and you will get some idea of the depths of misery and discomfort to which we sank in those early days.

"Keep it cheap" could have been Morrison's motto. His management commission (20% plus VAT) came out of our net earnings. The lower we kept our overheads, the higher his cut of what was left. Sometimes in an emergency we had to supplement our meagre wages by going through the record cupboards in Polydor's offices, often furtively leaving the building with 50 newly-released albums under our coats or stuffed into guitar cases, which we would immediately sell for a pound a shot to Cheapo Cheapo records (where I had once worked and been considerably better paid).

* * *

Our first headline tour followed almost immediately after the BeBop Deluxe tour, to coincide with the release of *Late Night Movies, All Night Brainstorms*. No longer able to handle the claustrophobia of the mobile home, but still constrained by Morrison's tight hand on the purse strings, we bought a 39-seater Bedford Duple coach for £1100. We took out half the seats so that we could also transport all our equipment with us.

The bus was part mobile hotel, part bordello and part pharmacy. If we were leaving a town after a gig and one of us had scored with a local girl, we would have to consummate the relationship in the fully-loaded bus, while Nigel gallantly stuck to a holding pattern on a ring road until it was obvious from the sounds emerging from beneath the blankets that some sort of animal satisfaction had been achieved and it was time to drop the girl somewhere close to where she could catch the night bus home. It was a shameful state of affairs seen from these PC days, and not especially gallant even in that pre-PC world.

As a vehicle of transportation rather than of fornication the coach was woefully unreliable, and without question it was totally illegal. Nonetheless, we drove it all over the UK and Europe. Nigel never did quite manage to gauge the width of that coach accurately, as a trail of damaged parked cars all across Europe will witness. Those narrow streets alongside the canals of Amsterdam are no place for a pissed, stoned and exhausted roadie to attempt to drive a 39-seater bus. But at least while we were in Europe we stayed in hotels, albeit flea-pit hotels, if only because the promoter of the gigs was contractually obliged to pay for them.

Back in England we thought nothing of driving home 200 miles after a gig to save on hotel costs. Those were those prehistoric days before cappuccino, before McDonalds and before the mobile phone. Fortified by amphetamine and adrenalin, our intrepid roadies drove back to London from Doncaster or Sheffield, from Cardiff or Exeter or Liverpool, to save us a few precious pounds. We invested part of the savings in speed, usually amphetamine sulphate, to keep us all awake and to reduce our appetites so that we didn't spend so much money on food, and the rest went to reduce our debt to Morrison. No wonder I looked skeletal in those live photos. Usually these post-gig drives were perfunctory dashes down whichever motorway led to London in the shortest possible time.

On one occasion, having just consumed some or other oil-slick-on-a-plate at a motorway service station, I wandered into the shop and was confronted by the bizarre spectacle of Captain Beefheart, a man who single-handedly defined the term "eccentric rock star", buying up their entire stock of tacky ceramic dogs. I watched in awe as the bemused sales assistant packed figurine after figurine in tissue paper and then into cardboard boxes. In the middle of this, Beefheart, these days better known as the painter, Don Van Vliet, looked at me, six foot three, thin as a whiplash, and blue-haired, and, with his mouth agape, remarked "Man, you are one weird cat!" I took it as a compliment, coming as it did from the "high priest of weird".

The gig venues themselves were, for the most part, awful rancid-smelling dives, which held anywhere between 300 and 1000 punters, who were pressed so close to you on the low stage that you could smell the beer and saveloys on their breath. The promoters at these clubs were always hearty men with hefty paunches who seemed to be forever sailing close to the extremities of the law. Some would greet us like long lost friends and offer us a drink before announcing, almost gleefully, that advance ticket sales were shit and that he had thought about cancelling the show and putting on a stripper instead, but the stripper had haemorrhoids and couldn't risk putting a G-string on, so we were going to have to play anyway. As the rain lashed down outside on a bleak Tuesday night in February, and 50 disinterested punters rattled around inside the desolate Nelson's Column club in Burnley, we rather wished that the stripper had got the gig, but still we played on regardless because there were 150 notes waiting at the other end.

Inevitably, the constant proximity of the band members to each other, and the tedium of criss-crossing the country on the same motorways for weeks on end to play every toilet in the provinces, led to the occasional explosion of frustration. The annoying little personal habits of a band member or a momentary lapse in personal hygiene would, over time, become irritating in the extreme, and would rapidly become the only thing you noticed about that person. Urban Blitz had an irksome habit of whistling a snatch of a tune through his teeth, and drumming his hands on his thighs, which always indicated that he was bored and possibly about to get into one of his violent interludes. Peter, never the most eloquent of people, would get tongue-tied whenever he tried to express an idea. The more enthusiastic he was about something, the harder he found it to express it. He used the English language with all the confidence of a blindfolded man walking backwards through a minefield. My defence mechanism was to get morose and withdrawn, then become arrogant and confrontational, and finally to get hopelessly drunk before going onstage and seeing what happened.

Occasionally, of course, the gigs were magnificent, and seemed to vindicate all the work that we had put in. When everything worked as we intended, when there was a large and vocal audience, the spirit and the dynamic of the performance transcended all the aggravation. On those occasions on stage we actually enjoyed being together.

The relationship between a performer and his audience is a complex one. I always felt that those kids who loved us didn't really know *why* they loved us, but those who hated us certainly knew *exactly* why they hated us. Bryan Morrison was not a man given to excessive theorising about performer–audience dynamics. He only ever gave me one piece of advice in that department – "My son, when you've got an audience by the balls, squeeze 'em!" I have always loved to polarise an audience – where I would stoke up the dynamic fury, and if there were hecklers in the club I dealt with them with great relish. They became my personal victims for the entire evening. It is no different from Nuremberg. Identify your hate-figure and sweep the masses along with your rhetoric.

We were starting to attract a hardcore, fanatical following who would not only come to see us in their home town, but would travel 50 miles to see us, usually arriving at the venue before we did, and chatting and helping out with the unloading of the van. We also were becoming just well enough known to attract our first groupies. They tended to fall into two distinct types: they were either fabulously sullen introverts, so pole-axed with shyness they could barely speak, or irritatingly extrovert girls with rasping voices, who wore too much makeup and home-made clothes that proclaimed the greatness of my band. It was usually possible to have frantic, half-dressed sex with one of these girls in the dressing room before or after the show and sometimes, even more exciting, coerce a few of them into participating in a large-scale orgy. Since there was precious little in the way of creature comfort on the road, I took what pleasure I could in those abandoned, pre-AIDS days and enjoyed it to the full. Rene had always known that I was a soft touch for casual sex, and was incredibly indulgent and forgiving. Amazingly, I never caught anything more life-threatening than a common cold.

Sometimes our excesses blew up in our faces, like the time we were onstage at Bridlington, in Yorkshire, tearing the house up, unaware that the drug squad were in the dressing room going through our belongings and finding Stoner's supply of finest weed. Exultant as we left the stage, with the thunderous cheers of the audience still assaulting our ears, we were brought down to earth with a thud as the gruff detective-sergeant asked, "Evening gentlemen. Sorry we're not on the guest list. To whom does this tin of marijuana belong?" Stoner had no choice but to own up, and was promptly nicked and taken to the local constabulary and charged with possession. Quite apart from the immediate inconvenience, it meant that he had to travel all the way back to Yorkshire for the court appearance and a £100 fine a couple of weeks later. Similarly, returning from a short European tour the van carrying our equipment was stopped just outside Dover and thoroughly searched, resulting in our roadie Joe having to make an unplanned return to the Magistrates Court in that unlovely city a few weeks later.

Our stage show on this tour was considerably more sophisticated and elaborate than it had been with BeBop Deluxe. We had more space to move, time for proper sound checks before the show and a sound system and lighting rig tailored to our own requirements. Visually we were a rather eclectic bunch. I usually wore a white suit that had been made for me by Tommy Nutter, one of Justin's pals. It was cut in Western style with a frock coat and high-waisted trousers. It made me look like a genetically modified Doc Holliday, an effect I rather liked. Sometimes I wore trousers with zips that ran the front length of each leg. Or a pair of thigh-high leather waders. Blue hair. Shades. Or sometimes silver contact lenses. Sometimes some make-up. You get the picture. I had also had a very flash, custom-made electric guitar whose body spelt out the name "kid". Urban Blitz favoured army combat fatigues. Stoner wore skinny T-shirts, and skeletal make-up, lovingly but perhaps a little over-enthusiastically applied by his wife, Elaine, which was more Max Schreck than Max Factor. Peter di Lemma bleached his hair and looked like a Californian surfer.

We played most of the tracks from the album, plus a couple of covers of personal faves: Dylan's enigmatic, paranoid, *Ballad Of A Thin Man* ("Something is happening and you don't know what it is, do you Mr. Jones?"), and Lou Reed's *Waiting For The Man*. We probably played more slow songs than any other band around at that time. The show was loosely structured to convey a narrative of a guy having a nervous breakdown onstage. Our closing tableau was played out under strobe lighting, ambulance sirens and smoke-filled bombast. As I went increasingly out of control on stage, the white-coated roadies would rush onstage and restrain me in a straitjacket. Amidst all the mayhem, a modified tailor's dummy vaguely resembling me, complete with straitjacket and a blue wig, would be substituted and as a final *coup de théâtre* it would be exploded onstage to close the show.

Finally, in March 1976, Polydor released *Late Night Movies, All Night Brainstorms*, our first album. We held our breath as the first reviews started to appear, as a favourable music press was absolutely essential for a band like us to be successful. The reviews were mixed, but came down rather more against us than for us. The disappointment an artist feels at reading a bad review of his work is unutterable. You feel dirty, cheap and exposed.

In *Music Week*, the industry trade paper, David Renshaw said, "This LP is a serious attempt to make more of the rock ballad form, with slow passages building up to brain busting tunnels of sound. The chorus hook on *Mainlines* is as good as anything Lou Reed ever wrote. Certainly not easy listening, the band deserves a break for trying to get new sounds into rock." *Street Life*, a newly-launched magazine that concentrated on newer acts wrote, "Though the album starts with the dense flailing amyl nitrate hyperactivity of *Waiting*, they're Gothic rather than Punk, with frequent frozen landscapes appearing, helped by Urban Blitz, one of their strongest weapons of attack. Kid Strange has the ability to write unusual but memorable tunes – heavy but with melody."

Melody Maker called it "one of the worst rock albums ever made. " The *Worksop Guardian* observed: "The playing is absurdly ham-fisted and clichéd, and a more inept, all-round performance would be hard to imagine. To be avoided like the proverbial plague." *Polly*, a colourful magazine for pre-pubescent girls, were scathing: "*Billy Watch Out!* for example is just a mess." While the *L.A. Times*, probably not for the first time, held a view that was diametrically opposed to that of *Polly*. The august West Coast journal wrote, "*Billy Watch Out!* is one of the most gripping tracks since Bowie's *Rock And Roll Suicide*."

* * *

We were delighted by the passion and polarity of opinion that our first record had aroused, but we would have preferred the support of the majority of the mainstream press rather than the idiosyncratic rump. However, given the nature of the music we were making, we were more or less satisfied. And, besides, we still had an ace up our sleeve: the NBC TV special about The Doctors of Madness was about to be aired coast-to-coast across the USA on network TV. In anticipation of this, Bryan sent telegrams to the heads of all the major US record labels urging them to cancel whatever plans they had for Saturday night and watch *Weekend* instead.

On the Monday following the broadcast, Bryan was in the office before lunchtime, an unusual occurrence. He was there to take the calls coming from the American record company moguls, who would all try to outdo each other by phoning London before their rival had even got out of bed. Strangely the telephone stayed quiet. After lunch Bryan was again there waiting, but again no calls. "They're playing hard to get. They want me to call them. Fuck 'em, let 'em stew" was his appraisal of the situation, "They always pay more when *they* call *you*". The next day was the same and by Wednesday Bryan was so perplexed and agitated that he phoned a friend in New York to see what the reaction to the programme had been. "Bryan, it was a disaster from start to finish," he said. "It was a complete assassination job on you, on Justin, the band. Everyone." It transpired that the film had been edited in such a way so as to make the band look like a talentless bunch of no-hopers being manipulated by a pair of Machiavellian Svengalis. Every shot was designed to reinforce this theme. The only live shots of the band were the ones taken at near-empty gigs, to pitiful audience acclaim. The out-of-tune rehearsals were shown as proof of a lack of musical talent. The footage from the Olympia show was used to illustrate the fact that we were the beneficiaries of a crass, but powerful, hype machine. The shots of Morrison and de Villeneuve were all filmed as they tucked into lobster and champagne, and were juxtaposed with me being interviewed in front of the one-bar electric fire. The voice of Greg droned monotonously over every picture, implying that we were a sort of manufactured, Monkees-style marketing exercise, rather than a band who had been playing live for two years before Morrison and de Villeneuve came along. All in all we had been totally and utterly stitched up by the duplicitous Greg and his amiable crew, who had come with an agenda and cut the film accordingly. Bryan was livid. We were devastated.

I have always had a great capacity to accept disappointments, to rail and to grieve, and get on with real life. This is what we had to do after the NBC fiasco. We had to put the idea of an imminent US release of the record out of our minds and concentrate on the UK and Europe. Unfortunately, this meant Polydor getting the marketing of the record right. And to get the marketing right, it was essential that Polydor understood the band. They had to "get it".

In popular music, where genre is all, to be non-generic is commercial and critical suicide. Polydor didn't understand it, didn't know what "it" was. Consequently, they had no idea how to market us. Pop music is very unforgiving in one crucial sense. If you aren't shifting product, you are a waste of time, money, vinyl and shelf space. Very few people in the business are prepared to stick out their necks and go for the long haul or the oddball act, since for the most part people in the record industry lack both taste and critical judgement. They seek consensus and the approval of their peers, since they are essentially herd animals. This is why they hunt in packs. When two record companies want to sign the same act, all the other companies are *de facto* interested too. Not necessarily because there is any unique quality in the act; simply the act been legitimised by the interest of the first two companies.

In April we returned to Europe to capitalise on our earlier success there, and we toured France and the Benelux countries extensively. By now we were earning better money, and could afford to take a proper truck and driver in addition to our regular road crew. Somehow or other a guy named Martin Griffin was pointed our way for the job, and I took against him immediately. He was big, powerful-looking guy with a huge handlebar moustache and an opinion on every subject. He was garrulous and cocky and had a chip on his shoulder. All in all he was much too much like me (apart from the moustache). I was horrified at the prospect of this guy, who everybody called Drumbo, being on the road with us for the next month. I tried every avenue to get him replaced, but he was the only person who was available and willing to do the job for the money we could afford. It went without saying that all the road crew were earning considerably more than the band at this point, and Drumbo, with his HGV licence, earned more than anyone.

That tour took us to every major French, Belgian and Dutch city, and we were playing to good sized crowds who were, for the most part, extravagantly appreciative. In Paris we played more consecutive shows at Le Bataclan than even Roxy Music had managed, and by the time we reached the large provincial cities such as Lyon, Marseilles and Bordeaux the word had already reached them that we were hot and we were selling out everywhere. The record charted first in Belgium and then in France, and we were getting dream reviews for all the gigs we played.

Drumbo came and sat with me in a bar one night and started chatting; six hours later we were the best of friends. I realised that my animosity towards him was totally unfounded and was based purely on the fact that I had recognised him as possessing an ego as large as mine. Since it was the first time this had happened in this touring party, I had felt threatened. I was so impressed and amused by Drumbo that I started travelling to gigs with him in the truck, leaving the rest of the band to travel by car. The conversation and the chemicals were so much better with Drumbo. He had a very healthy appetite for amphetamine sulphate and together we consumed vast quantities of the stuff as we thundered across the major roads of Europe. We spoke for hours on end, pausing only to refresh our nostrils every 50 miles or so. Drumbo was a fabulous Falstaffian character, a true English yeoman. He told me he was really a drummer, but after getting thrown out of Oxford he took an HGV course and became a bus driver. In those days, of course, you could always drop out because you knew you would always be able to drop back in.

That whole tour was enormously enjoyable, both for the pleasure of Drumbo's company and for the success and the acclaim that we were garnering. Arriving back in England I transferred back to the car to complete the journey home with the band as Drumbo had to take the truck to the warehouse where we stored our equipment to unload. Exhausted and out of chemicals, Drumbo fell asleep at the wheel on the motorway up from Dover and only woke up when he crashed into the central reservation at 70mph, tore the entire side off the truck and took half a mile of central reservation with him. Miraculously he survived unscathed. We kept Drumbo on the payroll for the British gigs that were lined up immediately after our return to the UK. In all the madness he had become my one link to the real world while we were on the road. I have known him for many years and he has never given me one bad piece of advice or a single opinion that wasn't thought through.

* * *

In spring 1976, we did a gig at Middlesborough Town Hall, as part of our UK tour. We got a call from Martin Hopewell asking if we would be prepared to let a band called The Sex Pistols support us for that one gig. They were a new, so-called "punk" band that had attracted an inordinate amount of media coverage, thanks to the astute manipulation of staged outrages by their self-proclaimed "situationist" manager, Malcolm McLaren. As yet they hadn't yet played any shows outside London and McLaren decided it was time for them to start. By this time we were attracting up to 1000 people a night. We were the only band around with any sizeable following that was prepared to risk of having them on the bill with us. Most of the other bands around were too "muso" and precious to share a bill with such an anarchic rabble. I liked what I had heard about their attitude and we agreed to give them the gig.

On arriving at the venue in Middlesborough, which actually turned out to be a large, drab Soviet-style functions room underneath the town hall itself, we did the usual stuff a headline band does – sound checking and dicking around, drinking and chatting to the die-hard fans who arrive at a venue even before the band does – while the surly, pimply-faced quartet sat in the auditorium behaving suitably obnoxiously. They farted, burped, yawned extravagantly and giggled. We were surprised how weedy they looked, like schoolboys bunking off school, muttering asides to each other that were designed to aggravate and provoke. We didn't rise to the bait but, like an irritating wasp buzzing around a picnic, they were impossible to ignore. They didn't dress as outrageously as we had been led to expect; their sole concessions to what became known as the punk look were their spiked-up hair, a few badges, a torn T-shirt and the odd safety pin. Johnny Rotten, the front man, had an extraordinary presence and charisma, and his nasal whine seemed to have been rehearsed to perfection. Glen Matlock, the bass player, seemed ordinary and unremarkable, Steve Jones was yobbish and Paul Cook was just a typical drummer, who seemed temperamentally to be just like Peter di Lemma.

Eventually we let them have the stage, and when they realised that they didn't have all the equipment they needed, they sheepishly asked if they could borrow some of ours. Urban Blitz flatly refused to lend them his guitar amp and I think the rest of us were none too keen to let them loose on our equipment. They had already attracted a certain reputation for trashing any equipment they borrowed that they didn't steal. Somehow or other they did a sound check, and it really was a God-awful racket that they made. It was desultory, half-hearted, out of tune and rhythmically all over the place. The funny thing with the Pistols was that if you took away Rotten's petulant, snotty-nosed vocal delivery and lyrics, you were left with fairly conventional up-and-down pub rock. An hour or so later, however, when the punters were in and the Pistols were on stage, they were electric. They spent their entire 25-minute set goading and cajoling the audience, daring them to trash the joint, provoking the most extreme reaction I had ever seen at a gig, yet all the while the band seemed almost comatose with boredom. It was a great act. Bryan Morrison would have approved – when they had the audience by the balls, they squeezed 'em.

The audience watched, open-mouthed and wild-eyed. They gobbed and they pogoed, the vertical take-off, Tourette's-Syndrome inspired dance of the time, and they were putty in The Sex Pistols' hands. Live, the Pistols mixed standards like Iggy Pop's Stooges song, *I Wanna Be Your Dog*, and the Monkees', *I'm Not Your Stepping Stone*, with their own nihilistic anthems that would soon make them famous, like *Anarchy In The UK* and *No Feelings*. It was a dreadful sensation, watching them from the side of the stage and knowing that we couldn't compete. There is a passage in George Melly's excellent autobiography *Owning Up*, in which he describes how, when witnessing the hysterical teenage audience reaction to 1950's British rock'n'roll hero Tommy Steele for the first time, a jazz colleague turned to George and said, "You hear that? That's the death of jazz. We've had it. In six months we'll all be on the breadline". I must confess that is exactly how I felt watching the Sex Pistols play that night. They were changing the rules, and the game was being snatched away from underneath our noses.

We followed them on to the stage after a suitably long interval, hoping that the temperature would cool sufficiently for us to get the audience going again. In truth, the gig we did that night was pretty good but we knew that we had not generated one quarter of the excitement that The Sex Pistols had. Our fans came backstage and were enthusiastic as usual, and many of them told us that they thought that the punk thing would blow itself out in a couple of months. I was neither comforted nor convinced. I was simply jealous. To compound what had been a very bad evening for us, while driving back to the hotel after the gig, we realised that we had all had some money stolen from our clothes in the dressing room while we had been on stage. It didn't require Sherlock Holmes to deduce that while we had been performing, The Pistols had gone through our pockets and scarpered. They didn't take a great deal, in truth there wasn't much to take, just a few quid from each of us at most, but we were livid. We weren't the final victims of that truculent, snotty-nosed bunch – the unholy trinity of record companies, EMI, A & M and Virgin, hadn't yet had the pleasure of their company, nor checked their back pockets to find that they had had hundreds of thousands of pounds filched.

Twenty-one years later, I was working as an actor in Germany on a regular TV show, travelling to Munich every weekend. I had a driver, a jovial, garrulous bear of a man called Ossi, who always collected me at the airport and drove me to the TV studio, and then did the reverse journey when I was travelling back to London. After our last show before the summer break, I asked him what he would be doing through the summer, and he replied that he would be driving bands around the different outdoor festivals in Germany. "That sounds fun," I said. "Who's coming over?" "Oh, I shall just be driving The Sex Pistols for their reunion tour."

I knew that the Pistols had reformed for this bank-snatch, sorry, reunion tour, and the rumour was that they would get a million pounds each for the summer. I took out a pen and scrawled a message for Johnny Rotten: "Dear Johnny, I have just been going through the pockets of a pair of trousers I haven't worn since you supported me in Middlesborough in 1976. I am afraid to say that approximately £12 seems to be missing. If you know anything about the matter, would you kindly settle with Ossi? Best wishes Richard "Kid" Strange." I gave it to Ossi and asked him to give it to Johnny Rotten at an appropriate moment.

In September, when I returned to Munich, Ossi was waiting for me at the airport, as usual. In the car I asked, "How was summer?" and he replied, "Oh, it was great. Lots of festivals and lots of fun. Oh, by the way, I have a letter for you." He slipped a tatty envelope over his shoulder to me, in the back of the car, as he drove. Inside, in ragged handwriting, was a short note:

"Dear Kid. Yeah. Sorry about that. I do remember something. Hope this will cover it. All the best John Lydon" Attached to the letter was a crisp new $50 bill and a receipt on which he had scribbled "paid in full". It was quite a nice touch and rather endearing. When I told Malcolm McLaren about this he laughed and said, "But I'm sure it was Steve [Jones] who nicked all the money that night".

EUGENE

For our second album, the archly entitled *Figments of Emancipation*, we talked Bryan and Polydor into putting us into the most famous recording studios in the world, Number 2 Studio at EMI Studios in Abbey Road in north-west London. It was where many of the classic rock albums were made, including The Beatles' *Revolver* and *Sgt Pepper*, and Pink Floyd's *Dark Side Of The Moon*. Rene and I had been there as sitters-in on countless late-night Roy Harper sessions in the late sixties and early seventies. While Peter Jenner rolled spliffs and produced the records (in that order of priority), John Leckie was the engineer, and we got to know him well. I managed to coerce Leckie into producing the record for us for a reduced fee and, since he was a friend of long standing, I knew that I could trust him with this important second album.

It was the fulfilment of any music-fan's lifelong fantasy to actually record their own album there. Apart from Abbey Road's pre-eminence as a studio, there was another reason I wanted to record in that part of London. Rene was by now on the point of giving birth and I wanted to be near to the Royal Free Hospital, in Hampstead, when the call came.

Against the prevailing musical style of the time, we were going into the studio to make an album of six long songs, rather than an album of 15 short ones. The songs were the 12-minute-plus *Brothers/Suicide City*, *Marie And Joe*, *Perfect Past*, *In Camera*, *Doctors Of Madness* and *Out!* The sound on this record was much bigger and weightier than on the first album (in studios, as in most things, you get what you pay for). We were paying something in the region of £120 per hour for Abbey Road, so we needed to be well rehearsed before we even went into the studio to begin recording.

One of my favourite songs on the album is *Marie And Joe*. It was a none-too-cryptic message to a girl I had a crush on at the time, who was married to the wrong guy. Lyrically and vocally, it owes a lot to Lou Reed in one of his more tender moments. It tells the story of two people *not* having an affair, but nevertheless the yearning and aching of the unconsummated lust is quite erotic.

I admit it's not exactly *White Riot* or *Anarchy In The UK*, but that song meant a lot to me at the time. Musically, I thought it was exquisitely languid, building through the verses with some achingly beautiful bass playing from Stoner and a great guitar solo played by Urban Blitz. What was essentially an acoustic song was transformed by the way Stoner and Urban Blitz took it by the scruff of its neck and magnificently kicked the living daylights out of it. Stoner and Peter provided some very nice vocal harmonies too, which lifted the later choruses and made the song soar.

The lynchpin of the album was the long two-song segue of *Brothers* and *Suicide City*. *Brothers* was an affectionate look at the way the lives of myself and my two brothers had diverged; *Suicide City* was a gaze into the abyss, provoked by an evening that I spent with Rene and Jacqueline, my 1966 French flame. In the song they are referred to as "The Giants".

> *And so it was when I spoke with the Giants*
> *With the night air of summer turning cold on our skin,*
> *And the talk turned to strangers and Doctors of Madness*
> *And to those on the outside who tried to get in.*

On the chorus coda we were joined by three female vocalists, Jill Mackintosh, Stephanie de Sykes and Clare Torrey. Stephanie had had a few bubblegum hits in the early seventies and became a session singer. Clare had been around for a while and had reached her apotheosis with her magnificent scat singing on Pink Floyd's *The Dark Side of the Moon*. Clare is that haunting, howling, pleading female voice that is heard emerging throughout the album, and which makes the record something very special. John Leckie had worked as an engineer on that session so he knew Clare and was able to get her in to work with us. They also sang on another of the songs we recorded for *Figments of Emancipation*, a straightforward love-ballad called *Perfect Past* (the song I had sung as a duet with Twiggy on her TV show.) It was Bryan Morrison's favourite song and it always reduced him to a quivering-lipped adolescent.

We were about a couple of weeks into the recording session, on 31 May. It was a bank holiday, and we were doing some drum overdubs on one of the tracks when the telephone rang in the studio. It was Rene saying that she had gone into labour and was on her way to hospital. I reckoned I had a couple of hours before there would be any real need for me to be at the hospital so I stayed at the studio, exhorting Peter to get these overdubs right as they were costing us £120 per hour. The drum overdubs complete, I told John Leckie to get on with Urban Blitz's overdubbed guitar parts, and one of the roadies drove me to the Royal Free.

When I arrived, Rene was already in bed, moderately comfortable, but the contractions were coming more and more frequently. Events seemed to accelerate through the afternoon and, by early evening, amid the maelstrom of Rene's howling and swearing, our screaming son was born. I was at the bedside, and in the excitement and the emotion of the moment I promptly fainted and had to be taken next door to be revived. Very bad for the image of the macho rock and roller.

When I came round and returned to Rene's bedside, she was lying in bed with a rosy-cheeked approximation of the Michelin Man, who looked about 80 years old with a few tufts of hair on his cannonball head. The nurse, a fabulously hearty Caribbean woman whom you would trust with your life, desperately wanted to say that the child was a spitting image of his dad, but as I stood there, ashen, blue-haired and skeletal, she could only say, "He's got big hands, like you."

Bryan and Greta Morrison arrived at the hospital within minutes of the infant's birth, armed with a bottle of champagne to toast mother and baby. For some inexplicable reason

Rene was not in the mood for a drink, so we drained the bottle between the three of us before Morrison, only half-jokingly said, "I hope they're fucking working at Abbey Road while you're here. It's costing me £120 an hour, my son."

When Morrison and Greta left, I stayed a while longer with Rene until she needed sleep and attention and the baby was whisked off to be weighed and washed and checked over. I returned to the studio, emotionally drained, but excited and thankful that the baby was fit and well. We had already discussed names for children, and we knew what he would be called. Rene was a big fan of the Irish writer, Edna O'Brien, and we called our son Eugene (who we nicknamed Geno), after the hero in O'Brien's book *The Girl with the Green Eyes*. His second name was Eyre, which was Rene's family name.

I continued the recording of the album, with daily breaks for hospital visits, until Rene and Eugene were discharged and went home to Brooklands Rise. Nineteen seventy-six was a long, hot, golden summer that started in May and seemed to last forever. I had never felt so alive or so excited in my life. To be doing good work, to have a wonderful partner and a healthy son, I felt that I was blessed.

We recorded three rock songs, *Doctors Of Madness*, which we had not managed to nail with John Punter first time around, *Out!* which was like a fourth part to the *Mitzi's Cure* trilogy from the first album – curiously, it was named by Joe Elliot, vocalist with the soft-metal megastars Def Leppard, as being one of his three favourite songs *ever* – and *In Camera*.

Working with Leckie was an absolute joy. Not only was he a producer full of great creative ideas and the technical ability to apply them, but he was also a man totally without ego or neurosis. It is this combination of qualities that has made him one of the greatest and most successful producers in the world. I am proud that I was the first person to engage him solely as a producer. He has subsequently gone on to produce such great albums as Radiohead's *The Bends* and The Stone Roses' enormously influential first album, as well as albums by Simple Minds, Spiritualized, The Cowboy Junkies, Kula Shaker, The Fall and The Verve.

No sooner had we finished mixing the album than we were back on the road, doing gigs all over the UK to keep our profile up. Morrison had the idea that Rene and I should take Eugene down for a day at the races at Royal Ascot, convinced that we would get our photograph into the papers. Since Royal Ascot is one of the great social events of the year, Morrison rightly reckoned that the sight of a blue-haired stick insect holding a baby in the Royal Enclosure was bound to be worth a couple of column inches in Nigel Dempster's Diary. I hired a morning suit and topper from Moss Bros, and Morry gave us a few quid to spend on champagne and strawberries. It was quite a hoot and Eugene was as good as gold. That night the Doctors were supporting Ian Dury's band, Kilburn and the Highroads in Sheffield, so as soon as we knew we had been snapped at the races we headed home. I changed out of the hired suit in the lavatory of the train, and emerged, like Clark Kent, dressed in more familiar attire of tight jeans and a leather jacket.

Summer is not a great time to tour the towns and cities of Britain. Dusty and hot, they are for the most part empty of record-buying kids, so Martin Hopewell hit on the idea of sending us round all the British seaside resorts for our summer tour. The weather that year was unforgettably good, the sun seemed to shine for months on end and we enjoyed ourselves, feeling that we had recorded an album that was really going to give our career a lift up to the next level. All through that blistering summer, though, I felt that we were being stalked by punk, like an assassin just waiting to kill us off.

* * *

Of all the punk bands Rene and I used to go and see at the Roxy, the 100 Club or the Nashville, The Damned always seemed to be having the best time onstage. They were a cartoon punk-band, like a new wave Screamin' Lord Sutch and The Savages. It was really Brian James' band. He wrote all their material and played a low-slung Gibson SG guitar with a craggy, leather-faced cool. He always seemed to me to be a lot older than the other three, and I always imagined that he had tried out every other style of pop and got lucky with punk. Rat Scabies was an explosive, pyrotechnic drummer from the Keith Moon School of Restraint. Ray Burns, aka Captain Sensible, the bass player and the most flamboyant of the bunch, always seemed to me to be a bit of a twat. It was the frontman and singer Dave Vanian who really caught the eye onstage, though, with his white Nosferatu make-up, black eye-shadow and lipstick, and immaculate Addams Family tailoring. He was like a loveable, toothless vampire. He couldn't really sing a note, but he had a busload of energy and prowled the stage like a man possessed, and really ripped it up. Off stage, typically, he was an absolute sweetheart, shy, amiable and embarrassed at his success, while Rat and Ray were totally brattish and obnoxious. Brian just hung out in the dressing room with his girlfriend, the American photographer Erika Eschenberg, and looked moody.

I got to know Dave pretty well and we used to hang out together whenever he was in London for a few days. The Damned toured a lot, and when he wasn't on the road he still lived with his mum in Hemel Hempstead. He was a big fan of the Doctors and got along to see us whenever we played around that part of the country. There used to be quite a few regular good gigs up there – St Albans City Hall, a club called Friars in Aylesbury and Hemel Hempstead Town Hall all used to be great audiences for us, and Dave came to them all. He was quite a bit younger than me and I was surprised when he told me he was going to marry his girlfriend, the Gothic clothes designer, Laurie. I was even more surprised when he asked me to be his best man. It was not a role I had ever taken before but I agreed to do it anyway, and we all assembled at Acton Town Hall Registry office on 7 September. I hadn't realised how strictly the dress code was still enforced in those days, and I was told that if I didn't wear a tie I would not be allowed to be best man. Laurie was looking a little anxious in her black lace and magenta wedding dress, and I didn't want to let her or Dave down, so when I saw a copy of *Woman's Own* lying on a chair in the waiting room, I found a nice colour photograph of an underwear model and tore it into the approximate shape of a tie, and stuck it to my shirt under my chin with a bit of chewing gum. The ceremony went ahead and the photos looked great.

Most of the artists who were on The Damned's record label, Stiff Records, came along to the reception afterwards, as did the label owner, Jake Riviera. Stiff were the first of the successful independent record labels, inspired by a combination of Riviera's marketing nous and the memorable record sleeves and graphics of the late designer, Barney Bubbles. Dave's mum baked a wedding cake, topped extravagantly with two black roses and, along with Elvis Costello, Ian Dury, The Adverts and Nick Lowe and 75 others, Rene and I got very hammered. The reception was at Pete Watts's house and went on for two days before Dave and Laurie left for their honeymoon in a chauffeur-driven hearse.

Nineteen seventy-six was a hectic year for The Doctors. We toured Holland (three times), France (twice), Sweden, Denmark, Belgium, Germany and Switzerland. In addition we played 86 gigs in the UK, including a big London show at the Shaftesbury Theatre. I was living the life I felt I was born to live, and for the most part my feeling was "This sure beats working", but the constant travelling and uncompromising lifestyle were starting to get to me.

While we were in France I called Rene one morning and she was in tears on the other end of the line. I asked what was wrong and she said that both she and Geno were in the Royal Free Hospital. She was frantic. She explained that Geno had been diagnosed as suffering from infantile eczema, which the hot summer had aggravated, and as he constantly scratched his tortured skin in his sleep, it had become infected. His entire body was covered from head to toe with a virulent scarlet rash, which had blistered and ulcerated. It was heartbreaking to hear both of Geno's condition and Rene's despair, and I felt so powerless, so far away, unable to comfort either of them for another 10 days, when the dates were finished. She was staying at the hospital with him, trying to soothe him while also trying to do her own illustration work. It was an awful time. I put the phone down, stunned. Then I burst into tears. I realised for the first time that I was probably suffering from exhaustion and couldn't wait to get home. We played out the rest of the shows, and they were great gigs, fuelled by the desperation of someone who is on the point of total collapse.

By the time I got back to London Geno was on the road to recovery, and I swapped places with Rene at the hospital for a couple of days to give her some time out. I needed the rest which staying at the hospital offered. The doctors and nurses were exemplary, and treated Geno with extraordinary care and tireless attention. It put the hedonistic, self-obsessed lifestyle of rock singer into a shameful perspective.

With the release of *Figments of Emancipation* in September 1976, we were back on the road again, doing gigs and interviews, radio and TV. Punk was now the only game in town, and although many of the punk bands who were getting a lot of media attention were self-confessed fans of The Doctors, (The Damned, The Skids, The Adverts, Penetration, etc.) we had just been around for too long to be thought of as being part of this new explosion. We were an anachronism, being neither old-style rock nor new-style punk. Timing is everything in the Music Business, and for reasons that were totally unforeseeable even twelve months ago, we were already starting to look old-fashioned; I was 25 years old and I belonged to a previous generation. It occurred to me that this is how it must have felt for Uncle Stan and the Radio Revellers, when the kids started screaming for the Beatles.

* * *

I went to see The Clash at the ICA in London in October and became even more depressed. They were sensational. Joe Strummer barked, Mick Jones prowled and Paul Simonon was a true rock god with impossible cheekbones. Their spray-painted combat-fatigue stage clothes made them look like heroic freedom fighters from the barricades of a future cultural war. The noise they made was like a B52 bomber taking off with a full payload; not a single word of the lyrics was decipherable, but the ritual of the experience took the audience to another, communal, place. In all honesty I never bought The Clash's politics, but boy, did I buy their rock. (Twenty-five years later, I feel that Tracey Emin's putative primitivism is only as authentic as the punk voice of Joe Strummer, Poly Styrene or Johnny Rotten was in those days. No less so, but certainly no more. Her primitivism is artfully and cleverly enhanced, burnished and heightened: it plays to the gallery and waits for its disapproval, and it cunningly focuses on the very elements she wishes to use to shock us. Her truest talent is the sharpness of that focus. Her work is conventional in its avowed unconventionality, but she has got it down pat, and in its own terms, it works supremely well.)

Despite the fact that the music press had moved wholesale into promoting punk rock, some of the critics were positive in their reviews of *Figments of Emancipation*. Phil McNeill in the *New Musical Express* said "[The Doctors] . . . are unusual, inspired and intensely committed to their obscurantist, neurotic–horrific desperately humanist view of inner city space. Their corporate understanding transcends structures." Sadly the most original and influential rock critic of the day, Giovanni Dadomo of *Sounds* magazine, was less enthusiastic. He demolished the record with a brilliant, typically minimalist, acerbic put-down: "So boring. No vision. So self-same. No Magic. So trivial. No aura. So eager. No action. So cloudy. No zip. So faceless. No freshness" etc. etc., before finishing with the *coup de grâce*, "So? No!" That review hurt like hell. Never believe any performer who says bad reviews don't hurt. They're either liars or they can't read.

It should be mentioned that the rock journalists who worked for one of the big three publications, *New Musical Express*, *Sounds* or *Melody Maker*, were enormously powerful and influential figures in the music industry at that time. A handful of them had the real capacity to make or break a band simply by writing a few pages of hyperbole. As well as Giovanni Dadomo, the biggest names in British rock journalism at that time were Nick Kent, Jonh Ingham, Julie Burchill and Tony Parsons.

Record companies thought nothing of flying one or several of these journalists half way round the world to do a piece on one of their acts. One of the big writers only needed to mention in passing that he or she had enjoyed one of the band's new songs and they would be on the next flight to Paris or New York to watch the band gigging at some or other dingy venue. Their flights, hotels and meals would, of course, all be paid for but usually there were added incentives. Sometimes a record company press officer would accompany the hack on the trip, either as an unpaid hooker or as a drug dealer. It was open season for the journalists and they took the record companies for everything they were prepared to offer. In return, an 800-word review or, occasionally, a 1500-word article was banged off, usually just as the hangover or comedown was making its presence felt. As often as not the perfidious journalist would enjoy all the venal pleasures the record company could offer and still write a stinker. They had so much clout that they knew that the company would always come back and send them out to cover the next Euro-gig of the next band of hopefuls.

The wonderful thing about this amphetamine aristocracy was that they had no more idea about what was really happening, or what was truly substantial, than any other Joe on the street. In their highly-acclaimed critique of punk rock, *The Boy Looked at Johnny*, Burchill and Parsons, the Herod and Salome of punk, having sounded off endlessly about their understanding and empathy, pontificated as to who posterity would prove to be the most significant acts to come out of "the movement". After much consideration these two precocious pundits of punk came up with two names – Tom Robinson and Poly Styrene. That's right. That nice broadcaster and the Loony. But, coincidentally, that's exactly what Tone and Jules became, too. He became the middle-brow mouth and she became the bonkers bitch. Er, the cigar stays in the humidor, guys.

I was so incensed by Dadomo's review of *Figments of Emancipation* that I wrote him a scathing letter accusing him of being a careerist parasite and demanded that we meet "to settle this like men". I hadn't really planned what I would do if he replied so I was astonished when he telephoned and said that he'd enjoyed my letter much more than my album, and asked if I would like to do an interview for *Sounds*.

We met at Bryan Morrison's office the following week. By now Morrison had moved his office to Bruton Place, behind Bond Street. A nervous, but distinctly cool, Giovanni Dadomo set up his cassette recorder and we sat across a table from each other and waited to see who would blink first. He had the dark, sunken eyes and gaunt features of an enthusiastic and single-minded drug taker. His skin was ravaged by the pockmarks of early acne or some other condition. The Damned always openly referred to him as "pizza face". Years later, my friend, the artist Brian Clarke, whom I met through Giovanni, told me his mother had taken him aside after meeting Dadomo for the first time and said, with heartfelt concern, "Ooh Brian, isn't it terrible what's happened to Lionel Blair?" to whom Dadomo bore a passing resemblance.

As we chatted, it slowly became apparent that we agreed on much more than we disagreed and that we shared a similar sense of humour and an almost identical set of heroes. We spent the entire afternoon together laughing at the scams we'd pulled, and enthusing about this singer or that band, and we emerged into the Paddington evening as the commuters were heading home. Unfortunately, there was no way back with his album review, but the article he subsequently penned was contrite. Within a few weeks of that initial encounter, Giovanni Dadomo, alias Joe Varnish, second-generation Italian junkie and founder member of his own punk band, The Snivelling Shits, had become a very good friend. He had a quirky writing style, and could turn his hand to anything. He had written lyrics for the Japanese percussionist Stomu Yamash'ta, poems, short stories and journalism, all imbued with a highly original approach and a memorable wit.

Despite the mixed reviews of the album, we continued a relentless touring schedule throughout the year. In the autumn, to promote *Figments of Emancipation*, we embarked on another tour of the UK, playing larger venues now such as universities, Top Rank dance halls and some of the smaller concert halls around the country. We publicised the tour with a manifesto I wrote about pollution, corporate greed and the arms race. We took to the stage in blinding white light, white noise and smoke, wearing gas masks! We opened with *Mainlines*, "This is the place the rats come to die", and got gloomier, ending with the musical equivalent of nuclear meltdown. It wasn't exactly an evening of dance music. We closed the tour on 28 November with the obligatory London showcase gig at the Shaftesbury Theatre, and it was a pretty good show. A lot of the kids who now had bands came along, and Dave Vanian of The Damned joined us onstage for an encore. It was a bit like being given the punk seal of approval.

Wherever The Doctors played now, our support bands were wannabe punk rockers. In Scotland we were supported by Johnnie and the Self-Abusers, who found rather more success after they changed their name to Simple Minds. They played a version of *Waiting For The Man*, which the chubby-faced singer Jim Kerr introduced with the words, "This song was written by Lou Reed and re-written by Kid Strange". In Manchester, at the Electric Circus, the warm-up band was Warsaw, who later became Joy Division, then became New Order. In Newport, South Wales, a pimply youth came into our dressing room after a show and brazenly introduced himself as Steve Harrington. He was gushing and sycophantic and announced to whoever was listening that from this day forth, he was changing his name in honour of the band in general and me in particular. "From now on", he announced to no one in particular, "I will be known as Steve Strange." I really didn't give it another thought as he was ushered from the dressing room, but three or four years later that night and that lumpy visage would come back to haunt me.

We played anywhere and everywhere. We played May Balls and deb parties, from nowhere to Knightsbridge. As a live band, The Doctors were pretty hot by now, and we had a loyal and committed following, but in commercial terms it was just too small to sustain us. In a review of one of our gigs at the renowned, but now defunct, Marquee Club in London's Wardour Street, which we sold out four nights running, the *New Musical Express* said:

> The blond, electric narcissus figure of Peter di Lemma crashes his kit into a relent-less train time and the Doctors slam into *Waiting*. It moves at an exhilarating, demented gallop, and it's still as big a surprise as it was first time I saw them to realise just how well this superficially superficial band can play. The music is all Kid's. He writes post-Velvets, romantic intellectual, virtually incomprehensible *cinema verité* of a blank generation from which his articulation disbars him and of sophisticated paranoia casualties from whom his aggressive self-confidence distinguishes him.

In November 1976 the record I consider to be the greatest single to come out of the punk rock genre was released. It wasn't by The Pistols or The Clash or The Buzzcocks, but by a highly literate poet from Kentucky who called himself Richard Hell. The record, made with his band The Voidoids, was entitled *Blank Generation*, and captured the stuttering frustrated nihilism of the punk ethos better than any other. Apart from the magnificently radical, angular music they made, It could be argued that Hell also invented punk fashion, wearing ripped T-shirts and spiky hair long before Malcolm McLaren and Vivienne Westward recognized there was a buck to be made from selling It. With *Blank Generation* Richard Hell kicked a hole in the cultural wall, and The Sex Pistols stormed through it.

On 1 December, The Sex Pistols appeared on a national tea-time TV show called *Today*, and established their career and created a legend. Following a three-minute long, foul-mouthed assault on the hopelessly out-of-his-depth presenter Bill Grundy, by the following morning they were public enemy number one.

Grundy, an old-style fireside presenter more at home covering the Crufts Dog Show, had attempted to bait the band and their entourage of hangers-on into giving the public a little bit of token anarchy. "Say something outrageous!" he taunted. He hadn't reckoned with the fact that the band were more than up for it, and were easier to switch on than to switch off. The belligerent Steve Jones was only too eager to oblige. "You dirty bastard. You dirty fucker. What a fuckin' rotter," he spewed. The TV station was deluged with protests from irate viewers. One lorry driver telephoned to say that he had been so outraged that he had put his boot through his television screen. Grundy had opened the Pandora's box of sensationalism and saw it destroy his own career overnight. The band cursed and swore and spat, they scowled and swaggered, emboldened by the free beer from the hospitality Green Room. In those three minutes their reputation was made and ensured that punk rock was no longer just a London cult but a national phenomenon. Celebrity is a fickle mistress and that same pro-gramme also ensured that Grundy was booked on a one-way ticket to provincial backwater TV obscurity. That is the harshest sentence imaginable for someone who is used to getting the best tables in the smartest restaurants and being fussed over by oily *maitre d*'s.

The following morning, all the newspapers led on the story – *The Sun*'s headline was "The filth and the fury". Outraged parish councillors up and down the country lobbied to have the band's concerts cancelled for fear of corrupting the morals of the local kids. For The Pistols and McLaren it was heaven-sent. They became martyrs to censorship and small-minded provincialism, and toured the country in a painted bus purely for the benefit of the journalists and photographers, turning up at the venues of the gigs only to be photographed against a backdrop of "cancelled" stickers. An "Anarchy Tour", featuring The Pistols, The Damned, The Clash and Johnny Thunders and the Heartbreakers was slashed from 19 gigs to three. It kicked off at Leeds Polytechnic on 6 December. That gig, plus a couple of shows in Manchester, constituted the entire tour. It didn't matter that no one could see the bands play. Punk rock was big news.

By mid-December 1976, The Stranglers, another bunch of old musos dressed up to appeal to the punks, had signed their post-Doors wet dream to United Artists. The Sex Pistols had signed to EMI on 9 October and were dropped less than three months later, on 6 January as a result of the TV outrage. By February 1977, The Clash had been signed by CBS (now Sony), The Jam had signed to Polydor, and in March Johnny Thunders and the Heartbreakers signed for Track Records. Any band with a spiky haircut and a pair of PVC drainpipe trousers could get a deal, and the record companies showed their herd instinct once again as packs of A and R men, still in their nylon tour jackets, scoured sweaty basement clubs like the Roxy, the

Vortex or the Hope and Anchor, looking for all the world like FBI men setting up a sting on the lower East Side.

Even Giovanni Dadomo's band, The Snivelling Shits, started more as a joke than a serious enterprise, had got a record deal and had released their double-sided cult classic *Terminal Stupid/I Can't Come* to considerable critical acclaim – in their case, rather easy to come by. Three of the four band members were rock journalists and they wrote slavering reviews of their own records, often weeks before they had even been recorded, and frequently awarded themselves the coveted "Record of the Week" accolade. They went on to record an extraordinarily verbose album, which featured what were possibly their two best songs, *Bring Me The Head Of Yukio Mishima* and *Isgodaman*.

Other bands who would soon be putting their names on the dotted line included Siouxsie and the Banshees, Squeeze, The Adverts and the all-girl band, The Slits. Rene and I frequently used to go to the Roxy to see all these bands. It had a strangely ambivalent atmosphere, like a youth club founded by the Marquis de Sade. It was run by Andy Czezowski and his partner Susan Carrington, two more South Londoners whom we got to know very well. They made all their own clothes and for the most part looked like extras from *Thunderbirds Are Go!* or *Joe Ninety*. When they walked, you expected to see the strings moving their legs. We got to know a lot of the bands too, but I always felt a bit old there even though I was only in my mid-twenties.

* * *

In the year ending December 1976, we had improved considerably on 1975 in our capacity to earn money from live gigs. We grossed over £25,000 in fees, but once again there was a £10,000 shortfall against expenses. It meant that the record advances, which should have improved our life style a little, (we were still only drawing £35 a week each as wages at this point), went towards servicing our debt to Bryan Morrison.

The music scene in the UK for this short period from 1976-7 was vibrant and exciting as never before. There was an extraordinary sense of energy and possibility, totally at odds with the oft-professed negativity, boredom and blankness of punk. In Europe, however, where musical tastes tended toward the more conservative and conventional, there was a massive resistance to punk and its younger brother, the so-called new wave music. We would frequently find ourselves playing huge outdoor festivals across the continent on the same bill as heavy metal acts like Black Sabbath or AC/DC, or paired up with jazz-rockers like John McLaughlin. It is hard to say whose fans hated us more – the denim-clad Dutch metal-heads, or the bearded German 40-somethings who clung on to McLaughlin's every last excessive note. It was a bizarre, bewildering time for us, and we secretly envied these bands that could be marketed with a convenient generic label: punk, heavy metal, glam or jazz-rock are so much catchier than "virtually incomprehensible *cinema verité* of a blank generation." We were feeling the pinch and I could see the writing on the wall, but I chose not to read it.

In March, we played an unpublicised show at the Speakeasy club while in the audience Sid Vicious, who had recently replaced Glen Matlock as bass player with the Sex Pistols in an atypically bloodless coup, took increasingly unfocused swings at anyone who was passing. I like to think that this was the night I saved Sid Vicious's life, since later that evening, after we came offstage, I walked into the gents toilet and was confronted by the gruesome sight of Sid with a needle in his arm, nodding off as he sat on the lavatory, the door wide open, his trademark leather jacket in a heap next to him. He was dribbling and his grey flesh looked like dough. Nancy Spungen, the American groupie, whom he would eventually marry and murder, threw up on the floor of the adjacent cubicle, oblivious to what was going on with Sid. Already aware through reports in the press of the legendary unpredictability of his temper, I woke him by slapping his face hard twice, and as his eyes flickered open, and seemed to roll back into his head, I fled before he could throw a punch back. As I left I heard him bellow the word "cunt!" after me.

April 1977 saw the UK release of the first Clash album, called simply *The Clash*. It contained all their best live numbers, such as *White Riot, Janie Jones, I'm So Bored With The USA, London's Burning* and *Police And Thieves*. It was a thrilling, pumped-up, 35-minute thrash, which managed to retain the live essence of the band's three-pronged attack of Strummer, Jones and Simonon. It didn't do a damned thing for *our* chances of survival, though. I was torn between loving that music and desperately wanting the whole punk thing to go away. We thought it might be the end of them when their American record company, CBS, refused to issue the record in the US, saying that the production was too crude and that it wouldn't sell. We were being over-optimistic and our *schadenfreude* was misplaced. In fact 100,000 imported copies of the record were sold in the USA before CBS rethought their position and released it domestically. On 12 May Richard Branson's Virgin Records signed the Pistols after A&M had followed EMI and dropped them. We all knew that if The Clash's album was a smash, The Pistols' would be even bigger. The juggernaut was rolling and we weren't on it.

* * *

In the spring Phil, the guy who was renting us the flat in Hampstead Garden Suburb, got into some minor difficulties and needed the flat back. It was a real wrench having to move house with a young baby but we actually weren't that sorry to be leaving the area. We moved back into my parents' house for a couple of weeks, which, with Dad at his most irascible, was purgatory. We quickly managed to find a garden flat in Streatham and, in May 1977, we moved in. It was owned by a 90-year-old, silver-haired, pink-faced woman named Mrs Normandale, who lived in the upstairs flat with her diminutive 65-year-old son Dudley. They were like an old colonial couple who had never left India when the Raj collapsed. Mrs Normandale, "Adele", sipped tea all day and looked out of the window. Dudley was given to wearing baggy Khaki shorts in all weathers, and to doing endless unnecessary odd jobs. His stock greeting was never "Hello" or "Good Morning", but "Are you winning?" I think they were rather nonplussed by my blue hair but they were happy to take the rent and watch us playing in the garden with Geno. He was a darling boy with a fantastic temperament who cried so little through his entire childhood that when he did, we knew something was genuinely wrong.

The flat had a bedroom, a sitting room and a dining room, with a small kitchen and bathroom and toilet. It was a bit tatty but it was self-contained and had a huge garden. It was a bit of a relief to be back in south London again. Getting all the way to Brooklands Rise with a baby on public transport from town, or from anywhere else for that matter, was becoming a chore. While Streatham is not exactly the centre of the universe, there were at least shops nearby, and buses and trains to get us anywhere we wanted to be.

On 7 June, The Pistols hired a boat on the River Thames called the *Queen Elizabeth* and had their own unofficial Jubilee party. It was a hoot. The band, selected journalists and hangers-on were marshalled on to the boat by a chirpy McLaren, intent on mischief, like Fletcher Christian hand-picking his own mutinous crew. The Pistols tried to play a set but had their power cut off, and then they were forced to return to their mooring by the river police. Malcolm was ecstatic. The band only had to get out of bed to ensure a slew of newspaper and television coverage.

Rene and I went to see all the American bands who came over, and they were frequently fantastic double-billed affairs where we got to glimpse first hand what all the press fuss was about. We loved The Ramones at the Roundhouse, but it was really their co-stars, the Talking Heads, who blew us away. They were so weird, so edgy, so artistic, so autistic. They were right up our street. Similarly we went to see a great New York double bill at the Hammersmith Odeon that featured the pure pop of Debbie Harry's Blondie, and the crystalline lyricism of Tom Verlaine's Television. All those bands were guitar-driven, but with a diversity of sound and approach which was much more adventurous than their British counterparts.

The British punks were all attitude – they acted dumb and made a virtue of the musical incompetence. The Americans could play. Tom Verlaine never acted dumb. Nor did Talking Heads' leader David Byrne. With the exception of The Ramones, who were happy to be characterised as "pinheads", none of those US bands fitted in with an English concept of punk rock, but they sat easily in the latest generic pigeon hole – new wave. Even the original American wild-boy, Iggy Pop, who had released his first album with his band the Stooges some 10 years earlier, found his career given an unexpected boost by the tributes paid to him by the British punk rockers. I saw him play a show at the Rainbow Theatre in London's Finsbury Park, supported by The Adverts, who were by now good friends of mine. T.V. Smith's girlfriend and bass player, Gaye Advert, punk's first pin-up and no stranger to the joys of amphetamine herself, listened wide-eyed with admiration as Iggy told me he had been up for 13 days straight. I was impressed. His claim would have stretched my credulity to breaking point had he not looked so wasted that one could easily have believed he had been up for 13 weeks straight.

In October, The Sex Pistols' debut album, *Never Mind The Bollocks*, was finally unleashed on an eager public. It featured all their single releases to date, *Anarchy In The UK*, *God Save The Queen*, *Pretty Vacant* and *HolidaysIn The Sun*, and was a hugely controversial smash, as McLaren intended. A record store manager was arrested in Nottingham for displaying the cover, which was deemed offensive, even though it was purely typographical. The top liberal barrister, John Mortimer QC, old "Rumpole of the Bailey" himself, defended the man, and called on a professor of English to explain the history and usage of the word "bollocks". The case was eventually dismissed.

By 1978, Polydor had all but dropped us. Contractually, we still had one more album to record for them, but we knew and they knew it was just a bank raid. Their energies were elsewhere. They were now enjoying some success with three big punk bands, Siouxsie and the Banshees, The Jam and the crudely-drawn cartoon punk rock of Sham 69. They had also just released a double soundtrack album from a 1977 movie called *Saturday Night Fever,* which was beginning to shift a few copies. It went on to sell over 30 million. The Doctors had finished the previous accounting year on something of a high note. We had made a touring profit. Having grossed £29,227.91 in appearance fees, we had paid out a mere £29,206.90 in expenses. We had made money – £21.01 to be precise. Between four of us. That was £5.20 each – or 10p a week!

This was the first time that I realised that the wonderful world of show business is unfair. Unlike other professions, you are not rewarded simply for sticking around. The music business thrives on novelty; if you stick around for too long without success you will notice everyone in the business starting to edge away from you like you are a bad smell or a contagious disease. Polydor was contractually bound to give us another big advance for a third album, and Morrison wasn't about to let them off that particular hook. I had written some very good new songs for the record, both alone and with T.V. Smith, the writer and singer from The Adverts, who had recently had a big hit with their quirky, darkly amusing song *Gary Gilmore's Eyes,* and I was keen to give the thing one last shot. We went back to Majestic Studios, where we had recorded our first album, and produced the record ourselves with Hobbsy, our soundman, at the controls. In some ways it was a reward for Hobbsy's uncomplaining loyalty to the band through all the shit and deprivations. We thought that it might help him make the transition to a less arduous side of the business, and since we really feared for his health sometimes we thought that could only be to his advantage.

The songs on the third album, which I entitled somewhat vaingloriously *Sons of Survival,* were actually some of the best songs I had ever written. The overall feel of the album was apocalyptic. We all knew it was to be our last but we never mentioned it out loud. The title track, *Sons Of Survival,* a rant against record company politics and big business machinations, was driven by a nagging one-note riff from Urban Blitz's violin and a goose-stepping bass line from Stoner. Chunky guitar chords underlined the vocal, and I even played a half-decent guitar solo on top.

Back From The Dead was a song I wrote with T.V. Smith, one of several we had written together over the preceding year. I think he came up with the title and we wrote the lyrics and music jointly. It was a furiously fast song, with lyrics spat out over a high-octane track. The Adverts recorded the song themselves on their second album but, if anything, our version was even more punked-up than theirs.

Triple Vision was one of the best songs I ever wrote for the Doctors, and I still like that song today. I especially like the residue of proud Nietzschean atheism and Marxist dialecticism. I even play it acoustically occasionally and it works – a sure sign of a good song.

*And there on the wall in words eight-feet tall they're advising you all to join
parties and watch the TV*
*And up in the sky is a vision of mercy but it might just as well be a fortnight
in Jersey for me*
*I'm so unconvinced by your saviours and princes, and since we got started,
your bleeding-heart love leaves me cold*
I'm either a century too soon or a lifetime too old.
*And down in the street is a man who's been blinded by visions of prisons for
some, and for others hotels*
*And he screams, "Could it be what you call evolution is nothing much more
than a multiplication of cells?"*
*I talk to my Revox about lonely millions, make tapes on the phone so it seems
I'm never alone*
The TV stays on while I'm out so I'm always at home.

The song, *Network*, was inspired partly by the recently released film of that name, about a TV
link anchor man who has an ongoing nervous breakdown on screen, and sees his viewing
figures rocket because of it, and partly it was my cryptic goodbye note to the rest of the band.

I'm through with the piecework
I'm through with the network

The album also included a punk-influenced song, *Bulletin*, which was a tirade against the
absorption of punk rock into the multinational mainstream.

Those were the best five songs on the album. Of the others, some were as appetising as the
warmed-up leftovers from a dog's dinner. I hadn't really had time to write all new songs for the
album, so I raided the archive and tried to beat *50's Kids* and *No Limits* into shape. In the end I
hated *No Limits* so much I got Stoner to sing the lead vocal. It didn't altogether improve it for
me, but it got the song off my back. The recording session finished with a live workout of the
song we used to close the live show with, *Cool*. Onstage we always segued it into The Velvets'
Waiting For The Man, but on record we didn't want to hang around to get permission from Lou
Reed's publisher, so we cranked our instruments up and thrashed the arse off it instrumentally,
and knew that no one would give a damn. It ends with screeching howling feedback and a
looped baying crowd. It was so obviously the last time we were going to be together in a studio
that we went crazy, unleashing all the frustrations of the previous three years.

When the recording was finished, Urban Blitz announced he had had enough and was
quitting. For me it was quite a relief. He had started to freak out on a personal level. He
became unmanageable on a one-to-one basis. But the great thing was, he was so screwed up
he had put all his neuroses on to this new record and made it really edgy. As soon as he'd done
his tracks and his overdubs, that was it. He was off. He wasn't interested in hanging around
for the mixing. As I said before, we had never been a particularly close band socially, but there
had always been a tacit relationship that was based on a common focus. The focus went for
him, and it got to the point where he was just turning up for gigs and going home after them.

Stoner, Peter and myself talked about what we wanted to do and agreed to give it a little while longer. We were reluctant to completely pull the plug because it felt like there was unfinished business. Not least because we had made a record of which we were all quite proud, and we wanted at least to promote it and give it a chance. We decided to give it six more months. The three of us really developed in that period. I was interested in filling the gaps that Urban left with tapes and electronics. It had been explored so little and it was what I had always intended The Doctors to progress into. I thought that where a fourth instrument was demanded, we would use sound – pure sound, sound effects and electronics – in an abstract way.

A few weeks later The Damned broke up, not for the first time and not for the last, and their singer Dave Vanian called me to tell me that he was at a loose end. It occurred to me that it might be fun to get Dave to tour with us as a second frontman and singer. I didn't mind sharing my limelight with him as I knew we would bounce off each other on stage, and that he would certainly galvanise us into positive action. We knew, too, that he would attract some of the Damned's following to our shows. It was really a last throw of the dice. Polydor stumped up a small amount of cash to put us into a studio with Dave to record a new song that I had just written with T.V. Smith, called *Don't Panic England*. We were panicking now. Dave Vanian and I shared the vocals. It was a pretty good song but it was all too late. The song was never released and Dave only did a handful of shows with us.

We decided to do one last tour of Europe as a three-piece and one last British tour. I set up a lot of the European gigs myself, spending days on the telephone with promoters in France, Holland, Germany and Scandinavia. Of course these European promoters wanted punk bands now, and it was quite difficult to set up a tour that would pay, but I finally got the dates into some sort of shape. One of the gigs we were most looking forward to was the Kant Kino, a cinema in Berlin that hosted gigs on an irregular basis. We had enjoyed a great deal of success in that city on previous appearances, and they booked us for two shows on consecutive nights. We always loved Berlin. It was our sort of city. The Wall was still standing and the city was like a depraved outpost of a time gone by. There was an energy and an atmosphere there unlike anywhere else in Germany. We took Giovanni along for the ride and played two of the best shows we had ever done.

Travelling home after the sold-out Berlin shows I told Giovanni that I thought we would fold up the band before the end of the year and he thought it was the best thing to do. "You've got such a talent," he told me, "you're bound make it when you find the right vehicle." I think it was while playing at a rainy outdoor festival in Chelmsford that I finally decided it was over. Not just for us, but for punk too. It was a dismal day, brightened only by a backstage visit from Rob Tyner, leader of the MC5, one of my great hero bands of the late sixties. He was wildly enthusiastic about the set that we had just played, and wondered if we could do some work together at some stage. My head was elsewhere, and I never even took his number.

The Doctors of Madness played their final show at the Music Machine, in Camden Town, on 26 October 1978, three and a half years after we had signed with Bryan Morrison and Justin de Villeneuve. Cabaret Voltaire supported. It was a miserable gig, in a venue that seemed like it had been sucked dry of all joy. We intended to play a very long set, taking in most of our favourite songs from the three albums plus a few others besides. It was as much for old times' sake and a sense of putting those songs to rest. We opened up with a 10-minute-long new song called *Trouble* that I had written some time back but never done with The Doctors. It kicked the set off with a howling agonised maelstrom of feedback, the rhythm slowly insinuating itself and then asserting itself until it was an insistent lobotomised jack-hammer. For a three-piece we made a most terrifying racket that night. The song ends with one of my more modest observations: "If genius was murder I'd end up in the chair, I've got a mind like Bertrand Russell and I dance like Fred Astaire." T.V. Smith joined us onstage for two songs that he and I had co-written, *Making Machines* and *The Last Human Being In The World*, plus a song called *Who Cries For Me?* that I had recently finished. I remember we also did a killer version of Lou Reed's Velvet Underground classic, *What Goes On?*, which we had first tried out in Berlin. But there was no real fun in the gig for any of us. We were so strung out on speed and booze that it felt like the people in the cavernous arena had just come to pay their respects to a corpse. Many of the critics reviewing that show took the opportunity to give the corpse a good kicking just to make sure it was dead – the music journalists Paul Morley and Jon Savage were two of the most vicious cadaver abusers.

The three and a half years since the Cabbage Patch had been a bumpy ride, full of excitements and disappointments and unfulfilled dreams. We had got tantalisingly close, we had been to the top of the candy mountain and seen the land of milk and honey, but we had been denied entry. We had somehow gone from being "ahead of our time" to being *passé*, without ever spending a single night between the crisp, clean white linen sheets of being "now". From dynamos to dinosaurs.

Pop careers, like political careers, always end in failure. Or death. Or, worse still, a reunion. Since there is no blueprint, no one knows what 50-year old rock stars are supposed to do. One thing is certain, though. They should not get up onstage, fat, flabby and flatulent, and try to convince themselves and us that they are still 22. No one in their right mind would ever say the records the Stones have made since the mid-seventies have been a patch on their earlier work. No one who saw The Sex Pistols or The Velvet Underground reunion tours would seri-ously suggest they served any useful function, except to provide an old-age pension for the participants. Would you swap your copy of *Revolver* for *Let It Be?* Or *The Clash* for *Sandinista?* Or *Ziggy Stardust* for *Tin Machine?* Snake-hipped Elvis' *Hound Dog* for bloated Presley's *My Way?* No, nor me. See what I mean? All pop careers end in failure.

By the time the band split I think I was on the edge of a nervous breakdown. It may just have been exhaustion or it may have been my ego reeling from failure and rejection. I found I couldn't ignore the amount of bad feeling directed at the Doctors and at me personally. I hadn't allowed myself to let it get to me while the band was working, but as soon as we split, and I decided I wanted to move on and do something new, it came horribly home to me.

I didn't really know what I was going to do next. I had a family to support and I was off the conventional job ladder. I was a failed rock and roller, but I wasn't one of those embittered failed rock and rollers who was about to hook up with "the enemy", the record companies, and find other young talent to crush on the wheel. I felt like I still had unfinished business in the "wonderful world of popular entertainment", and also my bloody-mindedness made it very hard for me to quit after so many people had written me off. I had in mind that snippet of Samuel Beckett: "Ever tried. Ever failed. No matter. Try Again. Fail again. Fail Better." (Worstward Ho!) I kept thinking about what Giovanni had said about finding the right vehicle. I looked around to see what my options were. I got together with T.V. Smith who had been through a similarly wretched run, and we started writing a lot of songs together. We didn't know what we were going to do with them, but T.V. used to come round to our flat in Streatham and we would write a song every day. Some good, some lousy, but we had a good working relationship; we were on the same wavelength and could work together without getting on each other's nerves. Despite the enthusiastic reception they got from both T.V.'s manager, Michael Dempsey, and from Bryan Morrison, nothing ever happened to any of those songs we wrote.

I also did some writing with Giovanni Dadomo. We were working on songs but for the most part we just got strung out. He was such an amusing individual that we spent more time laughing than working. We kept coming up with great titles for songs but not developing them. Among the classic songs that never actually got written were things such as *I'm On The Menu*, *"Woof!" Said The Wife*, *Murder By Cadillac*, *I Shot My TV*, *I Wanna Be Your Biro*, and *Your Architecture* (*brings me to my knees*). What an amazing A-side of an album they would have made, if only we hadn't been incapable.

In a strange variation on what had gone on six months previously, when Dave Vanian briefly joined the Doctors, The Damned asked me to join them, since they still didn't have a frontman vocalist. I joined them for one day. After one embarrassing evening in a rehearsal hall in Croydon with Captain Sensible, Rat Scabies and a guitarist all frantically scratching around to find some common ground, I said, "Thanks, but no thanks". I didn't pursue their offer.

Drumbo, ever a supportive and loyal friend, got a bit of money together and suggested I go into a London studio and record something with a new bunch of musicians. On 3 May 1979, the unspeakable Margaret Thatcher won the General Election, beating the governing Labour Party under Jim Callaghan by 70 seats, and became the new British Prime Minister. It was a fearsome prospect, having this right-wing harridan in power and I suggested to Drumbo that we seize the moment and record a version of Bob Dylan's *Maggie's Farm* before anyone else did. He thought it was a great idea and we assembled a sturdy group of musicians from various sources. We rehearsed for an afternoon and recorded two songs in the same evening in a 24-track studio in Central London. *Maggie's Farm* thundered along with a non-too-subtle lift from the Pistols' *Anarchy In The UK* riff, and with a scorching sax solo from Dave Winthrop, who was playing with one of Morrison's bands, the reheated mod-revivalists Secret Affair. Everyone sang on the choruses and it sounded very meaty and very live. We were extremely happy with the second take and, when we listened back to it in the control room at maximum volume, it sounded pretty damn hot. For the B-side I wanted to record *Trouble*, which The Doctors had never recorded, and we did a total re-working of it with Steve

Swindells playing a complex, discordant, barrelhouse piano figure, and Drumbo and Paul Martinez combining to make a rock solid, stuttering rhythm section, while my rhythm guitar chopped out the offbeat. It was weird, unlike anything I had ever recorded before. I really loved it.

We called the band Dumb Billions, a sort of pun on Bob Dylan. Astonishingly, we couldn't find a single record company who were prepared to release this double-sided potential monster. No one was interested in doing a one-off singles deal with a band that wasn't really a band. We sat on the masters and they are still gathering dust to this day, awaiting discovery by some earnest young future musicologist and completist. Part of the trouble, once again, was timing. The record companies, having been caught napping when punk broke, were now desperate to sign British-based, multiracial bands such as Madness, The Specials, The Selector and The Beat, who were all enjoying chart success with their ska-lite blend of Jamaican rhythms and off-the-peg retro threads. A rock version of *Maggie's Farm* didn't exactly fit that bill.

I wasn't unduly worried about the lack of progress my career was making in these few months since breaking up the band. I was happy with the stuff I was writing, and a three-year-old child is such a joy that I was glad not to be on the road all the time. Rene and I worked in the same room in Streatham, and Geno amused himself with Lego and building bricks and the usual stuff.

In 1979, however, almost out of the blue, I got another break. I had bought a cheap synthesiser and had written a lot of songs using its basic analogue sounds, which moved me away from a purely guitar-based music and method of writing. I could set up drones and atmospheres on the synth and doodle away on top so it was like having an accompanist. It was such a cheap synth that its oscillators were very unstable and so it was almost like playing with a person. I set up a groove on a drum machine and played over the top, and wrote a song called *International Language*. It emerged from a lyric idea I had got when Geno was in hospital. Lying in bed in the middle of the night, occasionally hearing a distant child crying, I thought that there are some sounds and ideas that are recognised universally, without the need for language: crying, laughing, screams of pain, even pained silence. I started writing a song about depression, for some reason (I am many things but, mercifully, I am not a depressive, but I knew the territory only too well). I placed it in a domestic setting. A woman waiting for her husband to come home, even though she knows he's having an affair, and probably won't be back. She has a breakdown and kills herself. Simple. All set to an irresistible electro-disco beat and a skipping bass guitar playing octaves, like Blondie's *Heart Of Glass*. It sounded great, and I made a tape of it for Morrison who was very enthusiastic.

I told him I didn't want to be with a major label again just yet, but that I would rather be with one of the smaller, independent labels of which, post-punk, there were many. This was one of the great legacies of punk. Bands could for the first time record, press and distribute their own records, and sell them through a network of specialist shops. There was a similar "democratisation" of the creative process in the nineties, when samplers and computers became affordable for all and kids in their bedrooms could make dance records that were of a high enough sound quality to press up records from, and to put straight in to clubs to test the reaction. In both cases it was not the creative process that was controlled by the majors, but the world-wide distribution which ensured sales.

One of the independent record companies operating at the time was a Wimbledon-based label called Cherry Red, which was started and run by Ian McNay. He was interested in doing some stuff with the slapstick singer John Otway, and got in touch with Morrison. Bryan played him my demo of *International Language* and he went crazy for it. A contract was drawn up and I went back down to Drumbo's studio to record the song. Drumbo co-produced it with me, as well as engineering and playing drums. A young guy called Sam Williams, the brother of classical guitarist, John Williams, played bass guitar. I played every-thing else, and the record was in the shops within six weeks. Rene and I did the sleeve together. We found a lovely picture of a dead Marilyn Monroe in the Kenneth Anger book, *Hollywood Babylon*, xeroxed it and used it more or less unchanged. A bit of typography and we were up and running. No committees to please, no egos to worry about except my own. It was heaven. The record got great reviews and made the independent record charts. It picked up some airplay in the UK and it also started to get played in the States on college radio stations. One of the most curious things that happened to *International Language* was that it got translated into French and covered by the Belgian one-hit wonder, Plastic Bertrand, who, as you might imagine, needed a lot of material to fill a *Greatest Hits* album. If ever an album title contravened the Trades Descriptions Act, that was it. *International Language* provided me with exactly what I needed: a low-key, re-entry into the loving arms of the music industry.

The wonderful world of show business may be unfair, capricious and fickle. It does, however, sometimes let you have a second chance. If you can roll with the punches, if your skin is thick enough, if you are hungry enough for it, whatever "it" is, if you are prepared to wade though the corporate shit and the ego shit and the personal shit, you can climb back on that horse and try to ride it off into the pay-dirt, celebrity, VIP lounge sunset. Like a gunslinger who has only taken a flesh-wound, you can always have another pop at pop. What was it that Nietzsche said on military matters in *Twilight of the Gods*? "Whatever doesn't kill me makes me stronger". Yeah! Let's rock! Nietzsche, eh? The *Übermensch*. Now that gives me an idea.

Chris Bohn was my press officer during my last days at Polydor. He was a young, shy, nervous figure in a totally inappropriate job. He was a genuine enthusiast and supporter who would have been much better suited to being "emeritus professor of left-field unlistenable". He was probably the only person at Polydor who, on being asked, "Who were Bert Brecht and Kurt Weill?" would not have answered, "Er, the Bayern Munich soccer team's midfield duo?"

He was, like me, a Europhile. We shared a lot of cultural heroes, from Fassbinder to Brel to the Polish absurdist genius, Stanislaw Ignacy Witkiewicz. The films of Francesco Rosi, *Illustrious Corpses*, and, in particular, *The Mattei Affair*, which Chris Bohn turned me on to, became the prototypes for a project I was starting to turn over in my head. It was to be a sort of political fantasy, in which a character called Richard Strange uses the marketing and promotional skills he has learned in the entertainment industry to become the elected president of a future united, federal Europe. While I understood that this was quite a long way from (*You ain't nothing but a*) *Hound Dog*, I thought I could write a provocative, edgy and intelligent rock album that could still be of interest to major a record company. My blueprint was *The Mattei Affair* meets *Citizen Kane* meets *Wild in The Streets*.

I modestly called the project *The Phenomenal Rise of Richard Strange*, and got to work on the narrative. Since I was suffering at the time from a rampant, amphetamine-fuelled egomania, the bare bones of the story came to me quite quickly. The story is essentially the following: a not-too-distant future scenario, where Europe is a federation governed by the EuroKongress from Frankfurt, and the president is elected by all the member states. The first EuroKongress has been a flop, the political situation in Europe is fractured and on the point of collapse. There are food shortages and civil disorder on an unprecedented scale. The people are crying out for a strong, charismatic leader who will sweep away the corruption and the bureaucracy and give an overworked population their leisure time back. The central figure, an entertainer and showman called Richard Strange, has grown bored with the banality of his life. He wonders if he can apply the techniques of self-promotion he has learned in show-business to building a political career. (This was before Ronald Reagan had declared his intention to stand for the US Presidency in 1980.) Richard Strange is totally amoral and wants to become president as a purely academic exercise. He sets up deals with the international bankers and the media moguls, offering them *carte blanche* when he is elected if they will just support his campaign. This they readily agree to and bankroll his political advancement.

The people fall for his fresh approach and his new ideas, and he is duly elected as leader of the second EuroKongress. Once in power, however, he becomes politicised, and from being a cynical manipulator he become a genuine crusader against injustice. He introduces a programme which utilises the new technology to free people from the drudgery of labour and, since the factories and services become much more efficient, Europe prospers and the people are encouraged to use their free time beneficially, on self-education and on community-based initiatives. The process of the redistribution of wealth, coupled with the curtailment of press and TV power start to rankle with his former allies, and a plot is hatched to kidnap him and to persuade him to slow down with his reforms. His captors threaten to assassinate him if he refuses to play the game by the rules of their original agreement. He refuses to do so and is probably shot. I say "probably" because I wanted to leave the ending ambiguous. I thought it was quite possible that such a character would get bored with the reality of political life, and orchestrate his own disappearance so that he could once again re-invent himself somewhere else

It should be remembered that this was written in 1979 and 1980, at a time when European political terrorism was at its height, and there was a real interface between predominantly left-wing terror groups and their natural enemies, the right-wing politicians, industrialist and high-profile capitalists. In Germany there was the Baader-Meinhof gang and the Red Army Faction. In Italy there was the Red Brigade. In Great Britain we had the IRA and the Angry Brigade. In addition, all over Europe there were the random strikes by the PLO (Palestine Liberation Organisation) and their many offshoot supporters. Kidnapped politicians would routinely be paraded by their captors in front of TV cameras, holding a copy of that day's newspaper to show they were still alive. The less fortunate were found riddled with bullet wounds in the back seats of abandoned stolen cars. Politics was everywhere, and in the UK Margaret Thatcher was already starting to batten down the hatches of repression.

I bought a Revox tape recorder and started writing furiously. I wanted the whole story to be told through the songs, with a varied musical canvas. I wrote about 15 songs that I thought would be included in the finished project, but some of them got chucked on the way. Although I didn't write the songs in a strictly chronological order, the opening title track was actually the first song I wrote for the piece. It was an insistent, minor-to-major melody, which serves as a sort of overture.

Walk a straight line to the landslide
Tap the walls with sticks and decide
Who you are, the slave or master,
Watch the race it's getting faster.
Walk a straight line, the road to ruin
You either end up screwed or screwing.
Change the time it's time for change
Europe welcomes Richard Strange.

I recorded the songs at home and I played every instrument as I had no desire to get into a band situation so soon after The Doctors fiasco. I hit on the idea that I could actually perform the entire show live just using backing tapes and perhaps a live acoustic or electric guitar. Later I decided it would be useful to have some film inserts, too.

My home recordings weren't of sufficiently high quality to use in performance so I telephoned Drumbo and arranged to go down to his studio at Roche, in Cornwall, to re-record all my backing tracks. He generously agreed and I travelled down with 10 songs to record with Martin and Sam Williams. I played everything else. Martin had a moderately well equipped 16-track studio then so the resultant tapes were pretty good. The vibes there were great, too, with Martin's partner, Sally, contributing in no small part to the generally fertile atmosphere of excitement and discovery. In addition to the title track, the songs we recorded were: *On Top Of The World, Hearts And Minds, Magic Man, Gutter Press, International Language, Who Cries For Me?, Premonition, The Road To The Room* and *I Won't Run Away*. I was re-energised when I got back to London with them, and anxious to get the project moving.

To showcase this new work I wanted to find a new type of venue. Since it wasn't a run-of-the-mill rock show, I wanted it to be seen outside of the usual rock club circuit of the day. To this end I hooked up with Andy Czezowski, whom I'd first met in 1977 when he opened the Roxy, and who now owns the spectacularly successful Fridge in Brixton. We scoured London for a new venue and after a while we found an intimate gay club in a Covent Garden basement, called Hell, which was dying on its feet on weekdays. We offered to take the club over every Wednesday night in April and May, promising rather recklessly to fill it within a month. To our total astonishment, we did. Our attendance rose from a first night of 40 to a capacity 250 in three weeks. It was at Hell that I got the first inklings of how enjoyable (yes, really!) live performance can be for both artist and audience. Normally only one or the other can feel valued. Either the audiences are treated like cattle or the artist is merely a product to be consumed. In addition, the logistical and technical shortcomings, which had so often come between The Doctors and our audiences, were not a factor in this stripped-down format. This was the beginning of a scene very different from punk, although many familiar faces from the punk days were also going through changes and walking through our doors and into Hell.

I tended to work solo, with occasional sax accompaniment from my *Maggie's Farm* colleague Dave Winthrop, who was a great foil for me onstage and endlessly amusing company off it. I got some good notices, too, which was something of a novelty for me. Hugh Blair of the *New Music News* wrote:

> In the middle of the set, as if to rip apart any bag we may be about to put him in, The Man picks up an acoustic guitar and plays a song called Triple Vision, written apparently when The Doctors of Madness were still alive. It ranks among one of the most electrifying solo performances of a song I have ever seen . . . Then back to the tapes, and the neo-disco of *International Language*, his only solo release so far. Tragic and Glorious.

Michael Dempsey, once referred to in *Private Eye* as "London's drunkest publisher", in itself no mean feat, was a close friend and stalwart supporter of what we were doing at Hell. Michael was a hugely likeable, but ultimately doomed Anglo-Irish Bohemian. He had left behind a wrecked relationship with the society authoress, Emma Tennant – with whom he had a daughter, Rose, a most exquisite child – and was still carrying the bruises. His capacity for drink and drugs was phenomenal, and as the manager of The Adverts, the talented but only briefly successful punk band, he found access to both in vast quantity. In addition to having a glittering career in publishing, Dempsey had also been a Labour councillor in Haringey and was as passionate about his politics as he was about his booze.

His greatest love, however, was Irish literature, and of all the Irish greats, best of all he loved W. B Yeats and Flann O'Brien. With his wild mat of thick, dark, unkempt curly hair and his ruddy complexion, blind as a bat without his bottle-bottom spectacles, lubricated with whisky or on fire with cocaine, he would quote huge slabs from either poet, and his soft musical brogue, exaggerated a little for the gallery, would replace the received pronunciation from his days at Cambridge. His small flat in the Fulham Road, next to Chelsea Football Ground would magically be filled with peat smoke, Gaelic mysticism and Dublin ghosts.

Whenever Michael came to Hell, he would bring along with him some fabulously exotic author or poet. Either they would be friends of long standing, or bar-room prophets he had just beguiled 10 minutes before. Michael Moorcock, Harlan Ellison and J.G. Ballard all came along at some point at Michael's bidding. Throughout the entire duration of my set I would hear Michael bellowing enthusiastically into their ears, "Strange is a genius! He must be heard!" Michael had an easy charm and a keen intelligence; he loved nothing more than a good argument and was as happy in a Soho saloon bar as in a Knightsbridge salon. In the short time that I knew him, maybe only five years before his awful death in 1982, he had been through his car windscreen three times and his face was sewn up like a patchwork quilt. That is not clever, but it is impressive.

The revisionism of the press corps had already started. Like an old Soviet apparatchik who had been out of favour with the Politburo but was now being rehabilitated, the music papers were revising their opinions of me and The Doctors of Madness. In the *Melody Maker* Paul Tickell opened his article by saying, "Punk had many Godfathers, and one of them was undoubtedly Richard Strange, guiding light of The Doctors of Madness. Who else in '75 was dying their hair blue and playing fast songs about urban psychosis? The Doctors helped pave the way for punk, but never reaped any of its explosive benefits."

For my one-man shows I had adopted a new guise, a new persona. The blue hair was long gone and so, too, was the punked-up spikiness of the last days of The Doctors. Now I adopted a much more austere look as befits a politician on the make. I wore a collar and tie, sharp suits, polished shoes, a trench coat and a hat. The ensemble resembled the result of a furtive coupling between a shady accountant and a 1940s private eye. The songs I played were principally the new ones I had written for the *Phenomenal Rise* project, plus some other songs I had developed since the demise of The Doctors. The programme was completed by acoustic guitar versions of a few favourite Doctors' songs such as *Triple Vision* and *Mitzi's Cure*.

The audience was partly comprised of former Doctors of Madness fans, partly some of the newly emerging British art school crowd and partly a new, as yet unnamed, group of flamboyant fashion victims who were later to be known as the new romantics. It was a more sophisticated, knowing crowd than I had played to before. These were people who read books and went to the theatre and saw pop music in a wider context. I liked the challenge of having to write songs that were both intelligent and entertaining. I also liked the format I was working in. It was mobile, flexible and potent. No more interminable tours of dubious value, artistic or financial. The backing tapes meant that I could play small venues that were not originally intended for live music. It gave a sort of intimate, cabaret feel to the performance, which I always enjoyed. It was also a very portable medium, which meant that I could travel with my entire show in a suitcase. Robin Denselow, of *The Guardian*, did an interview with me and asked, "How would you describe your current show?" I replied, "Neo-survivalism. That means keeping your head above water and staying one step ahead of the dogs."

I began to really enjoy working with Dave Winthrop. He was sociable, professional and adult. Musically his saxophone added an appropriate colour to the songs, and a live element that was obviously missing from the tapes. Personally he was a perfect companion for me. He was educated, amusing and self-reliant. He was very low-maintenance. Winthrop had been a musician most of his life, and had been an original member of the band Supertramp. Unfortunately and untypically for Winthrop, he misjudged his exit, leaving just before they hit the jackpot.

Dave and I were like the "odd couple", travelling everywhere by public transport, with sensible shoes and sensible suitcases. We went to Holland on the coach from London to play some shows arranged by a maverick promoter named Hans Eijses. Everything was done on a shoestring, but we had great fun and the gigs were always eventful. Winthrop was a very accomplished artist, and used to do wonderful pen and ink drawings while we travelled to gigs. Usually they were minutely observed caricatures in gloriously surreal scenarios. Hans Eijses was full of enthusiasm and bluster but we forgave him everything because his girlfriend, an artist named Bea de Visser, was the opposite. Where he was bluff and bonhomie, she was cool and collected. Oh, and incredibly beautiful. Winthrop and I were totally under her spell, like two adolescent schoolboys. We egged each other on but neither of us ever made a move on her, mainly out of fear of being rejected. Somehow or other Hans worked the Dutch system for the next 30 years, getting the government to part with vast sums of money to bankroll Bea's ever more wonderful and extravagant flights of fancy. We returned home after the shows and went our separate ways until the next trip.

The Eighties

FIRST US TOUR

We spent many happy and amusing days and evenings in Streatham during the seven years that we lived there. Life with Rene and Geno was very good, despite the fact that very little money was coming in, and it was mainly the combination of a hefty bank overdraft and Rene's college grant that kept us afloat. (Aah, the college grant. Remember them? The generation of politicians who recently abolished them certainly do. Those loathsome hypocrites who introduced the student loans (i.e student debts) were the principle beneficiaries of the grant system in the seventies.)

When I was happy with the songs I had written, I called John Leckie, who had produced Figments of Emancipation, to ask him if he would come round and listen to the new material and tell me what he thought. He agreed but, as he was with a couple of people, he asked whether he could bring them also. His friends were Richard Jobson and his new girlfriend, so I told him to bring them for dinner and we spent a very enjoyable evening. I had known Jobson since his band The Skids first came to London from Scotland; that night he was in a boisterous mood, playing it up for the girl. She was a young blonde about 17 or 18 years old, with a very sexy, husky voice. She was intriguing, wearing a rather bizarre Fair Isle sweater, which no one really wore at that time, and she seemed very self-assured for someone so young.

When Jobson was out of the room, Leckie told me that whenever Jim Kerr (of Simple Minds) and fellow Scot, Jobson, got together, they would argue over which was the best gig The Doctors ever did in Scotland. Kerr held that it was the Manniquie Ballroom in Falkirk, while Jobson insisted that it was when we had supported BeBop Deluxe in Kirkaldy. John had been working in the studio with both Simple Minds and The Skids recently, and told me that whenever these two front men talked about me, I was always referred to as "the legend". I was embarrassed so, to change the subject, I asked the girl, rather unfairly, "What's with the hideous Fair Isle sweater?" She said "Oh, Richard bought it for me." "I think he wants me to look like his mum." she added with a wink. I couldn't quite place her accent. She told me that her father was Norwegian, her mother was Scottish and she had grown up in Ireland. And that her name was Mariella Frostrup.

* * *

In the summer of 1980, I realised one of my lifelong dreams: a coast-to-coast tour of the United States. Thanks to the NBC TV débâcle, The Doctors of Madness had never been signed to a US record label and the expense of touring made the likelihood of The Doctors ever crossing the Atlantic without record company support very remote indeed. In June, I was approached by the leading agency representing British new wave acts in the United States, a company called Wasted Talent, who asked me to do an eight-week-long tour of the US and Canada, sharing the bill with an English lunatic named John Otway. I think another English band had pulled out of the tour at the last minute and, because I had no drummer with domestic problems, no bass player with a fear of flying and no mountain of equipment to carry across, I was able to accept.

Otway is a quirky, distinctly English fruitcake, given to writing and delivering songs in a *faux-naïf* style, while displaying onstage all the timidity of King Kong on steroids. He thought nothing of climbing to the top of a 15-foot-high PA tower mid-song and attempting to do a double somersault into the audience from the summit, while still playing his battered acoustic guitar. That he never ever broke his back is more of a testament to good fortune than to good judgement.

A former dustman in his native St Albans, he never lost his exuberance at having effected his escape. I had known Otway from the seventies. Indeed, Bryan Morrison had published all his songs, including his screwy, double-headed 1979 chart hit *Cor Baby! That's Really Free* and *Beware Of The Flowers* ("'cos I'm sure they're gonna get you, yeh"). As neither of us was exactly straight out of the conventional rock star mould, we were billed as the English Eccentrics and we toured the country like a freak show. Otway had a three-piece guitar–bass–drums rock band behind him, and I worked with the Revox tape recorder and a guitar. I was contracted to appear on all of the 40 or so shows, and would receive £150 a week plus all travelling and hotel expenses. It was irresistible and I sweated for about a month after we closed the deal, wondering if the whole thing was actually going to happen.

When the final confirmation came through I was as excited as I can ever remember being in my life. I phoned Bryan Morrison who wished me good luck and told me to come by for a drink. By now he had a young talent scout working for him, a cocky kid called Mark Dean, who travelled in every day from his mum's home in Watford, to listen to the demo cassettes that are forever dropping through a publisher's letterbox, and which, for the most part, sit accusingly in a huge cardboard box for months on end, unheard. Dean had golden ears. He could hear hits in the box where other people only heard bad demos. It was Dean who, digging deep into that cardboard box one day. found something that prompted him to call out, "Hey Bryan, come and listen to this. I think I've found something!" It was like one of those old prospectors panning for gold by the side of the river for years on end without success, then the keen eye spots a nugget in the mud and suddenly it's the Klondike. The tape he found was a demo of a song performed by two kids who lived just down the road from him, in Bushey. One kid was called Andrew Ridgeley and the other was called George Michael. The tape just had one word in Magic Marker on the outside of the box – Wham!

Morry ambled in and clamped the headphones of the first Walkman I had ever seen to his ears. Dean pressed "play" and within 30 seconds Morry was beaming like a child on Christmas morning. "My son, we have cracked it. It's a fucking smash," he enthused, with that too-loud voice you use when you have headphones on. He then slipped the cassette on to the hi-fi in the office and turned it up to the max. "Get 'em in 'ere this afternoon. I wanna sign 'em," he bellowed to no one in particular, though Dean took it as a personal order to him. Morry started a weird, spastic dance, which he performed with all the innocent enthusiasm of a man who can hear a thousand cash registers ringing in the distance.

"Have a listen to this, my son," he yelled at me, as if I had any choice. "I could probably sign these kids for a £150 publishing advance on this single". It was a dreadful, insipid, white-boy rap. He asked, "What do you think?"

I said, "Bryan, save your money. It's awful. It's third-rate fake black music."

He didn't take my advice and that wretched record, called *Wham Rap*, was George Michael's first hit with his band, Wham! Bryan still publishes him and in his best year he made $40 million worldwide.

A week later I went by Morrison's for a good-luck drink prior to my departure for the States. He was buoyant and played me the Wham! demo again. Over a glass of champagne he told me he was going to sign them, despite my lack of enthusiasm. In addition, he was paying for Mark Dean to join me in New York at the end of my tour, as a token of his appreciation of Dean's discovery at the bottom of the cardboard box.

The US-Canada itinerary was finalised at last, and it made thrilling reading for a boy from Tooting Bec. It took us by road from New York to Los Angeles and back again, taking in all the major cities – Toronto, Montreal, Chicago, Dallas, Detroit and San Francisco, as well as some real backwaters like Lawrence, Kansas and Tulsa, Oklahoma. Every place name seemed so exotic to me, these towns having been mythologised by all my heroes from Jack Kerouac through Chuck Berry to Bob Dylan.

We flew out to New York on Freddie Laker's low-cost airline from Heathrow, all on standby, all of us on different flights, all in the interests of dirt-cheapery. I travelled out with Otway's guitarist, Steve Boltz, a very stylish Lancastrian with a quiff like a tidal wave breaking on Morecambe sands and a great wardrobe. I quickly learned, standing by the side of the stage on the first dates of the tour, that he was also a 24-carat original guitar player with a sound like no other, and an oh-so-cool stage act. In more than 30 years as a professional musician he has had more than his share of the vicissitudes of the rock business. He has played with just about everyone, from the soul legend Rufus Thomas, through heavy prog-rock with Arthur Brown's spin-off band, Atomic Rooster, to Scott Walker, taking in sessions and tours with The Who, Paul Young, David Bowie, Dr John, Keith Richards and Marianne Faithfull. He has enormous charm and a great, self-deprecating sense of humour. We got on enormously well throughout that entire trip and he is still my first choice guitarist for any new musical project I embark upon.

When I first stepped through the arrivals lounge at JFK Airport in New York, and out through the swing doors on to the street, the combination of the intense heat, the humidity and my exhaustion nearly flattened me. Imagine spending four solid months in a jam-packed Marquee Club on a hot summer's night – that is New York in summer, with a minimum temperature (at 2am) of 85°F, rising to 105°F around mid-afternoon. Add to that 75% humidity and every air-conditioning system in the city pumping out hot air into the street, and you start to get some idea of what Fifth Avenue was when I arrived.

I decided, insanely in retrospect, to attempt to take in as much as I possibly could in one go, and to do so on foot. So I set off on a 15-mile walk, with temperatures in the high 90s, taking in the Village in the south of the island, going up as far as 125th Street in the North – Harlem. It is black. The music is rap, jazz-funk and ethnic stuff like reggae and salsa, and it seeps out on to the street from every store and every house like a gas. And the locals sit round talking, laughing and making time. Up here there are no white faces, except the occasional junkie looking to score ("Up to Lexington/125/feel sick and dirty more dead than alive/I'm waiting for my man" – Lou Reed). I turned down Lexington Avenue, the music still in my ears, the heat on my back and the soles of my feet scorched though my shoes. I walked back to my hotel, The Iroquois on West 44th Street, where James Dean used to stay.

A week later, I was gigging in Canada and the first US reviews started to come through. I was referred to as a "Marxist Superman" and a "champion of the little men who have had enough of economic repression, who has risen up against the ruling class and all its means of mystification, including pop music". Pretty accurate, as it happens. America welcomes Richard Strange. I did an interview with a local magazine in Toronto. The girl said to me, "Did you try experimenting with drugs while you were on the road with The Doctors?" I said, "Yeah, got very involved for a while. I was doing bits of everything." She said, "I'd never do anything like that because I am terrified of losing control of myself. What did it do for you?" I answered, "It helped me lose control of myself."

The reviews for the Toronto shows were great. Anita Mara Alksnis wrote: "Strange's vigorously convincing performance is like chasing someone though a hall of mirrors . . . After only one listen his songs seem superior to anything that Bowie has written since *Ziggy Stardust*. A really severe character and one worth watching."

It was in Toronto that I witnessed bunji-jumping for the first time, and I thought it was over-rated as a participation sport. The poor unfortunate who leapt from the top of the CNN tower, the tallest building in Canada, was putting in simultaneous appearances in most of the suburbs when the elastic broke and he hit the sidewalk at 500mph.

Week three found me in the back of a car driving slowly down Dealy Plaza, in Dallas. Sliding past the Texas School Book Depository, where one window on the sixth floor is boarded up. Past the grassy knoll to the left hand side, then suddenly accelerating away. This, of course, is the last drive John Kennedy made, nearly 40 years ago now. Like so many other people, I still remember the day. But on that Saturday afternoon it was eerie, quiet and deserted. For a few dollars you could experience the assassination in a *son et lumière* show. I gave it a miss. Instead I found a flea market and bought some old records: Wilson Pickett, Tammi Terrell and Jan & Dean. In Dallas it was 110°F, but not as humid as New York. Uncomfortable but not unbearable. That night I played to an audience of cowboys who were slowly coming to terms with the end of the sixties. After the show someone told me that the first two Doctors of Madness albums fetch $20 each among the Texan cognoscenti. I worked out that Polydor would only need to sell 10,000 copies at that price to recoup all the money they ever lost on that band. I thought of the Kennedy connection, how both JFK and The Doctors were never more popular than the day after they died. I laughed myself to sleep in a motel with a rancid pool and a dead armadillo in a bush nearby.

From Dallas we started the 200-mile drive to that evening's gig in the state capital, Austin, and quickly found ourselves behind the clock with a lot of miles to make up. It was a Sunday and the roads were quite empty so we put the foot to the floor of the tour bus and hurtled through the unremarkable Texas landscape at 80mph instead 55mph, the maximum permitted in this time of oil crisis. We were thundering past the Lyndon B Johnson Ranch, creating a dust-storm in our wake when, to our horror, in the rear-view mirror we saw a Texan Police Department car bearing down on us with its lights flashing and its siren wailing. We pulled into a layby and the cops pulled in behind us. Over the loudspeakers on their car they ordered us all to come out with our hands up and to lie on the floor, arms outstretched. Rather worried by the belligerence of the voice, we duly obeyed and two cops with shotguns hovered over us. They demanded to see the papers for the bus, which the tour manager John Rummens had left in the glove compartment. As he moved to get them, one of the cops barked, "Do not move or aaah will shoot!" Rummens explained from his prostrated position that the papers were inside the vehicle and with a gun at his back he was allowed to get them.

Once the cops realised we were British and obedient, they relaxed a little and told us they were issuing us with a ticket for speeding. It was a great relief when they lowered their weapons and seemed more amenable. We explained that we were heading on to do a gig that night, and would no longer be in Texas on Monday. "Then y'all have to go to the courthouse now to pay a fahn," said one of the two state-troopers. They were wearing those tall dome-crowned hats that boy-scouts used to wear, and they had pink fleshy faces and mirror shades. They looked terrifying to anyone who had seen the film *Easy Rider*. We drove with them in convoy into the nearest small town, stopping on the way to pick up the judge. Stopping in front of an impressive-looking house, complete with white picket fence and an apple tree, one of the state troopers got out of the car and rang on the front door bell. A white-haired man in paint-splattered overalls and carrying a paintbrush opened the door. The trooper explained the situation and the old man stepped outside, closed the front door, climbed into his pickup truck and joined our convoy to the courthouse.

Once there, he fumbled in his pocket for the keys, and we were all ushered into the deserted room. Sitting at his bench the judge, still in his overalls, pounded his gavel and announced, "This court is now in session," and called on one of the officers to read the charge. "If it please the court," he started, "We followed the defendants over a distance of two mahls and clocked their speed as being in excess of seventy-fahv miles an hour in a fifty-fahv mile an hour limit zone. We pulled them over and read them their rights and issued them with a penalty ticket. They explained that this was their last day in Texas and that's why we had to disturb you today, Jerdge."

The judge looked at us suspiciously, a ragtaggle band of dishevelled rock and rollers, and asked if we had anything to say in our defence. As spokesman, I explained that we were rather over-zealous in our desire to fulfil a contractual commitment, that we hadn't been fully aware of the prevailing speed limit and that we were, of course, dreadfully sorry for the inconvenience we had caused to all. The judge looked down his nose at me and then turned to the state-trooper who had detailed the offence and asked him, "Do y'all have anything to add before Aaah pass sentence, Trooper?" and he replied, "Yes Jerdge. Aaah do. I would just lahk to say that ever since Aaah arrested these fellows they have all been right courteous to me." The Judge's face brightened a little and he looked at me and said, "Please drahve friendly from now on. Ten dollars fahn." And with that he brought down his gavel again and declared the case closed. We convoyed back to the highway and the three of them, looking like extras from the *Wizard of Oz*, waved us off and wished us well. We made the gig with time to spare.

Week four found me staying at the Tropicana Motel on Santa Monica Boulevard, Los Angeles. They said, "Tom Waits lives here, but he's away right now." It was the only motel I have stayed in with a black swimming pool. Macabre but very chic. We spent our days and our free nights there, drinking and relaxing, and catching up on reading and correspondence and doing the laundry. Our favourite pastime was The Brian Jones Memorial Swimathon, in which we ingested large quantities of drugs and drank tequila and saw who could lie longest on the bottom of the pool. It amused us for hours.

Our show in LA was to be at the fabled Whisky-a-Go-Go in Hollywood. Our agent had heard that the advance ticket sales for our show were going well and suggested to the club that we do an extra show, a sort of early evening matinee around 7pm, to pick up the younger kids. The Whisky agreed and the extra show was added. Somewhere between the telephone conversation and the matinee, however, there had been a communication breakdown, and the club had clean forgotten to publicise the early show. The result was that when I went on stage at 7.45 or so to open the evening, there were only six kids in the entire club. Now The Whisky is not huge, but believe me, when there are only six people, they rattle like coffee beans in a biscuit tin. I did my show and headed for the bar to fuel up for the main performance. Poor Otway, though, had a pretty song that he always featured in his act, called "Genève". With two teenaged girl looking bored at the foot of the stage, and four acned jocks and myself at the bar, Otway sang the deathless lines from the song which he had so longed to deliver in this town: "For I am still young, and my dreams will see me playing to the screaming ladies of Los Angeles." I shared a rueful smile with Steve Boltz onstage and chuckled into my beer.

By the time we had got back to New York, after eight weeks on the road, Otway's mob were completely shattered, but I was just starting to get into the America thing. I decided I would stay on in NYC for a while longer on my own, to see if I could get anything happening out there. I reckoned I could afford at least another week at the Iroquois. I only had one contact in Manhattan, a guy called Mark Josephson, who was a friend of a friend. I called him and introduced myself and he invited him over. He lived and worked in a second floor space in the Puerto Rican part of the Lower East Side, on Delancey Street. He was a serious, driven young guy who had started up a business called Rockpool. The concept was ingenious and, like all the best business ideas, essentially simple. With his partner, Danny Heaps, he offered a service to record companies that saved them a fortune. Instead of the companies needing regional promotional men all over the 50 States, pushing their new record releases to clubs, local radio stations, college radio stations and local press, and monitoring the response, Rockpool built up a database of every major club, radio station and publication in the country, hundreds and hundreds of them, and serviced them direct from New York by parcel post or courier.

Otway and I did one last show together in Manhattan, at a big club called the Ritz, and we were both on top form that night. Afterwards I had a couple of visitors to my dressing room. They were a young, glamorous couple of uptown New Yorkers who had been watching the show. The guy, short, boyish with tight dark curls and olive skin, introduced himself as Michael Zilkha, and his diminutive, but exquisite girlfriend as Cristina Monet. He told me how much he had loved my show and how he had been a big fan of The Doctors of Madness. He explained that he had been to school at Westminster and had completely missed the NBC hatchet job that had torpedoed our fledgling career in the States. I was flattered. He went on to explain that he owned a smallish, independent record label in New York, called ZE Records, which specialised in putting out alternative, left-field material. I knew all about ZE records. It was painfully hip. He casually mentioned that ZE had released records by Suicide, James White and the Blacks, James Chance and the Contortions, Kid Creole and the Coconuts, Was Not Was and Cristina. That was, and remains, quite a impressive roster of out-there artists.

"Cristina," I thought to myself, "ZE Records. Of course!" This Cristina, standing in my dressing room, was *the* Cristina who had put out a deliciously knowing, punked-up version of the Peggy Lee song *Is That All There Is?* the year before. A record so vulnerable, but so tough, you wanted to simultaneously throw your arms around the vinyl and tell it to keep its distance. The song was originally written by the great sixties hit-machine, Leiber and Stoller, and was a sassy cocktail-bar ballad, but Cristina Monet had deconstructed it and restaged it in coke-sniffing, cold-fucking seventies-disco Manhattan, where medallioned Lotharios beat their girlfriends black and blue, and the girls said, "Thanks".

Leiber and Stoller were less than impressed by her reworking, but I told Cristina what a fan I was of that record. I must have gushed embarrassingly, but I was genuinely thrilled to meet her. So often girls who make records like that are a disappointment in the flesh but she was the real deal. Elegant, intelligent, beautiful and the wittiest girl I have ever met. In a zestier, brighter, funnier world, Cristina would have been Madonna.

Michael, half-Lebanese with the good looks to match, was a very cool, undemonstrative man with impeccable manners. "How would you feel about doing a live album for ZE?" he asked. I tried to be cool but I was so excited at the idea I just blurted, "Are you serious? I would *love* to. Thank you", without giving it any thought. He said asked me to come by the office the following day to discuss it and gave me his card. "I have to go to dinner now," he announced, and then, to Cristina, "Do you want a lift home?" She replied, in a voice that seemed to be forever pitched between two octaves of breathless sexual arousal, "No, darling. I think I will stay here for a little while longer."

Cristina and I saw a lot of each other over the next two or three weeks, and got to know each other very well. She was an intriguing and perceptive girl, aged about 22, and better read than anyone I have met before or since. The sort of girl who, in conversation, will say unpretentiously, but out of sheer enthusiasm, "It's just like what happens in chapter eight of Madame Bovary" or who will recite verbatim a favourite page-long paragraph from Henry James. In some people this facility would be merely tedious, like a precocious child performing a pointless party trick, but with Cristina it was always apposite, perspicacious and illuminating. She used her extraordinary talent with words sparingly, writing occasional reviews of books and the theatre for the New York publication, the *Village Voice*, and the odd, unfinished song lyric.

We arranged to work together on some new songs when I got back to London. She said she would be coming to London shortly and we should hook up. I was excited by the prospect and agreed. I wrote a song for her immediately, called *Let's Flatten Manhattan*, and started work on several more ideas with titles such as *I Ain't No Hotel* and *The Beast Goes On*. Cristina, the Queen of uptown New York disco, by way of reciprocation, started sending me scraps of paper covered in her spidery handwriting, with lists of fabulous titles for songs like *Do It And Call It Love*, and *Don't Mutilate My Mink*, and exhorting me to "Now write the song, dahling."

My meeting with Michael on the day following the Ritz gig was amiable and informal. He told me he would like to put an eight-track mobile recording studio into one of the most fashionable New York clubs for a couple of nights and record my entire show for release. He offered a derisory sum as an advance, saying we would make all the money on royalties. Back in Delancey Street I told Mark Josephson what Michael had offered and he laughed at his tight-fistedness. "That is so typical of the rich" he said. "Is he rich?" I asked, thinking no one ever got seriously rich from *Was Not Was* or *Suicide*, and Mark explained that Michael's father was Selim Zilkha. I looked blankly. The name didn't ring any bells. "He owns Mothercare and The Bank of Zurich!" Suddenly I felt that I had been rather short-changed by the charming, boyish enthusiast with the office over Carnegie Hall. Mark advised, "Don't worry. Do it anyway. ZE is the best label in the world for you." He asked where I would do the concerts to be recorded and I said I had no idea. He called Zilkha for a chat and together they decided that a club called Hurrah, on West 66th Street would be a suitable venue. A couple of calls were made and I was booked in for the following week for two nights, for a pretty good performance fee. These guys were certainly connected.

That night I wandered up to Hurrah to check it out, and an English band called The Psychedelic Furs were playing that night. I had always liked that band, especially the sneering vocalist, so I stayed to the end of their show and then had drinks with them afterwards. There is a sense of fraternity among touring English rock bands in the States. Despite the rivalry and the bitchiness, they always end up going to see each other's shows.

After the band left I was still at the bar drinking with a few stragglers. I got talking to a stunning black girl, over six feet tall with an incredible presence and an extraordinary capacity for chemicals. Her mouth was big enough to build an apartment in, and she had a fabulous raucous, dirty laugh. We hit it off well and chatted for a couple of hours. She had this thing about fur coats and was wearing some outrageously politically-incorrect specimen on her back. She said she was a singer, too, and had to go to the studio to record some vocal tracks. As she was leaving I said, "By the way, we never introduced ourselves. My name is Richard Strange." "It was a great pleasure talking to you, Richard Strange," she answered, flashing a wonderful smile, "My name is Grace Jones." The trouble with me is that I never recognise the rich and famous until they have left the room and someone says. "Do you know who that was?"

Later I met up with Mark for a nightcap at an after-hours club in the Village somewhere and I told him about my evening. I liked Mark for his seriousness and his application and his dry, typically New York sense of humour. He was also very generous and helpful to me for the whole duration of my stay. He never seemed to lose his cool even though his office was piled from floor to ceiling with boxes and boxes of records, press releases and photographs. Because of the different time zones in the States he worked a 16-hour day, in a space that, in the New York summer without the benefit of air-conditioning, was like a Neapolitan pizza-oven. I slept naked on a sofa, drank iced tea and fell feverishly in love with New York. And Cristina.

By now Mark Dean had arrived from London on his first visit to New York, and he looked like his mum had dressed him and told him not to talk to any strangers. I had good audiences because I was sharing a bill with Tuxedo Moon, a band with a good cult following of their own, and Michael Zilkha seemed very pleased with the results. The record cost less than $2000 to make, including the cost of mixing. The engineer simply recorded a stereo feed from my Revox, plus my vocals, my guitar and two microphones on the audience. There is something patently absurd about recording a live album that uses backing tapes, and that really appealed to my sense of the ridiculous. Michael dipped a little deeper into his pocket and had the shows videoed, and got a director, Ed Steinberg, to produce a promotional video for one of the featured live songs, *International Language*. We shot some additional footage for it in his apartment and Cristina appears in the finished film looking radiant as a tragic suicide on an unmade bed. Always a rather uncompromising and unpredictable girl, she showed me her wardrobe and asked me what I would like her to wear for the shoot from her impressive collection. We chose a few things and I left saying, "Whichever of those you feel most comfortable in will be fine. Any of them except the yellow dress." I asked her to arrive at the location for the shoot at 7.30. At ten o'clock she arrived. Wearing the yellow dress.

In the 20 years since then I have known people to miss flights, trains, concerts and hospital appointments, and threaten murder and suicide, because of Miss Monet's rather fleeting acquaintance with punctuality. Invariably her late arrival is accompanied by a story that fabulously details a highly unlikely Baroque chain of disaster and misfortune. That she is a genius and one of life's true originals is beyond reasonable argument. That she can be a pain in the arse and impossible to work with is equally incontrovertible. She does look great on film, though.

No major record company could have turned the project round in less than three months; Michael did it in a month without even appearing to have broken sweat. We put together a press release and a few photos, and he was already thinking about his next project. He asked me what we should call the album, and I suggested *The Live Rise of Richard Strange* since it featured half of the songs from *The Phenomenal Rise* project, and I wanted to use it as a teaser for the future full-length studio version.

I played a few more shows in New York over the next couple weeks. I was finding it increasingly difficult to leave the city. I really had fallen in love with the place. My favourite place to play and to hang out was a club called Danceteria, on an upper floor industrial space on West 21st Street. Ruth Polsky, a booking agent based in New York, offered to get me a few gigs, and the Danceteria were keen to do some shows. It worked out well. I only wanted enough money to keep myself afloat while I was there, and to try to build a profile in New York. Danceteria was the hippest and the most louche of all the Manhattan music clubs that month. It was reached by a small caged lift, like something from a Hitchcock movie, and although it was staffed by a hot-panted bellboy, the ascent to the club would routinely be accompanied by the rapturous groans of a fornicating couple whose lust had overtaken them in transit. The place was owned by a blonde German guy called Rudolph and his pneumatically voluptuous wife, the model and singer, Diane Brill. They held nightly court in the club's VIP lounge, like a mythical couple from the golden days of Hollywood.

Most of Danceteria's day-to-day administration was handled by Jim Fourrat, a fellow who was a fervent music fetishist. He had an impressively catholic taste in music, and booked acts as diverse as the rockabilly Levi Dexter and the Ripchords, the experimental Suicide and Tuxedo Moon, the mongrel jazz of James Blood Ulmer or the infectious salsa of Tito Puente. Thanks in no little part to Fourrat it was the most happening place in New York City. It was at Danceteria, a year later, in 1981, that Madonna first came to the public's attention, when the house DJ, Mark Kamins, started playing her tapes. It was Kamins who took Madonna's demo to Sire Records and produced her first club hit, *Everybody*.

There was just so much great music around in New York then, and as an English musician I could always somehow get on to the guest list to see the bands I wanted when they played in the city. I saw The Waitresses and the Bush Tetras play at the Peppermint Lounge on West 45th Street and the magnificent Bavarian oddball, Klaus Nomi, perform his castrati opera excerpts at a dismal club, appropriately called Exile, on Long Island. I met Nomi on my way to ZE Records one day and we had a coffee together. We talked about his days at the Deutsche Oper in Berlin, where he worked as an usher, and he told me how he had always wanted to be a singer. He was eventually sacked for demanding that he should take over the lead role one night when the diva was indisposed, insisting he was a far better singer than the replacement soprano. He was a truly delightful, articulate man, passionate about his music beneath his Rocky Horror-meets-the-Bauhaus shtick. He was the first man I knew personally who died from Aids, in August 1983. Sadly he was not to be the last.

Eventually, with all the preparations for the release of *The Live Rise of Richard Strange* completed, my stay in the USA came to an end. Michael told me that he and Cristina would be coming to London in a few weeks and we would stay in touch by telephone and fax until then. I packed my bag, and gathered up all the gifts I had bought for Rene and Geno on my trip, the baseball jackets and the cowboy boots, and all the souvenirs and records and press cuttings I had accumulated, spent a last evening with Cristina and flew home.

CABARET FUTURA

Arriving back in London after being away so long was a jolt to the system. A combination of culture shock, anticlimax, jet lag and fearful depression conspired to send me into a spin. After the initial homecoming, the distribution of the gifts and the telling of the news about the tour and ZE Records, I became withdrawn and non-communicative. Anyone who has been away on tour knows what this strange feeling is like. While you are on the road you are without responsibilities, without history. You can be whoever you want to be because no one knows you. It is a truly liberating feeling, to be able to re-invent yourself every day in a new town. To wake up, to adopt an accent, a persona, an attitude and try it on for size with your first cup of coffee.

Slowly I adapted back to life in London, the life of a man with a partner and a child, and Rene gave me the space to do it in my own time. She was happy to share in my excitement and to immerse herself into her own work as an illustrator. She knew, as women instinctively know – and Rene is more instinctive than most – that I had not been faithful to her, but she didn't make a big deal out of it. It must have been hard for her every time I enthused about how great Cristina was, though.

Geno, by now four-and-a-half years old and as bright as a button, was an absolute joy at that age. He loved my music and my stage clothes of trench coat and slouch-hat, and would entertain himself for hours in his room, with an old tape recorder, a raincoat and a hat so big you could barely see his mouth under it, let alone his eyes. Phonetic snatches of my lyrics would emanate from his room and, once in a while, at a particularly dynamic point in his show, he would hurl a pack of playing cards into the air, just as I did onstage, and shout "Premonition!"

Michael and Cristina came to London as agreed, and I met up with them a few times. The record was ready for release in the States and Michael told me that the buzz was good. I knew that some copies would naturally come to Europe as imports, but he was aware that I didn't want him to release it in Europe in case it prejudiced my chances of getting a record deal with the studio version of *The Phenomenal Rise Of Richard Strange*. He asked after my future plans and I told him that I was going to write some songs for Cristina and that I also had an idea about opening a sort of mixed-media club in London. He thought that sounded interesting and suggested I met with Mary Harron, who was an old friend of his from Oxford who was freelancing for the BBC Television arts programme, *The Late Show*.

Mary, a Canadian, had impeccable credentials. Before working in TV she was a rock journalist. She helped start *Punk*, the first punk magazine, and was the first North American journalist to chance her arm at interviewing the Sex Pistols when no one cared to or dared to. She wrote a history of the Velvet Underground for the *New Musical Express*, as well as a history of Andy Warhol and the Factory for the *Melody Maker*. Additionally, she was a music critic for *The Guardian*, a theatre critic for *The Observer*, and a television and rock critic for the *New Statesman*.

We met several times and, as I explained to her the sort of cabaret club that was evolving in my mind, she was enormously encouraging and supportive. "It sounds great," she said, "It's just the sort of cultural kick up the ass this town needs." She assured me that if I got it off the ground she would make sure it got media coverage. "Was she a girlfriend of yours at Oxford?" I asked Michael Zilkha later. "No," he replied, "She hung out with a creep called Tony Blair."

Mary was an extraordinary woman, intelligent and analytical, she was easily carried away with the excitement, enthusiasm and madness of being a fan, too. Her irrepressible energy served her well in the nineties, by which time she had decided to be a film-maker. In 1996, she wrote and directed the excellent film, *I Shot Andy Warhol*, the story of Valerie Solanis, the writer of the feminist SCUM manifesto, who tried to kill Warhol in 1968. Never one to play it safe, she followed up with the film of one of the most controversial books of the decade, Brett Easton Ellis's *American Psycho*, a horrendously difficult book to film (and to read). I thought the finished film was well made, with the sinister, predatory Christian Bale and the superb young actress, Chloe Sevigny, both giving impressive performances, but ultimately the film was unsatisfying, since it suffered from all the same shortcomings of the book – it wasn't quite sure if it was a satire or a gore-fest splatter-pic, and consequently fell somewhere between the two.

While I was turning the cabaret idea over in my head, I decided that I wanted to put together a nucleus of musicians who would record the studio version of *The Phenomenal Rise of Richard Strange* with me and do some gigs where the budget and the venue permitted. Mark Dean (Bryan Morrison's helper, the kid who really discovered George Michael) told me he had three friends in Watford who had a band called The Quiffs. He said they looked good and they could play OK, but that their music was going nowhere, and suggested I considered using them for my backing band. I thought it was a good idea and suggested that we meet as soon as possible. A couple of days later, the three of them turn up, looking painfully young and nervous. I sat them down and chatted to them, outlined the concept of the album and then played them a few of the songs on an acoustic guitar.

Peter O'Sullivan, the bass guitarist, seemed to be the most self-confident; Angus McLean, who played guitar, was frail and shy; and Rob Sutton, the second guitarist, was brash and brattish and abrasive in a way that marked him out for early departure. I told them they had to be absolutely dedicated to me, they would have to work like demons and be prepared to have a lot of fun for little financial reward. They all thought about it long and hard for about five seconds and said, "Yes". I telephoned Drumbo to tell him that I had a band and wanted him to be my drummer – I was delighted when he agreed.

We rehearsed in a studio owned by Andy Czezowski in Clink Wharf near London Bridge. The boys were as good as their word. They arrived on time, worked hard and did as they were told. Angus was the most musically gifted of the three, able to take a simple guitar part and make it sound oblique and new. Sadly, he was given to wearing a grey cardigan, which made him look like an 18-year old, middle-aged insurance salesman. Pete got by with a lot of enthusiasm and the ability to throw good shapes, and to hit the right notes more often than not. Pete was very into the new romantic thing, and wore huge, voluminous trousers that made him look like a galleon under full sail. Sutton was more old-style rock and roll, one of a million kids who wanted to be Keith Richards, and thought there was nothing more to it than playing with a cigarette jammed in the corner of your mouth. Drumbo was solid as a rock and brought his unique good humour, intelligence and practicality to the enterprise. He even took my insistence that he shave off his prized handlebar moustache in good part, thinking that I was joking. He quickly realized I wasn't and arrived at a rehearsal one morning clean-shaven and consequently looking half-naked. It was a truly heroic sacrifice on his part.

Within a couple of weeks we had worked on all the songs for the studio album, and had banged them into pretty good shape. We were all feeling good about the noise we were making, and when ZE Records released *The Live Rise of Richard Strange* in autumn 1980, it did wonders for our morale when the reviews started to come in. The *New Musical Express* wrote: "*The Live Rise of Richard Strange* is the US, shortened version of his soon to be recorded political fantasy. The chance to hear the work in progress before the complete opus arrives is comparable to hearing the first draft readings of *The Waste Land*." Even I thought this was a *slight* exaggeration!

Sounds enthused "*I Won't Run Away* – a sentimental and gloriously defiant ballad – is one track that convinces me Strange isn't just another musician with a novel publicity angle. Stage character and live person unite, and some of the pain and determination required for such an enterprise chokes its way out of the grooves . . . *The Live Rise* . . . gets five stars because Strange has proved he has the guts and energy to go out and do something dramatically different." *Zigzag*'s Ian Blake wrote: "The song, *The Phenomenal Rise Of Richard Strange*, is a song brilliant in its simplicity, while *I Won't Run Away* could well become one of the great torch songs of the 80s . . . I rate *The Live Rise* as one of the first great albums of the decade."

I set up a few low-key, out-of-town gigs to try out the band away from the prying eyes of the music press and in October we did our first show in London, at the Scala Cinema. We topped the bill of one of the enormously popular all-nighters that were promoted there each month. Six or seven bands would play one of these extravaganzas and they quickly became the most prestigious showcase a band could play in London. The hordes who came to every show were a baroque collection of white faced, bouffanted, velvet-clad Goths and new romantics. Both the audience and the bands were sustained by vast chemical intake, and there was a wonderful sense of communality and common purpose.

I made sure that we had the prime spot, around two or three o'clock, before people started to drift away to catch the night bus home or start to go on the nod. We hammered the set hard, augmented on a few of the songs by Dave Winthrop's sax, and the rasping and wheezing of his playing added an edge that greatly enhanced some of the songs. The reviewer from *Sounds* magazine enthused, "Strange carries off a dangerous idea with class and professionalism. A sizzling set, enough elastic to wind up compulsive foot-tappers, visual entertainment and food for thought for *Time Out* intellectuals. The single, *International Language*, should make a dent in the charts and Strange's concept should be investigated by all concept-goers."

The applause at the end of our 50-minute set was rapturous and I knew that we were on our way. The fact that the guest list showed that Spandau Ballet, Adam and the Ants, Simple Minds and Michael Moorcock had all been there that night only added to my feeling of satisfaction. The journalist Jessamy Calkin was as enthusiastic as *Sounds* had been. She wrote in *Record Mirror*: "[Then came] the brilliant Richard Strange. It became immediately obvious that here is a professional, despite the fact that his band has only been together for a few weeks. Tall and thin in ravaged evening-wear and dark glasses, he is a very physical and imaginative performer, combining confidence and a nicely sick sense of humour on stage." I was convinced that before too long, major record companies would be beating a path to my door, telling me how much they had loved The Doctors, and offering vast sums of cash for the privilege of releasing *The Phenomenal Rise Of Richard Strange*.

On 9 December, Rene and I were woken by our radio-alarm, which seemed to be playing an inordinate amount of Beatles music. It was not until the end of a four-record Beatles sequence that we learned why. A presenter interrupted the music to announce the news that John Lennon had been murdered the night before in New York, and we listened in stunned disbelief. The announcement recounted the bald facts of the murder – that John and Yoko were coming home late from a recording session. Outside their apartment block, the Dakota Building, Lennon was hailed by a fan to whom he'd given an autograph earlier that day, Mark David Chapman. Lennon turned and Chapman shot him five times with a .38 revolver. He was rushed to the hospital but pronounced dead on arrival from a massive loss of blood. We were truly devastated. Lennon had been so much a part of our growing up together that it really was like losing a limb. The grief-fest that followed was unseemly and crass, with Bryan Ferry's cynically opportunistic release of the Lennon song, *Jealous Guy*, which gave the ageing Lothario a number one hit, the most sickening act of cashing-in imaginable.

* * *

I had given my cabaret club idea a lot of thought, and throughout November I searched for a venue. I was incredibly fortunate to find a smoky, gay, Soho bar in Rupert Street, called the Latin Quarter, with an appropriately down-at-heel decadent feel and an avaricious but adventurous proprietor. I negotiated a deal with him, and Cabaret Futura was born. I opened Cabaret Futura on 14 December 1980 and I closed it on 25 May 1981. In those six months the club was host to many of the most interesting and adventurous artists working in live performance at that time. Its success was wholly due to a new mood of participation replacing the entertainment as spectator-sport ethos, which had prevailed for so long. What made it unique was its accessibility to artists and its highly charged atmosphere of expectancy, which seemed to lift performances from the mediocre to the magical, and from the stage-bound to the sublime.

It was in New York that I had really started to get ideas for Cabaret Futura. At that time there were some very exciting performing arts spaces in Manhattan. Places like the Kitchen, PS1, the Artists' Space and the Franklin Furnace would have regular events featuring the likes of Laurie Anderson, the dancer–choreographer Karole Armitage, the avant garde

musician– composer Rhys Chatham and the proto stand-up–monologist Eric Bogosian. I
had the idea to present this sort of collaborative and fringe work in a mutated European
cabaret environment.

Arriving back in London from New York, still flying on adrenalin, I didn't even consider the
difficulties involved in running a weekly club that would feature anything up to 10 different
acts, performing in a number of different media on any given night. I just thought it was a
great time. After all the cynicism and nihilism of late punk, art was cool again. It was a case
of needing somewhere for myself to play and, since it didn't yet exist, inventing it. I told the
journalist Simon Fellowes at the time, "Rock clubs pride themselves on the pathetic
perpetuation of crass rituals and stale values, which are of no use to me"

I did all the administration from home, booking acts and organising equipment, with Rene
helping out with artwork and publicity. I remember the agonising wait to see if anyone would
actually show up that first freezing December Sunday night. The line up for the first night was
eclectic. An extravagantly bequiffed Richard Jobson reading poetry he had rather freely
adapted from Sylvia Plath and Marguerite Duras; a two-piece synthesizer band called
Blancmange; a mime artist whose name I no longer remember; stand-up comedian (now
actor), Keith Allen, who performed naked, with a steak and kidney pie that he fashioned into
a surreal Lord Charles-type glove-puppet, and Rene and I performed a four-minute long
dance-performance version of the DM Thomas novel, *The White Hotel*, which she had
choreographed and I had written some deconstructed music for.

Cristina, still in London, had agreed to perform something. It was to have been her only
London show, but characteristically some real-life, last-minute *Madame Bovary*-inspired
drama intervened and she didn't make it. The atmosphere that night was excited and conspiratorial, and enough people turned up to cover costs – although if everyone I have
subsequently met who assured me they were there that night had actually turned up, I would
have needed to have booked the Albert Hall instead.

After an actual, as well as a proverbial "month of Sundays", we transferred to Monday
nights, in a much larger room downstairs. Although it was in the same building, it had a
different entrance and a different address – 13 Wardour Street. It is this space that I always
remember now when I think of Cabaret Futura. Down a tacky mirrored staircase to a small
lobby, all gilt and red flock wall paper like a Louisiana whorehouse, where our enchanting
door girl, Giussepina de Camillo, would meet and greet. She always arrived for work accompanied by her pet, an 11-foot-long python named Sainsbury, who would lay dreamily coiled
at her feet under the cash register for the entire evening. Once past the slumbering serpent
the guests would pass through a small archway and into the main performance room, dimly
lit with a small, raised stage with steps leading up from the floor. Tables and chairs ranged
halfway back, a pall of blue cigarette smoke hung over the bar, and the exquisite thrumming
of gossip was everywhere.

It had always been my intention to style the physical space of the club on the German
model immortalised, if not invented by, Auden and Isherwood. In her book, *Cabaret*, the
writer Lisa Appignanesi wrote in 1984:

Of all the Cabarets to spring up in Britain over recent years, it is Soho's Cabaret Futura, the brain-child of Richard Strange, which bears most atmospheric resemblance to its Weimar kin. Cabaret Futura became the focus and meeting place for the energy that fed the explosion in fashion, photography, film-making and music. More than that, it suggested a reaction to television, the growing demand for a live venue to serve specific, not standardised tastes.

Michael's friend, Mary Harron, was as good as her word and as soon as we were up and running she wrote a very favourable piece in *The Guardian*. She wrote, "Richard Strange brought the right touch of eccentric glamour to the proceedings . . . Onstage some murky drama is unfolding to the insistent rhythms of the tape machine. Strange gives a wonderfully stylish performance with just the right amount of caricature to keep the emotions in check." She followed up by bringing an entire BBC TV crew down to film an evening, an operation that was not without a certain amount of attendant hassle.

Many reviewers typically took the easy way out and described the club as decadent, but I never really thought that it was. I mean, *I* was decadent, but I didn't think the club was. It was debauched, but not decadent. I acted as a *conferencier* as well as an occasional performer. Sometimes I would perform one or two songs solo, sometimes a short set with a pick-up band. There were also times when, paralysed by drink, I would watch transfixed from the bar, a spectator at my own party, as the evenings seemed to run themselves.

The regular audiences of 300 or more were drawn from an extraordinarily wide age-range – anything from 17 to 50 on a typical night. The style was dressy and eccentric, but not elitist, and so was thought to be more relaxed than some of the contemporary peacock palaces in London. *Sounds* magazine wrote: "Civilisation in a cellar in Soho. People of every stripe – and none – cram in without crushing each other, show mutual respect in the small courtesies needed to keep a packed crowd sweet, flaunt their individualism and yet point no fingers at the substantial minority in the crowd who choose to make no extravagant visual statements about themselves." Its popularity and singular atmosphere meant that I had an extensive choice of performers who were keen to appear there. Since the entrance fee was only £1.50, budgets were tiny, and because there were so many performers each night, nobody was ever paid more than £25.

The true and quintessential character of Cabaret Futura was indelibly established when the Event Group did their first show for me. The Event Group was a performing arts-living theatre collective of indeterminate number, based around the inspired visionary, Tom Castle, and the physically insane Mick Jones. In addition to the nucleus of these two members, the group could also feature, for example, eight electric bass players, or 22 cricketers in full kit. After their first show they were ever-present regulars who would seep into the club in the afternoon like a patch of damp, to prepare for their evening show. They infiltrated the club like a virus, altering the space with installations, costumes, confrontation and cruelty. Sometimes they were like Antonin Artaud on absinthe, other times the Marquis de Sade on Mandrax. One of their masterworks, *Haircut, Sir?*, centred around a four-hour long ritual head-shaving of one unfortunate group member, lashed horizontally upside down to a pole, like an awful scene from *Lord of the Flies* that had ended up on the censor's floor. As each of the other acts that night finished their set, (it was rare for anyone to play a set of longer than 20-minutes) the lights would come up on the Event Group in another part of the building, their soundtrack cranked up to ultrasound, and the naked writhing figure would be shorn of a few more locks.

Another of their performances was *Run Out – They've Got Johnny*. To the eerily repetitive percussion of a revolving cricket wicket, amplified like some Mephistopholean marimba through the PA, they performed a stylised game of cricket in full paraphernalia, which featured frenzied running at top speed through the packed club, and a large quantity of fruit being thrown. Sort of cricket ball meets Hugo Ball. The late, great *galleriste*, Robert Fraser, veteran of the infamous Rolling Stones drug bust in the sixties, drinking at the bar with the artist Brian Clarke, regrettably got in the way of a flying Jaffa, catching it full in the face as it hurtled through the miasma. Incensed and lubricious after a polishing off a couple of bottles of Bollinger, Fraser looked around for something to hurl back. Finding nothing to hand he took off his exquisite handmade shoes and threw them at the man wielding the electric cricket bat, with the immortal line, "Dada lives. You die", and walked off into the night bare-foot. (Untypically, he missed his target that time. He once speared an unfortunate Punjabi waiter with a dining fork from 10 metres across a crowded restaurant while ordering Bang Bang Chicken!) Mick Jones survived that particular attack but shortly afterwards was hit by a flying table. He was taken to hospital in need of stitches, while still wearing his cricket pads and batting gloves.

Alcohol was certainly the preferred drug at Cabaret Futura, so it was perhaps appropriate that Shane McGowan should have performed his first-ever Pogues set there. Since hearing him that first time, Shane has been one of my favourite songwriters. He has an exquisite lyrical gift and a highly original "voice". The tragedy of his recent demise is all the more poignant because of his enormous, mainly wasted, potential. His determination to join his Irish heroes in an orgy of self-destruction is almost too pitiful to witness. That night, a much younger Shane and his pal, Spider Stacy, stumbled to the stage with borrowed guitars and delivered a blistering, rollicking set of Irish rebel songs and protean Pogues ballads before yielding the spotlight to a traumatised young Marc Almond and Soft Cell. Marc, resplendent in red sequinned two-piece and a pearl neck-lace, composed himself, picked up the gauntlet and played a memorable and haunting set with his partner Dave Ball. That night we all went home whistling *Tainted Love* and *The Tricolour Ribbon*.

It was an insane and exciting time. Paul Morley, who at that time was star journalist at the *New Musical Express* and still had a fine sense of humour, appointed himself unofficial cheerleader for the Cabaret. For the whole lifetime of the club he never again wrote an article for the *New Musical Express* without somehow mentioning Cabaret. It was as if he was trying to make amends for the savagery of his tirade against The Doctors of Madness. He remembers:

Us Northerners quite like flights of fancy, and digging up poetry, delving into twentieth-century art movements. It wasn't about showing off to each other. For quite a while it was an edgy, cool place to go. I remember seeing Depeche Mode there for the first time. I remember turning up onstage myself one memorable night with this incredible lost American pop group called The Bongos, playing this weird instrument which, whatever key you hit, was still in tune with the music. So I pretended I was Brian Eno, as I often did in those days, and had an ace time. My latter-day memories were quite drunken; you ended up in strange corners, pawing young women.

Bill Stewart, an anachronistic music biz figure, being a former Guards officer who just happened to sign U2 to Island Records, telephoned me one evening and told me he had been coming along to the club since the start and that he genuinely loved the place. He told me that he wanted to record a couple of evenings with the Rolling Stones' 24-track mobile studio and release it on his own label. We talked about assembling a mixed bill that would work as a purely audio recording and ended up with music from myself, Depeche Mode, Eddie Maelov and Sunshine Patterson and The Distractions. In addition, there was poetry from Richard Jobson and Giovanni Dadomo, and a "pure sound piece" by Capalula (the writer Ken Hollings). Rene produced a cover that was a pastiche of a poster designed for the Viennese Cabaret Fledermaus in 1907 (Futura, huh?), and the album was called *Fools Rush in Where Angels Dare to Tread*. It was released in the spring and actually sold pretty well for what was essentially a curio.

The great and the good (and the merely desperately trendy) flocked in. Some made it on to the guest list (William Burroughs, Keith Haring, David Bailey, Julian Cope, Harlan Ellison, Michael Moorcock, etc.) Others didn't (Richard Branson, Spandau Ballet, Steve Strange). On a good night the club was incandescent. Keith Allen, stark naked on stage, delivered terrifying, seething, stream-of-consciousness tirades. He was a palpably dangerous, thrilling act to watch. At that time he was the nearest thing to Lenny Bruce that this country had ever produced. He was that good.

Writers such as Anne Clark (in her first ever live performance), Ken Hollings, Giovanni Dadomo and Adrian Dannatt read excerpts from their works in progress. Dannatt, then 16 years old, now the New York-based art and opera pundit for a number of international publications, as well as one of the funniest men on earth, called himself Ezra Electrix and wore a fetching velvet beret and matching pantaloons, evoking nothing so much as a 16-year-old Rembrandt. He was still flushed from his TV success, starring as the eponymous hero in *Just William*. A reviewer of the day wrote of him "He is a courageous youth. He read aloud to a healthy mixed response: groaning derision, nay, irritation, alongside sincere appreciation. He has a good poem about bringing extravagant American TV to starving people, and others about the environment where (I suppose) he lives – Kings Road dandies, Oxford Street dummies and London Transport straphangers." John Hegley and Simon Fanshawe, now stalwarts of BBC Radio, both performed solo stand-up spots to mixed approbation.

The club was a great place too for oddities – one-offs who fitted into neither the mainstream music camp nor into the precious, self-satisfied world of high art. The sculptor Richard Wilson, nearly six years before he filled the Saatchi Gallery with sump oil in his magnificent installation work *20/50*, played to great acclaim at Cabaret Futura with the pyrotechnic noise merchants The Bow Gamelan. The shambolic good humour of the place saved the lives of many performers who would have been strung up by the balls at the more conservative and pompous ICA. One evening the stage became Winston Churchill's operations bunker for The Disco Winstons' only live performance. A portly chap with a cigar declaimed that "this was our finest hour", while four backing singers in the uniforms of the Allied and Axis armies performed an extraordinary (and possibly illegal) dance routine behind barbed wire. A thunder flash nearly removed the forearm of someone sitting close to the stage and, to top it all, thieves stole that night's takings from Giussepina and Sainsbury. As soon as word got around about this misfortune, someone organised a cash collection to make sure all the artists got paid and the snake got fed. It was that sort of place.

It would have been impossible to sustain the furious intensity of Cabaret Futura for more than six months so I closed it while the place was still blazing. Giussepina said later: "The acts just got wilder and wilder, and short of actually throwing Christians to the lions, there was nowhere left for it to go." I was offered a large amount of money to set up in other West End nightclubs and do whatever I wanted, but I felt it had run its course in London. I toured the USA with a selection of the acts that had appeared at the club but it was a disappointment in all ways but financial. Ultimately, the Cabaret was not a movable feast but a luncheon on the grass of that London moment, given by those who performed there and who supported it so whole-heartedly. Even now I am often asked why I don't start another club, just as Picasso was probably urged to bang out another *Guernica*, or Stravinsky cajoled into knocking off another *Rite of Spring*.

I occasionally listen to the 24-track tapes we recorded there. One of my favourites is of Depeche Mode, all cherubic-faced and full of nervy swagger as they tried out their first songs, wonderful three-minute anthems such as *New Life*, *Factory* or *Dreaming Of Me*. The first time I played the tapes back I was puzzled by what seemed to be a splashing sound on one of the tracks. Then I remembered it was the night that The Event Group did something fairly unspeakable with hoses and fake urine on the balcony while the band played underneath.

* * *

It was on the very first night of Cabaret Futura that Giovanni Dadomo introduced me to Brian Clarke, an artist friend of his who had just come down to London from Oldham. We met in a pub just up the road from the Cabaret as we steeled ourselves for our opening night. Brian and I hit it off immediately. He had been a child prodigy in the North and, under a system introduced in Victorian times by philanthropic industrialists and cotton barons, he had benefited from the British art school system since the age of eleven. Reminding me of how I was inspired by my English teacher, Bev Woodroffe, Brian once told me about his days as a 15-year-old student at Burnley Art School. He said, "We had a teacher called Donald

Matthews who, I believe, is still there. He did for me something that I can never ever repay, which was to teach me life drawing. I spent two years at Burnley doing life drawing, that's all I did, because of this man who'd chosen to become an art teacher as opposed to an artist. He filled me with such enthusiasm and I've never lost it."

Clarke was physically a slight, puny, post-punk sort of guy, gay but not faggy, with curly hair and piercing eyes. I recognised immediately that he possessed a fierce intelligence, an extraordinary energy and a sense of humour identical to my own. He had one very exotic claim to fame: his godfather was Albert Pierrepoint, the last official British executioner. Since arriving in London with his wife, Liz, he had been taken under the wing of a group of reprobates who included Mick Jagger, David Bailey and Robert Fraser. He took to the London social world of the early eighties like a man on a mission, and was soon more likely to be seen at a party or in a gossip column than actually working in his studio. His star was so much in the ascendant that he had a monograph written about him by the academic, Martin Harrison by the time he was 30, and the art world, it seemed, was his oyster.

Except that it didn't quite happen like that. On the contrary, the art world took against him with a vengeance, accusing him of dilettantism and a lack of substance. Although his arrival in London from the North of England preceded that of Damien Hirst by a mere 10 years, he was a contemporary of an earlier generation of the art establishment who were not yet prepared to cede power to the "young pretenders". They envied and loathed his exuberance and his ability to mix a glamorous social life with a substantial body of work. His output was phenomenal. He was not producing just paintings, but drawings, prints, stained glass and tapestries, too.

Today, nearly 20 years later, a high social profile is, it goes without saying, a *sine qua non* for artistic success. Interestingly, in an interview in 1983 about his showbiz years, Brian candidly says,

> I got far too much exposure when I was young. Really that wasn't healthy for me and, in all honesty, if God came to me and said "what did you do between the years 1977 and 1980?" I would have to admit that I behaved like a piece of shit . . . I got far too involved in cocaine and the whole number. I wouldn't advocate that kind of ridiculous lifestyle for one moment – not only is it vulgar and absolutely unforgivable in an artist, but it's also destructive".

Eighteen years or so later those exact words could have been spoken by Hirst, Tracey Emin and any number of the Young British Artists.

Brian was a fervent supporter of Cabaret Futura, and would arrive, week after week, with a seemingly an endless stream of celebrities in tow. Often he came with Robert Fraser, but on other occasions he brought Helmut Newton, David Bailey and the American film producer, Lynda Obst (*The Fisher King, Sleepless in Seattle, Flashdance*), who loved the place and referred to it as "the synagogue of sin".

From those very first meetings to the present day, Brian has remained an intimate. He is forever loyal, generous and supportive. Mercifully, he has never bothered to try to offload either his Lancashire accent or his old friends.

That same week, the journalist, Paul Morley, who later went on to found ZTT records and unleash *Frankie Goes to Hollywood* on to the world, interviewed me for the *New Musical Express*. He wanted to make amends for the rough deal he had given The Doctors of Madness in print four or five years previously. He was contrite when we met, and told me that he intended to set the record straight. In the *New Musical Express* on 24 January 1981, he wrote in his trademark baroque style (ending in the typical, but irresistible hyperbole of the religious convert):

> The Doctors were a perverse, concealed gift in the pre-punk vacuum: whilst punk was worming and warming around them, helping to kill them off, they were a warped, garish hint of modernist and romanticist things to come . . . [Theirs was] an obsessive search for realisation through some kind of Zen-Burroughs-ism . . . The Doctors were Pioneer Mutants . . . And in my version of Rock History, Richard Strange looms a lot larger than Pete Townsend.

* * *

On 25 January, my birthday, Michael Dempsey called to invite Rene and me to dinner at Zanzibar, a trendy but rather overpriced restaurant and nightclub in Covent Garden. When we met him, he was clearly as high as a kite and our suspicions were confirmed as he announced proudly that he had just taken enough drugs to kill a small horse, and with that we made our way to the restaurant. We got a prime table in the middle of the room but could not understand why Michael had booked the table in a bogus name. He explained that it was because we were all about to become celebrities and we had to get used to subterfuge. He was in fantastic spirits and held us spellbound with his stories and his general bonhomie. "Order whatever you want," he announced, "Tonight there is to be no holding back." Meanwhile, he ordered first one then a second bottle of vintage Krug champagne, to follow the large gins with which we had begun. As we ate he constantly toasted my birthday and my success with Cabaret Futura. "I always knew you would come good, you old bastard!" he announced, and introduced me to several of the other diners in the restaurant. He seemed to know everyone. "This is Richard Strange," he announced, "He is going to revolutionise the way we think about entertainment." I don't know who was more embarrassed – me or the people he introduced me to, but his enthusiasm and generosity were infectious, and soon other tables were sending over bottles of champagne to our table and raising their glasses in our direction. Needless to say, by the time we had finished dinner we were completely plastered and called for brandies and the bill.

Michael chose this moment to reveal that he was completely skint but explained that he had desperately wanted me to have a great birthday. Leaning conspiratorially over the table he whispered, "I am going to slip outside and flag down a taxi. I will get the driver to pull up to the door and when you see me, quickly leave the table and get into the taxi. I will settle up here another day." Rene and I were dubious but so far gone that we were up for the crazy idea. We fiddled nervously with the bill and our brandies while Michael slipped outside. Within minutes a black cab slid up alongside the entrance to the Zanzibar with Dempsey grinning in the back seat. I said to Rene, "Ready?" and, nodding that she was, we rose and headed for the door, with the well-wishers at the adjacent tables waving us on our way. Walking as calmly but as purposefully as we could, we got to the door, left the restaurant and hurried to the waiting cab. Our hearts were pounding as we pulled away, and we were exultant as we reached the corner of the street.

Disastrously, we hit the late-evening Covent Garden traffic, and the taxi drew to an ominous halt. Looking through the window we saw the *maitre d'* of the Zanzibar running after our cab, accompanied by a large waiter. As they reached the cab, the *maitre d'* opened the near side passenger door, which was Michael's cue to open the offside passenger door and effect a getaway. We followed. He sprinted off across the Piazza with Rene and myself in close attendance. The *maitre d'* and the waiter used the back of the taxi like a public thoroughfare, as in a scene from a Keystone Kops movie. Entering through the nearside, they exited through the offside and gave chase. By now we had twenty yards on them and reaching the far side of the Piazza, we darted down by Joe Allen's restaurant and waylaid another cab.

We were pulling away to safety, with our pursuers about to give up the chase when Michael, swept along by the drama of the moment, slid open the window which separates the driver from his passengers, and shouted to the driver, "Drive like the wind, you fucker! Drive as if Satan himself is on your tail!" It was a line he had heard in a Hammer horror film (the second half of it, at least) and had wanted to use it himself for years, he told me later. It was almost our undoing. The driver, unsurprisingly, took umbrage, and ordered us out of his cab, saying, quite rightly "I don't have to take this abuse". As we got out, our pursuers saw they had gained a second chance to catch up with us again. We dived into Joe Allen's, raced downstairs to the far end of the bar and waited there for the heat to die down. "Shall we have some champagne to celebrate our escape?" asked Michael, ominously. "No, Michael!" We drank beer. Rene paid.

Covent Garden was home to the Blitz, a tiny dive that was becoming London's newest most fashionable haunt. On entering the club you checked your coat with a hilarious young drag queen called George O'Dowd, who called himself Boy George and always had a bitchy word for everyone. The narrow, dimly-lit room looked like a brothel and attracted the Blitz kids – a suitably colourful, dressy crowd of poseurs, perverts and post-punks whose musical tastes had moved away from the frenetic guitar-driven rush and fury of punk rock, and had sought out something different. The music these kids most favoured was derived from the early German pioneers of electronic dance music, the so-called Kraut-rockers such as Can, Faust, Tangerine Dream and, most importantly, Kraftwerk. To the simple analogue synthesiser patterns borrowed from these bands they had added the rococo production and the extravagant dress sense of early glam-rock era David Bowie and Roxy Music.

The Blitz kids wore more make-up than Barbara Cartland; on occasions looked like they had raided their mothers' dressing up boxes during a power cut. There was a dramatic sense of mixing and matching, a combining of styles as disparate as old-style Hollywood glamour, pirate chic, the Battle of Culloden and the Moscow State Circus. All outfits were finished off, regardless of sex, with a gravity-defying coiffure. The bleached-blonde quiff of Richard Jobson, as he took his first tentative steps on the social ladder, was certainly among the most extravagant to be seen in London at that time. Sometimes I would see him struggling through the wind-tunnel that is the Tottenham Court Road, his hair caught by an unexpectedly strong gust and looking like he might be whisked into orbit any second. On other occasions his quiff would turn a corner a good three seconds before the rest of him.

Jobson was a regular at the Blitz, as he had been at Cabaret Futura. He was chummy with Rusty Egan, one of the guys who ran the place. Rusty was another old muso in search of a makeover. He spun the records and was the "mouth" of the Blitz, while his co-host, Steve Strange, was the pan-sticked "face". Steve Strange? Does that name ring a distant bell? Yes. It is the same guy who had come into the Doctors' dressing room after a gig in Newport, Wales and told me that from now on he would be known as Steve Strange. He was true to his word, and for the next two or three years I wish I had done the decent thing and strangled him in that dressing room the first time I set eyes on his pustulate face. The trouble was, you see, he became more famous than me and I was forever being asked if I was related to him. The embarrassment was confounded by the fact that, superficially at least, we both worked in a very similar area of the business. It was as if an admirer of the Bard of Avon had changed his name to Shakespeare in homage and then gone and written a Broadway smash based on an indecisive Prince of Denmark. It was irritating and inconvenient and he deserved to be strangled, but Fate had a more prosaic fall from grace in store for him. Years later, podgy and all-but-forgotten, he was arrested in a Welsh shopping mall for shoplifting a Teletubby. The fool – he could have just claimed he had mistaken the toy for a close relation and almost certainly got away with it.

The Blitz kids started to grow in number. They were now referred to as new romantics or the futurists, and other clubs sprung up in London to entertain them. For more exotic tastes there were fetish clubs such Skin Two and the transvestite dive, Madame Jojo's, in the heart of red-light Soho. Having been brought together originally by a love of the retro synth music and the theatricality of the dressing-up, bands started to form who wrote and played music specifically for the new romantics. It was the "new thing".

Even though Cabaret Futura wasn't, strictly speaking, part of the new romantic scene, its success had been noted and its formula appropriated by the guys who ran the Blitz and the other clubs springing up. The idea of the one-nighter, the once-a-week club run by an outside promoter, was a novel one. Clubs tended to promote in-house. Spandau Ballet's manager, Steve Dagger, expressing surprise at the runaway success of Cabaret Futura, was heard at the Blitz, asking no one in particular, "'Oo is this bloke Richard Strange? 'E seems to 'ave come from nowhere", which was rich coming from that particular parvenu.

As always happens with a new thing, some distinctly old bands tried to attach themselves to the "movement". The insipid Ultravox was one such band. They were exact contemporaries of The Doctors of Madness, and therefore had been around at least six years. They attached themselves to the new romantic bandwagon, bought a couple of drum machines and, lo and behold, a rotting corpse of a band was brought lumberingly back to life like a superannuated Frankenstein's monster after a particularly nasty thunderstorm. Their biggest hit, *Vienna*, a song which singularly and spectacularly misses the whole point of that city, has as its coda a phrase that succinctly sums the thought processes that went into its composition – "It means nothing to me, Oh, Vienna". It really was a case of nice video – shame about the song.

For the most part, though, the members of the new bands had barely started shaving. Spandau Ballet, Duran Duran, Soft Cell and Depeche Mode probably needed notes from their mothers to get into any of the London clubs but they were snapped up by the record companies and pushed into recording studios anyway. Even Steve Strange and Rusty Egan got in on the act, co-opting a couple of the guys from Ultravox into their new band, Visage, and recording *Fade Tto Grey*, one of the dreariest song ever to smear its way across a side of vinyl. As always, the major record companies threw the most money at the wall, but the mavericks were the more interesting.

There was a guy called Stevo who approached me at Cabaret Futura when the band he managed, Soft Cell, were playing there. Stevo's real name was Steven Pearse, and he was a 19-year-old kid from Dagenham, who worked weekends as a club DJ. He had made a sort of name for himself as the chronicler of the futurists, as the provincial Blitz kids called themselves, and compiled a weekly futurist music chart that was published each week in *Sounds* magazine. He decided to start his own record label, Some Bizzare [sic], releasing music that fell loosely into the futurist category, and started to sign up bands for his first release, the compilation *Some Bizzare Album*.

He asked me if I would be interested in licensing him *International Language* for inclusion. It did, after all, fall vaguely into the electro-disco category. I was tempted but there were some rather unsettling stories going around about him at the time and he seemed less than savoury. His older brother was Joe Pearse, who had been a leading light in the neo-Nazi National Front in the seventies, and I didn't want to lend my name to anything that might have had that poisonous taint to it. I confronted him about it and he was enigmatic in a non-committal, "Am I my brother's keeper?" sort of way, but in the end I didn't like the smell of it and declined. Many others accepted his shilling, though, and when that album came out early in 1981 it featured at least four bands who went on to chart success – Soft Cell, Depeche Mode, Blancmange and The The. Do you know what those four bands had in common? They had all played at Cabaret Futura for £20 each. And Depeche Mode had told the *New Musical Express*, "We don't like to be tagged as futurists. What's really looking forward is what's happening at Cabaret Futura, not us."

While Stevo was no Marinetti, he did like to outrage and taunt the music establishment, and as the bands he managed or released enjoyed ever-greater success, he found he was more and more frequently allowed to indulge his schoolboy sense of humour. When he signed The The over to CBS for a very large sum of money, he arranged to meet the company's chairman, Maurice Oberstein, at Tottenham Court Road tube station at midnight. The two of them then walked down Charing Cross Road to Trafalgar Square and signed the contract perched on one of Landseer's lions at the base of Nelson's Column. On another occasion he couldn't be bothered to attend a meeting with a record company, so instead he sent his teddy bear in a taxi, and round the toy's neck he hung a cassette recording of his demands.

It was around this time that Richard Jobson married the 18-year-old Mariella Frostrup. As I was not at the wedding I can only assume that, as she walked down the aisle, the lovely Mariella was no longer dressed to look like Jobbo's mother. The happy couple had an apartment near Kensington High Street and I used to see quite a lot of them. Richard and I often used to do gigs together. We were so frequently seen together we thought of calling ourselves *The Two Richards* like the TV comedy show, *The Two Ronnies*.

I always liked Mariella, quite apart from her radiant looks and heart-melting voice, she was always amusingly feisty and, like many who grew up in Ireland, she could tell a good story. My favourite was the one she told me about her new husband and to which she swore me to secrecy. Well, the statute of limitation has passed and now it can be told. Over coffee one afternoon, she confided that Richard was desperate to "improve" himself and widen his cultural references, with a view to being taken more seriously by the media. To this end, he had a sort of highbrow *Supermarket Sweep* through the HMV record store. His first port of call was the classical music department, where he bought a large quantity of Bach, all the Beethoven symphonies, *L'Après-midi d'un Faune* by Debussy and some Wagner operas. Next he went to the spoken-word department and bought the complete works of Shakespeare, performed by Olivier, Gielgud and the rest, plus poetry by Shelley, Keats and Donne.

Arriving home with his precious vinyl booty, he respectfully and ceremoniously placed the first disc on to the record player, installed himself on to the sofa and sat back to enjoy and improve. In that position he listened to the first three Beethoven symphonies, back-to-back, cooing appreciatively now and then at the subtlety and beauty of the music. Next came Bach's *Brandenburg Concertos*, which again elicited countless murmurs of reverential appreciation of the anvil-chinned Scot. Warming to his personal odyssey of discovery, he enthused to Mariella. "This is what we should be listening to all the time. No more of that simplistic, boring rock music. Classical is where it's at." Mariella agreed.

As dusk fell outside, Jobson decided to sample the joys of his spoken-word purchases and chose a recording of Richard III. He was dumb-struck when the first voice he heard, intoning that memorable opening speech "Now is the winter of our discontent made glorious summer by this sun of York", sounded less like Sir Laurence Olivier and more like a helium-charged Pinky and Perky. He realised to his horror and his acute embarrassment that he had spent the entire afternoon listening to his classical music collection at the wrong speed. He had been playing them at 45rpm instead of 33rpm. I visited him often around that time and remember admiring his new bookshelves, stuffed with an exemplary collection of classic fiction and biographies. "You see all those books up there, Strangey?" he asked, gesturing to the newly acquired library. I murmured my approval of his choices. "I have read the first page of every one of them."

While Jobson was busy improving himself, I was experimenting to see how much amphetamine sulphate I could put up my capacious nose. I had several willing co-experimenters but the most enthusiastic were Rene, Giovanni and his wife, Eve. Giovanni's behaviour was getting more and more unpredictable as time went by. I suppose it was almost inevitable that he would become a smack addict and he duly did. His addiction eventually landed him in prison, where he played the Italian card and got a job in the kitchens – it was assumed that, as an Italian, he must be a prince of pasta. Most nights he would clock off from his shift with a roast chicken stuffed down his trousers, which he would then trade with another con for heroin. After he was released from prison he did a number of hack jobs, including selling records in the Record Exchange on Notting Hill, and writing for third-rate music papers with titles such as *Hi-Fi User*. He was one of the few rock journalists to transcend the form but he never wrote for one of the major newspapers as many of his less talented but more ambitious career-minded contemporaries did.

In 1981, Brian Clarke introduced me to Lynda Obst, the LA producer who had been to Cabaret Futura several times and was interested in making a film based around a club like it. She asked me to write a treatment for a film, but since that was something in which I had absolutely no experience I thought I would work with Liz Finch, Brian's wife, who was a gifted, if quirky, writer. Somehow Keith Allen muscled his way in too, I don't remember quite how. Liz and I started writing what was essentially an absurdist hybrid of *The Phenomenal Rise* and *Cabaret*. Whatever we wrote Keith found a problem with it, and although Lynda stuck with us for a while, in the end I think she found Keith so obstructive and disruptive that she just couldn't be bothered any more. Keith loves to make mischief, no matter how self-defeating or auto-destructive that might be.

Lynda returned to the States. She became a major producer at Paramount, and wrote a very amusing book about Hollywood irresistibly entitled *Hello, He Lied and Other Truths from the Hollywood Trenches*. By the time Liz withdrew and was writing for herself, I was already involved in my next project. I knew it wouldn't be the last offer to come my way because, thanks to Cabaret Futura, I was now a "celebrity".

Of course, when celebrity visits, you embrace it like a dear friend and hope it will stay for a while. I was as enthusiastic as anyone, and for a while I was invited to every party and opening, every reception and every media event. Rene and I had an amazing time. It was impossible to buy a drink because there was always someone who wanted to send me champagne. We never paid to go to the cinema because we got free tickets for every preview.

Nothing ever prepares you for the jaw-numbing tedium of celebrity. You never get used to the interview treadmill. The sheer bloody repetition, the knicker-wetting predictability of the questions, and the familiar feel of the words of your answer, as they form yet again in your mouth, like a meaningless mantra. From every direction I was pursued for my words of wisdom, for my analysis of the state of British culture or the meaning of life. Every time I picked up the telephone it was someone calling from the radio, a TV show, a newspaper or a magazine. I would be confronted face-to-face on the street. People would even come cold calling to my home. Publicity is the fuel of celebrity, and is very seductive when it first comes knocking at your door, but after a short while it becomes a bore and a nuisance. The interviews and the interviewers quickly lose whatever unique identifying features they may once have had and all start to merge into one. All you are left with is the irritation when they over-run and the sense of affront when they under-run. You end up wondering what is the more distasteful – the chippiness of the interviewer, or the obsequiousness?

Robin Denselow of *The Guardian*, neither chippy nor obsequious, a man totally oblivious to trends and fads, wrote a piece for his newspaper about the burgeoning London club scene, entitled "Striking poses in the night". Comparing the respective merits of Cabaret Futura and the Blitz he observed, "Richard Strange is Bertolt Brecht to Steve Strange's Liza Minelli." I liked Denselow very much, both before I knew him and since, but I chalked his article up like another bedroom conquest, like another notch on the handle of my gun.

With media interest so intense I knew that this was the time to get cracking with the new album, *The Phenomenal Rise of Richard Strange*, to try to get it finished while there was still a buzz about my name. I financed the recording of the album with a bank loan, intending to pitch a finished album to record companies, rather than a collection of demo recordings. I sent Angus and Pete down to Drumbo's studio in Cornwall to rehearse with a few quid in their pocket for beer money, while I did some gigs in Europe alone with the Revox to earn the rent. I had briefed Drumbo as to what I was after in terms of sound and atmosphere on the record. In any event he knew most of the songs from when I had recorded the backing tracks for my one-man show with him.

Angus and Pete, who were barely in their 20s, and Drumbo, the veteran, worked like devils while I was away. By the time I returned they had not only learned all the songs but Drumbo had got them to start recording some of the basic backing tracks as well. When he had taken the boys as far as they could go in his studio, he loaded his unwieldy 16-track tape-machine up on to a flat-bottomed boat and sailed it up the creek to Sawmills, his friend Simon Fraser's studio, near Fowey. There they transferred the backing tracks on to 24-track, two-inch tape, which was at that time the industry standard, and recorded the acoustic piano parts played by a talented local kid called James J. Hallawell. They recorded basic backing tracks for all 10 songs while I was away, and I was very satisfied with the results. I was also very satisfied with the fact that I had completed a large chunk of the recording at a fraction of the price of a London studio. It amused me to be recording in the same seaside town where my ancestor, Sir Arthur Quiller Couch, had once been mayor.

The next stage was to bring the tapes up to London and book myself into Matrix Studios, round the corner from the British Museum. While recording I was aware of a familiar-sounding voice emanating from the next-door studio. It was only when I went to make a cup of tea in the kitchen that I met its owner, Marianne Faithfull. She was in the studio recording her follow-up album to the delicious, bittersweet, *Broken English*. I remember her going over and over a song called *The Bitter Truth* for days on end. Polishing and overdubbing, adding vocals and scrapping them, and finally starting again. It's a rather lovely song.

The songs on *The Phenomenal Rise Of Richard Strange* are, stylistically, quite diverse, but all are driven by their lyrics. *On Top Of The World* is pushed along by the drums and bass in a repetitive pattern; *Hearts And Minds* is a jazzy, piano-led European cabaret-style song; *Magic Man* has pure noise and a sledgehammer intensity; *Gutter Press* is mutant rockabilly; *International Language* is mutant disco; *Who Cries For Me?* is almost folksy; *Premonition* is like a drugged-up James White and The Blacks; *The Road To The Room* is like a modern-day religious epic and *I Won't Run Away* is a huge, self-indulgent, torch-song ballad in the style of *No Regrets* or *My Way*.

I found the whole process of recording it immensely enjoyable, not least because I was able to make all my own decisions without worrying about other band members or record company hacks putting in their two-pennyworth. Winthrop and Boltz added fabulous top-line colours to the songs and the cinematic power of the music was sufficient to be able to carry some over-wordy songs like *The Road To The Room*, the song that describes the scene when the main character is kidnapped.

> *I carry my cross 1988-fashion*
> *In the back of a car, a motorised passion,*
> *An anonymous Pilate washes his hands at the wheel.*

Or in the closing song, *I Won't Run Away*, where the eponymous hero chooses death over dishonour:

> *I won't walk out now on the things I believed all my life*
> *I won't turn my back on the things I believe to be right*
> *I may end up beaten, I may end up dead,*
> *Stretched out on this floor with a gun at my head*
> *I don't care*
> *I won't run away.*

Once I had finished mixing the last of the tracks, I ran off some cassette copies to play at home and listened to the mixes for a week or so to be sure that they sounded as good as we could get them. There had been a lot of record companies sniffing around since I came back from the States, and especially since the success of Cabaret Futura, and I knew I was in with a really good chance to become the Comeback Kid.

In spring 1981, I got the telephone call that confirmed my optimism. The girl on the other end of the line introduced herself as a secretary at Virgin Records and asked me if I would take a call from Richard Branson. Richard introduced himself in that affable, informal way that has since become his trademark. We exchanged a few pleasantries and then he cut to the chase. He wanted to know whether I had signed my new album to anyone yet. I told him straight that we hadn't, but that there was a lot of interest in me. None of the "interest" had yet manifested itself as a firm offer from a major record company, but that was by the by; anyway, I thought, just a matter of time. "Why don't you come to my houseboat tomorrow with a tape for me and Simon Draper to listen to?" he suggested, "Who's Simon Draper?" I asked, and he replied, "My cousin. He is the head of A and R at Virgin." I agreed then, as a cheeky afterthought I added, "Will you send a car to pick me up". Not missing a beat he asked, "Rolls Royce or Daimler?" I chose the Daimler. It was less tacky.

I was extremely excited to have been approached by Branson himself as it confirmed to me what I secretly suspected, that I was "happening". I told Rene about the conversation when she came home from college and we went out to a restaurant to celebrate the news, even though it was, at this stage, only a telephone call expressing interest. We talked animatedly about the new possibilities that a new deal would offer and how this time I would make sure the record company did things properly. All through the evening my head was turning over how I would play the meeting the following day, whether to be cool, enthusiastic or enigmatic. We had a few drinks and decided that I should not seem to be in any great hurry, but that it would be useful to at least get a hard and fast offer from Branson if I could, if only to use it as a lever to get a better offer out of another company. However, at that time it was a standing joke in the record business that Virgin would pay more than other record company because Branson was so keen to build up his roster of artists.

The following morning I listened to the mixes of the songs once more, and set off in the chauffeur-driven car with Geno as my five-year old companion. I thought if things got sticky I could always bale out with a kid! We arrived at Branson's houseboat in Little Venice mid-morning, and on board it seemed to be a normal family set-up, with his wife making some coffee amid a general hubbub of domestic activity. Richard arrived with an enthusiastic smile, an unspeakable pullover and a handshake. He was bristling with energy and spent little time on formalities. He was accompanied by Simon Draper and immediately began to explain that the stereo on the boat had broken down, so he and Simon would take my cassette and listen to it in his car parked just alongside. I handed over the tape, and sat back to see what would happen. I picked up a magazine about ballooning, which was lying on the floor, and nonchalantly pretended to read it, though I was much too nervous to take in a single word. It was like waiting for the doctor to come back with the results of some awful examination.

After three and a half minutes, Branson came bounding back down the gangplank with a broad grin on his face. "We loved the first track, *The Phenomenal Rise Of Richard Strange*, and on the strength of that one track we are prepared to offer £50,000 for the album," he announced. "You don't have to take it but the offer may go up or down or be withdrawn completely depending on our response to the next track!" This was not at all what I was expecting, and it was a brilliant ploy by Branson that put me completely on the back foot. Whatever negotiating strategy I had formulated was blown out of the water by this maverick approach. He was treating the whole negotiation like some appalling TV game show with, I am sure, a final figure in his head at which he would ultimately arrive. I was totally off guard, but sent him away to listen to the next track, *On Top Of The World*.

Again he came bouncing down the gangplank. "Bad news. We didn't like that quite so much. £45,000." I sent him away again, and so the whole negotiation was played out like a game of stud poker. Raise you, see you or stack. Forty minutes after we had started he and Draper had listened to all the tracks. *Hearts And Minds*, *International Language* and *I Won't Run Away* all increased the offers; *Who Cries For Me?* and *Premonition* decreased them; the other tracks maintained the *status quo*. "Well," he said, when the two of them arrived at the end of their listening session "Our final offer having heard the whole album is £65,000." This was considerably more than I was expecting, but I thought it would be best if I played it cool. "Put that in writing and I will think about it for a couple of days," I told them. Branson went to his desk and scrawled out an offer on a sheet of paper and signed it. "Call us if you want to clarify anything," he said, and with that we parted.

I hadn't once got the impression that morning that Branson was really interested in the music, simply that he wanted to agree a price with me so that no one else could sign me. A spoiling tactic. Draper, on the other hand, gave the impression of being much more of a music fan and, as I got to know him better, I learned that he was a much more cultured man than the boisterous Branson, with a genuine love and knowledge of the arts.

Feeling exultant that Virgin had made a firm offer, I made a fatal mistake. I wandered down to Bryan Morrison's office in Hyde Park Place and told him about what had happened and asked him what he thought I should do. As he chomped on his Monte Cristo Number One, he first congratulated me, ("Well done, my son!") then poured a glass of champagne for each of us, ("Let's celebrate!"), then called out to his secretary, the unflappable, long-suffering Cora ("Cora, could you bring me the contracts relating to The Doctors of Madness.")

Morrison knew immediately what my talk with Branson meant for him. He knew that the record production deal I had signed with Morrison de Villeneuve in 1975 was a five-year deal with three renewable options of one year each, which Morrison had chosen to exercise. It meant that effectively Morrison was entitled to half the net advance that Branson or anyone else was about to give me, for doing nothing but sitting on his arse and a six-year-old contract. My heart sank when I realised I had been ambushed but it was too late. He offered to negotiate the details of the deal, to get the royalties up and to increase promotional budgets and so on, but it basically meant that when I signed with Branson and Draper at the Virgin Office a couple of weeks later, Morrison copped about £20,000. This was 50 per cent of the net after the studio and musician costs had been deducted from the gross of £65,000. Remember F. Scott Fitzgerald? "Let me tell you about the very rich, they're not like you and me." How right you were, Scotty.

One of the more amusing and classically Branson-esque touches to the contract I signed was the clause about "the territory", which means the country or countries covered by the terms of the contract in which the company has the right to sell your records. Typically, a record contract will refer to the UK, or the UK and Europe, or The World as being "the territory". But with Branson, as with James Bond, The World was not enough. His definition of the territory in the contract I eventually signed was "the world and any other planets which may be colonised by humankind." With business partners like Morrison and Branson, who needs enemies to screw you?

Two weeks later Branson called me again. I was still running Cabaret Futura, and had just had a big piece written about me by Robin Denselow in *The Guardian*. It was an enthusiastic piece, championing the club, its ethos and its unique atmosphere and sense of the *Zeitgeist*. Richard Branson also owned a club, the much bigger, flashier but slightly old-fashioned discotheque, Heaven, just under the arches at Charing Cross Station. He had been using a promotion company called Final Solution, headed by a thin-faced speed-freak called Kevin

Millings, to put bands on at Heaven on an occasional basis. He said he wasn't happy with what they were doing and offered me the job of running Heaven for him. I thought about it for a couple of seconds and then I quoted back at him the line from a recent Talking Heads song, "Heaven is a place where nothing ever happens."

I thought it was a very odd proposal since I had no desire to become a full-time club promoter, still less a club manager. I politely declined his offer, saying I thought it might be best if we concentrated our energies on making sure that *The Phenomenal Rise of Richard Strange* was a hit album. I offered to go along and talk to Kevin Millings on an informal basis. I had been to a couple of these Final Solution shows and I thought Kevin did a good job in a fairly restrictive and unhelpful environment. He tended to promote the newest, hippest bands such as New Order, A Certain Ratio, The Human League and Pere Ubu, on mixed bills. I went to see him, and told him if he wanted to widen his scope, taking some of the performance art and installation ideas I had been exploring at Cabaret Futura, I would be happy to put him in touch with some of the artists who had been working with me. Kevin was pleased with the offer and took several of my artists to Heaven with great success. The Event Group, in particular, thrived in the modular nature of the architecture at Heaven, where they could find small or large rooms to set up events and keep a continuous themed performance rolling throughout an evening.

By now my mind was fixing upon the release of the album and the attendant promotional work I would have to do. I also enjoyed playing with the band more than I ever had before since they were such a relaxed and amusing bunch, and were always great company. Although the nucleus was Drumbo, Pete and Angus, we were usually joined by Dave Winthrop and Steve Boltz if they didn't have a better-paid gig elsewhere.

I went into the Virgin offices on Portobello Road from time to time to jolly them along since I didn't have a manager to do that job for me. My A and R guy there was a suave chap called Jeremy Lascelles, who was reputed to be twenty-third in line to the throne by reason of some royal inbreeding far too complicated for me to understand. I imagined a rogue meteorite hitting Sandringham at lunchtime on Christmas Day, wiping out 22 prominent members of the Royal Family as the port is being passed, and Jeremy telling me, "Sorry, I won't be able to act as you're A and R man any more, I have to be King."

Whenever I went to see Simon Draper he was always looking for his next band, his next project. He was always pleasant and polite but never gave the impression that he was committed to my record, even though he had been instrumental in signing me. He had this habit when he spoke to you, of doing a sort of finger juggling with a pen or a key. He could pass an object from knuckle to knuckle across the back of his hand and then across the palm, so it would re-emerge between the thumb and index finger. It was mesmerising. I saw the actor James Coburn do something similar in one of those spoof secret agent films in the sixties, *In Like Flint* or *Our Man Flint*. I wasn't the only one who was hypnotised by Draper's manual dexterity. When The Human League first had meetings with him, prior to signing, they were so taken by his party trick that Phil Oakey practised the same digital acrobatics for eight hours a day for an entire week, so that when they returned for their next round of

Marc Almond fronts the band Soft Cell at Strange's Soho club Cabaret Futura in 1981. In the background is shadowy figure of Shane McGowan, who premiered his band The Pogues at the club that night, and Richard Strange, in hat.

Having signed with Virgin Records, Strange's promotional lunchtime concert at Virgin's Manchester Megastore went horribly wrong, due to a surfeit of hospitality, 1981.

Strange leaves Fiona Thyssen's house with the artist Brian Clarke, after a particularly enjoyable evening, 1981.

Andy Warhol and Michael Dempsey. London.

negotiations he could match Draper trick for trick, and hopefully unnerve him with his own variations on the manoeuvre.

Virgin were spending bucketloads of money at this time, and seemed to be signing every big act that moved. In addition to The Human League and their offshoot, Heaven 17, they signed Simple Minds, Boy George's band, Culture Club, David Sylvian's pretty art-doodlers, Japan, and Howard Devoto's band, Magazine. In some ways it was a good label to be with because they had so much clout and such a roster of artists. The drawback is that inevitably the most successful acts on any label will cream off the budgets, and the most creative people at the company will want to be associated with the fastest risers.

Consequently, an artist like myself, who will never get big record sales immediately, relies on a gradual popularity, spread by word of mouth. Such an artist needs to be nurtured, handled carefully, allowed to slowly grow into first a national, and then an international, attraction. But that all takes time, and the record business is rarely in for the long haul. After a couple of shuffles in the personnel of the company, you can find that you are marginalised and fending for yourself. The Human League and Culture Club both hit the big time soon after signing with Virgin. Japan, Magazine and myself, all harder acts to establish, fell victim to the ruthless Darwinianism of the business. For the first few months it didn't matter. I was enjoying the ride. The perks of being on a big label are not negligible – a generous budget that allows for good photographers, top designers and advertising, extravagant parties, more exposure, and lots of drugs.

On 22 May 1981, Virgin released the album *The Phenomenal Rise of Richard Strange* and a new version of *International Language* as a single. I was especially gratified to read the reviews when they came out because for the most part they were wildly enthusiastic. Dave McCullough, now one of the star writers at *Sounds*, devoted the best part of a whole page to his review, commenting:

> Richard Strange has, despite the fashionable hype, made an album quite outstanding in its truly panoramic vision. The music on show reflects the satire on self. It's eclectic to the "nth" degree, but manages to come together and prove integrated in a way that is reminiscent of Bowie's *Ziggy Stardust*. This album has the same incompleteness, that same make-or-break all-out effort, and this results in a record that makes up for itself over and over again by its bold wordiness, its feeling of inhibition despite the overt pressure to succeed. This is the sort of album that is hard to defy.

The journalist and broadcaster, Mark Ellen, wrote: "Richard Strange survives – currently thrives – while remaining two steps ahead of his own expectations and one step ahead of the crowd's. To fully understand Strange you need to digest what he says in newsprint, buy this LP and go down to Cabaret Futura and stand on a chair for about three hours. An ever-increasing number is doing all three, which is proof enough that its well worth it."

I still liked the idea of playing offbeat venues so I was very happy when the Vienna Festival offered me a couple of gigs. I was even happier when I learned that one was to be in the outdoor Metropol Kabaret and the other in the Steinhof Psychiatric Clinic, playing to the patients and their visitors. We treated the whole thing as a jaunt, and to make more of an event of it, five of us boarded the boat train at Victoria to travel all the way to Austria over-land: Me, Rene, Winthrop, Kevin (my roadie) and Liz Finch, who was coming along for the ride, but suggested she might do a performance if the mood took her. The trip itself even warranted a mention in *The Times* Diary.

The train journey went smoothly until Frankfurt. We had reserved a whole sleeping compartment to ourselves, and our possessions had spread out like a fungus, filling every inch. Instruments, clothes, books, refreshments were strewn on every available space. It was like a bacchanal. We had all stripped down to our underwear and the whole scene was unspeakably degenerate. At Frankfurt, believing we had a 15-minute wait, I gave Kevin some Deutschmarks and sent him to go to buy sausages, fresh coffee and a bottle of schnapps. Indolently he pulled on his jeans and, wearing only a vest and carrying the Deutschmarks, he trudged along the platform. No sooner had he disappeared from view than, to my horror, the train started to pull out of the station. The next stop was Linz, in Austria.

Kevin had no shoes, no ticket, no passport, no money and no knowledge of German, and there was nothing we could do for about three hours. We asked the conductor what he suggested but he said nothing could be done before Linz. The four of us went into a sort of hysteria, alternately giggling uncontrollably and fearing for Kevin's safety. By the time we got to Linz we still hadn't formulated a plan but as we pulled into the station, a little miracle had happened. We were told by the conductor that, because the train from Frankfurt to Vienna was so crowded, a relief train had been laid on, and it was just 10 minutes behind us. And so it was that Kevin, unfazed by the whole episode, calmly climbed down from the relief train, crossed the platform and boarded our train, and joined us for the remainder of the journey to Vienna, with the sausages, coffee and schnapps.

The gigs themselves were glorious – hugely successful at the Metropol, and comically surreal at the hospital. The organiser told me that one of the patients was a schizophrenic who believed he was Elvis Presley. He had asked if he would be able to sing a few songs as our warm-up act. It was irresistible and he took the stage in pyjamas and a dressing gown, and belted out unaccompanied versions of *Jailhouse Rock*, *Love Me Tender* and *Are You Lonesome Tonight?* All were delivered in an unintelligibly heavy Viennese accent and were received by his fellow patients with riotous acclaim, as if Elvis himself had performed them.

The Steinhof itself is a bravura, secessionist building, built in Art Nouveau style. It has its own church, St Leopold's, which is a true masterpiece of the style, built by the great architect, Otto Wagner, between 1905 and 1907. It is bewildering to think that when British institutions for the insane were at their most grim and foreboding, the Viennese were building such an enlightened and aesthetic clinic. The whole trip increased my taste for continuing to play less conventional venues.

The next European trip was to Brussels to play at a Jean Cocteau Festival. I have always been a big fan of Cocteau since my early Francophile days in the mid-sixties. As a man, I suspect he was probably a total shit, but as a towering figure of European art in the twentieth century I think he is with few equals and deserves greater recognition. While in Brussels I did a mixed media show with slides and films and music. I hooked up with old chums like Bill Nelson, from Be-Bop Deluxe, Blaine Reininger from Tuxedo Moon, who lived in the city, and Richard Jobson who was reading poetry. Someone else played the entire piano works of Erik Satie, non-stop, which lasted about three days!

I was thrilled to be doing so much interesting work although I wasn't sure whether any of it was actually helping to sell my new album. To promote it, Virgin arranged for me to play a lunchtime concert at their vast new record megastore in Manchester. They said the week of shows that they had planned, featuring many of their artists, would be very well attended and we would "shift a lot of product", as they so charmingly put it. I loaded the trusty Revox on to the train at Euston, along with my suitcase of stage effects, and took my seat alongside the faithful Kevin. The journey was pleasant but uneventful and we arrived at the store with hours to spare. We set up our equipment on the small scaffolding stage, which they had erected especially for the week, and did a short soundcheck. Everything sounded perfect and I was looking forward to doing the show.

Then disaster struck. Kevin and I were led to a room that was to be my dressing room. Expecting a whole band, rather than a singer and a tape recorder, the management had generously laid on a vast buffet and a disturbing amount of alcohol. We picked at the cold cuts and I started to lace into the vodka. It all seemed to go down so easily with the orange juice and within an hour and a half I had drunk the best part of a bottle, and realised I was totally pissed. Kevin had abstained but had not been around to prevent me from drinking, and when he came to collect me, saying "show time", he recognised the symptoms, and said "Oh dear, Richard. You have drunk rather a lot haven't you?" I meekly agreed that I had and asked what we should do. "Well, we'll just give them a short show shall we? Twenty minutes or so? Are you up to it?" I didn't really answer, as I couldn't get my lips to move the way I wanted them to, but I must have said "Mmm," because the next thing I knew I was being introduced to a tumultuous sea of expectant faces by the store manager, and Kevin was man-handling me up to the stage.

As I mounted the stage, I was so drunk that I thought I was hallucinating when I saw the monitor speakers on the edge of the stage first start to smoke and then burst into crimson flames. I looked at Kevin for corroboration and he confirmed that what I saw was actually happening, and he hurried me back to the dressing room while the sound equipment engineers set about replacing the faulty equipment. Kevin started pouring cup after cup of black coffee down my throat, administering the occasional slap to the face and the odd word of encouragement. Twenty minutes later they were ready again. Kevin collected me up and we headed for the stage. "Why are we here?" I asked him, genuinely unable to remember. "To shift a lot of product, Richard," he replied. "Oh." I said.

Once onstage with the whiff of cordite in my nostrils, and a bit of other stuff, too, I bucked up a bit but only because I always started my show sitting on a chair, smoking a cigarette and singing *The Phenomenal Rise Of Richard Strange* in a particularly louche and lascivious manner. Things took a turn for the worse when, in the second song, *On Top Of The World*, I attempted a rather ambitious dance move, lost my footing and felt my legs buckle and then give way. I hit the floor in a most ungraceful way and decided to deliver the rest of the song from that position while trying to work out how I would ever get up again. I was like a tortoise on its back, all flailing limbs and no prospect of correction. Under the guise of straightening the microphone stand, which had bent alarmingly under the impact of my fall, Kevin came on stage and helped me back to my chair.

With the abstract notion of "shifting product" rattling around my brain, I took a few tentative steps down into the body of the store, microphone still in hand. I started grabbing armfuls of albums from the browsers and handing them indiscriminately to members of the audience. No copies of my own album seemed to be close to hand so I think I distributed Duran Duran's and Demis Roussos's latest offerings to the perplexed crowd and mounted the stage once more. Somehow or other I was able to complete the show, mostly from a seated or prone position, and Kevin led me back to my dressing room like a fighter who had just taken a hell of a beating. More coffee and the manager came in and congratulated me on my show. "Very, er, different", he enthused, and gave me a cheque for my expenses. Kevin meanwhile dismantled the equipment and I gazed into space.

There was a knock on the door, and a friend who lived in Manchester came in. She was, at the time, a dear friend who had seen me in this state a few times before and said, "Oh dear, I'd better get you home," and, like a guardian angel, she told Kevin she was going to look after me. Thereupon, this angel, who was a big wheel in television, set me into her open top sports car, drove me to her apartment, put me under the shower, gave me some more coffee, put me into her bed, stripped, joined me in bed and fucked my brains out. Later she put me on the train to London and by the time I got home I must admit I felt pretty good. Less than a year later I repaid her with a shabby betrayal, for which I still feel guilty.

Whether or not a report of the gig ever got back to Virgin Records I don't know, but nothing was ever said. It wasn't to be the last time that drink got the better of me. My personal record is three separate and distinct hangovers in a 36-hour period. In July 1981, I was invited to Paris to perform at a glitzy nightclub called Le Palace as part of the festivities organised by the left-wing newspaper, *Liberation*, to celebrate the recent election of Francois Mitterand as President of France. I was to share a bill with Grace Jones, not a lady known for her qualities of restraint. As I didn't want to be in Paris alone, I took Winthrop with me and we flew out together business-class from Heathrow to Paris. Winthrop, a man who loved a drink, needed no encouragement to avail himself of the hospitality on board; by the time we arrived at the gig we were both pretty much smashed.

We did a soundcheck early in the afternoon, and spent the rest of the day and the early evening drinking ourselves to oblivion. We had some dinner to try to get our equilibrium back but it was to no avail. I fell asleep in my dressing room for a couple of hours before I was due on stage and awoke with the most appalling hangover. Winthrop and I did a show which for some reason was very well received, and to celebrate, guess what? We got drunk. We did some chemicals with Grace and we drank champagne, and when we woke up in our hotel the next morning, after two hours sleep, we felt wretched. We almost missed our flight to Manchester, where we had to fly to in order to film *The Old Grey Whistle Test*, the only influential television rock programme of the day, which Virgin had managed to get us on to. The flight was bumpy and, to steady our nerves, Winthrop and I had a couple of bloody Marys each. They seemed to do the trick so we followed them up with a couple of beer chasers. We reached the BBC TV studios in Manchester's Oxford Road in good time for a drink before we were required to rehearse, and after rehearsal we all adjourned to the pub across the road for a long lunch.

We did a pretty good show for the *Whistle Test*, playing *The Phenomenal Rise Of Richard Strange*, *Hearts And Minds* and *Premonition*, and the presenter, Annie Nightingale, gave us the big hello. We shared the bill that week with Duran Duran, who were at that time a new young band with their first release imminent, and we celebrated our success after filming the show in a predictable way. By the time I got back to London that night I had my third hangover in 36 hours. Throughout that whole indulgent period I never once considered myself to be an alcoholic, but I knew I was a drunk.

My next TV appearance was not so successful. I had written a chapter about Cabaret Futura for a book called *The Cult With No Name* and had been asked to go to the BBC TV studios at Pebble Mill, Birmingham, to do a piece on live TV to plug the book. The book was essentially a cut and paste job which had been hurried out to cash in on the new romantic–Blitz kid thing. Waking that morning at home to the news that the police had mounted a massive operation in nearby Brixton that had infringed the civil liberties of countless innocent black families, I was not in my best mood. Arriving at Pebble Mill, my mood darkened further when I saw that I would be appearing on the programme with a mob of asinine kids who looked like they had been eliminated in the first round of a Spandau Ballet look-alike competition. Furthermore the presenter, a bearded man in a bri-nylon shirt and an egg-stained tie, had not read the book and was winging it. As it was live TV, going out at six o'clock in the evening, I thought I might have some fun. In rehearsal the Beard had said to me he would ask me three questions about the "London scene" as he so quaintly put it. I said OK, no problem. He showed me the mark on the floor where I should stand, then went off to talk to the Blitz kids.

When we went on the air, around 6.15, the Beard was even more oily and patronising than he had been in rehearsal. He hit me with his first question. "Richard, tell us a little about the new romantic club scene in London." I did. Then, "Richard, tell us a little about the new romantic music" I did. Finally, "Richard, tell us a bit about the clothes." He was so pleased. He had got his three questions out without fucking up. "No," I said. He didn't even hear. I continued, "I find it vaguely indecent that we are standing here talking about such trivialities as the clothes when the London police this morning mounted a raid on innocent families in my neighbourhood which was almost fascist in its disregard for civil liberties." The Beard looked like all the blood had just been drained from him, his eyes scanned his clipboard for assistance, but none was forthcoming. He stammered, "OK, Richard, er . . . great. Er . . . let's leave you for a moment and talk to these kids about the clothes . . . er . . ." "And freeze me out?" I chided. "Er, well. Fine." Then, to a silly girl in badly-cut lycra and chiffon, "Miss, tell us about these clothes you are wearing . . ."

By now there was panic in the studio. I called across to him from off camera, "Why are we talking about such fucking irrelevancies when there is a real problem out there?" Then the director slipped an Adam and the Ants video into the VCR machine and pressed "play". I was hustled offstage and someone hissed, "I will personally make sure that you never work for the BBC again." I took the train back to London with the adrenalin pumping and my career fast going down the tubes.

Virgin were furious and immediately, but tacitly, withdrew any further support from me. They felt betrayed that I hadn't played the game. I still don't know whether I was out of order by biting the hand that feeds, or whether the sham of such a "live" programme deserved to be undermined by the gritty irritant of a little spontaneity. Either way, Virgin decided that I was a loose canon and set about gently letting my contract expire. I got a call from Annie Nightingale who, as well as presenting the *Old Grey Whistle Test* also had a night-time radio show on BBC Radio One. She had seen the Pebble Mill fiasco and thought that I had been right to do what I did, since the programme itself was essentially worthless anyway. She invited me on to her *live* radio programme to chat and play records for three hours with the simple request, "You won't say any rude words will you?" I promised her I wouldn't and we both enjoyed the show enormously. Since that day I have had a great deal of respect for Annie, a colourful character in her own right, for sticking her neck out when she didn't need to.

Brian Clarke had also seen the TV show and thought I was heroic, sacrificing my career with a single pointless gesture. He presented me with one of his screen prints with the dedication "For the pestilence of *Pebble Mill*". Bryan Morrison, exasperated, was less supportive and more prosaic. "Silly cunt. You've blown it, my son."

Driving home from the studio late one April night after a fractiously unproductive session with Tom Robinson, whose record I was producing, I was puzzled and bemused by the inordinate amount of debris and garbage that seemed to be strewn across the main road as I reached Brixton, on my way home. There seemed to be a huge police presence everywhere too, despite the fact that it was 3am, and I thought a terrorist bomb must have gone up. I learned that there had been a full scale race riot the previous night, triggered in no little part by the heavy-handed policing that I had complained about at Pebble Mill.

SOPHIE McEWEN

On the strength of the London success of Cabaret Futura, and the media frenzy that accompanied it, I had been booked to appear for a week at the Edinburgh Festival in August of that year. I had never been to Edinburgh before and I was very much looking forward to sampling the delights of the city. I had managed to negotiate myself a good deal with a promoter who wanted me to present seven nights at his venue. I could perform every night or not, as I chose. I only had to MC the event and lend my name to it. I was able to select some of the bands who performed and in addition I got a pretty good fee plus all expenses. I arranged to stay with Jim Telford from Everest the Hard Way, who had a nice apartment in London Street, very near to the Edinburgh Playhouse where I would be working. Everest had played at Cabaret Futura in London two or three times, and I liked their music. They were a sort of Calvinist Talking Heads, but without the gags. They played dour, rigorous, austere but muscular music that was totally without charm. I gave Everest a gig that week, plus Nick Cave's band The Birthday Party, who were always favourites of mine, and James King and the Lone Wolves. The mighty Jackie Leven's gothic terror Doll by Doll played a night, as did the awful fake-futurists Huang Chung, and the final spot was taken by a bunch of Notting Hill trustafarians called Funkapolitan.

I spent most of my time in Edinburgh drunk and was certainly in excellent spirits when, after the Funkapolitan show, where I performed a short set, a shy but very cute girl came to my dressing room and asked if she could interview me. Her name was Sophie and she was working for a local newspaper and wanted to do a piece on my week at the Playhouse. I gave her a drink and we chatted for a couple of hours. I was enjoying her company so much that we were still there at closing time. She was very cool, very bright, had a great sexy voice and was incredibly posh. Even more importantly she laughed at all my jokes and she could flirt for Scotland. She told me that she had come to see Funkapolitan because a couple of her cousins played in the band. By the time we finished the interview she was sitting on my lap, and the whole thing just disintegrated into an evening of debauchery. I went back to her flat, where we talked a whole lot more and I started to fall for this adorable 20-year-old. I was flattered by her attention and she was flattered by mine. It was perfect commerce.

From that evening on I spent just about every minute that I was in Edinburgh with Sophie, and started to learn about her extraordinary family, the McEwens. I was sucked in, like Charles Ryder being sucked into Sebastian Flyte's exotic but dangerous world in *Brideshead Revisited*. The McEwens are legendary for being the most hospitable, the most bohemian and the most doomed of all the great Scottish Catholic families. Their family home, Marchmont (tantalisingly close to "Marchmain" the family name in *Brideshead Revisited*), in the Scottish Borders, was a palatial property that had recently been inherited by her young cousin, James. She told me her father, Alexander, had played guitar with her uncle Rory in the sixties, and they had been on the nightly BBC TV show *Tonight*. I remembered them well. She told me Rory was a painter of the most exquisite watercolours, as well as being an extraordinary guitarist and songwriter, and that her other uncle, John McEwen, was the respected art critic. I learned that her mother, Cecilia, was a beautiful Austrian princess, who had worked in leper colonies in south and south-east Asia while her children went to school. And she told me about her countless cousins and second cousins whose names read like a *Who's Who?* of middle-European aristocracy. Frasers and Weikersheims, Hohenlohes, Fürstenburgs and Roxburghs. I thought that I had seduced her that week, but in reality it was she who seduced me and by the end I was totally under her spell. Whether I had fallen for the person or the idea I wasn't sure, but I was intoxicated, and knew that I needed more of her. Over the next two years, I came to understand what Sophie meant when she told me her family was "unlucky". In this short bleak period, three of her close relations committed suicide. The accumulation of sadness was almost too much for Sophie to bear.

When my first trip to Edinburgh was over, I knew I wanted to get back there as soon as possible, and through a combination of fortuitousness and manipulation, I started working with Jim Telford, the keyboard player with Everest The Hard Way, on a new musical project, which necessitated my frequent visits to Edinburgh. We were working on new musical material for a project as yet unformulated. Whenever I went to Edinburgh I stayed with Sophie, and although I knew it was breaking Rene's heart I couldn't help myself. While my attraction to Sophie was in no way purely physical, I am a man who has spent much more of his life as *Homo erectus* than as *Homo sapiens*. Steve Boltz came up to Edinburgh to work with me and slept on Sophie's floor. One morning, unable to sleep, I wandered around the small flat and accidentally trod on him as he slept under a mountain of blankets, so thin that I thought I had snapped him like a pile of dry twigs. His quiff emerged from the covers first, followed by his nose and chin. He looks like a cartoon version of myself, after I had been flattened by a runaway steamroller and peeled off the road in aHanna-Barbera animation.

When she thought she knew me well enough, Sophie took me to meet her parents at Whiteside, their house in Greenlaw, Berwickshire. I wore a tomato coloured suit and transparent jellies with bare feet. They were at once horrified but fascinated. We hit it off immediately as they are both blessed with enormous charm, good humour and intelligence. The fact that they are also very good-looking seems somehow just unfair.

Gradually over the next few years, I was introduced to a part of British society that I had hithertofore only ever observed from a guarded distance. In this world, if your name is Durham, Warwick or Somerset, as it often is, it's because your family owns or owned the county (unless, of course, your name is David Essex). Spending a country-house weekend with some of these people is like doing a crash-course in "Understanding the French Revolution" or "The Origins of Class War". But with others, to my socialist horror, I experienced only feelings of great respect, admiration and intellectual stimulation.

* * *

On 2 February 1982, in St. James's Hospital, Balham, Dad died. He had been ill for a while with emphysema and bronchitis, caused by a lifetime of smoking. I had visited him that day and he already looked like a corpse. His white hair looked thinner and sparser than ever, and all the blood seemed to have drained from his face. He lay in the bed, his face grey, like putty, his teeth in a jar on the bedside cupboard and his eyes hollow, absent and frightened. It wasn't possible to converse with him, because he was drifting in and out of lucidity. Sitting by his bed, I was neither overcome with a desire to make my peace, nor to have a formal leave-taking. It was as if I was sitting by the bedside of a stranger, a man with whom I had so little in common in life that I couldn't even be upset by his dying. I felt as if I had been cheated out of a natural, healthy, human response to the death of a father. I wanted to feel something, anything, but I felt nothing. Even in death he couldn't give me what I needed – a feeling of kinship, or closeness, or loss. He came to for an instant, opened his eyes, seemed to stare at me in alarm, or bewilderment, or supplication, muttered the words "Oxtail Soup", and slipped away. I never saw him alive again. He was 64. Just seven weeks short of drawing his pension.

I hadn't seen much of him, over the previous 10 years. Why would I? In truth, it wasn't the emphysema or the bronchitis that killed him, it was the fact that he had decided to give up living. A man like my father is so totally defined by what he *does* rather than what he *is,* that as soon as he no longer *did* anything, once he became unemployed, he had no reason to live. I believe it is different for women, and I think that explains why women tend to live longer, and seem to survive their husbands more often than not. It is because women are more at peace with themselves, their instincts are sharper, they know the role, or roles, that they will play in their lives and they do not necessarily have to look for anything external to bestow meaning on their lives.

Dad's funeral and cremation, the following week, was, needless to say, a quiet affair, with only family members and a couple of Mum's friends in attendance. Since Dad had no friends, who else would have come? Brian came over from Copenhagen, but John, whom we had not seen for a few years, did not show up. I think Mum was hurt by that, but I always sort of understood why John had disappeared. I knew well that feeling of wanting to get away from the family, to re-invent yourself as someone you would rather be, among people who do not know who you really are. To free yourself from the shackles of family, of your own history, is to free yourself from the only ties that bind you to your past. If you can sever those ties you will be truly liberated. Ah, if only it were so easy.

Dad's ashes were scattered in a garden of remembrance and that was that. Even now, years later, while I can begin to understand the psychiatric reasons for his shortcomings as a father, I still find it hard to be reconciled. The total absence of love, the lack of encouragement, the inability to show affection and the arse-clenching tension in any room in which we sat with him are the strongest memories I carry of my father, and all are negative. Even in his will he managed to show his absolute contempt for Mum by ensuring, by meticulous wording, that he would be able to control much of her life from beyond the grave.

* * *

Through February and March I took another short Cabaret Futura tour out on the road in the UK. We played universities and art schools. It was really just a way to get some cash, as I suspected that the Virgin honeymoon was over and a divorce was imminent. The shows were always fun, because it was just a gang of pals going round the country, showing off, making a mess and getting paid for it. How could we resist?

In the middle of that short tour I got the most dreadful news. We knew that Michael Dempsey had totally cleaned up his act and was getting back into serious publishing. Rather than having his nose in a pile of chemicals he was now more like to have it in a new manuscript. He would stop reading once in a while to stir a vast bubbling pot of Bolognese sauce on the hob, or a put on a new record for his young daughter Rose to dance to. His musical taste extended far beyond punk rock, into the wilder shores of reggae and country. He was living in Gledhow Gardens now. He had managed to keep the wolf and the bailiff from the door by packaging and commissioning books with ever more bizarre titles. *Is Your Cat Psychic?* was perhaps his finest hour, but he had decided that he wanted to return to the world he truly loved and to publish new Irish writers of fiction.

He wrote to the Irish government with a proposal, suggesting that they might be interested in helping to fund his start-up. Although he had been through the mill over the previous six or seven years, he thought that his reputation might still be enough to get a contribution of some sort from the Minister of Culture in Dublin. He sent his proposal off to them, but got no reply. Undeterred he carried on with reading manuscripts and making his plans, determined that one way or another he would realise his dream. "Fuck 'em," he said with typical bravado, "I've swept the streets before and I'll sweep the streets again if I have to." He was more together than we had known him for some years, and we all shared his excitement and optimism. One night, arriving home late from a party to his third floor apartment, and unusually sober, he noticed that the lightbulb on the hallway had blown, and, public spirited as ever, he let himself into his flat, got a lightbulb and a ladder and set about changing the bulb. He must have plugged his fingers into the live socket, and received an electric shock, because the following morning he was found at the bottom of the stairwell, where he had bled to death through the night. None of his neighbours heard a sound, and although he had broken bones it was actually the internal bleeding which killed him. He had landed on his liver, apparently, and given that organ one last, fatal shock. The bitterest twist was that, unseen on his doormat, he had stepped over a letter from the Irish government expressing "great interest in your proposal," and suggesting a meeting at his earliest convenience. The irony of his death was too awful and too arbitrary. This, after all, was a man who had been through his windscreen three times and survived. How many publishers does it take to change a lightbulb? One too many.

At his funeral service in the convent church in Brompton Road, a ragtaggle band of mourners, friends and family sat in total numbed silence. On the pew behind me, two Irish nuns, who had only come in for the mass and decided to stay for the funeral, had a brief exchange. "Who do you think he was?" asked one of the other. "I don't know," replied her holy sister, then, looking around at the picaresque congregation, muttered under her breath, "But I think he was a bad one." Michael, that crazy, inspired, generous, chaotic, whole-hearted giant, that true friend, that source of so much encouragement and intellectual intoxication, would have loved it. I half-expected to hear him telling that story himself in the saloon bar of the pub afterwards, so much better than I ever could, his too-quickly-shaved face looking like steak tartare, his clothes looking like the victim of a hit and run accident, his blarney tones and his love of life seducing all who would listen. We knew we would never stop missing him. I guess he just couldn't face another eight years of Thatcher.

* * *

By early 1982, in an unspoken withdrawal of affection, my Virgin contract had slipped into silent obsolescence. I played a riotous St Patrick's Night in Dublin, after which on the night ferry home I had all but gambled away my entire fee for the gig on the Black Jack tables, before a run of good luck doubled my profits for the trip just as we put into Holyhead harbour. It felt like the hand of Dempsey had done one last trick.

Cristina sent me a pre-release copy of her new album *Sleep it Off*, and I was blown away by the new material she had co-written. The songs were all little masterpieces of Upper East Side snide; spiteful, sarcastic and caustic as a vodka and quicklime. They reveal the lives of the international white trash in a documentary style that few other writers could have dared to attempt, let alone managed to pull off. Like lifting up a stone and seeing what crawls out, her characters put the filth into filthy rich. With titles like *Don't Mutilate My Mink, He Dines Out On Death* and *Let's Live The Lie Oof Love* she slinks her way from Madison Avenue to the polo playing fields of the Argentine with a retinue of unlovable characters in tow like a coke-fuelled Canterbury Tales.

* * *

In the spring of 1982, Ruth Polsky, my agent in New York, asked me to put a Cabaret Futura package together to tour the US and Canada, much as we had toured the United Kingdom. I had so enjoyed my first visit to the States with Otway in 1980 that I was delighted to tell her to go ahead and book a tour for June and July.

The economics of putting such a show together are not stacked in the performers' favour. To put together a package, you are by definition taking quite a few bodies around, and bodies cost money. I tried to combine several priorities as I was assembling my troupe. Firstly it had to be representative of what Cabaret Futura was about, i.e. a three or four hour-long, modular, mixed-media show. Secondly, it had to be sufficiently portable to pack performers and equipment into a single, large minibus. Thirdly, the performers had to gell with each other into a unit with a single purpose, rather than be a disparate, factional rabble. Fourthly it had to be affordable. While I wasn't expecting to make money from the tour, I wanted to enjoy it without losing a fortune.

My first decision was that I would work with backing tapes and Dave Winthrop on saxophone. That was two people. I wanted Rene to come as by now she had her own dance company called Pulse, which comprised of Rene plus two other girls. They would do three separate dance pieces, plus a couple of numbers with me. That was five people. I wanted Liz Finch to come to perform her own unique brand of absurdist performance poetry. That was six. I knew I needed another musical element for the US, because once outside of New York City there just wouldn't be the interest in the rather esoteric world of performance art. There were a few solo artists whom I thought would be suitable, and I settled on a guy called Thomas Dolby, who had a bit of an following in The UK and was looking to get across to the States. He worked with synthesizers and backing tapes too, but he was a very different sort of artist from me, and I thought the bill would be able to accommodate us both. That would be seven. Perfect.

I spoke to Thomas in the spring, detailed him the set-up and he was keen to join us. I spoke to Ruth again and told her the line-up and she thought it was perfect. She set about booking the dates from late June to early August. We were to do a loop, not right across to the West

Coast this time, but New York, Boston, Canada, Detroit and Chicago, then heading south through the college towns of Madison, Wisconsin and Norman, Oklahoma to Dallas, Austin and Houston, Texas. Then out through New Orleans to Atlanta and up through Washington and Philadelphia. It was a good itinerary, not too gruelling but taking in all the major cities in the eastern half of the country. Eight thousand miles in six weeks. The dates came in and the money was looking like it might work out. It was tight but just about OK. For a bit of fun I inserted into the rider a clause that I was pretty sure no US promoter would have seen before. It read: "The Management agrees to add to the ambience of the evening by providing such items as stuffed animals, potted plants, works of art, free-standing sculpture, mirror balls, pre-war paraphernalia and other items never normally found at a rock concert." Most of them did their best, but many were not exactly imaginative. Potted plants were considerably better represented than free-standing sculptures.

A week or two before departure I got a call out of the blue from Thomas Dolby's manager saying that Thomas' album release had been brought forward to June, and that he needed to stay in the UK for the summer to promote it. It was a real blow. It meant that I had to get back to Ruth and tell her, and then try to find a replacement artist for Thomas. Ruth was cool, saying, "Get the replacement artist first and then leave it to me to sell to the promoters."

Finding a replacement for Thomas was never going to be easy, I knew, least of all at such a late stage. There was another guy, Thomas Leer, who was making some indie waves, and I spoke to him, but again the dates didn't work for him. Finally in desperation I rang my old record company, Cherry Red, which had originally released *International Language*, and asked if they had anyone on their books who needed a short American tour for expenses and pocket money only. He came up with one name: the Manchester-based three-piece band called The Passage. I didn't know the Passage's music or their pedigree, nor did I know any of them personally. Ian McNay assured me they were a good bunch and having little choice, I offered them the gig. Mistake.

I told Ruth about the change and she said, with characteristic New York Jewish bluntness, that she had never heard of them, but understood my problem and agreed to go ahead with convincing the promoters that The Passage were a good substitute for Thomas Dolby. By the time she came back to me, all the guarantee fees for the gigs had been reduced, as the promoters were no more familiar with The Passage than the rest of us were. The change of bill shot a huge hole into my budget. Instead of touring with seven performers, I would be touring with nine. And, because of all the extra equipment, instead of one roadie I would need two. I took Kevin and the Passage provided their own. A party of eleven. Eleven return flights, eleven hotel beds, a 12-seater minibus (by this time Rene and I had decided to take Geno with us rather than leave him with his grandmother for six weeks), petrol, insurance, legal expenses for 11 work permits, 11 *per diems* – the day-to-day living expenses paid to performers on tour to cover food, laundry, postcards, dope, whatever. For forty-three nights that comes to a lot of money. Ruth had managed to get us between $1500 and $2500 a night for the shows, with PA systems and lights provided by the promoter. It was touch and go, and we touched and went.

Meeting the Passage for the first time at Heathrow airport was slightly depressing, as they seemed to be a surly and incommunicative bunch. The two younger members said nothing, and their older leader, a short northern vegetarian with plastic trousers and a personal hygiene problem, by the name of Dick Witts, said too much. I truly believe you should never trust a man with a limp handshake, and his had all the warmth and humanity of a three-day-dead haddock. As soon as we met I had a grim sense of foreboding. My fears were not unfounded. The Passage were an unmitigated, whingeing pain in the arse from the beginning of the tour till the end. Their main problem was actually Dick Witts, who was emotionally and personally balanced only by the expedient of having a chip on *each* shoulder. He had once been in a (pause for effect) "major national orchestra", and consequently thought this whole pop thing was slightly beneath him. But his career with the orchestra had come to an untimely end, so he had to get by slumming it. His band made spectacularly ugly music, and he just could not come to terms with the fact that he was not Mark E Smith and his band were not The Fall. When the music fell flat, which it frequently did, he tried to inject a bit of visual interest by making sub-Laurie Anderson hand gestures in front of a light to throw shadow-shapes onto the backdrop for no apparent reason. Whenever I saw that shadow I remembered how if felt to shake the hand that made it and felt instantly nauseous.

We attempted civility for the first week, but these northern boys had already adopted a sort of siege mentality in the minibus, and at times it seemed as if they had been surgically joined at the hip. They did absolutely everything together, like some bizarre act in a travelling mute freak show. The two privates were cowed by their little corporal, and most often gave the impression that they would much rather be tucked up in their Salford beds than crossing the New World on their maiden voyage.

My sanity was maintained by healthy doses of Winthrop and Liz, always game, always interested and interesting, with Rene providing emotional support and Geno providing endlessly amusing distractions.

The shows themselves were variable. The Passage always opened the show, which of course they hated doing. They were as snippy onstage as they were off it, and Witts, in particular, could never resist a dig at me while he was on the microphone. The silly boy was either not smart enough to realise that I was on the mike for much more of the evening than he was, or he was getting his retaliation in first. Either way his anodyne asides proved that his surname was nothing but an empty boast.

Next up either Winthrop or I would welcome the audience and introduce the first piece by Pulse. Their dancing was physical and enthusiastic, rather than cerebral and accomplished, and in their black PVC catsuits they tended to go down pretty well with the crowd.

Liz was always the highlight of the evening for me. She would prepare a new piece to perform in every town we went to. She has a uniquely English take on the absurd, as befits the daughter of a clergyman, and is best imagined as a sort of northern post-seventies Edith Sitwell. Her poems are truly inspired pieces of irony-laden, late twentieth-century angst. She would declaim her memorable verses like *The Nostalgia of Smegma* and *Spread the Word! Eat* the Bird while wrapped in a stole she had fashioned from a roll of discarded linoleum she found in a skip, and wearing a sequinned bra top and stiletto heels.

Rene and I performed a deconstructed adaptation of the poem *Don Giovanni* from *The White Hotel* as a dance performance piece, as we had done on the opening night of Cabaret Futura in London. I played Freud and Rene danced the part of the female hysteric in the book. It was actually quite a good piece and we always enjoyed performing it. Liz would then do another spot and then the dance group would perform a second piece. I closed the show with Winthrop, playing a 50-minute set of old and new songs, with the dancers augmenting the line-up on a couple of songs, such as my *Heart of Darkness* number, *The Beast Goes On*, and Liz grooving away on the edge of the stage. It was a difficult show to do in the USA, because it had very much a European, non-rock edge to it that took it into unchartered territory, commercially speaking. Inevitably, it worked best in the big cities and least well in the sticks.

It is not always easy travelling with your family, performing with your partner and trying to be producer of the whole event at the same time. It is not easy to clock off after you come off stage, because you still have to collect the money from the promoter, assuming they will pay. After a poorly attended show in Chicago, I went back to the manager's office to collect our $1500 guaranteed fee for the show. The promoter, a cauliflower-eared brute flanked by two enormous goons, announced that we had lost him money and that consequently he was only going to pay us $300. In that situation there is really nothing you can do. You hope your agent will sort it out later and forward the money to you. In a tight budget production like this, a sudden loss of $1200 from the cash flow is an enormous blow. Coming as it did when we were exhausted and tetchy, it was enough to reduce me to tears when I got back to the hotel – but with a credit card you get over these things.

By the time the tour finished I was truly glad to see the back of The Passage, if you'll excuse the expression. They were the sort of people who make you understand why it always rains in Manchester. On the plane home from New York, Dick Witts oozed himself into the seat on the plane next to me and said, "Sorry we weren't much fun to be with but we really enjoyed it anyway. Thanks for everything you did, we really did appreciate it. We would never have got to the States without you," and with that he handed me a cheque for £1000, which was what I had paid out on their behalf over the preceding six weeks, lending them money, hiring them kit and paying for equipment repairs. I was slightly bemused by his sudden friendliness – and slightly suspicious.

Back home in London, after banking the cheque, I was not at all surprised to find that it bounced. It happens a lot in the music business. I re-presented it, and the same thing happened again. It was only when I telephoned the Passage management office to tell them what had happened that I realised I had been duped by the duplicitous Witts. They never had any intention of honouring the cheque, they told me, and if I didn't like it I could sue them. I did. And I won. It wasn't because of the money; it was the principle of the thing that really galled, and most of all the slimy obsequiousness of the foul-breathed Witts. Enough about him. I refuse to dignify the contemptible runt any further by allowing him to stay on the same page as me. Goodbye.

Ruth Polsky wasn't at all surprised when I told her what had happened. She just said, "I could tell the guy was a jerk-off the first time I set eyes on him. Legs too short, ass too big." You live and learn. I should have checked the ass and the legs before booking them on to the tour.

GOLDEN YOUTH

Throughout the early eighties I met a brand new bunch of people, some of whom I found exciting and inspiring, and others simply amusing. They were the golden youth of Thatcher's Britain, and they seemed to be everywhere. With this group, the paradox of conspicuous wealth and a penchant for slumming it went hand in hand. The sons and daughters of the aristocracy, of politicians and of wealthy industrialists, they were happy to be seen in the company of working class artists and self-made men, and they affected accents and attitudes to match, the better to blend in.

Everyone seemed to be on something at that time. Smack was the most fashionable drug for the bright young things, followed by cocaine and spliff. Hardly a day went by without some MP's daughter getting busted for coke, or some viscount's son being found blue and dead from a smack overdose. These kids, all of whom were born with a silver spoon in their mouth, seldom seemed to have a silver spoon more that half an inch away from their nostrils.

I often think that London in those days were totally hedonistic and vacuous, creatively speaking, but then I think about who was around and I realise that it was not so. It was a time when the Holy Trinity of British architects, Norman Foster, Richard Rogers and David Sterling, were first making their collective presence truly felt. Katherine Hamnett, Scott Crolla and Body Map were making beautiful clothes. Michael Clarke was dancing like a faun, Michael Nyman and Gavin Bryars were writing extraordinary new music, Tom Dixon, Ron Arad and Jasper Morrison were producing astonishing designs for furniture that would become classics, and Gilbert and George and Bruce McLean were showing major art work.

Wherever I went at that time I seemed to bump into a young galleriste by the name of David Dawson. David's B2, in Wapping, was a cutting-edge gallery that showed the best and most interesting of the new British and American artists and photographers. I remember Debbie Harry and William Burroughs arriving by boat from Chelsea to attend an opening of a show by Genesis P.Orridge, like a latter day Elizabeth and Essex. I loved the space and the neighbourhood, and so, in association with David and the art critic, Waldemar Januszczek, I organised a special one-off Halloween event, which we called "Witches Fly South". It was a 12 hour-long all-nighter, featuring many of the best performers and artists around. They included David Cunningham's weirdly skewed covers-band, The Flying Lizards, which featured the cut-glass vowels of Sally Peterson singing *Money (That's What I Want)*; the French chanteuse and performance artist Hermine; the artist Kerry Trengrove; performance artists Sylvia Ziranek and Sonia Knox; The Event Group; The Klaxon Five, the group formed by Pete and Angus after I no longer had full-time work for them; Virginia Astley and The Ravishing Beauties – and a host of others.

The event was a sensation, which we could have sold out three times over. The only black spot on the whole evening was when an irate art lover, unable to gain admission, lost his temper and head-butted poor Waldemar, knocking him to the ground, before storming off. Waldo, who later became commissioning editor for the arts for Channel 4 TV, was stunned and shaken, but stuck to his task of tearing the tickets like a professional.

With the success of the Halloween show fresh in the memory, I decided in November to start a regular venue again. This time I moved out of Soho and into the more salubrious area of Mayfair. I found a tacky discotheque–nightclub, more often used by Arab princes, travelling arms salesmen and hookers, owned by a very dubious character who almost certainly had friends given to carrying violin cases – though not because of their musical talent. The club, dressed in red plush and mirrors, was called Gulliver's. I renamed it "The Slammer – an Artotheque" (Artaud-theque? 'Eart-attack?) It has more space than the original Cabaret Futura and was on two separate floors, so I was able to put on longer, more elaborate performances. I also decided to go for fewer acts to save myself some work.

Because my reputation was good, and I cared about enabling artists to show their work in the best possible way that the space would allow, I was able to get some very good artists to perform at the Slammer. The Hull Truck Theatre Company came, as did The Yorkshire Players. Both performed full-length works with live music. The composer, Jeremy Peyton-Jones, brought in his small orchestra, Regular Music; we featured a gamelan orchestra from Bali; and The Frank Chickens, a kitsch but highly amusing Japanese outfit. From the London art scene we had Lumière and Son and Ian Pussycat, who gave absurdist cookery demonstrations with Liz Finch. There was comedy from Keith Allen and The Oblivion Boys (Steve Frost and Mark Arden), and more music from Danielle Dax and The Lemon Kittens. I found the whole project very exciting because it took a less scattergun approach than the original Cabaret Futura had, and there was more scope for artists to show more substantial work. Lisa Appignanesi wrote of the Slammer, "Designated as an artotheque, the Slammer is a regular, sympathetic space where performers are being judged as working, developing artists, not as hip novelties on the rock circuit nor as precious icons of the 'serious' art–dance circuit, nor even as potential fodder for sycophantic Channel 4 arts programmes."

Sometimes the audiences were so large that they were almost sitting on the stage with the performers. I remember one dreadful evening when David Rappaport, the dwarf actor from the *Monty Python* films, was sitting right underneath a PA speaker, which, for no apparent reason, collapsed on to him and concussed him. It was a heart-stopping moment, which in other circumstances would have been highly comic, as we manhandled the speaker off the diminutive, pole-axed Rappaport. Fortunately no lasting damage was done. I apologised profusely to David and the following week he came back for more. I put him at the best table with a bottle of champagne and he was as good as gold.

I was by now quite adept at organising multi-disciplined, mixed-media extravaganzas and had a nucleus of performers I could rely on to deliver the goods. I worked a lot with The Event Group, those stalwarts of Cabaret Futura since its earliest days; Mick Jones in particular was a willing and amusing collaborator. It got to the point where I could put a good bill together in my sleep, and so Richard Strange, Rene Eyre, The Event Group and The Klaxon Five became something akin to a working co-operative, operating both individually and jointly, fashioning continuous shows that could run for anything from an hour to a whole night. Costumes, slides and tape loops were constantly recycled and butchered so that they could be used and reused in brand-new ways, and through it all ran a fantastic group camaraderie and good humour.

While the clubs, the gigs and the record production were keeping me busy and bringing in some money, I was keen to get over the Virgin Records débâcle as soon as possible, and to start releasing some records again. Apart from that, I was feeling a bit like a baby seal – I was clubbed to death.

A small label, Albion, better known for releasing records by pub-rock bands, offered some money for a one-off singles deal. I had already written the song I wanted to record. It was a "list song" called *Next!*. Its eventual release fortunately coincided with the launch of a new TV arts programme called *After Image*, and they asked us to make a video at their studio for the song. It was a good deal. They would get a video to show on their opening programme and I would have a promotional video free of charge. At that time the going rate for a promotional pop video was anything between £20,000 and £100,000. Rene choreographed the video, which was basically a disturbed man interviewing a series of females (all played by Rene) and becoming increasingly crazed and irate, bombarding the hapless women with increasingly nonsensical questions. The lyric contained such crucial questions as:

Is this a trial? Or a deal? Or what?
Is this love at first sight?
Is this the Last Post? Reveille? Or What?
Or just a song at Twilight?
Can you swim? Do you dance? or what?
Are you afraid of the dark?
Do you faint? Do you paint? Do you cook? Any children or what?
Are you a friend of Brian Clarke?

Brian was delighted to get a mention in the song, not least because he was about to open a big new show of his paintings at Robert Fraser's new gallery in Cork Street. It was an enormously important show for both Brian and Robert. For Brian it was his first big solo show in London and for Robert it was the inaugural exhibition at his new gallery. The private view was a real bunfight with more celebs per square foot than any other show I had ever attended. With their impressive address books, Fraser and Clarke had pulled out all the stops and invited the whole of smart London to the show, and the rooms were throbbing.

Andy Warhol, Mick Jagger and David Bailey rubbed shoulders with Marie Helvin and Paul and Linda McCartney. Brian is engagingly and unselfconsciously proud of his northern roots and never misses an opportunity to involve his mum in his successes. His mum is an enthusiastic, but none-too-precise, celebrity-spotter, who had once mistook Giovanni Dadomo for

Lionel Blair. Seeing Paul McCartney in the corner of the gallery she hissed to Brian, "Oooh, Brian, you must introduce me to "you-know-who"." "Sure, Mum," Brian agreed, and taking the elderly grey-haired lady by the arm, guided her through the mêlée. "Excuse me, Andy. Excuse me Bailey," he gently pressed on. Eventually he arrived, with his mum, still in tow, at the former Beatle. With his usual ineffable charm he said to McCartney, "It gives me enormous pleasure to introduce my Mum, Mrs Lilian Clarke." Paul thrust out his hand. "Mum, it gives me enormous pleasure to introduce you to . . ." "Oooh, Brian," she interrupted, not wishing to be thought of as a country bumpkin, "Derek Nimmo needs no introduction."

Robert Fraser was one of the key figures of the sixties art scene, showing early pop artists such as Andy Warhol, Richard Hamilton and Peter Blake at his Duke Street gallery. The son of a successful merchant banker and an Old Etonian, Fraser's life was a complex and sometimes contradictory one, achieving many of the goals that were expected of a man of his social standing – and many that were not. During his colourful life he served as an officer in the King's African Rifles, most notably serving in Kenya at the time of the Mau Mau uprising. He was also a hedonist and a notoriously promiscuous homosexual, whose liaisons included a fling with the Ugandan dictator, Idi Amin.

In 1966, his show of works by the American pop artist, Jim Dine, was raided by the police. His next, more publicised brush with the law was when he was arrested along with Mick Jagger and Keith Richards in the infamous 1967 Redlands bust. He served four months in Wormwood Scrubs for possession of heroin and his arrest, handcuffed to Mick Jagger in a police car, is immortalised in the Richard Hamilton print, *Swingeing London*. It was Fraser who introduced Paul McCartney to Peter Blake, and it was McCartney who commissioned Blake to create the cover artwork for The Beatles album, *Sgt Pepper's Lonely Hearts Club Band*. Whether or not it was Fraser who negotiated the fee for his artist, rumoured to be a paltry £200, no one seems to be sure, but I do know that Peter Blake is ambivalent about that one single piece of work by which he is best known. It was as much a curse as a blessing as it has inveigled its way into every interview he has ever done since, like a pushy relation jockeying for best position in a wedding photograph.

Robert Fraser's next major show at the gallery was for the New York graffiti artists who were starting to make such a splash, and after the opening night there was some serious partying to be done. All the major New York graffiti artists were in town and Robert threw a party for Keith Haring at Titanic, which was a blast, with a lot of champagne and cocaine. For a while it was the best club in London, despite being up against some formidable opposition from Café de Paris, Legends, Gossips and the Embassy.

I liked Keith Haring very much. He was six or seven years younger than me and he had a wonderful energy and *joie de vivre*, and was producing so much work that it was impossible not to know who he was. He was the quintessential graffiti artist who became the symbol of all the others. In two years he had gone from chalk drawings on the black paper that covers expired advertisements on the New York subway, through an inaugural solo show with the typically perceptive Tony Shafrazi in New York's Soho, to being included in the Whitney Biennial. In the few short remaining years of his life he would paint a mural on the White

House lawn, design for ballet, opera and Swatch, and collaborate with artists as disparate as Andy Warhol, Jenny Holzer and Grace Jones. His style became one of the most instantly recognisable of any twentieth-century artist. In London recently I visited an exhibition of his 1985 series of paintings, *The Ten Commandments*. I expected to be sorely disappointed and to find that time had not treated his work kindly. On the contrary, these massive canvases had a certainty of line and a spirited vigour that was timeless and thrilling. They transcended Keith's initial idea of graffiti art and were something quite magnificent and awe-inspiring.

* * *

In July, Sophie wrote from Edinburgh to invite me to the wedding of her cousin Christobel, which was to be held at the other big Scottish house the family owned, Bardrochat, in Ayrshire. Christobel was to marry Ned Durham, the son of Lord Lambton, the former Tory minister who resigned from Edward Heath's cabinet in 1973 after another sex and security scandal, at which the Tories seem to excel.

The wedding party at the big house was an appropriately lavish affair, as befits the coming together of two of the great Borders families. Carloads of guests from all parts of the world climbed the steep hill that leads from the village church up to the house. It was a gloriously hot summer's day and the party, so discreet, so tasteful and so perfect, looked like an art director had been given too much money to recreate a sense of the last days of the British Ruling Class for some never-to-be-made big-budget Hollywood film. Beautiful children played on the croquet lawn, overfed dewlapped dukes and earls threatened to burst out of their too-tight waistcoats, and creamy-faced English girls with names like Charlotte, India Jane and Victoria draped themselves on the arms of high-cheekboned, pink-faced boys called Hugo and Rupert and drank too much champagne.

It was all somehow bizarre and compelling. This was the class that was born to rule but they never would. A whole generation without a role. No wonder so many of them ended up hopelessly addicted to smack and shopping. I felt like a complete outsider, an interloper, but I was fascinated by this world. Despite my natural antipathy to privilege and ostentation I was intoxicated by the champagne, the sunshine and the prettiness of the scene. I began to develop a desperate fear that I would be found out as a fraud and be humiliated and ejected. I wasn't. I stayed with Sophie at Bardrochat for three blissful nights then headed back for London bracing myself for Rene's righteous and justifiable anger.

For the next three-and-a-half years Sophie and I were lovers, and I trampled over Rene's heartbreak and humiliation time and time again. It was three-and-a-half years of torment for her. We had huge fights, Rene took lovers, too, but like a typical male who wants the best of both worlds it never occurred to me to leave Rene and, despite her feelings of anger and betrayal, I don't think she ever got really close to leaving me. For Geno's sake she tried to make light of her pain, never tried to turn him against me and never sought to use him to get me to stop my philandering. All in all, she behaved considerably better than I did, but the bouts of manic-depression, to which she had always been susceptible, started to rear their heads more and more frequently.

I saw in the New Year, 1984, at Bardrochat. Deserting my own family for the New Year's festivities, I went to Ayrshire and listened to the chimes at midnight with Sophie's. It was a tradition with the McEwens to have a large family celebration, lasting two or three days, at the big house. Aside from the immediate family, the guests were a colourful mix of the more eccentric members of the British upper classes.

The New Year's party was great fun, with Alexander (Sophie's father) playing a mean, finger-picking style on his guitar, and singing a selection of old blues songs, with Leadbelly, Blind Willie McTell and The Rev. Gary Davies numbers being particular favourites. Vocal support came from an unlikely source – Bunter Somerset, otherwise known as The Marquess of Worcester, the heir to The Duke of Beaufort, who displayed a remarkable pair of lungs and an accomplished, if bizarre, talent for vocal improvisation. It sounded as though Joe Cocker had been given a *Monty Python* script to sing. The more Scotch Bunter drank, the more uncertainly he swayed on his feet, and the ill-coordinated, six-foot six-inch Marquess would occasionally come crashing to the floor, taking a priceless piece of furniture with him.

On 3 January 1984, Sophie drove me to Manchester, where I was suing the unctuous Dick Witts of The Passage in the Small Claims Court. It was a miserable couple of days. We drove down and back in a blizzard that had caused a complete white-out on the roads. Sophie drove heroically and I was nervous and fractious. We spent the night in a dismal motel on the edge of town with a bottle of Scotch for comfort. Arriving at the court the next day we saw that The Passage's manager, Laurence Beadle was there, but Witts hadn't shown up. Fortunately the judge went ahead with the case anyway and, despite the fact that Beadle had obviously clued-up on *Perry Mason* courtroom drama re-runs and seemed to be intent on testing the judge's patience to the maximum, I got judgement against Witts for the sum he owed me, plus costs. As soon as the case was finished, Sophie and I headed back for Bardrochat, in considerably better spirits than we had made the journey down. The snow was still falling, but it was daylight and the anxiety of the court appearance had been lifted. I stayed another couple of days and travelled back to London.

* * *

The following year I was back in Edinburgh again. I was working quite intensively with Jim Telford on new material, and both the writing and the recording were going very well. I worked all day every day, till late at night, then I spent the nights with Sophie. Jim would give me backing tracks, I would write melodies and lyrics, then give them back to him, to adjust the key or the tempo, or to change a few chords, or to write a middle-eight, then we would record it. We had a good pool of musicians we could call on around Edinburgh, but mostly we just worked by ourselves with Wilf, the engineer.

Jim programmed the drum machines and the synthesizers, because I could never be bothered. I hated the way technology was beginning to take over music. Jim was smart. He had sussed the way the whole MIDI revolution in music was going, and got on to the first rung of the ladder. I felt intimidated by the technology and couldn't be bothered to learn it; besides, I was working with someone who knew how to do it. It took me many years to take the leap myself, and even now I still work with a technology that is continually out of date. I was finally galvanised into taking some courses in computer music when I walked into a studio in the late eighties and realised I didn't know what a single piece of equipment did any more. I hated that feeling of relying on an engineer to tell me what sounds were available, what structural tricks could be played and how many different drum patterns could be composed. I felt like a painter who could no longer see colour and was forced to rely on a stranger to tell him what colours were on the palette, while all the time suspecting that the colours which I was told were available were simply those that were easiest to access.

We wrote a whole bunch of good new songs, and both felt that we were really getting somewhere. Jim was the first musician I had ever really collaborated with. He had no interest in writing lyrics so I had free rein to dictate the narrative, the titles and the vocal style. He worked on churning out great instrumental backing tracks, mainly just chord sequences, for me to work with and to refine.

My thirty-third birthday was spent in Edinburgh, and Rene and Geno came up to join the party. My birthday, 25 January, is also Burns Night, which is a cause for great celebration in Scotland. Traditionally, haggis is eaten with turnips and potatoes and a great deal of whisky, and the haggis is piped ceremoniously to the dining table by a bagpiper. As Jim plays bagpipes he provided the appropriate skirl, and then several verses of Robert Burns's poem, *To A Haggis*, were recited while the dubious delicacy was dissected and served. It was an evening of enormous merriment, and I resolved to adopt the Burns Night formula for my birthday for the future, regardless of whether or not I was in Scotland.

With Jim and I working all day every day, the music was coming thick and fast, and we got a local girl singer named Julie Hepburn in to do some vocals. She had sung with The Deltones, a local band, and was painfully shy, but had a very lovely and unusual voice. I had written a lyric called *Wild Times,* inspired by the notion of the British aristocracy in general and the McEwens in particular. It was written to be evocative rather than specific. It was about class and cocaine, and the idea of a generation without a role to play.

> *Take a look, kings and queens,*
> *In the red, in the snow-white scenes*
> *Make no mistake these are Wild Times.*

Julie Hepburn's voice gave the song a lilting, nostalgic quality that was absolutely right and when she got her part on tape it sounded fabulous. We demo-ed about six songs and came to London looking for a deal. Jim played the songs to a guy called Max Tregonning, who had managed Everest the Hard Way and, before that, Adam and the Ants. Max flipped, or came as close as a dour Yorkshireman ever comes to flipping, and asked if he could manage us. We didn't have a manager (I had managed myself since the demise of The Doctors) and as I didn't want to spend my life going from one record company to another, I agreed, and Max became the manager of the band, which we called The Engine Room.

The first thing he did was to take the tape of the new songs to Bryan Morrison to offer him my half of the publishing. The plan was to sell Jim's half somewhere else so that we effectively got two publishers working for us. I suppose I must have agreed but I can hardly believe it now that I went back to Morrison again. I must be a glutton for punishment. Morry loved the songs, like he always did with my stuff, and wanted to get involved immediately. He drew up a publishing contract and told us he would oil the wheels of a recording deal meanwhile. He was hand-in-glove with David Simone, the MD at Arista Records, and I suspected that would be his first port of call. I liked the idea, because Arista were a good, fresh pop label, and the music I was doing with The Engine Room was essentially fresh pop.

A couple of days later I was woken by the telephone after a late night. It was Morrison. "Where's that fucking publishing contract?" I knew the Arista deal was in the bag. I took the signed publishing contract into Morrison's office that day, and he was cock-a-hoop. "I did a fucking snow-job on him!" he announced. I didn't and still don't know what a snow-job is, but it seemed to have done the trick. Arista wanted to sign the Engine Room for a two albums and two singles deal, and Max was despatched to iron out the details. Now I remembered why I kept going back to Morrison. He makes things happen.

On the home front, we were having difficulties with our ageing landlady, Mrs Normandale, and her baggy-shorted son, Dudley. They wanted to sell up and move out, and to maximise the sale price of their house they needed vacant possession of our flat. In short, they wanted us out. We were given notice to quit, which sent us into a bit of a spin. We knew it would go to court but we had to stall for time while we tried to find somewhere new to live. As the days and weeks ticked by our situation became more desperate.

Geno was eight years old and was about to start at the junior school which was attached to the infants school he had been attending. We needed to stay in the area if he was to do that, although I must admit I was starting to fear that the education he was getting was not sufficiently challenging and that the peer pressure from his schoolmates was not having a beneficial effect on him. He was under-achieving and was frequently getting into trouble – nothing desperately serious, but with an increasingly irritating regularity.

I slowly came round to the idea of looking for an out-of-town school. I couldn't afford to pay school fees, but I had heard of a few schools that had scholarships and bursaries for certain kids, either because they were academically gifted, or possessed a certain musical or sporting talent, or because their parents had fallen on hard times. I did some research and found a couple of schools that looked suitable. One was the Edgarley Hall, the prep school of Millfield, the great sporting and music school near Glastonbury, and the other was a small prep school in Kent called Northbourne Park. I telephoned the schools and asked them to send me application forms, filled them out and returned them. To aid my cause I invented a hyphenated name, ending in Strange, thinking that if I was going to play the system, then I ought to do it properly.

I was surprised that both schools responded quickly and positively, and both invited Geno down to sit a short assessment examination. We went to Edgarley Hall first, and he sat the exam while I wandered around Glastonbury and climbed the Tor. At the end of the exam I collected him and as we travelled home I asked him how it had gone. He told me the maths was hard but he had written a good essay and felt the interview had gone OK. "What about drawing?" I asked. He was a very enthusiastic and talented young artist, a talent inherited from his mother. I nearly hit the roof when he told be what he had done. "I drew Pluto," he replied. "What!" I was incredulous. My son, a budding Giotto, a burgeoning Botticelli, a nascent Matisse, had drawn a Disney cartoon character for his exam. I didn't even ask why. I didn't want to upset him. That's the thing with kids. They sometimes don't quite get it. As soon as I got home I bundled up a load of his best drawings and sent them off to the school, but to no avail. Only work done on the day of the exam was considered valid for assessment.

Predictably at this time I was having extreme financial difficulties. That was nothing new for me. The gloom was lifted, however, in April, when I signed The Engine Room to Arista Records for a healthy advance, plus recording costs. The deal was for two albums in three years but I knew by now that recording contracts are not worth the paper they are printed on. If you are a success, the company will bend over backwards to keep you happy, by extending the period, increasing the royalties, reducing the product requirement or letting you have your own label, as long as they still keep control of the distribution. But if it isn't happening, then forget about the two-album, three-year deal. You will be given the heave-ho just as soon as it looks like you are not going to make a profit for the company. Cruel and simple. The record business is just the market economy in microcosm.

ACTING UP

One April evening Rene and I arranged to meet Perry Ogden, a photographer friend, and a very nice, very posh girlfriend of his, called Carina Cooper, for dinner. I had always liked Carina, with her pretty English face, blonde hair and intelligent, lively conversation. We were chatting about nothing in particular when she asked me what my plans were for the summer. I told her I didn't have a clue, and she suggested I should come along to Shepperton Film Studios "to meet Franc".

She explained that Franc was Franc Roddam, the film director who, in 1978, had made *Quadrophenia*, an interesting teen-flick inspired by the 1973 album of the same name by The Who. The film was a moderate commercial hit, and its grittiness and swagger had influenced the teen-flick genre for several years to come. Carina was working as a personal assistant to Roddam, who was currently in pre-production for his new movie, a remake of *The Bride of Frankenstein* called *The Bride*. "We're shooting in France through the spring and summer," she told me, "and there's loads of small parts which haven't yet been cast. I'm sure you could get something. It will be so much fun to have you along."

Now at that time every Tom, Dick and Harry in the pop world was trying to be the new Brando. Bowie had been in films. Jagger had been in films. Sting had been in films. Curiously enough, it was not something that I had ever considered. The evening progressed and when we parted she took my phone number and said she would call me tomorrow about meeting Franc.

Carina was true to her word and the following morning she called to say that Franc was desperate to meet me. Could I come along to the studios at Shepperton that afternoon at about 3.30? I hadn't really had time to decline the invitation so, I got the train out to Shepperton station and found my way to the film studios. It was the first time I had ever been to a major film studio, and I was overwhelmed by the size and the rambling nature of the buildings, and the huge outdoor sets that were either being built or demolished. I managed to locate *The Bride's* production office and as I arrived Carina swooped down on me and said how glad she was that I had agreed to come. She led me through to another office, where a good-looking, casually dressed guy was sitting at a desk, and introduced me to Franc. He got up and we shook hands and he looked me up and down. "Wow, how tall are you?" he asked.

My mind went into overdrive. Franc Roddam is not a tall man. He's probably five feet seven, eight maximum. (He might disagree, but trust me.) A bell rung in my head from the previous night – "It's a remake of *Frankenstein*", Carina had told me and it suddenly occurred to me that they possibly hadn't yet cast the actor who would play the monster. I stood to my full height, looked down at Franc and, adding a couple of inches to my own height said "Six foot seven". I reckoned that anyone under five foot nine would believe that anyone over six foot three could be six foot seven. "Pity," he said. I knew I had blown it, but I didn't know why. "The actor playing the monster is only six foot two, and I am looking for a peasant to quake with fear in front of him". I knew I couldn't suddenly lop eight inches off my height but I had a moment of inspiration. "Put me in a wheelchair", I suggested enthusiastically but over-optimistically. He laughed and said it wouldn't really be appropriate.

At that point a fabulous-looking woman walked into the room and Franc introduced her as Joyce Gallie, the casting director of the movie. "Wow, how tall are you?" she asked. Back-pedalling a little, I said "Six foot five" and Franc smiled. "And who's your agent?" I had to come clean and say that I didn't have an agent, that my acting career was as ephemeral as my inches, and that only a friendly gesture by Carina had brought me here. Franc said, "I tell you, with your bizarre look and that great voice you will always get work as an actor". Joyce agreed, and told me she was sharing an office with an agent and that I should call to arrange a day to come along and she would introduce me.

We chatted a little longer, but it was clear that there was nothing for me in *The Bride*, but I promised to phone Joyce the following week and arrange a meeting. Franc wished me good luck, Carina said "Sorry, but it was worth a go" and I headed back for London. I didn't feel dejected, because 24 hours previously it had never occurred to me that I would one day become an actor. But as I sat on the train Franc's enthusiasm started to play in my head. "I tell you, with your bizarre look and that great voice you will always get work as an actor", he had said, without prompting. He needn't have said anything except "No thanks". He didn't owe me anything but he had opened my mind to a whole new possibility and I was thrilled and excited. I didn't know at the time that the meeting would have the direct effect of changing my career, and the indirect effect of changing my entire life.

The following week I *did* phone Joyce Gallie and she invited me along to her office to meet someone. At that time she was sharing an office in a grubby little alleyway, which always smelled of piss, called Blore Court, just off Berwick Street market. Nowadays it is a brothel but then Joyce shared a slightly sour-smelling, upstairs, two-roomed office with an agent named Michelle Braidman. She took me into Michelle's room and said "Michelle, this is Richard Strange, the chap I was telling you about from *The Bride*." Michelle sat me down and offered me a cup of coffee and gave me the once-over. She was a petite, fine-featured woman with intelligent eyes and a good hearty laugh. Her husband, Alan, was also in attendance. He was a jovial man who seemed like he had recently enjoyed a good lunch. The telephones in her room and in Joyce's were constantly interrupting us, but she sailed on. "How much acting have you done?" she asked, and I had to honestly answer, "None."

Unbowed she asked for a few details and measurements between taking telephone calls, and asked if I had any particular skills or unusual talents. I explained that I was a musician, I could play guitar, I could sing and that I knew my way around a recording studio. Reluctantly I admitted that I could *not* tap dance, sword-fence, juggle or eat fire. For some inexplicable reason she offered to take me on to her books on the strength of my unusual looks and brass-neck alone. "We'll give it three months," she said, "And if nothing happens then none of us are any the worse off." I agreed immediately and thanked her for taking the time to see me. She was thoughtful and sensitive, yet business-like, and I got the impression that she would not waste my time. "Do you want me to sign anything?" I asked – I would probably have signed whatever she had asked me to. She said, "No, we have to trust each other in this business." She told me the percentage she would take from any job she got for me and that I was free to do whatever I wanted with my music as that was none of her concern. I left the office and went for another cup of coffee in Soho and thought about how lucky my life has been. I had an agent. Therefore I was an actor.

With the formalities of the Arista contract completed I received the cheque for the first instalment of the advance. That night Rene and I enjoyed a good, celebratory dinner with Brian Clarke at his home in Notting Hill. The other guests included the art consultant Anthony Fawcett, advertising tycoon Frank Lowe and Marie Helvin, the model. It was the first time I had really met Marie, a stunning Hawaiian girl who was married to David Bailey. She was radiant, with the most extraordinarily translucent skin and a delightfully relaxed charm. Fawcett had worked for John Lennon at one stage and was now a sort of PR guy as far as I could comprehend.

After an indecently short time on Michelle's books I was actually offered my first part in a film. It was the first audition I had been to and when Michelle sent me to a small office in Soho to meet Mike Hodges and Mel Smith, I thought it was just too absurd and too easy. They were casting for a film entitled *Morons from Outer Space*, a dreadful film as it turned out, indeed one of the all-time worst, but Hodges was a director with a very good reputation. He had directed the gritty 1971 British thriller *Get Carter*, one of Michael Caine's three halfway-decent movies, and one of the best British films of the late twentieth century. Mel was best known for his TV comedies, first, with *Not The Nine o'clock News*, and later with *Alas Smith and Jones*. There is a long and regrettable tradition of British TV stars attempting to make the transition to the big screen and not managing to pull it off. The remainder racks in any video store bear appalling testimony to this fact. I felt that *Morons from Outer Space* would be no exception but accepted a small part as a first foot on the acting ladder.

Soon afterwards I did an episode of a spoof cop-show called *Dempsey and Makepeace* and a commercial for something or other, and I was on my way. It was just as well that some money was coming in because after a court appearance on 25 April, we were served with 28 days notice to quit Babington Road. The Normandales had succeeded in getting a court order, despite a stunning courtroom performance of heart-rending pathos by myself. Our situation was desperate because we really had nowhere to go, and anyone who has lived in London knows that 28 days is not a long time to find affordable accommodation for a family. I had also recently heard from Edgarley Hall, Millfield's prep school, that Geno had not done sufficiently well in the examination to be offered a scholarship, but they would be prepared to give him a place as a fee-payer. As boarding fees at Edgarley Hall were somewhere in the region of £4000 it was out of the question.

We entered him for a scholarship at the other school, Northbourne Park, near Deal in Kent. It was an idyllic setting: a rambling, Edwardian family country house in its own woodland, once owned by Joyce Grenfell's family, run in a slightly shambolic but caring way by a staff who seemed to be a throwback to the days of Alan Bennett's *Forty Years On*. The enterprise was watched over by the patrician eye of Lord Northbourne, a man I later found to be genuinely decent and enlightened, who lived nearby. Geno sat the exam and we were both surprised and delighted when he was offered a scholarship, with a place at the school for the term commencing in September.

We explained to Geno what was involved with boarding, how he would be living away from home with all the other children, but that we would visit frequently and he would come home for holidays and that our time together would be all the more special. It was heartbreaking for all of us but especially for him. He said he would like to try it. We promised him that if he became miserable we would bring him back to London and find a local school for him. Neither Rene nor I had ever had any experience with private schools, and with the English class system so much part of the English education system we agonised about what was the right thing to do. I still believe it was the right decision at the time; the fact that Geno even now visits the school whenever he is passing that way suggests that his time there was happy.

As our date for eviction from Babington Road got ever closer, I was writing letters to every housing association in London, trying to find one that could offer us a flat. Eventually my persistence paid off, and a Catholic association (No, I'm not) offered us a three-bedroom flat in Herne Hill, near Brixton, available immediately at an affordable rent. The lady who lived downstairs was a little difficult, they explained, but apart from that it was fine. We moved in and Geno finished the remainder of his last term at his old school without any further upheaval. Rene and I painted up the new flat with some help from Mick Jones and Rene's brother, Dave, and we felt that despite all the dramas, we had landed on our feet.

Jim Telford and I went into the Scorpio Studios, beneath the Euston Tower at Warren Street, to begin work on the first Engine Room single, *Wild Times*. I had chosen Scorpio because the previous year I had produced The Way of The West's hit single *Don't Say That's Just For White Boyss* there, and I decided to use the same engineer who had worked with me, the American boffin, Dennis Weinrich. The reason I went to that particular studio in the first place was because Scott Walker had recorded his epic song, *The Electrician*, there with Dennis as engineer. The performance by Scott on that enigmatic ballad had always been one of my favourites. When I asked him about that session Dennis told me,

> "We had already recorded the entire backing track, and it had taken forever to get it to the level of performance Scott required. One morning he arrived at the studio and announced that he would record the lead vocal in one take at quarter-past one that afternoon. He said he would eat a whole roast chicken just prior to singing. We ordered the chicken. It arrived at 12.45. Scott ate the chicken and lay down on his back on top of the grand piano. I arranged two microphones above him where he lay and at 1.15 he recorded the lead vocal, straight through, faultlessly, in one take. It was awesome."

I can't pretend that there were any such exotic arrangements for the recording of *Wild Times* but the first couple of days went well. Gradually, though, we started to lose the essential poignancy of the song, and we ended up with half a dozen long and short mixes but nothing really excited us.

We told Arista that we weren't happy with the finished record, but they listened to it and convinced us that it was fine, even though we knew it wasn't right. Record companies are sometimes in a wretched position with bands, as the recording process can sometimes be a case of throwing good money after bad, trying to capture a certain atmosphere or performance on a record. Max, our manager, was a lovely guy but never quite tough enough when it came to a difference of opinion with the record company. He was just too nice. Consequently he was steamrollered. With a sub-standard recording we had not got off to the best of starts with Arista.

I had a lot of ideas about the video I wanted to make for the song. I wanted to shoot it at Marchmont, the McEwens' house in the Borders and started to make plans. Arista told me to wait and see how the reviews and radio plays went before they committed themselves to a video. I could understand their point – it cost upwards of £20,000 to make even a simple video of sufficient technical quality to get it on to TV, but in the mid-eighties promotional videos were an absolutely essential part of the marketing and promotion of any record release. The reviews and radio plays were OK, but no more than that, and the video never actually got made.

* * *

I was called to do my two days' filming on *Morons from Outer Space* early in July. *Morons* was an unhappy cross between a sci-fi spoof and a satire on the pop business, and the mainly British cast starred Mel Smith, Griff Rhys-Jones and Jimmy Nail. It was naff in every detail, but I found the experience of working on it fascinating. On my first morning on set I went to hair and make-up, got into costume, went to my dressing room and got my first taste of the realities of film making.

The realities are that a film typically takes 12 weeks to shoot and lasts for two hours. Is doesn't take a genius to work out that this means they shoot ten minutes screen-time a week. An actor will, however, be on set for maybe 12 hours a day, sometimes longer, sometimes less. So what happens for the 10 out of 12 hours when an actor is on call but not actually in front of the camera? He waits. In his too-small dressing room, alone or with others, he waits for the knock on the door of a young third assistant to the director, the same youth who brings him his first bacon sandwich and cup of rancid coffee at 5am as he arrives, bleary-eyed, on set. The same youth who tells him at one o'clock that he can have lunch and apologises that he hasn't done a single shot yet. The same youth who will rouse him from his mid-afternoon torpor saying, "They're ready for you on set" and escort him into the brightly-lit, bustling studio to meet the director for the first time.

While they are lighting the set for the scene he is about to shoot, the director will ask. "Have you had a look at the script? Shall we run the lines?" He will then meet whichever other actors he is doing the scene with, sometimes for the first time, sometimes not, and attempt to "act" under the half-watchful eye of the director. Only half-watchful, because the director is constantly being bombarded with questions about where he wants a light to be, where the tracking for the camera dolly should be laid and which wig he prefers on the actress: the blonde or the brunette? When the director does have a minute to talk to the actors, he will give a thumbnail sketch of the way he sees a scene being played, the way the lines are to be delivered, the movement within a scene, the entrances and exits of the players, the use of props or special effects. When you are playing a small part, as I was in *Morons*, you will quite often only see the pages of script that your lines appear on. You will have no overall idea of what the film is about and that can be quite disorientating, especially when the crew and the principle characters *do* know what's going on, and have already built up a camaraderie over the preceding weeks. You feel very much like an outsider on every level.

Given all this, it was a nice gesture when Mel Smith knocked on my door to introduce himself on my first day at the studio. I was reading *The Times* and checking my *Times* Bingo card. *The Times* was running a competition based on the daily movement of share prices on the London Stock Exchange. You had a blue and white plastic card, the size of a credit card, with a dozen or so numbers printed on it that corresponded to a dozen different listed companies. You had to match the total gains or losses of your 12 shares with a total printed in the newspaper each day. If you matched it you won £1000 or something like that.

When Mel came in and saw me he was amused, because he and Griff had been responsible for the TV ad campaign for that promotion. As he sucked on a huge cigar (at seven in the morning) he told me that the chances of winning were minuscule (a fact I had already deduced), but that the cards were not altogether useless. With that he took a large mirror from the wall and put the card to much better use. We quickly got chatting and he started to enthuse about the merits of different forms of gambling. His preference was for horse racing. He announced conspiratorially, "I will see if we can make ourselves some money today. I just have to make a couple of calls," and with that he left my dressing room. Ten minutes later he returned. "Pity," he announced cryptically, "None of the gee-gees are trying today."

In my naiveté I was surprised to learn that such information could be gleaned from a couple of phone calls to stable lads and trainers. It was an eye-opener for someone with only a passing acquaintance with the sport of kings. Later that day I shot my first scene as a film actor. It was not a particularly memorable debut but I was happy just to get through it without major embarrassment. I don't actually remember whether my scenes even survived the editor's cut. I had enjoyed my day though, in a perverse sort of way, and felt that I had acquitted myself sufficiently well to seriously think about taking the acting side of my career further.

At the end of the summer it was time for Geno to start at Northbourne. The cost of buying all the component parts of the school uniform, the various items of games kit, a musical instrument and the new luggage to carry everything in it was pretty well ruinous, but we knew that the culture shock for Geno of going from a Lambeth inner-city state school to a home counties prep school was going to be big enough, without lumbering him with a shabby suitcase full of inappropriate clothing. At that age, more than at any other, a kid wants to be invisible.

As I hadn't yet learned to drive, we all went down on the train to the nearest station, Deal, then got a cab to the school. It was a beautiful late summer's day, with golden light pouring through the trees and the warm fragrance of the English country side hanging in the air. At the school, all was bustle and frenetic activity. Large cars were crunching up the gravel drive-way and disgorging apple-faced children at the school's door. Those veterans who were returning after a school holiday had the luxury of familiarity. To Geno and the other first-timers, all was new and bewildering. He was immensely brave, refusing to betray any sadness or reproach, and when he was whisked off by a kindly matron, it was Rene and me who were closest to tears. We climbed back into our waiting taxi, stunned into silence and biting our lips, then driven back to the station to wait for our train back to a silent empty house. We were advised not to call for the first few days as the settling-in period would be that much more difficult if tearful parents talk to tearful children about the agonies of separation.

For the next few weeks we grasped what little comfort we could from snatched telephone conversations with him and weekly letters that we anticipated and devoured many times over with morning coffee, scavenging what crumbs of consolation we could from them. We missed him appallingly and were riddled with guilt. Little by little, though, he settled in, and we visited him as often as we could, and lived for the times when he came home for weekends, half terms and school holidays. We would make the six-hour round-trip just for the chance to see him play an hour-long football match and possibly to share a glass of warm orange squash with him at half time, or to crane our necks in order to catch a glimpse of him as he sang in the school choir.

As the summer ended and the leaves fell, Jim and I began the recording session for *Going Gone*, the first Engine Room album, and our follow-up single. We had found a new producer with whom we got on incredibly well, and were looking forward to the sessions enormously. The producer, Dave Allen, had produced the latest records by The Cure and The Sisters of Mercy, and had engineered The Human League's recent hits. In addition to being a highly competent engineer and producer, Dave was a great guy to be with. We began the sessions at Tony Visconti's Soho studio, Good Earth, where Bowie often recorded. Dave got fabulous big, meaty sounds on to tape, and understood perfectly the sort of album we wanted to make.

We wanted to make a record that was eclectic, using elements of ethnic music, electronics, samples and pure pop, a record that combined high and low technology. Jim recorded the basic tracks with synths and drum machines, and then we added broad washes of colour as we progressed. Jim was pretty efficient with his writing and had a good feel for a muscular bass line and a solid beat. My skill was for lyrics and melodies and we combined well together. We used the mighty Boltz for a lot of the guitar parts, Winthrop for saxes, Rene and Julie for lead vocals, plus the three black divas known collectively as Afrodiziac; for brass parts we enlisted a section called the Kick Horns.

We went for a Middle Eastern feel on the opening track, *Damascus*, using samples of muezzins and Arab singers, and real Arab violins and percussion. It was a song that sought to conjure up the steamy claustrophobia of a Middle Eastern town after dark.

We had also written a song called *Your Kiss Is A Weapon*, which was very light and catchy, and we decided to go for that as a single. Dave did a great job of making a mid-eighties pop record out of that song, with drum machines, synths and big brass parts, and it sounded like it had as much chance as anything else around as a single. Arista were pretty taken by it, too, and it was agreed that it would be our next single to be released with a launch party for the band in February. Everyone was very positive and enthusiastic. When I played Morrison the track at Hyde Park Place, he sucked on his cigar, grinned his toothy grin and came up and put his arm around me. "My son," he said, exhaling a Hiroshima-like mushroom cloud of Monte Cristo smoke, "You have fucking cracked it. That song is a smash." Little by little over the next nine turbulent months we assembled that album, fitting in with Dave's availability among his other commitments, and piecing together a record of which I was really proud.

The school Christmas holidays arrived and Geno came home. Eight-years-old is a great age for a child, but he was special. He was great company, always truthful and never whinged. We spent Christmas at our new home, with a tree and decorations and all the trimmings, and friends and relations came and visited. It was idyllic. Or almost. All Rene saw was the spectre of Sophie everywhere, like the Ghost of Christmases to Come.

Like me, our former next-door neighbour in Streatham, Judy, a 70-year old woman with a taste for drama, was also drinking too much, and over Christmas and New Year she would call me on the telephone with increasing frequency, and deliver long, rambling diatribes about some or other perceived snub or insult from a neighbour or, more worryingly, from me. She would remonstrate with me about Sophie, about my lifestyle or about some or other topic and, between sips of whisky, she would launch tirades of abuse. She became increasingly inebriated and her speech more slurred as the conversation progressed. On occasions, most alarmingly, she would become flirtatious, and adopt a baby-doll voice, which she seemed to have picked up from the films of Barbara Stanwyk or Carole Lombard, and coming from a seventy year-old woman was really quite scary. Generally speaking, I do not want a graphic description over the telephone of every single item of clothing a woman of that age is wearing. The following day she would either not remember what she had said, or be distraught, embarrassed and apologetic. On such occasions she would occasionally announce some or other outrageously extravagant gift she had bought us by way of an apology.

The most extreme example of this was when, the morning after a particularly ferocious verbal tirade about my morality, she announced that she had bought me a second-hand car and a course of driving lessons. "It's time a man your age could drive," she announced, not altogether unreasonably. "You can't afford it and I can, so I will not hear another word about it. The car is waiting for collection [at one of the used car dealers on the High Road]. Here is the number of the BSM driving school. I have already lodged a cheque for a course of lessons with them. All you have to do is arrange the days to suit you." She was given to such acts of extreme generosity between her plotting, her planning and her playing off one neighbour against another.

I collected the car, a bronze Vauxhall Chevette (an unreasonably capricious and spiteful little car as it turned out), called the driving school number and started driving lessons. I was 34 and had assumed that I would never drive, because Dad never had. I failed miserably on my first attempt but passed second time. My failure was not as embarrassing as that of Rene's brother, who was failed because he was timed-out. You only have five minutes to get the examiner to your car from the test centre and, in his nervousness, Dave had forgotten where he had parked his car. After marching the exasperated examiner up and down six different side streets in search of the missing vehicle, he was eventually told that he had failed because of the time-out clause.

* * *

In January 1985, I commissioned Andy Earl and Robert Fairman, who had photographed and designed the cover of *Wild Times,* to design the cover for *Your Kiss Is A Weapon*, and also to give some thought to styling a live show with us for our launch party. I didn't want musicians with me on stage; rather I wanted Rene and Julie to sing live with me with a taped backing. I knew that it wouldn't be easy to sell this idea to Jim, as all performers love the limelight, but somehow I managed it. Andy and Robert came up with a vaguely *News at Ten* sort of vibe, with myself as an anchor man, the girls as assistants and the songs delivered like news items, with slides and videos adding visual enhancement. I liked the idea, and they got down to designing a television news studio stage set, with TV monitors, minimalist clean lines, desks and logos.

With the record finished, the artwork ready and a release date for 6 February fixed, we set about finding a venue for our launch party. We decided on Heaven (the club that Richard Branson had asked me to run for him three and a half years previously) for reasons of location, suitability and cost. It has a low, wide stage and allows for video projections without obstruction. We decided that we would preview just three songs, *Damascus, Your Kiss Is A Weapon* and the dance track, *Love Scare*, in a very stylised, stylish segment, using lots of projected images and choreography.

Max and I went to look at Heaven to take measurements and to get a feel for the place. We went over costings for the show and the party. After Arista put in their share, we calculated that we would need to stump up about £1000. However, since the costumes, slides and set would be re-usable, that was a one-off cost. In any event, the money was academic because I was still in so much debt that an extra £1000 really made very little difference one way or the other. We flew Julie down from Scotland and rehearsed for a week, first practising vocals and Rene's choreography, and then working with a technician on the visual elements – the slide projections and the video inserts. By the end we were very confident that we had a great showcase performance for The Engine Room and that the *News at Ten* idea was working well as a concept.

Next we filmed a video invitation to the party. For this we went to Heathrow airport and had Rene and me faking our arrival in London to do the show. We swanned through customs and across the arrivals hall, with Rene executing fabulous pirouettes and *jetés* through the air to a bewildered public, while off-camera a breathless interviewer asked questions, culminating with the exchange, "And finally, Richard, will you be going straight to Heaven?" to which I reply, in my finest Noël Coward voice, "My dear boy, I hope we will *all* be going straight to Heaven." The video invitation was only about two minutes long, but it was very amusing and totally whacky. When we sent them out we attached a written invitation which read, "Your presence is requested to witness the world premiere of the Engine Room at Heaven on 6 February 1985. See the global patriots at work, rest and play! Hear their songs of love, honour and duty. Sex, jealousy and greed. Whack the old regime with the new big sound." We mailed out about 300 to press, radio, friends and celebs.

Throughout all the preparations for the launch party at Heaven, Jim and I continued to record the tracks for the album with Dave Allen. The next three songs we started were *Dominoes*, a song about celebrity and television that I had written for my guardian angel who had rescued me from the Megastore debacle in Manchester; *Pride, Time And Inspiration*, a thunderous dance-rocker that was driven by a percussion part played by Jim Russell on broken bottles; and *The Lion's Den*, which was a sort of bastard hybrid of Philip Glass and ZZ Top that featured a mind-melting one-note guitar solo by Steve Boltz. By now, Boltz was earning proper money and enjoying the sort of success that he had always deserved with Paul Young, who was having hit after hit. Boltz is an unwaveringly loyal friend who has been unaffected by his success and who is always prepared to do a session on whatever I project I happen to have on the boil.

The recording sessions were fantastically enjoyable because the three of us, Dave, Jim and me were all firing on maximum creativity and total focus on the project. In Scotland Jim and I had written and recorded a bizarre track called *Pioneering Surgery*, which we decided that, due to its extreme lack of commerciality, should appear on the album. It took a long time to record and even longer to mix because it didn't really have a regular structure; it was more of a declaimed stream-of-consciousness lyric sung over a stuttering, juddering soundtrack. With lyrics like:

Richard Strange with Louisa Buck 1996.

Richard had to execute John Cleese in five different ways in two days for a Scandinavian chocolate bar commercial, 1991.

Christmas at home, 1998. Clockwise from top: Malcolm McLaren, Charlotte Skene Catling, James Birch, Charlotte, Sachiko Hamagashi.

Joined at the hip. Strange played the butler of top German TV host Thomas Gottschalk in *Gottschalks HausParty* on German TV. This picture of Strange aping the blond curls, teeth and flamboyant dress-sense of Gottschalk is from one of the less embarrasing episodes, 1996.

Also from *Gottschalks Haus Party*. The job was not without its compensations. Here Richard is seen fighting off the attentions of Anna Nicole Smith, before learning that she had inherited $450,000,000.

Strange with Charlotte, 2000.

The absurdist play *The Beelzebub Sonata* was a great hit in 1998. Among others; Janusz Podrazic (composer, extreme left), Katrine Boorman (actress, with horns), Richard Strange (actor and co-producer with skullcap), Roddy Maud-Roxby (actor, back with straw hat), Duncan Ward (director and co-producer, extreme right) and Demian Burger (actor, with ruff and pyramid of Ferrero Rocher chocolates).

Damien Hirst, Richard Strange and Danny Webb enjoy a quiet Saturday night at Hirst's North Devon farmhouse, 1998.

Strange performing with the absurdly talented, multi-instumentalist David Coulter at The Queen Elizabeth Hall, London, as part of Julian Cope's festival, *Cornucopeia*, 2000.

Strange compares haircuts with the artist Gavin Turk at the Apocalypse show, Royal Academy, London 2000.

The art dealer Jay Jopling and his artist Tracey Emin try to turn water into Champagne, while Strange and the artist Darren Almond look sceptically on. Taken by Louisa Buck at the launch party for her book *Moving Targets* at the Tate Modern, London 2000.

I'm off to California in the morning she said
Don't you weep don't you moan don't you drop down dead
I wanted to punch her but instead we kissed
It might have been kinder if I'd just used my fist

The song was pretty much about me and Sophie but I didn't really know it at the time. That happens quite frequently with me. A song lyric can be like an almost mystical personal prophecy or tarot reading. You don't always know what you are writing about at the time. Sometime you understand it later. Sometimes you never get it.

We took one afternoon off from the studio to go down to Andy and Robert's workshop where they were building the sets for the show. We needed to check them over and they looked better than we could ever have imagined. They had decided that only two colours would be used on stage, grey and orange, and the desks they had made were painted in a matt-grey with cut out logos at the front illuminated with neon orange. They looked stunning. Cool and slick and very classy.

The only fly in the ointment was the increasing frequency with which I was having rows with Rene over my affair with Sophie. Rene is not one to lie down without a fight and we fought more or less every day. I knew that eventually something would have to give but I didn't want it to be just now. Sophie was already planning her own heroic, Captain Oates-style exit but we didn't know that yet. At one point Rene threatened to pull out of the *Heaven* show, but after some persuasion she relented. I really needed her input and I told her so.

We took the video invitation along to Bryan Morrison's office, as Bryan was my publisher for The Engine Room material and I wanted to keep him on the enthusiastic high that *Your Kiss Is A Weapon* had put him on. We slipped the video-cassette into his VCR and sat back, desperate that Bryan would like it. He was ecstatic; he was doing his spastic dance again. Suddenly I was a genius again, and the "whacky bird" in the video (Rene) was a star. It was always good to get Morry excited about something, because one phone call from him to Arista was worth 10 from Max. He phoned his chum, the MD, David Simone, and told him about the invitation and told him to make sure the catering was good at the party because anyone who saw the video was sure to turn up.

We sent out more invitations and when I phoned Max to see what news he had from Arista, I was astonished when he said that not a single person whom they had invited had confirmed that they were coming. I told him I would get on to them myself and give them a rocket. It is so demoralising to do so much work, to deal with so much shit only to have the record company fuck it up by their inefficiency or lack of co-ordination. I was absolutely livid and would have told anyone whom I spoke to as much. Max talked me out of any precipitous course of action, saying that he himself would get on to them again. Miraculously, the next time we spoke they had confirmed 20 or so top journalists and radio DJs so I felt better. I never felt there would be a problem getting friends and celebs to come – that was the easy part because I was doing that. We needed Arista to get the press and radio people along, which was why they had press officers and radio promotions departments – to build a relationship with those people and keep them sweet. It was looking for a moment distinctly wobbly, like an out-take from the *Spinal Tap* movie.

On the day of the show we arrived at Heaven at two o'clock, giving us five hours to sound check for the seven o'clock show. Everything was running perfectly. The set, assembled immaculately the night before looked ruinously costly, even though it had been fashioned out of the most inexpensive materials imaginable. Max, Robert and Andy were all on hand to reassure us, and we had booked a hair and make-up girl for the day for Rene and Julie. All our nerves and worries seemed to disappear the moment we went onstage. That night we played to a huge audience and the sound was crystal clear. The slides and videos were all in perfect sync. Julie sang like a bird and looked pretty and vulnerable. Rene danced like a dream and acted like a goddess, and I sang as well as I had ever sung in my life. We got a terrific ovation and left the stage on a towering high.

A throng of friends and well-wishers came back to our dressing room to congratulate us afterwards. Jobson arrived with Philip Core, the American artist and critic, and an efferves-cent blonde girl called Louisa Buck. David Cassidy and George Michael both rolled in. Brian Clarke came and Sophie brought Bunter Somerset. Peter O'Sullivan, followed by the rest of The Klaxon Five, staggered backstage and announced, for no particular reason, "I am not a bastard, I am a drunkard," and collapsed. Everyone was wholeheartedly and unreservedly enthusiastic about the show. I think I do this job as much to impress as to succeed. We adjourned with about 30 close friends to Andy Earl's studio in Clerkenwell and celebrated until the early hours. It had been a great night.

The next morning we were woken to the sound of *Your Kiss is a Weapon* being played on the Radio One *Breakfast Show*, the most important of all the daytime pop music programmes. Despite our king-sized hangovers Rene and I leapt out of bed and danced to it like teenagers, the radio turned up to top volume. At the end the DJ referred to us as "media personalities who make great records" and then said something like "everyone is talking about them". I remember thinking, "If only", but it was a great feeling, and for an instant we had no problems. Over the next few days the record was played quite a lot, enough to get Arista to agree to stump up £12,000 for a promotional video, which typically they wanted made by the following week.

Twelve thousand pounds was not a very big budget even then so we put Andy and Robert to work on devising a storyboard for the video that would develop the *News at Ten* idea. I knew that we could save some money by using the stage set that we had built for the live show; with judicious lighting it would look great. I didn't want the video to be too dry or too neutral so shot some outdoor stuff, too. In the end we ended up with something serviceable if not especially exciting, and we brought it in on budget.

A week or so after we completed the video, the plays and sales of the record had all but dried up. That is one of the many reasons record companies are so infuriating. Their short-term outlook and lack of foresight means that, even when they do spend money, it is often wasted because it is either too late or it is misdirected. Had they invested their £12,000 in a video a month earlier so that it was ready for use as soon as the record was released, they would have been able to have capitalise on the initial interest in the record, get the video played on some essential TV programmes and possibly have secured a lower regions of the chart entry. From then it is so much easier to build a record than it is from a standing-still position.

The big pop and rock TV show at that time was *The Tube*, on a Friday evening. Early in March I was invited up to Newcastle, where it was made, for an interview and a screening of the video. It was a good opportunity to get the video seen by a large audience so Max and I travelled up on the train to do the live show. There were two principle interviewers on the show, both of whom I vaguely knew. Jools Holland was the main one and Paula Yates was the secondary presenter. Neither of them were known for their "in-depth" style of interviewing and besides, *The Tube* was not the sort of programme that cared to expound on the human condition. Paula wittered on for a few minutes about this and that, I talked about the band and my new acting career, and they played the video. And that was that.

* * *

During the first week in March, Sophie revealed her exit strategy. She had for some time been planning a year-long, round-the-world trip to give herself some space and to try to get out of the messy triangle I had fashioned with her and Rene. She was only 23 and it seemed to me that she was being incredibly brave and noble. I had dragged her into my confused and selfish life and she had decided that she would make the sacrifice and take off into the unknown to help me sort it out. Sophie's father drove us to the airport. We kissed once, held each other tightly and said goodbye. She was heading for Rio.

As the year went on I spent endless days in the studio with Dave and Jim. Working on a record must be one of the unhealthiest activities that a sentient human being can willingly agree to. You spend 18-hour days in a dark, smoke filled control-room, breathing bad air, eating pizza, drinking coffee, taking drugs and listening to too-loud music over and over again. You get no exercise, you start speaking in code and when you do get home you cannot speak and you cannot sleep. Then you do the same thing the next day, and the next. And for the next three months.

It sometimes happens that you start to behave like a spoilt child in that situation, and I would admit to being as guilty as anyone of that charge. On one rare evening off, Rene and I were at the opening of a new nightclub near Oxford Circus. We had arrived quite early and had been putting away a lot of drinks when a girl came up and said something less than flattering to me. I was drinking a glass of champagne and rather ungallantly told her to get lost, and, as an added incentive, I tipped the contents of the glass over the front of her dress. It was a boorish, rather than a violent, act.

A couple of hours later Rene and I were sitting in sofas opposite each other, still drinking with some friends, when Ian McNay of Cherry Red Records came over with the girl and another guy carrying a bottle of red wine. Ian asked me if I would like to apologise to the girl for the earlier incident, and I refused since she had deliberately provoked me. At that, the other man upended the bottle of red wine over Rene's head and held it there while the contents drained out over her. I rose to my feet, bellowed, "You, Sir, are a cad!", took one step towards him and, for the only time in my life, wound up my fist and hit him square on the jaw with an almighty right hook. He crumpled and seemed to go down in slow motion, and lay on the floor as if he had been felled by Muhammed Ali. The manager of the club came over and, rather than remonstrating with me, he said, "Sir, I saw everything. I am so sorry. I will have these people thrown out immediately and I hope you will accept a bottle of champagne on the house. And please do us the honour of sending us the good lady's dry-cleaning bill." We thought the whole episode was hilarious, until it was pointed out that the person I had just concussed was a journalist, Spencer Bright, who wrote for the *Evening Standard's* entertainments page and would certainly get his own back in some way. We drained the bottle of champagne and eventually left the party.

Hailing a cab outside we got as far as the Houses of Parliament when I started to be violently sick. The cabby threw us out of the taxi and I leaned over the moat of the House of Commons and threw up again. Mistaking me for an MP in my black tie, a kindly Westminster policeman came up, put his hand on my shoulder and asked solicitously, "Are you alright, Sir? Was it a late night sitting?" I answered that it was and he hailed me a cab and put us in it. By the time we were halfway across Westminster Bridge I was vomiting again and once more we were ejected by an unhappy driver. Finally we got a cab to take us the rest of the way home. It had been an eventful night.

I knew that I was drinking too much, smoking too much, and that Rene and I were still arguing too much, despite Sophie's departure. These last two years had been terrible. We rowed all the time. Mainly it was about my infidelities, but if it were not that, I truly feel it would have been about something else. I felt a sense of incompatibility starting to creep into our relationship that I had never felt before, because I had always felt that we were basically compatible however much we fought. Had I been more sober and less cavalier I may have stepped back and taken stock of what was happening to us, but I wasn't and I didn't.

Back in the studio Jim and I worked on a tumultuous dance track called *Love Scare*, a sort of R&B song unlike anything I had ever recorded before. It was sounding epic when we started to deconstruct it and put it through the mincer. We added sound effects, break beats, percussion and snatches of T.S. Eliot reading from *The Wasteland*. It was demented, like an audio disaster movie, but I really loved it. While we were in the studio I heard from a mutual friend that Cristina was moving to Houston, Texas. It sounded just about the most unlikely place I could ever imagine that uptown girl living, short of living rough on the banks of the Ganges or in a yurt in Mongolia. While Michael eased his way into Houston society with his glamorous, intelligent, but wasp-witted, wife at his side, Cristina's recording career ground to a halt. The record she made with Don Was in 1982 remains to this day her swan song, a tragedy in itself.

By now Rene and I were seeing a lot of Louisa Buck and Philip Core, and once again the social centre of our world changed. Now it seemed to revolve around a gallery in the World's End, Chelsea, run by a friend of Louisa's called James Birch.

LOUISA BUCK AND KATHY ACKER

James was an extremely amusing fellow, sexy and attractive in a louche, feral sort of way, and his private views quickly became the stuff of legend. James Birch and the guests at those parties, a lively bunch of misfits, quickly became close friends – Louisa and Philip, Richard Jobson, the artist Gavin Jones, the galleristes Dominic Berning and Thomas Dane, George Melly, the writer Molly Parkin, Mary Lemley, The Neo-Naturists (a group of three voluptuous female performance artists who were never seen in public wearing anything more than body paint), the ceramicist Grayson Perry and the theatre producer David Johnson. At one of these openings I met the American writer, Kathy Acker. She made a tremendous impression on me and we hit it off from day one. She was tiny but tough, tattooed and pierced, and drove a motorcycle, but had a girlish fragility and a depth of reading and knowledge that all combined to make her fantastic company, someone from whom you learned something every time you met.

Michelle called me one morning to say that there was a casting session for a big Dr Pepper commercial that was to be shot in London. They were looking for a *Mad Max* vibe and wanted to see me for one of the parts. The director, Bob Brooks, was one of the biggest commercials directors in the world. Michelle told me not to hold out too much hope for this one, but that it would be good to be seen by Brooks anyway. The casting session was at a new club that had just opened in Soho called The Groucho Club. That evening Michelle called with the welcome news that I had got the part.

English private schools not only skin you for huge amounts of cash, they also give the children longer holidays than the state system, so when Geno arrived back from Northbourne on a Saturday morning in July, the whole summer seemed to be stretched out ahead of us. He had completed his first full year at the school. I remember the day – it was 13 July, the day of the Live Aid concerts world-wide. Geno loved music and we watched the TV for hours. I will never forget the point at which, after the Bowie performance, they played The Cars' song *"Who's Gonna Drive You Home?"* as a background to the most harrowing footage of the Ethiopian famine we had ever seen, and Geno and I were in floods of tears on the sofa. He announced that as soon as the banks opened on Monday morning he would be sending all his pocket money off to the appeal. He did, too. I was immensely proud of his sensitivity and his generosity. He was just nine years old.

Throughout that summer we spent a lot of time together. Geno loved cricket and was rapidly becoming a useful player for his age. He soaked up both the technique and the subtleties like a sponge. He could bat, bowl and catch better than 95 per cent of the kids with whom he played. I started to play a lot of cricket that summer, too. Every weekend I would turn out for a team called the Occasionals, which had originally been the Arts Council's team, but now no longer had any affiliation. I was an enthusiastic, but unreliable, number 10 batsman, in a team that included the artists Mark Wallinger and John Riddy, the gallery owners Robin Klassnik, Anthony Reynolds and his brother Mike, and later, Peter and Donald from the Klaxon Five.

I have derived enormous pleasure, mixed with a sense of frustration, from playing the game socially ever since.

* * *

With a lot of enthusiasm emanating from Bryan Morrison and Dick Leahy over our track *Love Scare*, Arista consented to paying for a 12-inch remix of the song. During the mid-eighties, club culture was really taking off and you could break a record in the clubs as successfully as you could break a record on the radio. A 12-inch remix of a song was a prerequisite if you wanted to break into the club scene, preferably one done by a club DJ or a remix specialist. As New York was the centre of the remix industry, with producers such as Shep Pettibone, Jellybean Benitez and Bob Clearmountain carving out lucrative secondary careers for themselves as remix experts, it seemed logical that we should look there for our man.

I telephoned Mark Josephson, my friend at Rockpool, and asked him who was upcoming and hot at the moment, as Arista would not pay the sort of money that the big three were asking, and he suggested a young kid called Ivan Ivan, who had been starting to enjoy some success in New York both as a club DJ and as a remix man. Mark gave me his number and I got Max to give him a call. Like all New York kids Ivan was keen to come to London, so we did a deal to bring him over and worked with him for three days at The Roundhouse Studios. Ivan was a typical New York club kid, very brash and cocksure, but fun to work with and totally on top of the technology. He suggested we got a percussionist in to overdub some tracks to give the track more swing, and to make it more dance floor friendly.

A friend told me about a Mexican guy called Pedro Ortiz who was based in London and had appeared with David Bowie at Wembley on the Live Aid show. I remembered the guy immediately as his high-octane playing and hyperactive performance behind the congas had threatened to overshadow even the Thin White Duke himself on that Saturday. It wasn't hard to track him down, and we booked him for a session on *Love Scare*. He was very relaxed, very amenable to suggestions, and brought a great new dimension to the track. Ivan did a superb job on *Love Scare* and transformed the song into something massive and irresistible.

The remix session completed, we set about putting a live band together for the show at the Fridge that Andy Czezowski had offered us. The Fridge was a great venue for us because they were all geared up for video transmission, with 200 screens scattered around the cavernous former cinema. We played the same venue about two years later as part of an Andy Warhol tribute evening (he died in 1987). It was a great show, and all the more memorable as we were sharing the bill with the former Velvet Underground chanteuse, Nico. You see – those schoolboy dreams *do* come true if you wish for them hard enough! Less than a year after the show we did together, the poor ruined beauty was herself also dead, falling off a bicycle in intense heat in Ibiza and suffering a cerebral haemorrhage. Her death was as unexpected as Dempsey's. One no more expected Nico to die on a bicycle than one expected Sid Vicious to die helping an old lady across the road.

It was interesting to be working both as a musician and as an actor, but I still saw myself as a musician first and foremost. The acting work that came in was a welcome and enjoyable source of money, but at that stage it was nothing much more. I still loved music and I was writing more prolifically than ever before. We took the live band into the studio to record three more songs for the album. *Turn It Up* ("I love that song") was a song about a music-fixated fashion victim. *Virginia*, was a paean to Virginia Woolf, one of Rene's favourite writers ("I could have warned you/all that summer she was mad/I could have told you/make the most of any happiness you had"). Finally, during that session we recorded one of the Engine Room's best songs, which I always thought was like the soundtrack for some unmade wide-screen gothic spaghetti Western.

You are the hill and the cross and the nail
You are the jury, you were the judge and the jail
You are the cave and the rock and the white linen shroud
You are the tongues of the flame and the overhead cloud.
You are my Bethlehem and my Calvary Hill
My Pearl Harbour, Hiroshima, smouldering still
You are the undeclared war between unprepared nations
You are my Salvador, you are my salvation.

Also using the studio at that time was a familiar figure from the seventies, whom the eighties had treated less than kindly – Noddy Holder of Slade. I went to make a cup of tea in the kitchen and saw him sitting on a sofa in the lounge. He looked dreadful. I was going to go up to him to chat and to jolly him along but then I realised he was on the phone. I heard him utter six words with a voice of such total dejection I thought he might string himself up. In bewildered Brummie he asked the person at the end of the line, "What do you mean, it's bounced?" It needed no subtext and no background. Those words just seemed to embody the entire perfidious, capricious, shitty business.

A series of disappointments, upsets and bad news started hitting me around that time. As Claudius says in *Hamlet*, "When sorrows come they come not single spies, but in battalions." I got a letter from Sophie telling me she had been bitten on the leg by a viper in the jungle in Java and that she was all but paralysed in a tiny room with her leg swollen to the size of a tree trunk and she was running a massive fever. There was talk of amputation and worse. Thankfully she was slowly nursed back to health by a local nun and a snake doctor, and eventually continued her trip.

The next blow came, inevitably, from a record company. After a year in the making, Arista listened to our finished tapes and decided they weren't going to release the album. No reason was given. What happened was an all-too-familiar story. Simon Potts, the A and R guy who signed us to Arista a year earlier, and who was a genuine fan of what we were doing, had moved on in the interim to another company. We were left at Arista with no one who really knew what we were up to. Consequently when we delivered the finished tapes there was no-one at the company who wanted to fight our corner, and with Max a decent but ineffectual manager, the project hit the buffers.

I managed to negotiate a deal with the MD of the company whereby the finished tapes reverted back to us, against a small over-ride royalty, otherwise legally it could have been construed as a restraint of trade on Arista's part, and reluctantly I sacked Max. I think in a way he was pleased to be relieved of the burden. It was all very amicable and we stayed friends, but I felt the change of circumstances required a change of manager.

The run of bad luck of that autumn ended when Michelle Braidman rang me to tell me of a casting session for a new film. The Irish director Neil Jordan, whose two earlier films, *Angel* and *Company of Wolves,* had received enormous critical acclaim, was in pre-production on a new project, called *Mona Lisa,* a tough but poetic film about a London hooker and an under-world minder. I met him at the production office in Soho and we hit it off well. He told me that he wasn't casting specific roles at the moment but was looking around for interesting types to people the film. He seemed to me to be very open and straightforward. A lot of people try to mystify the creative process in order to appear more enigmatic or remarkable, but Jordan cut straight to the chase and said, "You have a great look. I am sure we can fit you in somewhere. Thanks for coming along." I left the office believing that he would use me and a couple of days later Michelle phoned to confirm that he had offered me a part. I was very excited because I knew I would be working for the first time on a film of real quality. My sense of anticipation was increased when I was told that the cast included Bob Hoskins, Michael Caine and Robbie Coltrane.

In November we shot my scene. I played a pornographer and originally I was supposed to be reading a copy of *The Sun* when the Hoskins character comes into my shop to deliver some dirty videos. In a typically wry Jordan touch, he swapped *The Sun* for Feodor Dostoevsky's *Crime and Punishment,* but equally typically downplayed it rather than making it a feature. That sort of touch is what makes Jordan's best films repay a couple of viewings. He is, at his best, a very subtle and slyly amusing film-maker. He is also a very un-neurotic one. (Incidentally, the only other time I saw *Crime and Punishment* being read in a film was in *Wallace and Grommet,* where Grommet reads the Fido Dostoevsky version.)

The scene was necessarily short since *Mona Lisa* was being shot on a very tight budget, and the location for the scene, the Sven bookshop in Old Compton Street, required us to be finished in time for the lunchtime rush. Even so, I was amazed at the number of disgruntled punters we had to turn away at 7.30am. I was surprised how nervous I was at working with Hoskins but he was a delight and, sensing my apprehension, made me feel completely at ease. It is so important for an inexperienced actor to get encouragement, advice or support from someone like Hoskins, otherwise his unease unsettles the scene for both of them. Between takes we ate bacon sandwiches and chatted about music; by lunchtime I was finished.

On 5 December, Ruth Polsky arrived in London and told me that a busload of revellers were heading north that evening to attend the opening of a new club in Manchester called the Hacienda. She convinced me that the evening would be a riot and that I would be a fool to miss it so, typically, when the coach set off from London with crateloads of champagne and other more exotic entertainments on board, I was on it with the Klaxon Five as my travelling companions. Long before we even arrived at the club we were completely smashed and The

Hacienda itself is consequently something of a black hole in my memory. I do remember, however, getting erotically involved with a delightful American girl called Maureen on the journey home, fired by some South American aphrodisiac. After we were disgorged from the coach as the milky winter sun was coming up, we slipped down the alleyway alongside the Victoria Palace Theatre and had a furious, furtive fuck. As the old sage himself, Sam Beckett, sagely observed, "One is no longer oneself with an erection."

* * *

For that Christmas and New Year, Brian Clarke invited Rene, Geno and me to Italy, where he and Liz were living in a hunting-lodge in Lunghezza, just outside Rome. Christmas Day was spent at home with Liz, Rene and Geno preparing lunch in the kitchen and Brian and I went in search of champagne. We exchanged gifts and were joined for lunch by Dado Ruspoli, an extraordinary man who is both a papal prince and a magician; and Lucian Freud's daughter Bella, who was in Italy studying fashion (having previously worked for Vivienne Westwood and Malcolm McLaren).

Dado is a lovely man, full of warmth and fun and a spectacularly colourful past. Often cited as the inspiration for Fellini's *La Dolce Vita*, he was either introduced to sex by Salvador Dali and to opium by Jean Cocteau, or the other way around, depending on who is telling the story. Dado's mythological status is further enhanced by his legendary endowment, a wine bottle being the most frequently used comparison. It always seemed somehow superfluous and nitpicking to ask, "Is that flaccid or erect?" Unable to contain his curiosity any longer, Brian confronted Bella directly with the question that had been disturbing his equanimity. "Tell us how big it really is." Bella thought for a few seconds and answered enigmatically, "Well, it doesn't fit in his shoe."

Two new guests, Anthony Fawcett and Jane Withers, arrived from London. In truth Anthony and Jane were not my favourite people at that time. I had met them several times before at parties, and it is always disconcerting to hold a conversation with a couple who are looking over your shoulder and taking in the whole room, in search of someone more useful. It became almost a joke between us. I am a foot-and-a-half taller than Anthony and he was obliged to try to look round me for his A-list prey. As the man behind the corporate sponsorship of British art for the last fifteen years, principally in collaboration with Beck's beer, I think he has done a sterling and invaluable job, and has actually mellowed to the point where he can laugh at himself now, something that would have been unthinkable at Lunghezza. These days we get along very well. He has been involved in projects with all the leading British artists, including Damien Hirst, Gilbert and George, and Rachel Whiteread, and also co-ordinated such events as the Beck's Futures Prize for new artists. It is not easy to forgive a man who was once the public relations man for The Eagles, but I think, heroically, I have managed it.

We celebrated New Year with a party at the house, and Rene, Geno and I left on the train for London on New Year's Day. Brian, who had warned that the train would be crowded, and therefore it might be difficult to get anything to eat on it, had generously prepared a hamper of the most delicious food and drink for our journey. From the Campari and soda aperitif, through the caviar, salamis, cheeses, meats, breads, cakes and chocolates, with appropriate wines to accompany each course, it was effectively a five-course banquet in a box, and as we heaved it up onto the luggage rack of our crowded compartment, we knew it would not be long until we would be heaving it down again to sample the delights of its contents.

We actually managed to resist for a couple of hours, but as our train pulled out of Livorno, we were overcome and hauled it down. All eyes were upon us as we fetched it down, and as we unbuckled the two straps the anticipation was almost too much to bear. Two nuns smiled beatifically as we removed the linen tablecloth and utensils that Brian had thoughtfully packed, but their smiles turned to horror as, out of its knife-sharp folds, a pornographic magazine of such vivid venality slid onto the floor, and fell open at a centrespread of almost impossible erotic athleticism. Brian had slipped the magazine into our feast as a little joke, but had omitted to warn us of its inclusion. The temperature of the carriage dropped by twenty degrees, and for the rest of the journey we were scrutinised by our fellow travellers as if we were the apostles of Satan himself. Dinner was partaken in silence, punctured by nervous giggles from us and a disapproving tut-tutting from the Holy Sisters. To save our blushes we drifted off to sleep as soon as decency would allow.

* * *

In January, 1986, Robert Fraser died of Aids. It was a miserable month. I was in extreme financial difficulty until Michelle rang to say they had just received $1200 from Dr Pepper. Almost as encouraging was the news that an agent friend of hers had seen a cut of *Mona Lisa* and my performance had survived the editor's razor blade. I didn't delude myself for a moment that my two minutes on screen would set Hollywood tongues wagging, but I thought that it might, at least, lead on to something else.

On the day that Sophie returned to London I went to spend some time alone with her. I rather spoilt the occasion by deciding on the way over that I would have to make some effort to put Rene out of her misery and to give Sophie back her life, which she had effectively given over to me for the last four-and-a-half years. I thought that it would be best to bring our affair to an end in the hope that I could keep Rene as a partner and Sophie as an incomparable friend. I wasn't being heroic, I was just being a bit less selfish than previously, that was all.

Poor Sophie was disorientated, jet-lagged and exhausted, and although she agreed and understood, it was clearly the last thing she wanted to hear just then. We wept together and clung to each other, but the saddest thing was the lost look in her eyes. It broke me up. Eventually we reassembled ourselves into moderately presentable adults and went to Adam McEwen's birthday party and dinner. Neither of us was really in the mood for it. The party was a largely family affair, but the McEwen family is so large it still makes for a huge crowd.

On a cold March morning Rene and I took a cab to St Mary's Church, Paddington Green, for Robert Fraser's memorial service. It was a very moving service with a simple church full of Robert's family, friends, acquaintances and admirers. There was a heavenly choir, and readings from *The Wisdom of Solomon* and from *Some Fruits of Solitude 1693* by William Penn. "Death is but crossing the world, as friends do the seas; they live in one another still . . . This is the comfort of friends, that though they may be said to die, yet their friendship and society are, in the best sense, ever present, because immortal." Fifteen years later the British Prime Minister Tony Blair hijacked the same text when he delivered a speech in the wake of the New York Twin Towers attack on 11 September 2001.

The address, which Brian, a wonderfully natural public-speaker gave, was genuine, warm and heartfelt, and had many of us close to tears with its simple affection and respect. The tone was perfect. The service ended with Gaz Mayall playing a tape of Louis Jordan's *There Ain't Nobody Here But Us Chickens*, a Fraser favourite, on a ghetto-blaster placed in the middle of the aisle. Despite the upbeat lunatic jollity of the song itself, those three minutes were almost sadder than anything else in the entire morning.

* * *

As a result of a chance meeting I renewed an old acquaintance with Michael Collins. Michael was a friend from the Dempsey-Czezowski days. He had managed the post-punk art school band, Wire, in the late seventies, but was now working as a freelance graphic designer, and only rarely dabbled in music when something really grabbed him. I told him about the Engine Room material and how we were trying to place it with record companies on a territory-by-territory basis. He expressed an interest and we arranged to meet the following day. At his minimalist-chic Islington office I played him a tape of the material that had reverted to us from Arista, the stuff that Dave Allen had produced, and he seemed genuinely impressed by both the music and the concept. We had lunch and agreed to meet after Easter to discuss specific details. I eventually signed a management deal with him, on my own limited terms: one year only, pop music only, net deal on live work and 20 per cent.

Over the next few weeks Michael negotiated a release for *Damascus* in Germany. A Frankfurt-based production team, Anzilotti, Münzing and Schmitt, responsible for big club acts like Snap! and Sven Väth, did a very impressive dance remix of the track, and it became a dance floor smash in Germany. Success followed in France and *Damascus* actually went to number three in Israel, of all places. It really felt that, at last, things were starting to move with the Engine Room. The record had taken over a year to record, had been rejected by Arista, had led to the parting of the ways with Max, but was now finally starting to enjoy a certain amount of success and justifying my confidence in it. We still didn't have a release for the record in the UK or the USA, but we were sure that was only a matter of time. Mark Josephson was plugging it for me in the States through Rockpool and was getting a lot of favourable feedback.

With financial contributions from two or three of our international record companies, we got enough money together to shoot a video for *Damascus*. I knew exactly who I wanted to direct it. George Stone had been a Doctors fan in the old days and we had stayed in touch as he had made a reputation for himself in advertising before coming up with the character Max Headroom, for a ground-breaking TV series of the same name. George had the killer combination of being media-savvy and techno-literate. He was the first person I ever heard mention the Internet. George looked like a cross between a boffin and Maggie Smith. A curious combination, I will grant you, but you will have to take my word that it is an accurate description. We had known each other for the best part of 10 years and he was always a fantastic source of tangential suggestions and iconoclastic ideas. He was the first person to turn me on to the joys of Louis-Ferdinand Celine's masterpiece, *Journey to the End of the Night*. Celine is an author so dark, so pessimistic, that he makes Conrad read like P.G. Wodehouse. The book contains the glorious lines, "We'd just arrived at the end – it was more and more obvious. You couldn't go further because after that there was nothing but the dead." I recognised them instantly as being a close cousin of the opening lines of my song *Mainlines*: "This is the place the rats come to die," and I was hooked.

George and I chatted about the video and decided that we wanted to set the action in a dance marathon in a dance hall in the kasbah at the end of the world. We wanted that Celine idea of "after that there was nothing but the dead". I had memories of the 1969 Sydney Pollack film, *They Shoot Horses, Don't They?* in my mind, with exhausted couples clinging to each other for support as they dance for days on end in an eliminatory competition for a couple of hundred dollars prize money. Apparently during the Depression of the thirties these dances to the death actually took place. (These days they are TV shows called *Big Brother* or *Survivor*).

We wanted a huge cast of spectators, sleazy, decadent and deranged, egging them on, and a Middle Eastern dance band that might have failed an audition for Rick's Bar in *Casablanca*. The more ideas we came up with, the more maniacally we laughed. George has a great sense of humour and an impressive ability to get things done. He had contacts in every sort of business so we could hire cameras, lights, costumes and technicians for next to no money. Rene choreographed a wonderful gestural procession of turbaned and burnoose-clad dancers (students from the Laban Dance School where she was now studying) to snake through the action like a malevolent serpent imagined by Pina Bausch.

I telephoned Andy Czezowski and asked if we could film at the Fridge for nothing and he kindly agreed. I got all my friends to come along in wild costumes of their own devising to play the spectators. By the time we had dressed the set it looked amazing. We had palm trees, birds and even Giussepina's snake, Sainsbury, made an appearance. We cast a wonderful looking dance band with the actors, Peter Geeves and Fred Aylwood ("Les" from Vic Reeves's early shows), joining The Temperance Seven's Alan Cooper onstage and managing to look both bizarre and menacing. Micha Spierenburg, one of the most high-powered merchant bankers in the world at that time, played a cocktail waiter in his own immaculate white-tie tuxedo. Poor Kathy Acker, who had only come to London to plug her book, *Blood and Guts in High School*, ended up in a leading role, dressed to look like a freedom fighter from a long-lost war. Carl Chase played a sort of Peter Lorre cameo role and Rene danced ina cage.

It was three days of the most magnificent chaos. George was both inspired and inspirational, like a crazed general fighting a valiant rearguard battle against the forces of reason. The cameraman, Marek Pytel, was equally heroic, submitting to every conceivable indignity and physical humiliation to get the shots we required. By the end of the shoot we were human wrecks, but the finished film looked fabulous. The experience of shooting and editing the video had forged an unbreakable bond of mutual dependency between George and myself, and we saw each other almost daily for months to come.

* * *

In July 1986 a Belgian record company, Crepescule, released both the Engine Room single, *Damascus*, and the album that I had entitled *Going Gone*. For the album cover artwork, Rene built a fabulous shrine in our front room, which was photographed. It was like one of those shrines you see by the side of the road in Spain or South America, but a very post-Chernobyl version. In this version the offerings to the saints are now so diverse, so random, as though people have forgotten the symbolism and significance of everyday objects, that they have been transformed into totems. The cover featured business cards, batteries, pornography and circuit board diagrams along with more conventional flowers and cash offerings. It was magnificent. It seemed to perfectly encapsulate the musical content of the album, with its mixing of old and new technology, and ancient and modern religion.

By now the band was called Richard Strange and The Engine Room, which didn't please Jim especially, but Mike was sure that in order to facilitate overseas deals we needed to capitalise on my name, which had, in the 10 years since the first Doctors of Madness album managed to accrue a little bit of credit and recognition. The reviews and sales in Belgium and Holland were good, and *Damascus* got a healthy amount of radio play. The French release enjoyed some success, too, and in Germany we found a company who wanted to release the album to cash in on the club success of the remixed *Damascus*. Michael shared an office with the great Dutch rock photographer, Anton Corbijn, and we had some new photos shot by him to accompany the foreign releases. Anton is a masterful photographer with a supreme understanding of the specific requirements of rock photography in the myth-making process. He is a true artist, rather than a mere snapper, and many of his images have become classics of the genre over the years. His pictures of Bowie, Beefheart, Miles Davis and U2 will be admired for as long as people wish to look at rock stars in all their enigmatic, egomanic diversity.

Early in September 1986, I heard of a tragedy in New York. Ruth Polsky, my US agent, had been killed. I learned that she had been queuing to get into the Limelight Club in Manhattan when a taxi mounted the pavement, ploughed into the queue and killed her. It was a pointless and arbitrary way for her to die. She was one of those people so in love with life, with her job and with people, it just seemed so premature. She could only have been in her thirties. I wrote to her mother to express my sorrow and to tell her how much Ruth had done for me in the States and how I always looked forward to seeing her. She wrote back thanking me with a letter of heart-rending sadness. I vowed *never* to queue to get into a club again.

Nineteen eighty-seven got off to a great start, which promised much for the year to come. Owing to the success of *Damascus* and *Going Gone*, we were doing TV all over Europe. While television is the most effective way of promoting a band worldwide, the actual recording of a spot for a pop programme is a pretty dreary affair. It inevitably involves a lot of waiting and making small talk with local promotions people from the record company, with a seemingly endless procession of press interviews to maximise the impact of your stay in any town.

Every once in a while something distinguishes one show from another, and it was in Amsterdam, while on a Dutch TV show, that I met someone who became a very close friend, the outrageously talented Sarah-Jane Morris, the Titian-haired singer with The Happy End and The Communards, with whom I have happily worked many times since. We were sharing a bill on the TV show and I recognised her watching us from the studio floor. When we finished, we were introduced by Michael Collins, who shared an office with her manager. After finishing recording the show we all had dinner together, and the following day spent the morning wandering round the Stedelijk gallery, where there was a massive exhibition of the works of the contemporary German artist, Anselm Kiefer, who was a great favourite of mine.

Sarah-Jane is great company and the only woman I have ever met whose singing voice is lower than my own. As we picked our way through the gallery, chatting about the work and our own projects, we realised that we lived only 10 minutes away from each other in London. She lived in Coldharbour Lane, Brixton, with her boyfriend, David Coulter, a musician in the noise-metal band Test Department. We spent hours exchanging stories until, after a drink at the American Hotel, we had to go our separate ways. We promised each other we would stay in touch and, unusually for these chance meetings on the road, we did.

For my birthday party this year I decided to celebrate with a Burns Night supper. As the birthday celebration progressed, fuelled by some good single malt whisky and the ballads of Burns, it declined into a bacchanalian riot. Our neighbour downstairs, Greta Knuckles, who had been described by our housing association as "difficult", lay newspapers all the way up our staircase, brandished a box of matches and screamed, "God has told me to burn you out!" We were so gone we could only laugh and kick the paper away. I fell into bed at three, leaving a trail of kilt, sporran and dirk (that sounds like a firm of Scottish solicitors).

* * *

On a beautiful hot English summer's day in the Cotswolds, at the height of Thatcher's years of misrule, Bunter Somerset, aka Harry Worcester, heir to the Duke of Beaufort and Badminton Castle, married the actress Tracy Ward, the younger sister of Rachel Ward. It was a society wedding the likes of which only happen in England, in the Cotswolds, in summer. In a scene unchanged for 500 years the local people waited at the gates of the village church to watch the toffs arrive in all their swank and finery. Two hours later they were still at the church's gates to send the bride and groom off with their good wishes.

Rene and I had somehow thrown outfits together which, while having the appearance of appropriate formal wear, were in fact bastardisations of our existing wardrobes. We were quite shocked that Bunter had invited us and, having been invited, we knew we had to go. I genuinely like Bunter. He is a good egg. Politically we disagree on just about everything, but have found an accommodation. It is proof that friendship does not rely on the mirroring of opinions. He is generous, hospitable and courteous. A gentleman without any pretensions. He happily lists his interests in *Who's Who* as music and sport, surely better than those of the Cuban dictator Batista, whose only interests, according to the great writer Norman Lewis, were "canasta and murder".

There is a braying, preening clique of international white trash whose entire year is spent following each other round to weddings, christenings and funerals all over the world, and this clique was out in force in the Cotswolds on that Saturday afternoon. It was amusing to be an observer, an outsider, indeed to be the closest thing to a black man at the wedding party. I was surprised to see Cristina had come over from Houston for the occasion and she seemed less than blissfully happy with her life. I couldn't help noticing that she had had a certain amount of, er, bodywork done, and her bosom seemed to have once belonged to someone else, someone rather bigger. We chatted fitfully and were parted by the shifting throng, only seeing each other from across a crowded room for the rest of the celebration.

The party in the evening was especially amusing for its rubber-necking value. First, Mick Jagger and Jerry Hall arrived, (Mick *loves* a toff and the toffs *love* Mick) to add some rock and roll glamour to the mix. Then Prince Charles and Princess Diana made a dramatic entrance, their way cleared by special branch men with suspicious bulges beneath their jackets. After much bowing and curtseying from the family, the heir to the throne was seated with his wife and a drink, and the party recovered from its moment of heart-fluttering excitement. As the evening progressed the dance floor started to fill up (a dance-floor full of toffs is never a pretty sight) and the school disco selection of seventies and eighties hits kept everyone happy. Later still, a tired and emotional Princess Diana took to the dance floor, pursued by half a dozen good-looking men but not her husband. As one woefully inappropriate song gave way to another, as *Hi-Ho-Silver Lining* gave way to *Dancing Queen* and *I Will Survive*, Her Royal Highness' dancing became more and more abandoned, perhaps echoing her innermost feelings, and she cut a dervish-like swathe across the floor, mad-eyed and white-faced, pausing between songs only to mop her royal brow on the hem of her royal evening dress.

The bride, on the other hand, who had been something of a schoolboy's fantasy figure for her role in the TV spoof drama, *CATS Eyes,* was a picture of decorum and restraint. Even as she exchanged a few words with Jagger, while he clutched Jerry's handbag outside a portaloo, she looked unflappable and in total control. Tracy is best known now for her evangelical promotion of green issues in general and sustainable farming in particular. Of course, this did not necessarily chime well with the majority of the green-wellie brigade, whose idea of green politics is to take a taxi to Harvey Nichols, not the four-wheel drive. Many of Bunter's friends thought that she was a bit of a space cadet, but to her eternal credit she put in the brain work, stuck with it and became an eloquent and enthusiastic supporter of environmentalism, and a stern and well-researched critic of globalisation. She doesn't only do the glitzy charity balls, either. One of my abiding memories of Tracy is seeing her leaving Badminton, dressed as a carrot, on her way to picket Sainsbury's in Bath on a wet Saturday afternoon. That is dedication.

* * *

I was lucky. I was failing upwards. From being an unsuccessful rock star to being an undiscovered actor may seem like one small step for a man, and in many ways it is, but through the seventies, the eighties and the nineties I was able to live a life that offered such riches of inspiration, of excitement, of enjoyment, of friendship and of travel, that I have much to be grateful for. In July, Mark Josephson invited The Engine Room to New York to perform at the New Music Seminar. The NMS was like a trade fair for the so-called alternative music business. Small independent labels and publishers pushed new artists while journalists and industry moguls pontificated in symposia on the "the future of the chord of D minor in rock music" or "are A Flock of Seagulls more relevant than Mozart?".

In the midst of all the humbug, though, were a lot of concerts, and we went over to play two shows at the Limelight. It was weird playing at the same club that Ruth had been queuing outside the night she died. I had met with Ruth every time I had visited the States, and it felt odd not touching base with her and exchanging gossip, her favourite pastime, before heading off to do a pointless soundcheck somewhere. We played good, hard shows those two nights – Rene, Pedro, a guitarist called Richard West and myself, although it was proving difficult to keep Pedro in check onstage. His natural exuberance jeopardised any subtle dynamics I tried to build into a running order of songs. *The Fall Of The House Of U,* a moody gothic ballad I wrote about the McEwen suicides, was a song that I performed solo in the middle of the set. My instructions to Pedro were "On this song you do nothing. Just chill."

I was astonished while singing the song on the first night that the audience didn't seem to be focused on me, but at something that was happening onstage behind me. Intrigued I turned around between verses to see what was happening, and to my horror saw the athletic Ortiz doing a perfect vertical headstand on a guitar amplifier. This was his idea of chilling. If I had said "I want you to make sure you pull the entire audience's focus off me for that song" I can only imagine he would have done something with dynamite, offal and underage girls.

At that time I had a beautiful Jean-Paul Gaultier overcoat. It was a lightweight, full length, navy blue number with a chalk stripe. While I was onstage it was stolen from my dressing room, presumably by an East Village junkie who would be selling it on the street for two dollars that same night to buy some smack. It was annoying and irksome, because the coat was a great favourite of mine and had not been cheap. In order to be recompensed by my travel insurance, I knew that I would have to report the theft, both at the club and to the police, and go through a lot of form-filling on the way.

My first port of call was the Limelight's manager's office. There was a guy, probably in his 30s, smartly dressed and looking impressive behind his desk, but not evidently over-bright. I told him what had happened and he was sympathetic. He reached into a drawer to get a sheet of paper with the printed heading "Report of Crime" at the top. I started to give him details as he asked for them, you know the sort of thing, my name, date of birth, my hotel, passport number, all that stuff. It seemed to take forever. Finally we came to the coat. "It was a Jean-Paul Gaultier overcoat," I began, at which point the telephone rang and he spoke in a bizarre patois for 20 minutes with someone I could only suppose was a dope dealer of some sort, before returning to me saying, "Sorry, Richard. OK, let me read this back to you," he said in an irritatingly faggy sing-song. "Your name is Richard Strange, you were born on the twenty-fifth of January nineteen fifty-one, etc., etc.," he droned on, charmed by his own voice. Finally he reached the point. "And you have lost a goat-hair jacket . . ." Oh dear, I thought to myself, this is going to be a long night,

The album *Going Gone* started making small waves in Britain, and was favourably reviewed by most of the music press. One review said, "This is the album that Richard Strange has been threatening to make since those early, earthy, trashy days of The Doctors of Madness. An album which addresses itself simultaneously to the head, the heart and the feet, with contributions from many of the most inspired producers and musicians inside and outside rock." Despite the enthusiasm of some music journalists, we still couldn't get a British or American record company to release the album, and I found that extremely frustrating.

* * *

In the first few weeks of 1988, I met a guy with whom I have worked with off and on ever since. David Coulter was the boyfriend of Sarah-Jane Morris and, as they lived in Brixton, I saw quite a lot of them. He is one of those characters blessed with an innate musicality, who can pick up a saucepan or a wooden spoon in the kitchen and get a tune out of it. As soon as we met we hit it off and I knew it was only a matter of *when*, not *if* we would work together. He has an energy and a curiosity of mind that can sometimes be quite unsettling. Just when you think you have settled on a way to tackle a song he will say, "But what if . . . ?" and unravel all the ideas you have agreed to the previous day. What is irritating is that his "But what if . . . ?" is usually a better idea than the one you had settled on. This is what happens if you work with Marc Ribot, The Pogues, The Kronos Quartet, Joe Strummer, The Band of Holy Joy, Boy George, The Communards and Pete Townshend. You absorb a lot of styles and your musical vocabulary becomes a lexicon.

Meeting Coulter gave me a lot of confidence about the future of my music, and when I got a call out of the blue from EMI Publishing asking me to go in to their Charing Cross Road office for a chat, I knew I could sell them a great new Engine Room project, even though we still hadn't had a UK release for *Going Gone*. I spent half an hour with Steve Walters and convinced him that he *had* to sign me, but that it was going to cost them a lot of money. It helped that he was a big fan of *Damascus* and *Love Scare*, and The Doctors material, and really he only needed to see that I could walk unaided and wasn't in a permanent drug-and-drink-induced coma to convince him to sign me. I told him the next Engine Room project would harness the skills of Jim and myself to the flair and the multi-instrumental talents of Coulter, which would bring a unique palette of sounds to the record unlike any that I had previously made.

Although the details of the deal with EMI took a long while to finalise, I knew it was only a matter of time as I had him well and truly hooked. I went straight to Morrison, the way one would go to an unfaithful lover who has slept with every celebrity, and told him that I was signing with EMI. It was like saying, "See, you are not the only one who can fuck a big name". He seemed indignant at first that I could be so perfidious, but soon got over it when I told him how much EMI were paying me.

Ninety eighty-eight was an eventful year, perhaps too eventful, with a great deal of travel, excitement, high drama and death. In March, Uncle Stan died after a long illness, and it was shocking to think we would never again enjoy his conviviality, his sense of fun and his gentle ribbing of Auntie Else's accent. He had been in many ways an inspiration to me, both professionally and, more importantly, socially, and his humour had been a godsend in our house during those childhood Christmases.

In May the EMI publishing deal finally came through, and I split the money with Jim, the not-so-canny Scotsman who always seemed to have a scheme to get the better of the business, but always seemed to misread the situation and miss out. Jim and I went straight to Germany to discuss the new album, which Uli and Wolfgang, from the band International Noise Orchestra, wanted to pay for and co-produce. In the event they ended up paying for it and mixing it, while Jim and I produced it ourselves, partly in Germany and partly in a studio in the East End of London.

No sooner was Geno back at school than I got a walk-on part in another film, *Getting It Right*, directed by Randall Kleiser. The film was a dog but it had a superb cast, including John Gielgud, Lynn Redgrave, Jane Horrocks and Helena Bonham Carter. My part was very small and, when I arrived on set in Bayswater where they were shooting on location, the crew were way behind schedule. The first assistant director said to me, "To be honest, we won't be shooting your scene till well after lunch. Grab yourself something to eat and wait in your trailer till we call you." I asked him which was mine, seeing that about a dozen were parked back to back around the leafy square. "The one on the corner," he answered, gesticulating in the general direction of a corner.

I went to the catering truck and, happy not to have to queue, picked up some lunch and walked to my trailer, prepared for a long wait. On entering my trailer I was rather surprised to find that the previous inhabitant had not cleaned up properly, as is the customary etiquette of the profession, but I was happy with its roominess and its facilities. It was considerably better than I was used to. Tidying myself a space amid newspapers and unemptied ashtrays, I lazily ate my lunch and read a newspaper.

I was vaguely aware of the sound of running water in the background but paid it no attention until, to my surprise and utter horror, a door opened at the end of the trailer and a totally naked Helena Bonham Carter emerged from the shower, like a ravishing, bush-baby-eyed brunette version of Botticelli's *Birth of Venus*. I leapt to my feet as she approached me and spluttered an apology while instinctively thrusting out a hand, "I'm Richard Strange, er, how do you do? I think I have made a mistake." She casually grabbed a towel to protect her modesty and sat down and said, "Don't worry. Finish your lunch," and she proceeded to chat as though she had known me for years, while she dried her hair and picked at my plate. She was a very amusing and very cool lady. I have liked her ever since.

A month after *Getting It Right*, Michelle left a message for me telling me about a casting session at the Warner Brothers office in Soho's Wardour Street. Quite frequently, for reasons of exchange rate, technical expertise or studio availability, films that we think of as American blockbusters are actually filmed in the UK. The James Bond films, for example, were done chiefly at Pinewood Studios, as were large parts of *Star Wars*, *Superman* and *Indiana Jones*. But it wasn't for any of these that Michelle had called me. It was to tell me that a full-length feature film based on the comic strip hero Batman was in pre-production, and that since they were planning on filming it at Pinewood, they were casting a lot of British actors in the smaller roles. This happens regularly these days. British actors have become synonymous with bad guys (something about our foreign accent, I guess). Consequently, when an American producer is casting the baddies for a film to be made in the UK, he doesn't need to bring a whole load of villains over from Hollywood with him, with the added expense of paying their air fares, hotels and other expenses. This is one of the areas in which we Brits score. We pick up a lot of the crumbs that fall from the big table.

BATMAN AND HAMLET

The more I learned about the film, the more exciting the prospect of working on it became. First, they were looking for guys who could start immediately, had no commitments for nine weeks and were British citizens. So far so good. I went along to Warner Brothers and their offices were full of the meanest-looking actors in London. Eventually my name was called and I went through and met the casting director, who told me a little bit more about the project. She told me that Tim Burton would be directing, Michael Keaton would be playing Batman and, most exciting of all, Jack Nicholson would be playing the Joker. They took a few Polaroids and put each of us on to video and then told us we would know by the end of the week. I was one of the lucky ones. By the time I had got home Michelle had called to say that I had got the job, and that Tim Burton wanted to meet me at Pinewood the following day. I am a notoriously superstitious actor. I never tell anyone about a job I am going up for until I know whether I have got it (although I don't mind talking about a job I haven't managed to get after I know). I told Rene about the job and then we went straight back into town with some champagne and had a good drink at Michelle's office.

At the meeting Tim Burton was very cool and laid back, looking like an LA Goth-kid. He just had a quick look at me and said, "You look great. Welcome aboard," and smiled a shy sort of smile, as if the whole project was as much of a blast for him as it was for me. One of the costume designers was called to measure me and Burton said, "See you on set" and that was that.

There is something unforgettable about doing your first big US blockbuster film. The scale, the egos, the money are all so different from any other type of film. There are reputations and fortunes to be made, and for a lot of the people involved it was their first really big film. For Burton, for example, who had had a couple of modest hits with his dark, cultish *Beetlejuice* and the quirky-pervy kiddie film, *Pee-Wee's Big Adventure,* it was a huge step up the ladder. For Michael Keaton, too, it was to be the picture that established him. Even the producer, Jon Peters, who had only made a couple of pictures previously, was better known as having once been Barbra Streisand's hairdresser.

Six of us were eventually cast to play the Joker's "goons" or henchmen. I had worked with one of them, Carl Chase, once before, on the *Dr Pepper* commercial. I shared a dressing room with him and a very engaging London-based American actor called Mac McDonald, and for nine weeks they were my constant companions. When we got our pages of script it soon became clear we didn't actually have much to say in the film, but we did seem to be in a lot of scenes, "doing stuff".

On our first day at Pinewood we all wandered out on to the back lot where they had actually built Gotham City. It was to be our home town and we got to know it in every detail: roads, shops, cinemas, the City Hall, diners, everything was there in fantastic faded-thirties detail. Some of the structures were two-dimensional flats; some were three-dimensional buildings that you could actually enter. The art department had gone crazy – every shop was stocked inside and out, and the cinema had a fantastically ornate foyer, just in case the camera caught a glimpse inside as it tracked past. The art director, Anton Furst, who had worked on *Alien, Full Metal Jacket* and *Company of Wolves,* was the hottest young designer in Hollywood, and he went on to win an Oscar for his work on *Batman.* It should be noted that Furst, who committed suicide two years later in 1991, not only designed the sets for the movie but also designed the greatest style icon of the film, the sleek, implausibly sexy Batmobile.

Although the set came close to stealing the finished picture, there was really only one star on set – Jack. We were all in awe of meeting Nicholson. At that time he really was the "big one", although he rather modestly confided in me later, "Every actor in the world will move up one place when Brando dies." Every morning that we were doing scenes, from October to December, we would spend hours in the make-up artist's chair having scars and tattoos and other facial adornments applied. Nicholson's make-up as the Joker took longer than anyone else's, as it was a full latex prosthetic underneath a complete make-up job. In comparison I got off quite lightly with just a nasty sort of hare-lipped scar, for which Jack nicknamed me "Tigerlips".

For the most part, Jack maintained his equilibrium as the morning transformation got underway. The East Coast boy has become the archetype of West Coast cool, and spent most mornings chatting in his inimitable drawl and occasionally singing along to the radio. There is something quite bizarre about sitting next to a star of Nicholson's calibre and hearing him sing along to The Beach Boys' *Good Vibrations*, but then it somehow seemed less odd when he explained that he had once been a lifeguard and "to be a lifeguard, you *have* to dig The Beach Boys".

Everyone knows that Jack loves to play, but it is none the less true because of that. It soon became clear that the reason we were hired to be on call for nine weeks was so that if Jack decided that he wanted to go to Paris for a couple of days to see a Jean-Paul Gaultier fashion show, for example, the production of the film did not have to grind to a halt. Because of Furst's clever design, the vivid purple colour that is associated with the Joker was echoed in the leather jackets of the goons. Consequently, if any skulduggery needed to be carried out in the film in the name of the Joker, it could be done using all six goons at a fraction of the cost of keeping Nicholson in town if he wanted to be somewhere else.

How much was Nicholson getting for his role? Well, one evening in the back of car we waited for clearance from the first assistant director that the day's filming was over, and that we were free to go. When it came, the Joker turned to me with a grin and said, "OK, Tigerlips. Another day, another $90,000". He wasn't talking about *my* salary. American actors know their worth and are not embarrassed to talk about money the ways we Brits are. In addition to his salary, incidentally, Nicholson was on a hefty percentage of the profits and the merchandising. There is also a rumour that, uniquely in this insane industry, Nicholson was on a cut of profits and merchandising from the follow-up Batman film, in which he didn't even appear. When I asked him a couple of weeks into the shoot whether he had seen the previous days' rushes (the rough prints of scenes shot the previous day) he answered, "Tigerlips, I only watch the rushes until I know whether it's going to be a good picture or a bad picture." "And?" I asked. "I think we are looking at $350 million gross," he replied, with an understandably contented smile.

There was a story going round the production at the time that typified the laconic leeriness of Nicholson at his wittiest. He was at a glitzy function in Paris and a beautiful girl at another table caught his eye. He spent much of the evening admiring her from afar and, when the band struck up, the girl, emboldened by the attention and a few drinks, sashayed up to Jack and asked, "Hi, Jack, would you like to dance?" to which the ageing superstar replied, without missing a beat, "Wrong verb, baby."

He was an amusing guy to work with and, unlike many stars of his calibre, he was always grateful for the support that the rest of the cast and crew gave him. But he wasn't above nicking a bit of "business" from one of his fellow actors. There is a scene in the Flugelheim Museum, where the Joker and his henchmen arrive and proceed to trash the art gallery. In the rehearsal before filming I made the mistake of showing my hand. When I got to the famous Degas painting of the ballet dancer in the tutu I went into a cod-balletic routine in front of the painting before trashing it. By the time we shot the scene, Jack had appropriated that bit of business for himself; I was just left to slap the Rembrandt self-portrait around a couple of times.

Jack's personal dresser on *Batman* was a guy from South London, Dave Whiteing, known to all as Dave the Dresser, a flamboyant character whose style was a cross between Clarke Gable and Harry Flashman. Dave is a very personable, very likeable man, who often seems to be doing the job he does just so that he can find increasingly outrageous costumes to wear himself. He and Nicholson hit it off immediately, as kindred extrovert spirits, and would often arrive on set together with matching or co-ordinated outfits, to be greeted to a spontaneous round of applause from both cast and crew. Nicholson valued Dave's attention to detail and treated him well while they worked together.

Some time after the filming had finished and Jack had returned to Los Angeles, Dave was unemployed. That is the nature of this business. It is famine or feast. Out on his motorbike one evening, he was hit by a speeding car that didn't stop and his legs were badly broken. He had to go into hospital for a protracted period of time and when he was eventually discharged, he arrived home on crutches to find a mountain of bills. In amongst all the bad news there was a letter with a Californian postmark. He opened it and there was a short note from Nicholson saying "Dear Dave, sorry to hear about your misfortune, get well soon. Love Jack."

Attached was a cheque for $5000. There are not many stars who would even remember the name of the guy who dressed them three months earlier, still less care. When the six goons were finally finished on the film, he thanked us all for our work and a few weeks later a parcel arrived at each of our homes from Jack. He had had purple leather jackets made for each of us, as mementoes, and thanked us again.

Not all the Americans were as amusing or secure as Jack. When Kim Basinger heard that both Nicholson and Keaton had double-sized dressing rooms, she wanted one too. Now in each dressing room block in Pinewood there are only two double-sized dressing rooms, for the "stars". That was not a good enough reason for Ms Basinger. The fact that she was seeing rather a lot of Jon Peters on and off set meant that she had the producer's ear, and probably other more intimate parts of his anatomy too. We were astonished when we arrived one Saturday morning to find half a dozen great British workmen hard at work in the dressing room block. "What are you doing?" I asked one of them. "'Er bleedin' Royal 'ighness wants an extension," came the none-too-impressed reply. But there was a problem. They had been ordered to knock down the party wall between two single dressing rooms, so that Ms B could enjoy the star status of a double dressing room.

Unfortunately, they had just demolished a supporting wall, and they were doing all in their power to shore up the ceiling and prevent the production office on the floor above from falling into Ms Basinger's fruit bowl. In the end the delightful actress had a double dressing room, but was unable to access one half from the other without going into the corridor and using the other door, as a metre-high wall had been built where the old wall once stood, scaffolding poles and beams taking the weight of the upper floor. The low wall was decorated with a few potted plants and everyone was happy. It was a classic Hollywood fix. Certainly it didn't prevent Jon Peters from making frequent visits to the highly talented blonde.

None of us Brits really knew what Michael Keaton looked like, and we had been working on the film for about three weeks before we actually met him. We had not been in any of the early scenes with him, so when the second assistant director told us one day that we would be working with him, we were intrigued. Once in our make-up and costumes, we wandered down to the set to see if we could catch a glimpse of him. To our absolute horror we walked in on this Californian hunk being absolutely obnoxious, throwing his weight around in every direction. We were aghast. He was pointing at spotlights and saying, "There's no way that can fucking well stay there. We just ain't gonna do the shot if that ain't moved. And no green gels, OK, or we will just walk off. Got it?" The British sparks are fairly used to the egos of the Hollywood stars but I thought this guy was going too far. "What a prat that Keaton is," I said to one, to show my nationalist solidarity. "That's not fucking Keaton," he replied, "That's one of fucking Kim Basinger's hairdressers." To put this in context, we should not forget that this was at the time when, before surrendering to the inevitable and shaving his folically-challenged head, Bruce Willis's scalp painter was one of the most powerful men in Hollywood.

A visitor to the set whom it really was a pleasure to meet, was Bob Kane, the creator of the Batman character. By now he was a frail old man, but walking around the set and seeing all his comic strip ideas materialised into a three-dimensional reality was clearly a thrill for him

– he wandered around, trying things out and being photographed with the cast just as any 10-year-old kid would have done.

Tim Burton was a fantastic guy to work with. As anyone who has seen his films will know, he is a toweringly imaginative and visual director (think *Beetlejuice, Edward Scissorhands* and *Sleepy Hollow*), a master of great picture-making, but not one who is over-interested in narrative and character-psychology. I think on *Batman* he was slightly overwhelmed by the occasion and the company that he was in. Nicholson takes direction but gives you five different versions. He didn't have a great deal to do, and much of his action shots were done by a stunt double; Kim Basinger squeaks and squeals her way through the movie; the veteran actor, Jack Palance, who played a cameo hood, once threatened to "punch [Burton] off the set" if he told him how to act (something he could quite probably have done – he used to be a fairground fighter); Jon Peters and his producers wanted much more of a conventional "action picture" than Burton was intending to make, and kept adding fight scenes and car chases. Burton had wanted to play up the dark side (to be enhanced by Furst's sets and vision) but instead, hamstrung by a fairly limp script, the movie ended up a big-budget, missed opportunity. But hey, it earned a fortune, and isn't that what the business is all about?

At the end of the job, I was able to go along to my bank and deposit a cheque that effectively cleared my overdraft for the first time in 15 years. Mr Harman, the theatre-loving manager who had supported me through a lot of lean times, was even happier than I was to see his faith in actors repaid, and insisted on introducing me to all his staff. "This is Mr. Strange," he announced to the slack-jawed workforce. "He is one of my oldest clients and is starring in the new film, *Batman*, with Jack Nicholson." Starring? Hardly. Total screen time for the nine weeks work, about three or four minutes, but what the hell?

My involvement in such a prestigious and high profile production didn't only earn me brownie points with the bank. With Geno, too, my stock went sky-high. It doesn't matter to your school friends if your dad is skint. But if your dad is in *Batman*, wow, that is *so* cool. By this time Geno was having to drag his own career as a schoolboy back from the abyss of poor reports and diminishing teacher support. He was able to turn his last year around thanks largely to three things. music, drama and sport. Through his own determination and competitiveness he became the leading chorister in the school, one of the leading lights in the school plays. and a reliable and occasionally inspired performer on the sports field. His non-academic achievements gave him a renewed confidence to make a new, albeit belated, start on tackling his academic work, and his improvement was as rapid as it was welcome. The teachers reported a metamorphosis and instead of speaking gloomily about his chances of passing the common entrance exam, they now suggested that he might be a good enough cricketer and badminton player to get a scholarship to one of the top schools in the country if he got a good pass mark.

With the joint pressures of shaky finances and poor school reports simultaneously eased, Christmas 1988 was a happy and relaxed celebration. We had a big Christmas Day lunch party at home, with Rene's sister and her lover joining Kathy Acker, Mac McDonald and his family around our table. Kathy was in great shape and, as always, was great company. She was now living in Barnes, alone except for a pair of love-birds, and arrived clad all in leather on a huge motorbike that looked three sizes too big for her. She was a sort of social chameleon who was at home in any situation. She could be a girlie, a fierce intellectual, a sexual predator or motorcycle disco-diva at the drop of a hat. That Christmas she gave me a tie. It sort of summed her up, she could do the most conventional things on Earth but still she was always different and special. OK, the tie was a Gaultier number with an embossed skull and cross-bones, but it was still a tie, and she gave it in such a delightful way, wide-eyed, like a kid who really wants you to like something.

* * *

I had almost given up looking for somewhere to park that January day in 1989. The ever-decreasing circles I was driving were becoming very irksome. I thought long and hard about cutting my losses and heading for home. I had received a message from Michelle Braidman, informing me that the great Russian director, Yuri Lyubimov, was in town for a few weeks, and was auditioning for a cast of British actors to tour his radical reworking of *Hamlet*, which he had originally directed for his own Taganka Theatre in Moscow in the early seventies, with the extraordinary alcoholic actor Vladimir Vissotsky in the lead role. This new production was to be part of the bold programming policy of the Leicester Haymarket Theatre, with tour support for the subsequent eight-month long world tour coming from the British Council and several commercial sponsors, principally the Ginza Saison Hotel group in Tokyo.

I must confess I was very surprised to be summoned since my acting experience at that time was limited almost exclusively to TV and films. In fact, it was in my small role in *Mona Lisa* that Lyubimov had noticed me. On the evidence of this scene, apparently, he had decided that I was an interesting, physical type, bookish pornographers being perhaps at a low premium at central casting.

As I had never, in my entire life, prepared a piece of Shakespeare for audition, there seemed to me to be little point in attempting to compete with the massed hordes of Royal Shakespeare Company and National Theatre hopefuls who were also keen to be part of this uniquely exciting project. I decided to eschew the obvious choices of audition pieces open to an actor of my age and sex, something from *Othello*, *Twelfth Night*, *Macbeth* or even *Hamlet* itself, in favour of a piece that would at least ensure a certain cachet in auditioning history, if not the immediate offer of work.

Two hours after the time appointed to meet Lyubimov in a hall at the Tottenham Court Road YMCA, time spent listening through closed doors to mellifluous renditions from fellow actors dispensing *Othello*, *Twelfth Night*, *Macbeth* and *Hamlet*, plus what seemed like an entire rendition of *The Tempest* by three NT actors who went in together, I was ushered into the presence of the "great man", and introduced. Lyubimov at that time could not speak a word of English and our conversation was conducted through a charming man in a designer-drab suit, an ill-fitting hairpiece and a curious mid-Atlantic-Estonian accent.

"Would you please tell Mr Lyubimov what you have been appearing in recently?" he requested. I didn't have the heart to say that I had just finished working at Pinewood as one of the goons to Jack Nicholson's Joker in *Batman*, but I did admit that not only had I not appeared in anything onstage recently, but that I had (deep breath) never appeared in a conventional stage play, *ever*. My stagecraft had been learned, I explained, as lead singer and frontman of The Doctors of Madness, a protopunk rock and roll band of the mid-seventies. While this may have lost something in the translation to Lyubimov – only the international Esperanto of "rock and roll" seeming to survive the conversion unscathed – he did not seem unduly abashed. But when Designer Drab asked me what I had prepared for an audition speech and I answered, "Cleopatra's speech, on hearing that Marc Antony had married Octavia" Lyubimov's body language needed no translation. It snarled, "This had better be good, boy!"

In preparation, in a bedsit in Wimbledon with Michael Crompton, a sympathetic and extremely talented director friend, helping out in my hour of need, the piece had dragged itself up from the nadir of village-hall, amateur dramatic awful to a zenith of Dame Judi-esque luminosity. Sadly, in the presence of Lyubimov, my performance erred more toward Dunstable than Dench, but to my astonishment and horror, he took a shine to me and requested that I prepare the part of the Player King from *Hamlet* for the next day. It was my worst-case scenario. I was so anxious about the audition in the first place that I desperately wanted him to say "yes" or "no". I did not want "maybe".

I went back to Michael and he was much more enthusiastic than I was. "Fantastic," he exclaimed, "now we have got something to get our teeth into." "But I have to go back tomorrow, Michael," I whined. "Bags of time," he countered, "Get over here now." He gave me another crash-course and when I returned to Lyubimov the next day, he was sufficiently interested to ask me to work on it some more. "Come back next week, please. And please, more operatic, like Wagner," was his suggestion. I explained that I would not be able to come back again as I was due to leave the next day for Germany to work on The Engine Room album. I told him it had been an enormous pleasure meeting him, and that I had found these last few days extremely educational and informative. He shook me by the hand and advised me that next time I audition for Shakespeare, I should do the Player King, "But operatic, like Wagner," he repeated.

I thought that was the end of the affair but a week later, while in Germany working on the record, Michelle rang me and told me that Lyubimov had offered me the part of the Player King. I was truly astonished. My sense of adventure had got the better of my sense of self-preservation and I had been offered the tour, reputed to be the longest ever undertaken by a British theatre company. In addition to securing the gig for myself, I was subsequently able to get Jim a part in the play as a musician, playing bagpipes and other assorted instruments.

Although that piece of news was both exciting and somewhat daunting, it didn't really sink in immediately as I was totally immersed in the recording. We moved the recording to a studio in the East End and set about making *The Rest Is Silence*. Jim and I had worked together for quite a while by now, and we knew each other's strengths and weaknesses. We were starting to write some very tough material and getting it on to tape the way we wanted it to sound. Some of the songs were quite ethereal and enigmatic, such as *Waterlilies* and *The Ghost Of Brian Jones*, while others were much more political and hard, such as *Endless Winter*,

Down Comes The Hammer and *God Help The Wealthy Man*. Coulter brought with him not only his own considerable talents, but also an address book full of interesting musicians who we could call on.

Waterlilies was a mysterious song, a bit like a Gothic ghost story. It details a series of weird manifestations of a spirit in a garden. The lyric is deliberately quite sparse and obscure, in an attempt to enable the listener to fill in many of the gaps.

> *Our lady of the spheres,*
> *Something swinging in the trees*
> *All the ghastly noises that the mask makes*
> *Our lady was here, tiny footprints by the lake*
> *How much can the rope take till the bough breaks?*

It sometimes happens in the studio that a song that has resolutely shown no inclination to reveal its full potential is jolted into life by the addition of a single sublime performance, or a moment of transcendental inspiration. *God Help The Wealthy Man*, a song of Old Testament fervour, is a rant against global capitalism. With Coulter's wheezing accordion, Kate St John's sexy, snaking soprano saxophone lines, and a rhythm track that skips along a treat, all the elements were there but the song refused to ignite. It was only when the mighty Zulu factor was added, in the form of Shikisha, three Zulu girls who had been regulars at Cabaret Futura, underpinning the rhythm track with their own scat-sung click-language, that the track had sufficient vitality to support what might otherwise have been a top-heavy lyric:

> *Christ died for foreign money*
> *God help the wealthy man*
> *In the mouth as sweet as honey*
> *Now I think I understand*
> *A plague on all your guilty houses*
> *Long and lonely nights*
> *One question begs another*
> *Why do I dream of body-snatchers?*

Rene's own career as a dancer and choreographer was starting to go well by now and she was booked with her company to perform her piece, *You In Your Small Corner* for three nights as part of the prestigious *Spring Loaded* Festival of Contemporary Dance at The Place in London in February. I helped her out where I could with music, driving and doing projections and so on, but our lives were just starting to take their own directions. She had her own dance company, Action Syndicate; when they weren't performing, she was either trying to raise finances for the next show from grant authorities or funding bodies, or she was teaching. We still shared a bed, and a closeness, and were mutually supportive of each other's work, but slowly, imperceptibly, I was moving away from her and thinking for the first time that we might not grow old together. It was odd, disturbing and slightly frightening, but I felt like we were entering the final act of our great love affair.

You In Your Small Corner was about childhood. Like all her work it was cinematically conceived and executed on a shoestring. For one scene, candles were the sole source of lighting, not for reasons of drama but for reasons of cost. Actually, the scene worked extremely well as it was played out in the candles' soft glow, to a hauntingly beautiful piece of piano music by Chabrier. She went on to show the work in Manchester, Brighton, Derby and Edinburgh. The Derby show could easily have been our last as, driving up the M1 near Northampton with the central prop of the piece – a double bed – tethered on top of the roof of our van, I was horrified on looking in my wing mirror to see that a sudden upward surge of wind had caused the bed to break free of its bonds and take flight. By some divine intervention no one was driving immediately behind us and those who were further back were able to take appropriate evasive action, but it was an horrifically dangerous moment. We gathered the battered prop together, all the while dodging between hurtling juggernauts, tied it once more to the roof and proceeded to Derby.

In April, Geno called me from Northbourne to tell me he had been appointed cricket captain for his final year. He was nearly 13 and understandably proud, but admirably modest, too. I was so thrilled for him to be given that honour in the last year of what had, despite the ups and downs, been a very happy five years at Northbourne. He repaid the faith the school showed in him by scoring 105 not out in a game that Rene and I had travelled down to watch on a beautiful summer afternoon. It was almost impossible for me to watch him batting as he entered the 90s, knowing how important a century was to him. When he hit the runs that secured it, it seemed like all the turmoil of his young life was lifted for this unforgettable intstant. Tears well up in my eyes even now as I remember the cathartic moment.

Throughout the first week of June he sat his Common Entrance exam and reported back each night by telephone. Generally his confidence grew with each paper he sat, and his nervousness, which sometimes prevented him from doing his best work in a high-stress situation, seemed to be under control. His last days at the school, sports day, speech day and playing the Artful Dodger in the school play, *Oliver!*, were among the happiest of his life to date. In the summer holidays he joined a local cricket club and seemed to be playing every-day. His Common Entrance exam result came through, and it was good enough to allow us to apply to Millfield School for a cricket scholarship, which, after a trial at the school, he was awarded. He had managed in two short terms to turn his entire life around and come out of a perilous situation and land on his feet. He obviously had inherited a lot of our genes.

I should have got an inkling of what was in store when I got a call in June from Sally de Souza, the producer of *Hamlet*, three weeks before the commencement of rehearsals. She said that the whole company had been recast, and asked me if I would consider doubling up roles and playing the first Gravedigger, a role which had been considerably expanded for this pro-duction, and one of the Players. Of course, after a suitably aggrieved pause, I agreed, and I was told that rehearsals would begin in Loughborough Town Hall in July. She asked me, in passing, whether I knew any multi-instrumentalists who might want to join the company for the duration, playing a variety of instruments live on stage and occasionally taking a small, non-speaking part. I offered up the name of the diminutive Scotsman who stood at my side in the studio, and after a short audition that week, he got the gig too.

This gave Jim and me just a week to finish off the album and managed it with a day to spare. We called the record *The Rest is Silence*; as these are the last words spoken by Hamlet, it seemed appropriate, and in July 1989, the album was released in Germany, Austria and Switzerland on Uli's World Music label.

* * *

I first met Charlotte in London with her sister, Dorothee, after the Cork Street summer party, when all the Cork Street galleries have an opening on the same night, and there are bands in the street and the drink flows all evening. If the weather is good, it is an enjoyable way to catch up with old friends. We went back to Dorothee and her husband Felix's flat for supper, then on to the Café de Paris to dance. A German, Dorothee was living in London, working at one of the major auction houses in the rare books department, but her baby sister was still living in Germany. I flirted with Charlotte and thought she was great fun. A tall, voluptuous brunette, with a fabulous big-mouthed smile, I thought she was very sexy, too. She was also the most un-rock and roll girl I had met in the previous 15 years. She was in London doing a short course – an introduction to English law – at the LSE as part of her Law degree at Munich University. My car at that time was a very old Volvo 240 estate, extremely robust but very heavy. Unfortunately, it no longer had a functioning reverse gear, which made parking a very precise science. I would always have to park facing up an incline, and use gravity as my reverse gear. When there was no incline, it called for brute force. Consequently, the English word that Charlotte heard from me most often was "Push!"

When the *Hamlet* cast were all convened in July to commence rehearsals, it quickly became clear that we were extremely fortunate that Lyubimov had agreed to direct for the Haymarket on two conditions. One was that we should have the finished set to rehearse in from the very first day. This is absolutely unheard of in British theatre. The set is usually completed in time for the last dress rehearsal, if luck is with you. The other condition was a demand for a rehearsal period of nine weeks (most British productions of Shakespeare rehearse for between three and four weeks). Both conditions were agreed to and it was with a mixture of excitement, anticipation and sheer terror that the cast assembled at Loughborough town hall that beautiful July morning.

At our first full-cast meeting with Yuri, an energetic, wild, white-haired inspiration in his early seventies, wearing ill-fitting blue jeans and horn-rimmed spectacles, he was anxious to explain his vision of *Hamlet* and to demonstrate the workings and possibilities of the set. The design was extraordinary, at once simple and breathtaking. It comprised a wooden floor with concealed lighting, and a wood and polished aluminium proscenium and backdrop, with a huge wooden cross from floor to ceiling on the back wall.

The single most striking feature, however, was a dun-coloured, coarsely-woven curtain, stretching the width and height of the stage. This curtain was suspended from a truss that could pivot through 360°, as well as being able to travel forwards, backwards and from side to side. It was an ingenious design with the ability to constantly change the performance space, to reveal and to conceal, and to sweep all before it. The grave, which was the fulcrum of the production, was hydraulically operated and set stage-centre front. In performance, a live rooster would be perched high on a proscenium upright and illuminated at key moments with a follow spot. It would either be encouraged to crow by the use of a stick, or a pre-recorded cock crow would be played.

Yuri said that the acting style would be the diametric opposite of Lee Strasberg, following more in the traditions of Meyerhold than Stanislavsky. He was very amusing when he talked about American actors and Method acting, which he described as "The unfortunate marriage of Stanislavsky to Freud". This style, he announced, produced too much talking and introspection. He wanted us to involve and engage the audience throughout, to lose the "fourth wall", and to be able to call upon the audience as supporters or witnesses at any time in the performance. The feeling in the company at the end of the meeting seemed to be one of heady anticipation for the work to come.

At the end of this first day we all separated and made our ways to our respective digs. I was determined to "pay my dues" on this project, so with the grim image of Tony Hancock drinking gin from a tooth-mug in my head, I headed for Fitzroy Street, Leicester.

My landlady had told me in advance that she would be away on holiday for the first week of my stay, but said that she would leave the front door key under a stone in her front garden. On arriving at the house I was wildly excited to notice a huge satellite dish in the front garden, angled towards the heavens. I retrieved the key from its hiding place, let myself into the house and unpacked the few clothes, toiletries and books I had brought with me. Taking a beer from the fridge, I decided to unwind a little with the novel delights of satellite TV. Zapping the remote control in eager anticipation, I was bitterly disappointed to find that the TV would only cough up the four terrestrial channels. Thinking that there was something wrong with the dish, I went outside into the garden to investigate, only to find to my embarrassment that the "dish" was, in fact, a round plastic garden table with a central hole for an umbrella, which had been blown over by the wind. It rather restricted my entertainment possibilities for the duration of my stay.

A few yards from my front door there was a sign on a meat-packing factory wall, which read, "When red light flashes, man trapped in deep freeze. please call police immediately". As this sign was rather off the beaten track, and as my hope of more orthodox entertainment had withered at the outset, I resolved to myself that at every available opportunity I would check to see if the light was flashing, and fantasised that I might possibly save some poor freeze-dried meat-porter from certain chilly demise, and perhaps even receive a judge's commendation for the quick-wittedness of my actions into the bargain. I also envisaged an eternally-grateful meat mogul offering me a lifetime's supply of fillet steak as a small token of his thanks. Sadly, for nine whole weeks that damned light never flashed once.

Every day seemed to throw up some new personal drama or another interesting story from Lyubimov, who loved to use them as a roundabout way to illustrate a point in the play, but as often as not he would tell them just to amuse himself and us. When directing Andrew Jarvis, a superb, shaven-headed actor playing Claudius, on the opening speech, which he wanted to be delivered like a speech at a political rally, he described the head of the KGB standing on Lenin's tomb after Stalin's death and making it perfectly clear that he intended to be the next leader. This story in turn led him into a merciless impersonation of Brezhnev, all clicking sounds, twisted mouth and bumbling incompetence. He remembered a time when Brezhnev's secretary had inadvertently handed Brezhnev three copies of the same speech, and was powerless to point out the mistake before the leader mounted the podium. He made the same speech three times and didn't even notice. The attitude and delivery was far more important than content.

By the first afternoon we were actually working on the set, and it became clear that Yuri loved playing around with sets like a child loves a train set. He told us:

> I once did a production of *The Three Sisters* in Moscow in a theatre in which the back stage wall was raised and lowered throughout the production, revealing a panorama of the whole of Moscow. One evening, the wall went up to reveal three tramps sitting just beyond it, with their vodka cups and sliced sausage all set out for the midnight feast. They looked like rabbits caught in car headlights. They bolted down the vodka, grabbed the sausage and ran.

He was a great source of advice about bits of business onstage, too. He described a piece of advice he had once given to a businessman friend who was cleaning his glasses. Without his spectacles, the friend's grotesque, bulging eyes were apparent. He was frighteningly ugly but completely normal as soon as the specs were replaced. Yuri advised his business friend that anytime he needed to grab a few seconds advantage in a business deal, he should repeat what he had just witnessed, stunning his adversary into silent passive observation, while he collected his thoughts and pulled a stroke. Some years later, the businessman attributed his considerable fortune to Yuri's piece of advice.

It was no surprise, then, that he told Lloyd Owen, who was playing Laertes, that his first scene in the play would be stood in front of an imaginary mirror squeezing his teenage spots. Lloyd is a hugely amusing person, simultaneously arrogant and insecure, but with a great sense of humour that ultimately rescues him from both his afflictions. I thought that this spot-squeezing scene was a bit much for any actor, but Lloyd told me with great glee that it was what he had actually done for Lyubimov in the audition. "And now the fat bastard is pretending it's *his* idea."

The early days were long but very absorbing, and usually the evenings were spent in the company of some of the other actors, eating, drinking or just exchanging stories. One night while we were rehearsing, the musical *Dames at Sea* was opening at the Main House, and we gate-crashed the party to enjoy the free food and drink. Spotting the star, the winsome Bonnie Langford, across the crowded room, I bet Lloyd a tenner that I could have her kneeling at my feet in five minutes. He was doubtful and took the bet on. I brought her over to where we were sitting, introduced her to the rest of the cast and asked if she would mind if we had a photo with her, as we were all such fans. She happily agreed and I said to her, "Would you mind kneeling here, just by me, so we can all get in the shot?" She gamely agreed, knelt at my feet and smiled for the camera. We thanked her, wished her good luck – and I collected my winnings from Lloyd.

At lunch the next day I sat with Lloyd and James Nesbitt, the Northern Irish actor who played Guildenstern (he has since become something of an unlikely heart-throb, switching on the blarney to shine in the hit TV show, *Cold Feet*). Yuri had announced that the first scene we would be rehearsing after lunch would be the Laertes scene, and Jimmy and I ribbed Lloyd mercilessly about the rough ride he was in for. Both Jimmy and Lloyd are brilliant mimics, and Jimmy was commentating on the imagined scene of Lloyd's rehearsal as if it were a sporting event – first in the voice of the Scottish rugby commentator, Bill McLaren, then as Richie Benaud, the Aussie cricketer. We were laughing hysterically and Lloyd was getting increasingly anxious.

We were horrified when we returned to the rehearsal, to find that Yuri had changed his mind and that the first scene would actually be the Gravediggers' scene, with Jimmy being told that in addition to Guildenstern he would also be playing the second Gravedigger. Unlike many of the other characters in the play, the Gravediggers speak in prose, not verse. Somewhere along the line some "additional dialogue" had been written for us, which was clumsy and ungrammatical, and we both felt uncomfortable with it. Jimmy, at least, is a trained actor and had some basic technique to fall back on, whereas I was like a fish thrashing around, convinced that Lyubimov would put me on the next train back to London, realising he had made a terrible mistake casting me.

Next up for the shock treatment was Jim. He played his bagpipes for the first time and they were completely deafening, only dropping to an acceptable volume when he was two rooms away. Yuri looked worried and surprised by the racket that they made, and a pow-wow was called to try to solve the problem. Other pipes were mentioned – Northumberland, Uillean and so on – and Jim was starting to fear an early return to Edinburgh was imminent. He hung on by assuring Yuri that if alternative pipes could be found, he would be able to play it.

He was whacked a second time when Michael Wassermann, Yuri's translator and assistant, announced that Yuri understood that Jim was also a highly competent one-man band, and that Jim had been practising for three weeks. Jim looked ashen and we tried to assemble on paper some sort of ensemble that he could master (bass drum, accordion, harmonica, kazoo) or failing that, a band that we could muster from the company's combined musical talents. We spent an afternoon in the theatre's studio trying out various combinations and eventually we constructed an ensemble for Jim to try, using a bass drum, a hurdy-gurdy, panpipes and a tambourine. His first attempts were cacophonous, but gradually he started to co-ordinate the various bits of his body needed to make the thing work. As he walked noisily through the theatre with the bass drum on his back and a hurdy-gurdy round his neck, he looked like a rampant medieval tortoise. He also looked a much happier man. He felt as though he was back on the bus to Tokyo, rather than the bus back to the Royal Mile.

I received two pieces of advice that day, which I have found useful ever since. One was from

Yuri, who advised, "Never stop yourself in a speech in rehearsal, no matter how badly you think you're doing it. By pushing yourself through to the other end you may pull something extraordinary out the other side." It is a wonderful tip and one that has been helpful in every acting job I have done since. The other piece of advice came from Danny Webb, the actor playing Hamlet, a generous, passionate and committed actor without pretensions. I told him over a drink that evening that I had found the day incredibly hard, and that I felt like a total impostor in this fine company of actors. He had noticed that I was struggling and quietly advised me, "In future, don't worry about trying to do to much in the first run-through you do, just familiarise yourself with the text, the situation you are in and why you are there. All the business can come later. You don't have to 'act' from the off. Let it find you." It was a suggestion that was as obvious as it was invaluable.

Rene sounded happy, too, that night when she called my digs. She had had a heavy rehearsal day, but had got a great review in one of the London listings magazine, and there was already interest from television in the next project she was about to start, a cricket opera in collaboration with Mick Jones from the Event Group. The choreography, she explained with characteristic enthusiasm, would be based on the movements used in cricket, and the "libretto" would be the names of the members of Mick's "dream England XI team" repeated *ad nauseam*. It would be called *A Perfect Action*. It is probably the only time in history that the names Boycott, Botham, Emburey and Edmonds have ever been sung onstage by a female chorale against a thunderous, hard-rock rhythm track. Did I say "probably"?

In time-honoured tradition, the female assistant stage manager (ASM) was the object of most of the unattached (and some of the attached) men's desires. She was young, blonde and extremely attractive. Unfortunately, she was the partner of the producer's son, who was also an ASM. The producer threw a party for the company one night after a rehearsal and most of the actors turned up on the off-chance that the ASM would be there. She was. Irish Jimmy and Scottish Jim were the main contestants, with one or two others in contention. It looked like she was out of bounds due to her rather delicate relationship to the producer, but this was not enough to deter Mr Nesbitt, who seemed to have something of the terrier about him now. He spent much of the evening turning on the charm while trying to keep the anxious boyfriend both amused and at bay. It was a sensational performance and, as we left the party that night, the smart money was on the boy from Belfast. The following morning he told us how he had gone by her bedroom window in the middle of the night and serenaded her with a couple of verses of *Danny Boy* in his finest schoolboy tenor, and we knew it was just a matter of time.

As the rehearsals progressed and time seemed to accelerate, inevitably there were occasions when tempers frayed and there were eruptions of temperament. These did not always come from where you would most expect them. Danny Webb, for example, seemed to take everything in his stride, despite the size of the part he had to learn and the unique significance that playing the Dane has in the English theatre. Andrew Jarvis seemed the most suited to the Russian's architectural, physical style, but we didn't know that below the surface he was having a rough time of it. Richard Durden, the actor playing Polonius, confided in me through gritted teeth after only a few days rehearsal, "If you can survive this, working with any other director will be a piece of cake!"

My relationship with Durden, who today is one of my closest friends, got off to a very bad start. During a break in rehearsals, I was flicking through a newspaper and my gaze fell on an article about Jonathan Aitken (the disgraced politician), the odious nephew of the newspaper magnate, Lord Beaverbrook. More to myself than to Durden I said, "Don't you find these Aitkens repulsive?" Richard looked shocked and said, "Why do you say that? Do you know I was married to Maria (Jonathan's actress sister) for seven years?" It was an inauspicious beginning to a relationship, but we became and remain the closest of friends, and for much of the time on the tour Durden and I were inseparable.

He is a charming and cultured man, with a wiry body and a craggy, weather-beaten face. He is blessed with impeccable manners and a deliciously waspish sense of humour. In addition, he is a wicked mimic and, like myself, a great lover of cricket. Unforgivably, he is a considerably better player than me. He didn't altogether enjoy the experience of working with Lyubimov, believing that the Russian was not sufficiently respectful of Shakespeare's text, and at one point the two of them had a memorable scorching row about some piece of direction that Durden felt undermined a scene. Lyubimov always respected Durden, though, because he had heard early on in the rehearsals that he had gone to Oxford, and Yuri was a great respecter of education.

I told Scottish Jim that, to avoid fraying tempers, he would do well the following week to stay in Leicester for the weekend and work with Gavin Bryars, the composer, who was acting in advisory role on the play, and build up some solid work to play Yuri. Gavin, a generous and fascinating man, best known for his minimalist orchestral works, *Jesus Blood Never Failed Me Yet* and *The Sinking Of The Titanic*, was Professor of Music at Loughborough Polytechnic at that time, and had offered Jim the use of the college's facilities over the weekend to develop some ideas for the play.

As rehearsals progressed further, the down-side of a "director's theatre" started to manifest itself, and many of the actors who were used to working in a very text-based style became exasperated by the seemingly endless interruption of scenes to adjust the position of the curtain, or for a music cue. Yuri works with the complete picture of a scene in his mind: the combination of text, action, lighting, costume and music. The British tradition, particularly when directing Shakespeare, is to work from the text upwards, adding visual embellishments to what is essentially a recitation of beautiful poetry. There are, of course, notable directors who are exceptions to this rule, but they have tended to have to look outside Britain or outside Shakespeare for critical acclaim. Most notably, the great Peter Brook comes to mind.

Lyubimov sometimes got exasperated if he thought we did not fully understand his vision. On one occasion, he wanted to illustrate a point about the nature of Rosencranz and Guildenstern's relationship with Claudius. He told an anecdote concerning Molotov's relationship with Stalin, which he thought would be helpful. Whenever Stalin summoned Molotov, his foreign minister, for a meeting, he would humiliate him by putting a cream cake on the seat on which Molotov, always wearing his best suit, would he obliged to sit. Molotov would stay in his seat for two hours or more, without registering the slightest facial response or reaction. It was an accepted part of the relationship between dictator and operative, and was repeated over and over without a word of complaint from Molotov. Time and again Molotov would leave Stalin's office with a cream cake stuck to the seat of his pants, a humiliatingly visible symbol of Stalin's need to dominate and Molotov's need to appear acquiescent and submissive. Stalin's nickname for Molotov was "Old Stone Arse".

Yuri once was drinking vodka with an old sailor who had served on a submarine in the war that Molotov had visited. The sailor assured Yuri that Molotov was "a good sort". "In what way?" enquired Lyubimov. "Well, that time he visited us he was walking through the submarine and hit his head on a door arch with such force that he dented the metal, but he didn't show a flicker of emotion or pain. A good sort."

On another occasion, to illustrate a similar point, Yuri told us of the time Stalin summoned the leader of the Soviet Composers' Union for a meeting, to tear him off a strip or two about some decadent formalist music that was being composed in Russia. The man was in such fear of Stalin that, as he was ushered into the great man's presence, he literally shat himself. Sniffing at the putrid air, Stalin ordered for him to be taken away, washed, changed and perfumed, and brought back in one hour. He referred to him ever after, with great distaste, as "shit-head". At the time of telling the story, that man was still the head of the Composers' Union. "Living in the West," he continued," you have no idea what it is like to live under a totalitarian dictatorship." Rather recklessly I got to my feet and said, "With all due respect, Yuri, after five weeks' rehearsals I think we're beginning to get some idea", and the company held its collective breath for a second. Yuri bellowed with laughter, shook my hand and fished around in his pocket for a coin, which he gave to me. I wondered whether it was a Russian theatrical tradition to give an actor a coin immediately before giving him the sack!!

While Lyubimov could be cantankerous, stubborn and a very difficult man to work with, he also had great charm, warmth and a disarming sense of fun. However peevish or exasperated one felt with him at times, it was difficult not to be won over by the geniality of this man who looked for all the world like a *Spitting Image* caricature of the British television comedian from the sixties, Harry Worth. He sent us home one weekend exhorting us to all be "off the book" (to know all our lines by heart) by Monday. "It is conceivable to rehearse prose with the book;" he declared." It is inconceivable to rehearse poetry with it."

As our opening night approached, and Yuri was keen to get the play moving at the right pace, he demonstrated a bizarre technique he had used in Russia to achieve this end. As we ran through the work in its entirety, he sat at the back of the auditorium with two torches in his hands. One of the torches had a green light, and one had a red light. Quite simply, when the play was moving too slowly he would flash the green light, visible only to us on stage, and when the play was going too fast he flashed the red. It was a crude but effective way of conducting the speed of the play, although it should be said that nearly *all* plays are played too slowly.

Because the play was a major theatrical event that year, a lot of television companies came up to Leicester to shoot scenes from rehearsals for broadcast in all the countries to which we would be travelling. When there were no TV cameras in, Yuri would direct from the back of the room, but the moment a camera started to roll he would be on stage, leaping into the grave or hanging from the curtain. He was a showman – some said a charlatan – who knew that he was bankable commodity and used the TV as his preferred medium for advertising. Sometimes, when Jimmy Nesbitt and I were doing the grave scene (a favourite for TV because it includes the famous "Alas, poor Yorick" speech), he would be lying on the coffin beneath us, artfully in camera-shot, "directing" the scene, while Jimmy and I did all we could to keep straight faces. (This was a problem we had for most of the tour. Nesbitt is an extremely amusing man, with a face that is funny without doing anything, the eyebrows permanently raised like two exclamation marks. He could convulse me with a twitch of the lip.)

The promotion of the play became a major consideration for the last couple of weeks of rehearsal and the theatre was keen to have me at the forefront of the publicity assault, despite the fact that my part was small, simply because they felt that they could use the *Batman* angle to sell the story. I must say I found it odd using *Batman* to sell *Hamlet*, but in the modern world anything goes. Even Lyubimov was impressed. Once, arriving inexcusably late for a rehearsal, I had prepared my apologies before I opened the studio door, and was about to blurt, "Maestro, I am *so* sorry. You see, what happened was . . ." He interrupted me, "Richard Strange – you are allowed. You are a superstar. *Batman! Batman!*" Like all good post-*glasnost* Russians, he can spot a brand-name or a label from a mile away.

While I continued to rehearse all through that summer, and Rene was doing performances and was in pre-production for *A Perfect Action,* Rene's sister, who lived in New York, invited Geno over to stay with them for a couple of weeks. It was a perfect arrangement, allowing Geno a holiday that we couldn't afford, and Rene and I the time to concentrate on our projects. The trouble with being freelance, as all artists effectively are, is that you cannot always choose the periods you will work.

We were fortunate to have a child as resourceful, undemanding and imaginative as Geno, who was always just as happy playing with inexpensive toys or sports equipment as his friends were with the latest designer models. Geno was growing up, and his identity and sense of self were becoming stronger and more defined by the day. Thirteen is a very important age for a boy. When he returned from New York, I was glad to spend a relaxed weekend with him and Rene, doing nothing special together, before driving him down to start his first term at Millfield. It was a sobering thought to know that, despite the scholarship award, I would still need to find the best part of £2000 a term, three terms a year, for the next five years to keep Geno at Millfield. But if you think about things like that too much, you could end up putting your head in the oven.

Hamlet finally opened, after a couple of successful previews, at the Haymarket Theatre on 19 September. Rene travelled up from London and it was great to feel both her emotional support and her physical presence again. After a frantic and delirious hour of reunion in bed at the hotel where we would stay the night, we strolled down to the theatre in time for lunch and I introduced her to whoever was around. After lunch we had to take notes from Yuri for an hour or so. He announced that he had been pleased with the previous night's final preview and his notes were delivered with relaxed good humour. He warned us that over the next eight months there would be a temptation to wallow in our roles as we became more familiar with them, but that we should resist the urge to embellish and decorate our performances; that we should go deeper into out characters, not wider. In subsequent years I have found this to be a very interesting and useful piece of advice.

There is a wonderful, mutually supportive vibe in the theatre, a genuine sense of common purpose. At worst this is what is referred to, with justifiable disdain, as "luvviedom"; it is superficial, self-congratulatory and bogus. But at its best you make friendships that last the rest of your life. In the nine weeks of rehearsal, we had effectively become one another's family. The closeness of the bond between actors during the creative process of rehearsal is a theatrical fact of life. It is, by definition, essential for us to form relationships with each other at a much faster rate than in any other profession, because the job we do is about, among other things, illustrating and describing relationships. When you add to this the fact that we were all separated from our partners or families and thrown together in a town unknown to us all for the rehearsal period, it is not surprising that it is impossible to explain even to one's nearest and dearest what the process is like. You are sustained by humour and stupid recurring in-jokes, which are, of course, meaningless or irritating to those on the outside.

We went up to a packed house and performed our best show so far. I was thrilled that I was actually doing it. The whole of the rehearsal period became real, and my terrible nervousness disappeared as soon as I was onstage. The energy level soared the moment the lights went down, and the power of the piece and our own adrenalin enabled us to overcome any exhaustion that we were feeling. There was a warm ovation at the end. Yuri joined us onstage for our second curtain call and milked it for three or four minutes. It was, for me, a truly unforgettable moment.

There was a lavish party at the theatre afterwards, with a constant stream of well-wishers. It was a fabulous end to an exhilarating day. As a leaving gift for Yuri, we presented him with a book of Gordon Craig's theatre designs, and his wife, Katya, paid us the compliment of saying that she thought the production was now as good as the original Taganka production of 1971. They departed for Budapest and thence to Moscow the next day. I knew that, despite all his exasperating foibles, I would miss his avuncular presence.

The sold-out run was accompanied by a bemused, bewildered and occasionally bitter press reaction. It was hated by *The Financial Times*, who rubbished every actor and the production as a whole. (I was called "clod-hopping," and I got off lightly). *The Daily Telegraph* and *The Times* were just as bad. *The Independent* was mixed, but liked Jimmy Nesbitt and myself for playing the Gravediggers with a "macabre gusto". Only *The Guardian* critic, Michael Billington was whole-heartedly positive. It seemed that many of the critics love the idea of "European director's theatre", but would rather not have it imposed on dear old Will, and certainly not in English!

None of the cast was surprised by the polarised responses that this production provoked and, indeed, we would have felt that we had rather failed in the brief if it had been reviewed as just another provincial theatre company doing just another *Hamlet*. But bad reviews really do hurt, no matter what anyone ever says to the contrary, and they have a most God-awful debilitating effect on the morale of a company. Any doubts that you might have had about the production are reinforced by adverse criticism, and one or two cast members took the reviews very hard indeed. It is not easy to commit yourself for a further eight months to a show that you have just realised you hate. In truth, Lyubimov had not devised this piece for the rarefied, class-obsessed atmosphere of English theatre, but as a vibrant, resonant and relevant production to tour the world. It was with some relief, therefore, that we left the Little England mentality behind us and set off on the world tour.

My tour started two weeks before anyone else's, as I had been asked by Uli to travel to Germany to do as much promotion for the album as I could before *Hamlet* took me away. In Munich one evening, the day's interview circus finished, I summoned up my courage to phone Charlotte, who was now studying Law there, to invite her to meet for a drink. She accepted and we met at a club called Schumann's, which was warm and crowded but somehow very cosy – *gemütlich,* as the Germans would say. Charlotte was there with some friends but seemed genuinely pleased to see me. We had some drinks and later walked back to her apartment. She made me supper, it was some sort of awful diet-menu ready-meal, but Charlotte presented it with such allure that I couldn't help but feel a certain stirring for her. She resisted my advances without a great deal of difficulty, but remained flirtatious and encouraging, and when I left her with just a chaste kiss on the cheek, I felt somehow curiously aroused and smitten.

I told her that we would be bringing *Hamlet* to Berlin in February and that she must promise to travel up to see it. She promised, but said that she might see me in London before then, as her sister Dorothee was be having a drinks party in December and she was sure we would all be invited.

The first shows we performed outside of the UK were in Rome, and while we were in that most beautiful, elegant and sexy city we were lucky enough to stay at the sumptuous Plaza Hotel on the via del Corso, right in the heart of the city. It is an extravagantly opulent hotel with a breathtaking, marbled ballroom that is lit by two hugely ornate crystal chandeliers. After depositing my bags and hanging up some very crumpled clothes in the closet, I made a quick telephone call to Dado Ruspoli to let him know that I was in town, and to invite him to come and see the play. I then set off on a grand walking tour of the immediate neighbour-hood with Jimmy Nesbitt and Jim Telford. Arriving back at the hotel there was a message from Dado saying that he had passed by and that I should call him.

We had a speed-reading of the play at lunchtime and then we had to do some scenes for Italian TV. I managed to speak to Dado and arranged two tickets for him for that night's opening. We agreed to meet for a drink at my hotel beforehand. I waited for Dado to show up at the hotel but, curiously, he didn't come, and I had to leave for the theatre without him.

That night we played a good, if not great performance, to a full house and the response was very warm. It was extraordinary to be doing the grave scene with the front row of the audience literally three feet away, and the highest tier of the boxes just 150 feet away. It did make knowing exactly where to pitch our voices a bit of a problem. With opera it would not matter, because the singers always need to be heard above the music, but with drama you need a rather subtler vocal dynamic.

The next morning I called Dado to find out why he hadn't made it along to the hotel or to the show and I immediately regretted making the call. He had not turned up at the hotel at seven, he told me, because his father had died at six. I felt awful for calling him, but he was very sweet. He obviously now had a great deal to do and I didn't want to take up any more of his time. I asked him to get in touch when he was next in London and he said he would. I expressed my sympathy and left him to get on with what must have been a very arduous and distressing day.

The Italian press were much kinder to us than they were to Rossini and the public reaction to the play throughout the 10-day run was a revelation. I have watched opera in Mediterranean countries before, so I was partially prepared for the spontaneous responses and partisanship that Latin audiences can bring to a performance, but I was really not prepared for the crescendoes of applause that would mark the end of a famous speech or the death of a much-enjoyed actor. These responses reached their peak during the Saturday matinee, performed to an audience comprised almost entirely of Roman youth, with an atmosphere strongly reminiscent of the Saturday morning pictures of my childhood. I kept thinking how much they would have enjoyed the live rooster, which had been an integral part of the run in Leicester, heralding from his perch high in the proscenium each momentous event onstage. Unfortunately, a combination of RSPCA inspectors and poultry-liberationists within the company had the wretched bird laid off. I couldn't help but muse on how many chickens would have given their right drumstick to work with Yuri Lyubimov.

The next day I telephoned Rene, who told me the sad news that Philip Core had died. It was not altogether unexpected as he had been ill with AIDS for a year, but it was still desperately sad to lose such an interesting and original friend. Ironically, two postcards, which I had chosen for Philip were next to my bed as we spoke.

A performance at 10am meant getting up at 7.30am, which was less than welcome. The show was actually (surprisingly) very well attended and, despite a bleary-eyed cast, well performed for the most part. There were fireworks, however, after my first scene, when Jimmy Nesbitt giggled once too often and I snapped. This had taken a while to come to a head, and I tore Jimmy's ear off for being a complete buffoon in every scene that we did together, for having no pride in his work, for corpsing every night and for trying to get me going. I told him that he was becoming a bore, that it wasn't just me who thought so and that he ought to grow up. He was stunned and shell-shocked by my outburst for the entire first act, but I thought it would do him some good. He had a respect for me that made him take the reprimand with some degree of seriousness. I subsequently felt terrible about the whole episode and apologised as soon as the show was over, but I told him that I had to get it off my chest and clear the air, as his tomfoolery was affecting my performances as well as his. He took it well and we had a drink together that evening and all was well. I do like him enormously but he had gone beyond the pale.

NEIL KINNOCK AND THE OLD VIC

Back in London again, I had time to unpack my suitcase, do my laundry and get to know Rene again. On Monday we moved into London's Old Vic theatre for a two-week run. As part of the promotion, we were invited by Neil Kinnock, the Leader of Her Majesty's Loyal Opposition, otherwise known as the unelectable Labour Party, to the House of Commons. Kinnock had gone a long way towards reforming the party but his destiny was to remain a spectator on the opposition benches, rather than rule as Prime Minister. Kinnock was one of a triumvirate of fundamentally decent men who would spend their years as party leader in the political wasteland of opposition – the others being Michael Foot, whose misfortune was to lead at a time when then cut of your politics mattered less than the cut of your suit, and John Smith, whose premature death led to the coronation of Tony Blair.

Kinnock received us warmly in his office at the House of Commons, gave us coffee and biscuits and talked with both enthusiasm and some knowledge of the play. It was impossible to imagine that his nemesis, Margaret Thatcher, had ever been in a theatre, or even read a book for that matter. His oak panelled room was hung with trades union banners, and for the hour we were there it was impossible not to like the man. Those of us who managed to drag ourselves out of bed early enough for the meeting included Yuri, Danny (with a name like Webb he was, of course, duty-bound to be a dyed-in-the-wool socialist), Lloyd, and a few others, plus myself. It was an interesting hour, which culminated with Kinnock showing us the empty chambers of both the Commons and the House of Lords. We sentimentally wished him well in the next election, but didn't hold our breath.

We opened at the Old Vic on the 20 November, and it was wonderful to be in London and to be able to invite our friends, families and agents along to see the play and to enjoy a drink with them afterwards. Rene, Sophie, Mum and Michelle all came to the opening night, which was well received by the public, less well by the critics. Geno came another night and was fascinated to be shown around that wonderful theatre, to stand on its hallowed stage, to get into the grave and to hold Yorick's skull. He also loved, like any 13-year-old, to be taken to a smart restaurant, be given a good dinner and be allowed to take the next day off school.

The additional benefit of working in London was that my days were my own. I did not need to be at the theatre until "the half" (the bell that sounds backstage half an hour before curtain up), to get into costume and into character. I spent my time with Rene or catching up with friends, doing general admin and resting, in the relative financial comfort of knowing that for the next six months, there was some regular money coming in weekly. This was a novelty for me, not having seen regular money since the £25 a week Morrison allowed us in 1976.

Rene was by now totally immersed in her own projects. It was inevitable. Being an artist is hard at the best of times and the only way to have any chance of success is to devote yourself to it 100 per cent, often to the detriment of personal relationships. Artists are driven people. Not very often driven by money, but sometimes by ambition or by a desire for celebrity, and most often because they are temperamentally unsuited to any other type of work. They will work hours, days, weeks on end on a project for no financial return, for no appreciation or acclaim, simply because it is the work that makes them feel that they are most alive. We knew that, at the end of the Old Vic run, I would be spending most of the next six months out of England, and we tried to see as much of each other as we could for those two weeks.

When we finished our run at The *Old Vic*, there was break of a few days, during which Dorothee invited us to a cocktail party at her house. It was her birthday and she had invited about 30 people for cocktails and some food. I went with Rene and as soon as we arrived I saw Charlotte across the room, and my heart leapt. I introduced Rene to her and we chatted for a couple of hours. The party was a very relaxed affair, full of the usual Eurotrash who always frequent those parties in Kensington and Gloucester Road – the minor aristos, the expat German, French and Italian bankers, the horsey home-counties girls who sell over-priced cushions to overfed dowagers, and preppy Americans doing a course in Art History at the Courtauld Institute before returning to work for pop. It was fine, but in that room, that night, all I saw was Charlotte.

In London for Christmas 1988, this time quiet and with the family, Rene, Geno and I headed for Scotland for New Year. The McEwens, generous and hospitable to a fault, accepted Rene and Geno into their house like long lost friends. We broke our journey north to stay with Danny Webb and his wife, Leila, who had rented a cottage in Lochgoilhead in Argyll. We spent a wonderful evening and night there, with delicious food and drink, and gentle relaxed company. Geno played tenderly with Danny and Leila's small daughter and it felt close to perfection. The following day we left for Bardrochat, where we stayed to see in the new decade with a houseful of guests including all the McEwens, Bunter and Tracy Worcester, James Fox (the author of *White Mischief* and *The Langhorne Sisters*, and a very accomplished guitarist to boot), and Jools Holland, who was by now living with Sophie's cousin, Christobel. The house was full of music every night, with Alexander McEwen, James, Jools and myself providing accompaniment for anyone who wanted to sing. It was that New Year at Bardrochat that rekindled my love of live music in private homes. I would so much rather hear a musician play the piano or a guitar, or a poet declaim a poem at dinner, than listen to the irritating subliminal muzak of Simply Red or Dire Straits, who were ubiquitous at that time.

The 1980s had been a thrilling, exhilarating decade for me, full of the excitements of success, travel and new friendships. I had been all but washed up after The Doctors' split at the end of the seventies, and somehow got through another 10 years without doing a proper job! Rene's solo career was slowly taking shape and Geno was in a school where he was able to develop his skills and talents as far as his own self-discipline and ambition would take him.

It had been the decade of yuppies, of greed and of solipsism. A decade where the twin doctrines of Thatcherism and Reagonomics had torn the heart out of communities on both sides of the Atlantic, and put in its place the veneration of easy money and cheap celebrity. All that is crass, ignoble and mundane, all that is self-serving, down-dumbing and blood-sucking found in the eighties a willing host. It was the decade of Keith Talent and Sherman McCoy and Bananarama, of AIDS and MTV, of Chernobyl and Tiananmen Square. The decade of Black Monday, *Rambo* and aerobics. And it was the decade of the worst excesses of *The Sun* who, tapping into the repellent jingoism and puerility into which the country had slid, led with headlines such as the sick *Gotcha!,* when the Royal Navy, at Maggie's request, sank the retreating Argentininian cruiser, *General Belgrano,* outside the exclusion zone with the loss of over 300 men, or *Freddie Starr Ate My Hamster* when there was nothing as amusing as a war going on.

The Nineties

FALLING IN LOVE AGAIN

As luck and the touring schedules would have it, I was back in London for 25 January, but we didn't celebrate my birthday that day because it fell on the same day as Philip Core's memorial service. It was held at Leighton House, in Holland Park, as befitted an aesthete like Philip, and the evening was distinguished by two beautiful French songs, Reynaldo Hahn's *L'heure exquise* and Henri Duparc's *L'invitation au voyage*, which were movingly sung by the soprano, Patricia Rosario. I spent the evening with Louisa Buck, whom I had originally met through Philip, and her boyfriend, Tom, who I liked more and more each time we met. We had a quiet dinner afterwards and went home. The following day we celebrated my birthday and Burns Night with a dinner for 10, followed by a very drunken party for 50.

The next leg of the itinerary took us first to Germany and then on to Copenhagen. I was glad that the production went to Copenhagen as I was able to meet up with my brother, Brian, whom I had seen only infrequently since he had moved there all those years ago to salvage his sanity. I also met up with Birgitte, my sixties sweetheart, who had brought me to Copenhagen (where I had bought that first guitar) over 20 years previously. Somewhere on a German autobahn, as we hurtled between Copenhagen and Antwerp in our legendary luxury coach, we heard on the radio that Nelson Mandela had at last been released from his prison on Robben Island. It was 11 February and the whole bus was elated. (Most actors are pinkos at heart!) While we all had great hopes for the eventual future of South Africa under Mandela, I don't think any of us, even in our most sentimental moments, dared believe that the proud, dignified figure who walked from his cell that day, freed after 27 years of imprisonment, would end the millennium as the most widely admired man in the world, and one of the few true international heroes of the late twentieth century.

A few days later I heard the distressing news that Keith Haring had died. With Keith the news did not come as much of a shock as we all knew that he was ill, and we were reluctantly getting used to so many of our friends dying from AIDS. What had been a trickle in the early eighties, when I heard about Klaus Nomi's death, had turned, if not into a flood then at least into a steady, relentless stream by the end of the decade; now it wasn't only happening to other people's friends, it was happening to mine.

From Antwerp we flew to Berlin, and in that week in Berlin my life changed. We were staying at the grimly functional Hotel Hervis (or Hotel Herpes as we soon dubbed it) on Stresemannstrasse, very near to Potsdamerplatz and the Wall. It was a featureless, glass building with featureless staff. I was astonished to be handed a parcel on my arrival by the receptionist and I had no idea who it was from as I made my way to my room. We were allocated single rooms as usual, and as I unpacked my suitcase in my tiny dark cell and lay on my bed, my gloom was lifted first by the package, which contained a silly belated birthday present from Charlotte, and then by the ringing telephone. It was Charlotte and she had arrived in Berlin, staying at her friend's house. "Would you like to come out with us tonight?" she asked. There was one small complication – she was with her boyfriend, but I was welcome to join them for dinner or a drink at Florian's on Grolmanstrasse. By way of encouragement, however, she did say that she had a lot of plans for the next day for just the two of us. Minutes later she arrived at the hotel with a girlfriend, both girls six feet tall and looking fabulous and exotic, and drove me away from the hotel. We had a good dinner and moved on to another bar before parting some time after midnight.

The following day Charlotte came to the hotel with a car planning to take me to Potsdam for an excursion, but my passport was at the Japanese embassy in Berlin awaiting a visa for Japan, and it was not possible in those days before reunification to travel in East Germany without a passport. Instead, she treated me to a wonderful tour of the city, which was in absolute turmoil since the historic breaching of the Wall the previous November. Everywhere we went the *Mauerspechte* (literally "the Wall-sparrows") were hammering away at the Wall, the all pervasive chip-chip-chip of their tools ringing in the crisp winter air as they removed fragments – anything between a flake and a boulder in size – for souvenirs or for resale to the thousands of tourists who were flocking in.

Being in Berlin that month put the whole tumultuous sequence of historical events of 1989 into some sort of graphic reality. Beginning with the election of Mikhail Gorbachev as chairman of the Supreme Soviet of the USSR in May, through Poland's first free election (June), Hungary opening its border (October), East Germany opening the Berlin Wall (November), the execution of the Ceausescus in Romania (December), and the election of Vaclav Havel as president of Czechoslovakia (December), the course of history had unfolded in a way that had been unthinkable only a year previously. It is perhaps surprising to learn that, according to Gorbachev, Ronald Reagan, that man we think of as a bumbling, ineffectual intellectual pygmy was responsible, more than any other human being on earth, for setting in motion the break up of the Soviet empire.

That bright, freezing morning Charlotte and I went to the Reichstag and the Brandenburg Gate, where thousands of East Germans were continuing to swarm, their eyes filled with wonder and disbelief, as they stood mesmerised by what had happened. In some of the stretches of the Wall there were holes big enough for a man to climb through, and they did it, over and over again like delirious children, through the hole from East to West and back again. And again. And again. Elsewhere they sat atop the wall their arms aloft, mimicking the heady scenes of the previous November that were beamed around the world. Bemused border guards, once so hated on both sides of the Wall, still armed but now redundant, were reduced to the role of uniformed extras in other people's home movies. They must have been wondering what the future held for them, too. I shot still photographs and super-8 movie films, eager to record the extraordinary scene for myself, to replay years hence when my memory has failed.

For every West Berliner I spoke to, the prospect of unification held no appeal whatever. The period of euphoria that greeted the breaching of the Wall in November was well and truly over, and the West Germans were now afraid for their jobs, their security, their homes and their economy. They found their Eastern brothers and sisters uneducated and unsophisticated philistines. It seemed that even the Turks and the Yugoslavs, the traditional under-class in West German society, were frightened that the East Germans would take their jobs because they would be prepared to do them for less money. It was a curious reversal of the normal.

And all the while, the beautiful Charlotte was at my side, chatting and laughing, supplying cultural information and historical background, her lawyer's mind adding an analytical dimension, and generally being the dream companion. Eleven years younger than me, it was odd to be with someone who hadn't grown up with the first Velvet Underground album as part of her own personal teenage soundtrack. We photographed each other at the Wall, scaling the Wall and going through the Wall. We drove to Kreuzberg, the punky, funky Turkish neigh-bourhood of Berlin, for coffee and the day miraculously warmed up to such an extent that we sat outside on the terrace for an hour. We then moved on to a muddy swamp that was home to the Polish flea market. The traders had makeshift pitches between the puddles, selling the sort of goods that anyone coming from Poland might bring with them – a carton of duty-free cigarettes, vodka, wooden chess sets, drab clothes and the occasional ornament. We bought some food in a supermarket and cooked an early dinner together. We sat down on the sofa like teenagers and shared a Walkman. Later she went out with her boyfriend and I went back to the hotel to read, but I couldn't really concentrate on anything. I was in Marlene Dietrich's city and what could I do? I was falling in love again, never wanted to, what am I to do? I can't help it.

The following day was our opening show, so most of my time was spent at the theatre doing a tech-run and getting back into the swing. The theatre, the Hebbel, was an attractive 1930s building that had been unused for years until it was bought by an independent production company that were determined to make it the most influential and ambitious theatre in Germany – and they succeeded. Apart from our *Hamlet*, over the years that I have been going back to Berlin they have shown new plays by Robert Wilson and Tadeusz Kantor, as well as dance and music from Pina Bausch and Laurie Anderson. The auditorium has an intimate feel, in stark contrast to the theatre we had used in Antwerp, which had the atmosphere of a municipal sports hall. The opening night performance was a huge success with the sell-out audience, but not with Yuri, who arrived backstage afterwards in a black mood and called us all for a notes session the following day. After the play Charlotte and I went for a drink with the rest of the company, then on to a quiet bar alone.

She arranged to pick me up again the next morning and we spent the day in the castle and gardens of Charlottenburg, in Berlin. Although parts of the baroque palace are very beautiful, I was rather disappointed with the building and the art that it contained. The gardens are mostly formal, in the French style, but we wandered through them and found an English-style oasis, much freer with brooks and streams and some delightful surprises. Once again the day was enjoyably warm and we stayed in the garden for two hours. I asked her incredibly impertinent questions about her love life, which she answered tangentially or enigmatically. Her answers to my most direct questions only served to confuse me further. Over coffee she told me she had to return to Munich the following day for an exam, and I knew that saying goodbye to her was going to be heart-wrenchingly hard.

She dropped me off at the theatre for the notes session and went off to her friend's house to revise for her exam. Yuri, looking older and tired said he felt a hostility from us at coming to try to reclaim his baby, but that hostility did not come from the entire company, just certain sections of it. I flew out of the notes session to catch a last hour with Charlotte who suggested that if the Hotel Herpes was too miserable, I could stay at her friend's house instead. I said I would love to do that, to get a bit of a break from everyone and to be alone to think. She drove me to the flat and showed me how everything worked. The boyfriend was there and it was torture saying goodbye as she handed me the keys, and not being able to take her in my arms and kiss her goodbye. Instead I was polite and charming, jollying her along and wishing them well as we parted, they to the airport and me back to the theatre for a rehearsal.

Yuri's notes were gruelling for most, but Jimmy Nesbitt and I had come out of the session smelling of roses. "The funniest Gravediggers scene ever" was his verdict but, unable to give a note without a suggestion for improvement added, "But Richard, put more salt on the egg." He was referring to the hard-boiled egg that I cracked every night on Yorick's skull during the scene. The notes session finished at five, and I had to immediately dash across Berlin to do an interview with someone who clearly wished he was elsewhere, and then sing two songs live for a TV programme.

The shows at the Hebbel were uniformly good, and it was a wonderful feeling having the audience so close to the stage and feeding off their excitement and enjoyment. After that night's show I took Nesbitt to the Schneecafé. It was a bar run by Bea and Martina, two girls I knew from my days as a musician, and at midnight they closed the place to the public and the four of us just drank and danced and goofed around until six in the morning. Nesbitt thought he had died and gone to heaven, having a bar almost to himself, and he asked the girls if they would let him be barman for the night. They readily agreed and I have never seen one man derive so much pleasure from washing glasses and pouring whiskies as Jimmy Nesbitt did for those few drink-sodden hours.

I slept that night in the bed that Charlotte had slept in just the night before, which I found incredibly erotic. The following morning, appallingly hungover, I wandered the streets of Berlin in an adolescent, lovesick daze. I went to a couple of galleries, the Martin-Gropius-Bau and the Bauhaus Archiv, and tried to get my thoughts in some sort of order. On returning to the hotel, I was greeted by a phone call from Charlotte, saying that she would be returning to Berlin on the first plane the next morning, and would meet me at the flat. I told her I would be sleeping there that night and she said, "Good". My heart soared, even though I knew I was heading for major trouble somewhere down the line.

The following morning she arrived, and our reunion was as wonderful a moment of matutinal ecstasy as I had dared imagine it would be. I wondered if and how I would tell Rene what had been happening to my heart in Berlin. I wondered if things would return to normal after a couple of days on the road, but I had a nagging suspicion that they wouldn't.

After we dressed we drove to the hotel for breakfast, then to the zoo to change some money into East German marks. We had decided that now that I had my passport back, we would spend the day in the East. We took the subway to Friedrichstrasse, the main crossing point from the West. We made our way to a smart restaurant where mediocre food was served in grand style on silver platters with huge silver domes, and devoured a vast lunch for the equivalent of £3 a head. Then we headed for the main event – the horse-racing track at Karlshorst. When we arrived at the track, we were hysterical with anticipation, and enjoyment of the ridiculousness of what we were doing – horse racing in East Berlin. By the time we arrived we only had time to watch one race, won by a 13-year old horse who looked like he should keep on going to the knacker's yard. The whole spectacle was completely ludicrous.

That night was our last in Berlin. After a dinner together, Charlotte stayed with me at the Hotel Herpes as I had to be up at the crack of dawn to depart. Despite getting up at 6.30 I still managed to be last on the bus at eight o'clock. As we parted, neither of us had any idea what the future held for us, but we felt sure that we hadn't just played out the last scene.

At Heathrow I was met by Rene and Geno. We had lunch together and by the evening I had told Rene everything that had happened but, in truth, not everything that I had felt. She took it in with a sigh of familiar resignation and that night we went to Sophie's for the whole evening, drinking, chatting and laughing. It was a brilliant evening to arrive back to, and Berlin had behaved true to form. I felt shattered, hyper, happy and mad. Rene looked beautiful and so did Geno. I thought, "What an undeservedly lucky bastard I am."

I was in London for the weekend before setting off very early on the Monday for the longest leg of the tour, to Australia and the Far East. Rene drove me to the airport in appalling traffic in time for a nine o'clock check-in. As we kissed each other goodbye I had no idea how final that kiss would prove to be.

From the airport, with practised deceit, I phoned Charlotte and pleaded with her to call me in Australia. She said she would.

Twenty-three hours after taking off from Heathrow, having watched the sunrise from the plane over Bangkok, a blood-red slit in the sky which started to haemorrhage daylight, we landed in Perth, Western Australia. It was early evening. We were transported to our hotel where we all had suites with kitchens and fridges, which suggested we might be able to save some money on restaurant bills. After a shower and a short rest, we headed down to the Perth Festival Club, where George Melly and Georgie Fame were playing. As we were participating in the Perth Festival, we got free membership to the Club (and reduced-priced drinks) for the duration of our stay.

It was such a joy to sit outdoors in a T-shirt in February, in the middle of the Australian summer, drinking a cold beer and listening to Melly's bizarre Bessie Smith-Fats Waller hybrid. We didn't stay too late, hoping that if we could get a good night's sleep we would defeat the worst of the jet lag. I called Charlotte from my bed to tell her that I had arrived and to give her the telephone number of the hotel. Chatting on the phone, hearing her attractively low, sexy voice, relieved my feelings of separation from her momentarily but ultimately served only to remind me of how far apart we were. Hanging up the phone, I gazed at the ceiling and realised how deeply in love I had fallen.

At His Majesty's Theatre, a most lovely late-nineteenth century stuccoed building, like a white wedding cake, the opening night show was sold out and was played by a cast suffering variously from jet lag and sunstroke with Nesbitt's face, in particular, a livid, vicious red, looking like it was on the point of self-immolation.

The next day began well with a telephone call from Rene, in good spirits, telling me she had won the coveted Bonnie Bird Choreography Award, for which she would receive £1000 at the South Bank Centre, and a commission to choreograph a new piece. It was great news and a fantastic boost for her confidence at this most crucial time. I was delighted for her and proud that she had made Action Syndicate a viable entity, but at the same time I was worried. Rene is, and always has been, to a lesser or greater degree, a manic-depressive and, as anyone who has lived with a manic-depressive knows, depression and sadness are not the same thing. That should be shouted from the rooftops for the benefit of all who don't know. Depression, when it strikes, can be triggered by anything, and by nothing. It is as likely to be triggered by good news as by bad, and I worried that the award and the commission might send her into the spiral. The award symbolised approval of her work and she could easily and illogically have felt unworthy of that approval, and feelings of inadequacy could have made her terrified at the prospect of having to choreograph a high-profile piece. Her condition may be genetic, since both her mother and her grandmother suffered from it, but either way, that is no comfort to her or anyone else. The feeling of powerlessness, mixed with frustration, which the partner of a manic-depressive feels in a relationship is indescribable. Watching a loved one sinking and soaring independently of the love, care or attention that she receives is both devastating and destructive. It requires the patience of a saint to take that on for life. I am not a saint.

Because of the time differences between Munich and Perth, Charlotte's telephone calls would wake me at unpredictable times. One night she called me at the end of a long session of studying. She was quite mad, very affectionate, criminally extravagant and was seriously talking about flying out to Hong Kong to meet me at the very end of the tour.

* * *

Our week in Perth passed all too quickly, swimming and fooling around when not working, or going to the odd cricket match with Durden, and we decamped to Adelaide for more of the same. Adelaide is a much rougher town than Perth, and Hindley Street, where were staying, has the reputation of being the roughest street in the whole of Australia on a Friday and Saturday night. It did seem particularly unsavoury at night: the sidewalks strewn with alcoholics, junkies and glue sniffers, and Aboriginals slumped in doorways, wretchedly poor and ruined by the drink that their bodies lack the gene to metabolise.

Once again we were playing in an international arts festival, the Adelaide Festival being considerably bigger than that of Perth, and once again we had enough time on our hands in the daytimes to explore the environs, enjoy the local wine and food and relax. The joy of doing festivals is that you meet up with old friends on the other side of the world who you didn't even know were there. Sarah Sankey was an actress I had met through Coulter and Sarah-Jane. She was a fabulously attractive, six-feet-two-inch, big-boned, fleet-footed, busty, shaven-headed Amazon, who was working in Adelaide with the French alternative circus Archaos. She was not in great shape, physically, covered with bruises and scratches, but she is so charismatic that when you sit with her on a terrace somewhere quietly chatting and sipping tea, you are automatically the centre of attention.

That night, at a desperately boring dinner in a Greek restaurant with our local sponsors, I telephoned Sankey, told her where I was and asked her to rescue me. She arrived 15 minutes later looking absolutely heroic, like a cross between an SAS commander and Tank Girl, all Kalashnikov machine guns and Chanel No 9. She entered the restaurant as if she were a stun-grenade, and every mouth gaped open, fork frozen in space, as the Amazon swept me out to her waiting jeep and we sped off to a barbecue being given for Archaos. Within 15 minutes of arriving I was under a table in deep conversation with a girl called Felicity; after a further 20 I was in the front of a sports car being driven by a drunk man I had never met along the main Adelaide street at over 100mph. It was terrifying and exhilarating. I remember thinking "Tonight I am going to die in Adelaide in dubious circumstances, intestate, insolvent and inebriated."

One thing you notice about Australian cities is how tenuously the wilderness beyond the suburbs seems to be held at bay. You feel that at the end of the last suburban street, the outback starts. Dark, mysterious and primeval. A savage terrain, a hostile climate and the remnants of an impenetrable earlier civilisation. You imagine that if the family in the final suburban house forgot to mow their lawn one Sunday afternoon, the wilderness would start to reclaim the city again.

At the main Adelaide Art Gallery I saw an exhibition of dreamings, Aboriginal paintings, while outside the gallery Aboriginals drank themselves to an intoxicated oblivion or a glue-induced catatonia. They are dislocated from their rural roots yet excluded from urban (meaning white) society, so they miss out both ways in what is essentially a deeply racist society. The Aboriginals share the same status as the Native Americans in the United States, that is, the status of the dispossessed, which is even lower than the status of the immigrant. There is no "ghetto fabulous" sartorial-style among the Australian Aboriginals, just a general sense of being down at heel for 200 years.

The whites, on the other hand enjoy enormous relative wealth and value-added lifestyle. Generally, they look unquestionably fitter and healthier than their European counterparts. They are leaner, leggier, have better teeth, skin and hair. They are not a brainy, intellectual nation though: they are good at "doing things" – medicine, engineering, publishing or business but seem, as a whole, to lack intellectual sharpness or curiosity. The television in Australia is truly appalling, with soaps on every channel, and the television news is more parochial, insular and isolationist than even that of the USA. They are, however, a genuinely generous and hospitable people, at least they are if you happen to be white, who are immensely proud of their country.

One show in Adelaide sticks in the memory. Out of sheer and wholly unprofessional bravado, I played an entire scene stark naked beneath a long raincoat. Every time I delivered my lines upstage I held the raincoat wide open so that the poor actors and actresses saw everything, but as soon as I turned down stage, towards the audience, I closed the coat and looked perfectly chaste. The poor company were trying to deliver their lines with tears running down their faces, as they struggled to keep it together. Offstage, an incandescent Durden, who had been more affected by the outrage than anyone, assured me that "Six years ago I would have physically put you offstage." It was unforgivable but symptomatic of the hysteria that starts to creep into a company after six months together. I felt bad about balling out Jimmy Nesbitt a couple of months earlier for unprofessionalism.

The show could not have been too bad, though, because at the reception afterwards a moustachioed businessman buttonholed Nesbitt and me, and asked if we would be interested in a small business proposition. Intrigued we asked him to elaborate. He said:

> My name is John Duncan. They call me Dunky the Death around here because I have the biggest undertaking business in South Australia. I have a big funeral up-country tomorrow and I couldn't help but notice the technique that you two showed in lowering the coffin into the grave tonight. I don't have any blokes on my books with those sorts of moves. I would pay you three hundred bucks each, fly you up and back in my private jet and assure you there will be some Sheilas around at the party afterwards. What d'you say?

It was tempting but since we had a show to do the following evening and there was just a bit too much scope for things to go wrong, we politely declined. I have always regretted that decision.

The morning we had to catch the first flight from Adelaide to Tokyo, I asked Charlotte to wake me with a 4.15am call. I suspect I was incoherent but we still managed to talk for a quarter of an hour. In the lobby a ramshackle, bleary-eyed assembly had mustered. Danny was looking 100 per cent feral by now, totally wired and hyper but never losing it completely. Killing an hour and a half at Adelaide Airport, the most boring airport in the world, is like spending a week anywhere else. I was by now tetchy, exhausted and withdrawn. I listened to three albums endlessly: Elvis Costello's *Spike*, Aztec Camera's *Love* and the second House of Love album, the one with *Shine On*. Three albums of beautifully crafted poignant pop. They soothed my aching heart as I yearned to be with Charlotte again, and wondered how I would resolve all this with Rene and Geno.

The 10-hour flight to Tokyo across the vast Australian interior, Papua New Guinea and the Pacific Ocean, offered little in the way of amusement. When I tried to sleep I felt too hyper, and when I tried to read my eyes refused to stay open. We finally touched down around six or seven in the evening, too dark to see anything and with a 40-mile bus ride from the airport to the city to set the seal on my exhaustion. It was with a great sense of relief that we finally checked into our hotel. I grabbed my key, headed for the elevator, found my room, crashed out and slept a dreamless sleep for 12 hours.

The following morning I felt restored and relaxed, and ready to start all over again. I met Lloyd and Terry Wilton, the actor who had replaced a disillusioned and exhausted Andrew Jarvis as Claudius, and by now known to all as "the Skipper", at breakfast, and the three of us decided to take advantage of three free days while the stage was installed at the theatre. We decided to head inland and make a round trip to Koriyama, Aizu Wakamatsu, Nikko and back to Tokyo. We bought guidebooks, packed rucksacks and headed for the station, all three eager with anticipation.

The culture shock of arriving in Japan after Australia is enormous. The feeling of confusion is heightened by the impenetrability of the Japanese language and alphabet. None of us really had any idea what we would see, how much it would cost or how we would cope outside of Tokyo without speaking a word of Japanese between us. On the underground train to the station we started to get our first experience of the bizarre diversity of Japanese life: school-girls in sailor suits; school boys in high-collared, brass-buttoned jackets with military style caps; Western-suited "salarymen"; kimono-clad beauties and pensioners; and venerable, traditionally-dressed monks or elders in their finely detailed clothes in the most dazzling of colours, and with divided socks and wooden soled sandals – all travelling on the same subway.

On the mainline train we headed north-east out of Tokyo. The suburbs sprawl forever, a mass of unco-ordinated buildings, neon lights, overhead cables and flyovers before you hit the first hint of rural life. Then we began to see paddy fields, already planted with rice, partially flooded by an elaborate irrigation system and worked by traditionally-clad farmers. It was like travelling in time. Here and there, trees were being trained to grow in a certain way, with the aid of a system of ropes and crutches, to coax the branches to grow upwards. In the setting sun it all looked very Dali-esque.

By the time we reached Koriyama it was dark. We found a hotel and shared a traditional-style room, with tatami mats and futons on the floor, rice paper screens and low tables. It was very simple, very minimalist and very comfortable. We drank overpriced beer in the hotel's top-floor bar high above the town, watching the bullet trains bisect the darkness and yearning to be on one, and wondering at how far from home we were and what an adventure this whole tour had been. Lloyd and Terry Wilton were great company in their very different ways: Terry older, more experienced and with a sort of home-spun wisdom and sensitivity; Lloyd young, brash, confident and exuberant, ambitious and seeming to know exactly where he wanted to go. I have rarely come across a 23-year-old so mature beyond his years and yet such a brat. He reminded me of my 23 year-old self. I felt that he would go far.

The following day we took the train to Aizu Wakamatsu to visit the fabulous Samurai residence from the Edo period. It is a fascinating, intact structure, perched on a hill and made up of temples, shrines, reception rooms and living quarters. I was struck by the simplicity of the structures, the clean lines and the restraint of the decor. It is easy to understand how

Japanese and Zen design has become the blueprint for western modernists. From Aizu our journey continued by train, with one of the best railway journeys I have ever undertaken, around Lake Inawashiro, through stunning mountain scenery, deep gorges, past bottomless green lakes and spectacular forests to the ancient city of Nikko.

We were only a couple of hours by train from Tokyo, capital of probably the most highly technological society in the world, yet here we were in a world of startling simplicity, with methods of farming, planting and irrigation that had remained largely unchanged for centuries. Babies were still carried in slings on their mother's backs. Buzzards circled high above the pine forests.

In our Nikko hotel we shared a corner room that offered two magnificent views of the surrounding mountains, including the spectacular Mt Nantei, snow-peaked and imposing. An added, unexpected bonus was that the hotel was actually a spa hotel with its own hot spring. Naturally, the three of us were in there like a shot. Observing the arcane rituals of Japanese bathing, the squatted shower, the soaping outside of the bath, the rinsing off on a low stool, we eased ourselves into the bubbling, boiling cauldron and gently simmered. It was pure heaven. After dinner we lay on our futons telling stories, until first Lloyd and then the Skipper drifted off, like bearded babies, into deep contented silent sleep. I slept fitfully, and thought of Charlotte and Rene and what to do.

At dawn I looked though the blinds and saw one of the greatest sights of the whole trip – the rising sun striking Mt Nantei and bathing it in a soft rose-pink glow, while everything was in dark-mauve silhouette. It was magical, breathtakingly beautiful. I woke the others up to share the moment with them. We took photos and went back to sleep for a couple of hours. It was a wonderful feeling of achievement and satisfaction, being here under our own steam, enjoying each other's company and the pleasures of such simplicity. Five trains and 250 miles from Tokyo, we hadn't seen another European face for two days.

Breakfast was brought to our room and prepared in front of us by a shy Japanese girl. Salad with asparagus, strawberries, eggs fried at the table, coffee and juice. We were like excited children, adoring every novelty that came our way, and over-praising every simple thing. If we had designed the view from our window ourselves we would have been accused of over-romanticising the picture – by now if was fully light and Mt Nantei was no longer pink but shining white, its foothills covered with pines and cedars, and a glorious cloudless blue sky with bright sunshine.

We explored the evocatively atmospheric town of Nikko on foot, taking in the perfectly proportioned Red Lacquer Bridge, the Rinno-ji Temple, the Temple of the Three Buddhas, each figure 15 feet high and exuding overwhelming serenity and strength, then along the avenue of towering straight-trunked cedars. We stayed as long as our schedule would allow, and caught the bus and train back to Ueno station in Tokyo and rejoined the company with our stories of exotica and wonder. We were on such a high that we felt like we had just scaled Everest. Over the next six weeks that we were in Tokyo I made various other trips around Honshu, and I have been back subsequently, but I think that three-day excursion was one of the greatest travels I have ever done.

The run of the play at the Ginza Saison Theatre was phenomenal. Every single night for six weeks was sold out. The audiences seemed to know the play inside-out and, despite the fact that they seemed to all be listening to a simultaneous translation which was just behind the live action, Nesbitt and I even managed to get a few laughs. They threw endless receptions for us, many of which were stiff and formal, but we always seemed to get them loosened up a bit. One night they took us all out to a karaoke bar and while the Japanese sang those mawkish, maudlin, melancholic songs that they always sing in karaoke bars, we tore the house up with everything from *Mack The Knife* to *Anarchy In The UK*. We had guys who could sing and guys who couldn't sing. You always could tell the difference. The guys who couldn't sing were the ones who wouldn't relinquish the microphone and always started a song in a key they had no hope of finishing it in.

One morning, after a particularly boisterous and indulgent night out on the town, I was awakened by what I took to be an alcohol-fuelled hallucination. I watched disorientated from my bed as large pieces of furniture were moved across the room by an unseen force. Pictures fell from the wall and glass bottles of toiletries in the bathroom fell into the bath like a round of machine gun fire. Then the very bed I was in moved, and yea, verily, I was sore afraid. Believing that it was Judgement Day, and that I was about to meet my Maker, I thought seriously about a quick death-bed conversion and a last-ditch attempt to make my peace with the Good Lord. After 10 hyper-animated seconds the torment stopped, and I realised to my relief that I had just experienced my first earthquake – and survived it. Apparently it was a minor one; they are so frequent in Tokyo that none of the locals even commented on it.

I kept in touch with both Rene and Charlotte as best I could while on the other side of the world, and sent letters and cards to Geno, but exchanges, in those days before e-mail and Internet cafes, were fitful and unsatisfactory. It was a strange feeling to be having so many unique and dramatic experiences and not having a loved one nearby to share them with, to compare experiences and to enthuse and rave. The solitary experience is a totally valid one, but the shared experience is infinitely more enjoyable.

The six weeks we stayed in Tokyo raced by – the cherry blossom was blown away by the fierce seasonal wind that always chases it up from the south-west, and the springtime arrived like a softly warming glow. Japan got to me like few other places ever had and I was loath to leave it, via the northern winter Olympics city of Sapporo, for Taiwan.

It was a bizarre feeling touching down at Taipei airport, being in China but not being in communist China. The regime in Taiwan is authoritarian, as it has been since the time of Chiang Kai-chek, the country's founder, whose overwhelming role in shaping the country is commemorated with statues, buildings and road names all over the tumultuous, bustling, polluted city. At the hotel I settled into my sensory-deprivation tank of a room and unwound. Charlotte called to check on my safe arrival. She also announced that everything was arranged and she would be flying out to meet me in Hong Kong at the end of the tour.

We did our shows in Taipei to considerable acclaim, despite Jimmy Nesbitt corpsing the entire company one matinee by doing the whole of his performance in a spot-on Ian Paisley accent, while Lloyd favoured the voice of Jimmy Saville for his Laertes. The unsuspecting audience watched with the simultaneous translations handsets clamped to their ears, hearing the correct text being spoken but blissfully unaware of why the accents might not be appropriate.

Our final show in Taipei was the last of the tour. At the end of the performance there were bouquets, presentations and speeches, and a party at the hotel by the pool. We swore to each other that we would keep in touch, and hugged each other in that emotional way much favoured by actors on programmes such as *This Is Your Life*. I knew that I would be friends for life with Durden and Lloyd after this, and that I had spent so much time with Jimmy Nesbitt, Danny and the Skipper, through good and bad, that we would always be happy to see each other when it was all over and laugh about it over a beer.

For all of us, though, 10 months after the first rehearsals in Loughborough, it was the end of the road and our minds were already checking out and thinking about the next step. For me it was Hong Kong. I had told Rene that, since we had to change planes there, I would take advantage of being there and stay for four or five days. I didn't tell her Charlotte was flying out from Munich to join me. I hated the deception but justified it to myself by saying, "If this is all a mistake, and comes to nothing, why should I hurt Rene now by telling her what I am doing?" It was probably a cowardly thing to do but sometimes I think that so-called honesty in a relationship is in fact mere self-indulgence. Nor could I face a row and tears on a long-distance telephone.

At Taipei Airport I was laden down with gifts and souvenirs and clothes that I had acquired since leaving London in February, 11 weeks earlier. I had bought a small synthesiser in Japan, some prints and endless artefacts from Harajuku as gifts, plus numerous T-shirts printed in that weird approximation of English so popular with Japanese fashion victims. Irresistibly proclaiming "Psychedelic Violence – Crime of Visual Shock" or "Good Boy Polly, Gun the River –Yea!" I knew they would be a welcome gift for anyone back home if I could bear to part with them. I was way overweight with my luggage, and had to off-load some on those members of my party who had not shopped with similar zeal. The problem was compounded by the fact that some were going directly to London and beyond, while others were also breaking their journeys and didn't want the encumbrance of extra luggage.

The short flight from Taipei to Hong Kong was uneventful, except for the heart-stopping approach to Kai Tak airport, as the plane swooped down and navigated a seemingly suicidal course between the tall office buildings, so close to some that you could actually see through the windows and see people working, apparently unalarmed. Grabbing my seven pieces of luggage I made straight for the exit, grabbed a taxi and headed for the Hong Kong Hotel.

There in the lobby on my arrival, like a vision that I had hardly dared imagine, was Charlotte, looking cool, serene and beautiful. I, on the other hand, looked like shit, sweating in the tropical humidity under the weight and bulk of my luggage but otherwise ecstatic but nervous. We went straight to our room and held each other for what seemed like an eternity. Gradually we unwound from our embrace and I started to dig deep into my cases and bags for gifts that I had gathered for her in Australia, Japan and Taiwan. She was the perfect recipient, expressing unerring delight as each new gaudy trinket or ludicrous item of clothing was produced from the apparently bottomless pit of my luggage. Charlotte, for her part, had brought some very good wine with her and, surrounded by the debris of the gift-wrap and gifts, we lolled on the bed chatting and holding one another, almost hysterical at what we were doing.

We spent every single minute of the time we were in Hong Kong in each other's company, deliriously, giddily in love. Every single thing we did was hopelessly romantic – from having breakfast overlooking the harbour, to taking the Star Ferry to Kowloon, from the Temple Street night markets to the Peak – it was all a dizzy adventure. When we were sure that we could do anything together, that we were invincible, we booked ourselves on to the night boat up the Pearl River to Canton, China, arriving in that seething maelstrom of a town at dawn, and hiring bicycles and spending the day in giggling bewildered elation.

We wandered through Qing Ping market, "not so much a food market, more a takeaway zoo" as one of the guidebooks succinctly put it, trampling slimy, squelchy, indeterminate invertebrates underfoot, like some disturbed out-take from *Eraserhead* as we went for hundreds of yards without recognising a single item that we would know as food. Caterpillars, centipedes, bobcat, tortoises and deer horn, yes, but not a chicken, not a potato – more poodles than noodles. The stench that emanated from the market increased with the temperature, which with the mid-afternoon sun soared from the oppressive to the unbearable. We climbed a pagoda and marvelled at the wonderful colonial architecture of the old town, and were swept along by the tide of a million cyclists, not really having a clue where we were going, nor caring.

And when it was time to return to Hong Kong, of course, we missed the boat and, of course, a taxi driver took us to the airport even though our sign language screamed "Station!" And once eventually at Canton Central Railway Station, bewildered by the crowds and the impossible process of buying a ticket, we thought we might never escape. Charlotte had the bright idea that anyone with a mobile phone on the station would be Hong Kong Chinese and, therefore, able to speak English. We descended on the first one that we saw and, naturally, her theory was watertight. He led us to the ticket booth, negotiated the price and handed us our tickets. Once on the train we could relax again and Charlotte slept on my shoulder as we rattled through tropical thunderstorms of biblical proportions to Hong Kong.

Charlotte had so much about her that I loved. Her intelligence, her very un-German sense of humour, her independence and her unspoilt, unforced way of being simply affectionate. She had been to Hong Kong once before with her boyfriend, and wanted to keep what they had done together special for them, so we didn't seek to duplicate their earlier visit. Instead, we formulated our own simple adventures. Out walking one evening we sat at a crossroads and talked. As someone interested in cannibalism and meat, I think she wanted to know details of my appendix operation. I was warming to the theme and noticed that she had fainted. She was only out for a few seconds but it seemed emblematic of our passion that I should actually make her swoon. It doesn't happen *so* often in one man's life that a beautiful woman faints into your arms in the Orient. On another day we took the boat to the pretty Lantau Island and sheltered in the Po-lin monastery when another violent afternoon storm caught us unawares. We bought blood-red Chinese writing paper overlaid with gold leaf, and ate mangoes and lychees as the rain crashed down around us, the elements conspiring to give the most dramatic backdrop possible to our tempestuous affair.

By the end of that week together I knew I wanted to spend the rest of my life with Charlotte. I knew that it was selfish, irrational and hurtful to Rene, but I knew also that if I didn't do it I would regret it forever.

We flew back to London together, me to go home, she to catch an onward flight to Munich. We clung to each other for the whole journey home, not saying a great deal now, preoccupied with the realities of re-ordering our individual lives. We kissed goodbye at Heathrow, both in tears, of course, but feeling that somehow we would work it out.

One glance back, a wave, and I was into the customs hall with my seven bags; of course, I was taken apart. Every stupid thing I had accumulated was inspected and anything of value was set to one side. Gradually, piece by piece, the articles were returned and I was given a import duty bill of £60 for the synthesiser – almost as much as it had cost in Tokyo. Out of customs and through the gate, and Rene was the first person I saw. I felt happy to see her but wretchedly treacherous. We went straight for a drink in the airport bar, and I told her my news, my stories, my adventures, but, in truth, I really told her nothing.

She told me how her life had been, how her career was starting to become exciting, how Geno was doing at school. We had been together for 20 years, and apart for one. And that was the problem. She drove me home and as I entered the house in Herne Hill, the enormity of the decision I had taken hit me. I was in turmoil. I knew that I couldn't possibly repeat what I had inflicted on Rene and Sophie, and that I would have to make a choice between Rene and Charlotte. Like a coward, I avoided broaching the subject for a few days, childishly hoping somehow that a decision could be made for me, in which no-one would get hurt and I would get my own way.

Returning home from the tour was like returning from New York the first time, after I had met Cristina, and I felt that feeling of dislocation, depression and anticlimax. Learning to act responsibly again, to consider other people's feelings and needs, took a long time. I slept with Rene as though nothing had happened, but gradually I found the courage to tell her what I was feeling for Charlotte. I hadn't yet found the courage to tell her that she had come to Hong Kong, but my good friend, Jim Telford, the guy for whom I got the job on the tour, took it upon himself to do that on my behalf. Devious and disloyal, with his own agenda, I have never forgiven him for his meddling at such a sensitive, delicate time. It triggered a period of abject misery for Rene and me, living under the same roof but no longer really living together. White-hot anger, mixed with a terrible sadness was all that Rene could show me, and I knew that nothing I could say could mend it or make it better. She pleaded with me to leave the house but I had nowhere to go immediately. I would make arrangements as quickly as I could.

I wanted us to talk it over with Geno at the earliest available opportunity. He was nearly 14. There is no perfect age to tell your son you are no longer in love with his mother, that you have found someone else and will at some point be leaving the home, but not leaving him. On a train back from Oxford to London, where the three of us had spent the day on the river with a school friend of his, I tried to tell him as gently as I could. He took it incredibly well, with a maturity and understanding that belied his tender age, but I didn't think for a minute that this was something that could be dealt with in an hour-long train journey. He was on a half-term break from school and we tried to give him as much love and attention as we possibly could. Rene and I even shared a bed, albeit a cold one.

One morning, with grotesque symbolism, she turned away from me and fell from the bed, which was seven feet above the ground. She landed awkwardly and broke her wrist very badly. The injuries resulting from a fall from that height could have been a lot worse, but the broken wrist compounded her state of total desolation. I took her to the hospital and waited with her until she was being treated. While Rene was accident-prone, a term often used to disguise an unconscious desire to self-destruct, I didn't believe she was suicidal. That was the only way I could excuse myself for leaving her. Charlotte was visiting London that weekend and I sped from hospital to her. I thought that I had to give Rene some space and slowly try to get out of her life. She wanted me to go because she couldn't bear me to be physically there but emotionally elsewhere; she wanted me to stay because she couldn't bear the thought that, after 21 years, I was leaving. It was a scenario that had never seriously occurred to me, either. Despite the inevitable upsets and irritations of living with someone that long, and the affairs and the occasional predictability, you do feel that when you have been together a long time, the relationship is actually bullet-proof, and that, come what may, you will get old together. It seems the only natural thing. This was not in the script.

Rene emerged from hospital with her forearm sprouting a dozen screws and levers, like a weird cybernaut, all holding the shattered bone in place. It was not to be her last post-break-up trauma. In the years that followed she would break several bones in cycling accidents, slip deeper into her lifelong spiral of mania and depression and slowly descend into alcoholism, with its two appalling bedfellows, dependency and denial, and then into a series of abusive relationships. I think I instinctively saw it coming and that was another reason I knew I had to leave. Could I have prevented it if I had stayed? Who knows? Yes, I was cowardly, treacherous and selfish, but I no longer loved her enough to stay and watch it happen. I only know that not a week goes past when I don't think that I treated Rene shabbily, and not a day goes past without thinking that I did what was best for me.

When Geno started school again, I travelled back to Munich to join Charlotte and to be out of London. I knew I couldn't live in Munich for any length of time as there was no way that I could work from there, but it seemed a good start. I continued to pay rent and upkeep on the flat in Herne Hill, made sure there was food in the cupboard, that the bills were being paid, and that Geno had everything that he had always had and, perhaps, a little more at this traumatic time. Five wretched months went by before I got another job and my money was running out. I would commute between Munich and London, signing on in London if I was there for a protracted period, and all the while knowing that I had to find a flat and start the true separation of our lives.

That Rene never stuck a carving knife into me, or bludgeoned me to an early grave with a cricket bat while I slept, spoke volumes for her patience and understanding. We were trying to have a "modern" divorce, both working desperately hard to keep the channels of communication open for Geno's sake as well as for our own. Separations like ours have so many unforeseen repercussions, not least with friends. Friends feel duty-bound to take sides, or otherwise are so embarrassed by the whole affair that they shrink away, hoping that the couple will soon come to their senses and return to the *status quo*. There is an awful period where no one wants to invite one or the other of you to dinner, for fear of offending the one who is not invited. And then there is the phase where tentatively they invite you and your new partner, not wanting to like her for fear of seeming treacherous to the wronged party.

I was lucky. My oldest and closest friends, Drumbo, Brian Clarke, Louisa Buck, Tom Dewe Mathews, Kathy Acker, Sarah-Jane Morris and David Coulter all stood by me, stayed in touch, didn't interfere and didn't take sides. They offered support when it was needed and advice when it was asked for. My newer close friends Richard Durden, Lloyd Owen and Jimmy Nesbitt had all seen what was happening at close hand and knew Charlotte better than they knew Rene, so were also supportive when I needed them to be. Most importantly of all, Geno never for a second withdrew his love or trust in me, and I hope I never gave him cause to feel betrayed.

* * *

The job drought was finally broken at the end of October, first with the trickle of a Scandinavian TV commercial, then with the comparative flood of a major Hollywood movie, *Robin Hood – Prince of Thieves*.

Originally called to a casting at Shepperton Studios to audition for the part of Little John, I took one look at the other hairy-arsed, man-mountains up for the part, and knew it was a wasted journey. I am tall but puny. I was about to make my excuses and leave, but Charlotte had come with me to the studios and convinced me to stick around anyway. When I was eventually seen they told me that, in fact, they had already cast Nick Brimble as Little John, but offered me the part instead of the Executioner. I was so hard up I would have taken the part of the Executioner's fourth assistant's sister's dog, and I was delighted when they told me that because the scene of the executions was one of the big set-pieces of the film, I might be needed for a whole week. I accepted immediately, knowing that Hollywood money is always considerably better than any other sort of film work. Charlotte was delighted and we felt as we drove back to London, that this was the change in luck that we had been waiting for.

Early in November I started my week on the film. It was a typically wet, grey, cold English November day and, of course, all my scenes that day were played outdoors in the main "town square" in a howling gale. It was my task to hang about half a dozen outlaws, one boy, and chop the head of another. A good day's work.

The film itself was even more ludicrous than most period romps. Not content with just telling the Robin Hood story, this version had to introduce that little-known character from Robin Hood, Azeem the Moor, and a witch, just in case there wasn't quite enough juice. In addition to a disastrously half-baked plot, the attention to historical detail was laughable even by Hollywood's high standards. Painted-faced Celts marauded their way through the action, having presumably got on the wrong chariot four centuries earlier and not been able to get off again. Robin himself, that master archer, was reduced to the dastardly ruse of relying on gunpowder to achieve his ends, a mere 200 years before scholars reckon it was introduced into Europe, no doubt by a distant descendant of Azeem the Moor. And there, in the middle of it all, like a bland, blond, beige blob, was Kevin Costner, an actor whose best role for many, myself included, was as the corpse in *The Big Chill*. To call him wooden would be unfair to the mighty oak or the noble cedar. He had put on a few pounds since *Horsefeathers*, sorry, *Dances with Wolves*, and spent the entire film fighting a losing battle with an elusive English accent.

His friend, the noble savage Azeem, was played by an embarrassed-looking Morgan Freeman, a truly impressive actor on his day, but this wasn't even his century. To his credit he didn't even attempt an accent. As a piece of miscasting, it was as bad as, er, Morgan Freeman in the monumentally awful *Bonfire of the Vanities*. (For a great laugh, read *The Devil's Candy*, Julie Salomon's account of the making of that quintessential $50 million disaster movie. Things never went well on that picture from the start, but they got noticeably worse when Melanie Griffith turned up halfway through filming with a brand new set of breasts which did not match her old ones.)

While the film was a turkey, filming it was a hoot. My one week turned into two and then three and then a fourth. This was not because I am in the film for any length of time but because someone forgot to write it before they started. Not knowing whether they wanted an adventure pic or a light romantic comedy, they got neither. When Costner attempts *gravitas* he is laughable. When he attempts comedy, sadly he is not. When Sean Connery appears for a few fleeting minutes at the end, for a fee rumoured to be a million pounds for a day's work, one is past caring. His Richard the Lionheart was paid for out of the promotional budget rather than the production budget. The scene has no narrative point whatsoever; its only function was to add the bankable name of Connery to the credits and the poster.

In the end, Alan Rickman's caricature Sheriff of Nottingham turns the tables on the Prince of Thieves by stealing all the best lines for himself and making off with the picture. Despite the extraordinary lengths that were gone to in the cutting room to cut Rickman's performance to the bone, poor Costner never had a chance against him for one simple reason – Kevin had never done panto.

Also in the cast was "the boy who would be Jack", Christian Slater. He was as nice a brat as I have ever worked with, and his boyish enthusiasm and recklessness came as a welcome relief on set after the uptight Costner. The career of Kevin Reynolds, the director, an alumnus of Costner, has not exactly flourished since *Robin Hood*. As the director of Costner's *Waterworld*, another of those films they don't talk about too much in Hollywood these days, out of respect for the dead, he didn't do himself or his boss any favours. He was a decent enough man to work for, though: polite, courteous and willing to share a moment and a joke with his actors.

I only had about three lines in the film and in an attempt to elongate my screen time by a few precious seconds I said to him, "These medieval executioners were a rum bunch you know," hoping to impress him with my knowledge of arcane social history. "Most of them were misfits, outcasts and whackos. They were the only ones who would do the job." "Really? I didn't know that," he answered, intrigued. "So I thought I might play the character with a stutter," I ventured. He looked at me, not altogether convinced, then reluctantly said, "OK, Richard, let's try it with the stutter." Unfortunately, I got rather carried away on the first take, as I wrestled Christian to the chopping block and with axe poised I told him, "The-the-the-there's a-a-a-a-al-w-w-w-w-ays r-r-r-r-rooom f-ff-or o-o-o-one m-m-m-more". At the end on the take Reynolds shouted, "Cut," (at least it sounded like "cut"), then, "OK we're going again. Take two. Er, this time without the stutter, Richard". Take two got the dribble instead. The famous dribble scene over Christian's lustrous hair. It was horrible. Shame the public never got to enjoy the stuttering version.

My death in that scene, felled by a flaming arrow as my axe was about to sever Slater's head, got the biggest cheer of the whole film at the night of the premiere, and it was reprised a million times in the Bryan Adams video, *Everything I Do*, on MTV screens around the world. I still have the arrow somewhere and use it as a conversational gambit to bore young children when they come to visit and get fractious. They look at me with contempt through their eight-year-old eyes and say, "What a sad man you are."

The last week of November 1990 was a particularly joyous week. Not only did my fourth cheque for wielding the axe in *Robin Hood* clear, but the British Prime Minister, Margaret Thatcher, was unceremoniously given the chop by a disgruntled Conservative Party, who rightly judged that she had become an electoral liability. Her cabinet colleagues looked on while they lined up lucrative directorships and consultancies for themselves for their old-age pensions, ineffectual, sycophantic or corrupt. Or, in the case of one or two, all three. To the surprise of many, not least to himself, her successor was not the perfidious, scheming, coiffed Michael Heseltine, but the grey man reckoned by the party to be a safe pair of hands, John Major, famously the only man to run away from the circus to join a bank. His term as Prime Minister effectively began in January 1991 with the Gulf War in Kuwait and Iraq.

As the defeated Saddam Hussein's crack battalion of republican guards turned their unwelcome attention to the Kurds and Marsh Arabs in the north-east of Iraq, with all the anger of a bully with a bloodied nose, Charlotte and I were moving our German base from the affluent, comfortable but uninspiring town of Munich to the funkier, edgier Berlin. Charlotte had got a very interesting job there, at the cutting-edge of the re-unification process, and we moved into a hotel room at the Metropol, in East Berlin, and watched events unfurl. She walked each day to her office, first in Alexanderplatz, and then in Leipzigerstrasse, and I walked the streets in the shattering icy winds that blow in from the Russian plains, wondering how to make it all work.

To stay in Germany and work as an actor was out of the question, as my German was very rudimentary. My music career had gone onto the back burner since falling out with Jim over his meddling, and I certainly had no intention of starting a club. As I walked through the East, watching history being made all around me, it occurred to me that there was a huge appetite for stories about the new Berlin in the press all round the world, and that I should write about life there as a resident, rather than just as a reporter.

I didn't know many features editors on British newspapers but I knew a few people who worked on the arts side, and so the first story I was actually able to place was a review of a big contemporary art exhibition at the Martin Gropius-Bau called *Metropolis*, which had been organised by the British curator, Norman Rosenthal. Fifteen hundred words of elegant bluff and I sold it to *The Guardian*. They only paid me £350, but seeing the article in print gave me as much of a thrill as signing with Virgin, doing *Batman* or getting the *Hamlet* job.

In writing the piece I had consulted Louisa Buck (who by now was earning her living as a critic and the arts correspondent for BBC Radio's *Kaleidoscope*) on a few points of fact, but otherwise it was all my own work. In journalism and art criticism, as in everything else I have ever done, I am an auto-didact. With a good pair of eyes, a good pair of ears and an inquisitive mind, there is not much that a man can't do. Writing about art is neither brain surgery nor rocket science. As Lou Reed put it "Opinions are like assholes – everybody's got one."

On the strength of *The Guardian* publishing my piece, I was approached by Mike von Joel, owner and editor of the art newspaper, *Artline*, asking if they could run the piece as well, for a fee. I cleared it with *The Guardian,* and a week or so after publication in *Artline* I was in London. I stopped off in Soho one afternoon to visit Mike von Joel at his office and to collect my cheque, and he said to me, "You know, we really liked that piece, and if you are resident in Germany, would you like to become European editor of the paper?" I had visions of comfortable chesterfields and three-hour-long lunches on expenses and so, never one to look a gift horse in the mouth, I readily agreed. Mike issued me with an official press card, a document that, along with my passport and driving licence, has accompanied me on every trip I have ever made since.

My first assignment in my exalted position as European editor was to travel back to Munich to review a show by one of my favourite contemporary artists, Anselm Kiefer. The show, *Die Bücher von Anselm Kiefer* (The Books of Anselm Kiefer), was almost unbearably sad. There was an overwhelming sense of human tragedy in those rooms, crammed as they were with images of the absent, of loss and of a country that no longer dared to allow itself to dream. Throughout the show Kiefer's work was nostalgic yet brutal, unsentimental yet profoundly disturbing. It persuasively questioned the Marxist critic Theodor Adorno's statement: *Nach Auschwitz ein Gedicht zu schreiben, ist barbarisch* (To write poetry after Auschwitz is barbaric).

It was a fascinating time to be living in Berlin. Every day there was incident, rumour and scandal. Germany was a society in flux, and there was never any shortage of topics to write about. The British have a soft spot for Berlin, which, thanks to the works of Isherwood, Auden and Spender, occupies a place in the British psyche unlike that of any other city. We love its perceived naughtiness and its perversity, but because we are an inherently prudish race, we like to glimpse it voyeuristically and from a distance. I quickly learned that if I could hang any story on the peg of sex, violence or resurgent Nazism, I would find a paper wanting to print it. Unsurprisingly, those stories were not hard to find in Berlin at that time.

In the two years that I was a semi-resident, I was enthralled by the variety and the vitality of life there. One thing is immediately clear – Berlin is not a typical German city, just as New York is not a typical American one. Berliners, like New Yorkers, are proud and independent.

For many Brits, Berlin conjures up images of the decadence of the twenties and thirties, and with a little imagination you can catch a whiff of those heady times. Try wandering around the Nollendorfplatz area of Schoeneberg – half close your eyes and you half expect to bump into Mr Issyvoo on his way to give an English lesson, or Sally Bowles hurrying to meet a wealthy admirer. My friend, the art dealer James Birch, was a welcome visitor to Berlin while I was there. He was in Berlin to buy a Trabi, one of the old East German motor cars made out of reconstituted cardboard and fibre, which were driven by an engine similar to that of a lawn mower. They came in a variety of colours, all of them repulsive, and could be picked up for a song. In 15 minutes he bought the car from a woman who had waited for 15 years to sell it.

It was not the first exotic form of transport that James had brought back from the Eastern bloc. A year or two earlier he had towed a decommissioned Soviet MiG fighter aircraft all the way from Moscow to London, and when asked by customs officials at Dover if he had anything to declare, he replied, "No". A maverick and an adventurer, James organised a Francis Bacon show in Moscow in 1988, took Gilbert and George there in 1990 and, emboldened by the experiences, he took Gilbert and George to China in 1993.

Throughout my stay in Berlin visitors such as James were always a valuable source of London gossip and entertainment. The artist, Richard Wilson, creator of *20/50*, the oil-piece installation in The Saatchi Collection, came to stay in Berlin for a year on a DAAD (Deutsche Akademische Austausch Dienst foundation bursary, a reciprocal exchange scheme for artists and academics between the UK and Germany). He arrived with his partner, Sylvia Ziranek and their son, and was a very welcome addition to the Berlin art scene. A lively flamboyant couple, who I had known separately through their appearances as performance artists in my clubs in the eighties, their parties became an eagerly anticipated monthly event. In the space of a couple of years, Damien Hirst, Rachel Whiteread, Richard Wentworth and Harland Miller all followed Wilson to Berlin, courtesy of the charitable arts body, the DAAD, to work in that exciting environment for a year.

While my journalism ensured that there was some money coming in while I was not acting, I knew that my principle source of income would continue to be films and television in the UK. I needed to do some mathematics. I had to work out how many castings I went to in an average year, how many jobs I got and how much I earned. I could then average how much each casting earned, whether I got the job or not. For example, if I went to 100 castings in a year, and earned £40,000 pounds in an average year, then even if I only got one in five of the jobs I went to castings for, I could calculate that, on average, each casting earned me £400. Further, if a return flight from Berlin to London cost £140 or so, then the maths suggested that it was worth me flying to London to go to any casting that Michelle happened to set up, so long as the job was for a minimum £400. Consequently, I got to know the departure lounge at Berlin Tegel airport pretty well, and I was saying hello and goodbye to Charlotte as regularly as an over-trained parrot at the Welcome Inn.

When I was back in London, I knew that I had to find a flat, and Louisa Buck came to my rescue. She told me her dad, Sir Antony Buck, the Conservative MP for Colchester North, sometimes known as the "silent knight" because he hadn't made a speech in the House for so many years, had a small house in Kennington that he would not be needing for a while, as he had recently taken up with a Spanish courtesan named Bienvenida. Sir Antony had vacated the tiny house in Kennington and moved into Bienvenida's St John's Wood pad; all he really wanted was someone to move in and maintain it, and pay the council tax and rent that he was being charged. In effect I was house-sitting for him but the arrangement suited me fine. It was a small but pretty house within easy reach of both the West End and my family. Louisa arranged a meeting at the house with Sir Ant, we signed a very basic contract over a bottle of claret and I was in within the week. He explained that he didn't expect to need the house back in the foreseeable future and that I should treat the place as my own. After we left, Louisa advised me not to be too sure about how long I would have the place as this Bienvenida was a bit of a loose canon.

I moved some clothes and personal effects into the house and for Rene it was, at least, the start of the real process of separation. It was also good for me to be able to slip back and forth between Berlin and London without having to make a lot of arrangements with other people.

No sooner had I moved in than the news of Sir Ant's *liaison dangereuse* with Bienvenida started to fill the gossip columns. This had the unpleasant and unwelcome effect of attracting grubby little men with cameras and notepads to my doorstep from the crack of dawn to lights out, in the hope of getting a story or a shot of the star-crossed lovers. Soon afterwards, proving, if proof were needed, that there is no fool like an old fool, Sir Ant married the blonde Spanish waif and the alchemical wedding changed Lady Muck into Lady Buck. Everything went well for the first few months as *Hello! Magazine* followed other publications with less intellectual pretensions in and out of the Buck House boudoir.

Tom Dewe Mathews, Louisa's beau, was writing a book called *Censored* about censorship in the British film industry, and asked if he could move his computer into one of my rooms to get him away from his child-filled home to work each day. He was a model co-worker, with only the Hiroshima-like clouds of whacky-baccy smoke emanating from his room causing any friction between us. He came every day and stayed for six hours, and was always happy to take a break to chat about this or that film, director or producer. His knowledge of his subject is extraordinary, yet he wears his knowledge so lightly and with such modesty that you have to drag it out of him. With his silvering temples, grey eyes and dimpled chin he looks like a cross between Kilroy and Christopher Walken. Women find him irresistibly attractive and he pretends not to notice. Over the next four months his fascinating and unique study of British taboos and prejudices took shape. I often thought he wasn't working fast enough and was rolling too many spliffs – or enjoying our exchanges more than he ought – but, in fact, he got the book finished in good time and it was very well received.

By now I was getting a lot of commissions from publications as diverse as *The Guardian, The European, Artline, The Face* and *Blitz* magazine, and I wrote stories on anything from the weekly jumble sales held at the former Stasi headquarters in East Berlin to picaresque snapshots of Berlin nightlife, plus pieces on architecture, music and food. I enjoyed hunting down new angles for stories, and keeping an ear open for local gossip. I overheard two young English squaddies discussing in a bar that the Russians were finally pulling out of their garrison in Karlshorst, in the Eastern part of town. That afternoon I was there, with camera and notepad, to try to intercept some of the shy young conscripts as the clambered aboard their personnel carrier to head home. Many of them seemed less than enthusiastic about heading back to Murmansk or Irkutsk just when life in East Berlin was about to become fun. A week afterwards I was back in the same deserted barracks to watch a Vivienne Westwood catwalk show, where she was previewing her spring collection to the wide-eyed bright young things of the Berlin fashion world.

Michelle was at this time getting me a lot of work, mainly television and commercials, which meant a lot of flying between Berlin and London. It was all enjoyable and acceptably well paid, and my relationship with Charlotte was deliriously happy and exciting, marred only by the protracted periods we spent apart.

* * *

One evening in December, back in London, I had a dinner at Brian Clarke's house, and the musician and TV presenter, Jools Holland, was one of a dozen or so guests. After we had eaten, Jools announced that he wanted to show us some slides he had taken a few days previously, of an hilarious day he had spent recording a television programme (*The Tube*, I think). He set up Brian's slide projector and a screen and proceeded to show us 20 or so slides of only moderate entertainment value. Emboldened by alcohol I threw down a challenge. I said "Jools, that was a real disappointment of a show. I hereby declare that my typical day beats yours hands down for entertainment value. I challenge you to nominate a date in the not-too-distant future, and everyone here will record that day in pictures. We will all re-convene here the following week to show our slides and settle the matter once and for all." Jools picked up the gauntlet and nominated a date, a week later, which we would all record.

It just so happened I had been offered a job working with John Cleese on a series of commercials for a Norwegian chocolate bar called Relax. The commercials called for me to put Cleese to death in a variety of gruesome ways, by guillotine, by firing squad, by hanging and by nailing to a telegraph pole. In each scenario, just at the point of death, an unseen hand or an act of God would save Cleese from certain extinction and he would turn to the camera and, with his most obsequious Basil Fawlty grin, would exhort the viewer to "Relax".

The filming took place over three days, the second of which was Jools's nominated day. I got on very well with Cleese on the first day. Although he tended towards tetchiness if he was in an uncomfortable position too long, and didn't suffer fools or make-up girls gladly, between takes with a cup of tea he was charm itself. He is, as is well known, a very intelligent, very serious man off-camera, but we shared enough interests to enjoy each other's company in those long periods where nothing much seemed to be happening. I told him about the challenge I had made to Jools and he found the whole notion of "competitive days" very funny. I asked him if he would object if I photographed the following day's filming and he was positively encouraging.

The next morning I arrived at the studios with my camera and a large wall clock, which I decided I would feature in each picture to illustrate the sequence of events. As we progressed through the day, I would frequently grab the clock, get John to hold it in some alarming, near-death pose and have someone photograph the two of us. As the day went on, John was clearly enjoying the shots we did together more than the shots we were doing for the commercial, and set up ever increasingly ludicrous tableaux around the guillotine or the chopping block. The same imagination that had ignited the best moments of absurdist humour in *Monty Python, Fawlty Towers* or *The Life of Brian* was mine to use in the pursuit of a slide-show victory.

On my way home from the shoot, as a final bonus, I drove down the Strand and saw a fire near to Somerset House with smoke billowing from a window and half a dozen fire engines outside. I pulled up, grabbed my camera and asked a fireman in full apparatus if he would mind holding a large wall clock for a moment. He looked bewildered, but kindly obliged and posed with the clock heroically before the blaze. I thought, "Victory is mine." Sadly, Holland, sensing imminent defeat, has never managed to agree on a date for the great mass screening. My slides remain in a locked safe, in case of subterfuge.

Back in Kennington, Louisa warned me that not all was well with Sir Ant and Bienvenida in Buck House and that I should be prepared for the worst. It was only when the Jaguar needed repairing and both hoped that the other would be able to pick up the bill that things started to go awry. At the garage when the bill was presented, they stood side by side, each hoping the other would blink and say, "Don't worry, darling. I'll pay for this." After what seemed like an eternity Sir Ant did the decent thing and coughed up. It must have been a terrible shock for both of them to realise that neither of them was actually loaded. Although theirs was clearly a love-match forged in heaven, the more mundane requirements of life on earth had started to drive a wedge between Sir Ant and Lady Buck.

A week later I was woken at two in the morning by someone knocking on my front door. I had no idea who would come calling at that hour and threw up the window to ask who it was. There on my threshold stood the forlorn figure of Sir Ant, wispy white hair blown ragged by the winter wind and a plastic carrier bag in each hand. I went down to let him in and he told me the sad story. "B and I have had a bit of a bust-up," he confessed, "Marvellous girl and all that, it will all blow over in a day or two. Thing is, old boy, I need somewhere to crash for a couple of days. Mind if I take the spare room?" What could I say? I poured him a drink and listened to his tale of woe, put him to bed and the next day I knew I would be flat-hunting again. I have been one half of several odd couples in my time, but this was not about to be one of them.

I quickly managed to find another flat to use as a base, again in the Kennington–Oval area. In Berlin, I covered the Berlin Film Festival for the *European* and continued hunting down obliquely-angled stories.

In May, I did a film with Gavin Millar, *Look at it This Way*. This time I was playing an animal rights activist and I had to do a couple of scenes with a real lion that I was liberating from a circus. On the day that the beast arrived on location, albeit a rather moth-eaten specimen in a semi-tranquillised state, I was taken with Gavin to be briefed by the animal's handler. He was a self-important, weasly man in an anorak, with an irritatingly nasal delivery.

"The first thing I have to say," he began, "is that these animals can and do kill." This particular specimen looked like he could barely miaow convincingly, but I took the handler's word. "In case of an emergency, I will be standing by with a tranquilliser gun." This instilled a short-lived sense of security in me. "However," he whined on, with all the communication skills of a British Rail announcer, "The tranquilliser dart takes 15 minutes to take effect on the creature". I didn't reckon my chances of survival after a 15-minute mauling from a kitten, let alone from a lion so I suggested, helpfully, "If there is an emergency, could you use the gun on me first so I don't feel any pain?" He didn't laugh.

Having survived the lion, and the far more serious threat of death by boredom from its keeper, Charlotte and I headed to Malaysia for a holiday together. We went to the east coast, to Kuantan and Tanjung Jara, stayed in the most perfect hotel and unwound in total serenity for 10 days. I liked Malaysia, its people, its topography, its climate and especially its food, but to have stayed there for more than 10 days would have seen me peeling the walls. It's a little bit boring, it must be said.

Charlotte returned to work in Berlin, and I headed straight to London, where I knew that my old friend, Duncan Ward, the smooth, chiselled and wholly unreliable South African, was starting to put a film project together. He was making a short, absurdist film called *Dead Men Don't Remember*. Since I liked Duncan and knew that the film would be an enjoyable and different experience from the run-of-the-mill, I agreed to take part.

The film was a hugely enjoyable piece of work, driven through in less than a week by a combination of Duncan's acid tongue, a prodigiously talented cast and a good coke dealer. The story, such as it was, centred on the mysterious death of Rex Dunbar, a victim, apparently, of spontaneous combustion in the library of a grand house. His only earthly remains, a charred foot in the middle of the floor, provided the central motif. A number of characters who were satellites to Dunbar's existence file through the room, reminiscing and bickering over what they remember of the dead man's life. Two beautiful lesbians, one half-cut, the other half-clothed, argue bitterly over which of them Dunbar loved most. Their argument is interrupted by the arrival of two fez-capped chefs, looking like Tweedledum and Tweedledee, demanding the money that Dunbar owes them, and menacing the lesbians. These weird negotiations are cut short by the spectral figure of a white Nigerian freemason, in bowler hat and apron, with a totemic ju-ju in his hand.

The lesbians were played by Sacha Hails and the luminous Rachel Weisz, a voluptuous peach-skinned, dark-haired goddess fresh out of Cambridge. The fez-capped chefs were my friend, Mac McDonald, with whom I had worked on *Batman*, and the great absurdist writer and performer, Ken Campbell. It will come as no surprise to you to learn that the white Nigerian freemason was played by myself. Rachel was fabulous to watch, playing even the most ludicrous scenes with intelligence, wit and sensitivity. When God was distributing the goody-bags, she was at the front of the queue.

We shot the film in a converted warehouse off the Walworth Road and Duncan, who has a great talent for getting people to work for nothing, managed to assemble a whole crew on a kiss and a promise. The finished film looked wonderful, and was intelligently and originally edited, but was marred by appalling sound. At several stages during the editing process

Duncan abandoned the project altogether, but kept coming back to it. I detected in him then a trait I have noticed in his work ever since, a desire to mask his insecurity with either a wilful obscurantism, or a tendency to blame technical imperfections for a flawed project. Duncan always loses confidence in his work then tries to fuck it up. The 10-minute film was shown at a few festivals and clubs, but never got the release that it merited.

* * *

Geno was playing regular cricket for Millfield and in one game dismissed the future England test opener, Marcus Trescothick, who was playing for a local rival school, with a canny leg-break. Despite that, he was not really making the progress that he might have done either on the cricket pitch or academically, owing to the fact that, as a 16-year-old, his attention was often elsewhere. Like most kids that age he loved music, and after trying his hand as singer in one of the local bands, he turned his attentions to DJ-ing and recreational drugs.

It may come as a shock to you, in view of all you have thus far read, to learn that I was horrified when I learned for the first time that he was taking ecstasy, the preferred drug of his generation. As I was no longer living at home, Rene learned about it before I did and, because they had a very close and mutually protective relationship, she kept it to herself. In all honesty, I don't know what I would have done had I learned about it earlier, except to try to encourage him to restrict his use of any drugs to school holidays and to keep his mind clear during term time. I think that if I had attempted to use shock tactics or threats of punishments, it would have been both futile and hypocritical. Millfield had, and for all I know still has, something of a reputation for drug use among its pupils. It is now so commonplace it is no longer even newsworthy.

Coming from a very modest background, I think that Geno felt that if he couldn't compete with his school chums by flashing money, clothes and cars around, he could compete with them in his consumption and his dare-devil attitude to authority, and that way win their admiration and friendship. Either way, the letters started arriving from the school informing us of breaches of discipline, poor academic standards and loss of form on the cricket pitch. The inherent threat was that his scholarship would be reviewed and possibly not renewed for his two A-level years, despite the fact that he had picked up ten GCSE passes. As the next few weeks went by the threat became a reality, and Geno enrolled at the Fine Arts College in London to do his three A-Levels, beginning in September. When Bunter's brother, Eds, was expelled from Millfield, his father the Duke of Beaufort was summoned to the school. "What's he been expelled for?" he understandably enquired. "Birds and booze," came the headmaster's reply. "Thank God it wasn't druggery and buggery," thundered back his Grace.

Geno didn't seem unduly perturbed by the change of plan and was confident that he could pass his A-levels wherever he studied for them. In that respect he was very similar to me – he had a tendency to drift and in and out of academic focus and, in the run-up to the exams, an ability to energise himself, to concentrate and prioritise, and to pass exams against all the odds. He continued to live at home with Rene and she continued to be a great mother, despite her ongoing personal problems.

When Michelle called me one morning to say that they were casting for a second series of a sitcom called *Men Behaving Badly*, I had to confess that I didn't even know there had been a first series. Television sitcoms do not feature very highly in my priority "must-see" section. She explained the basic plot idea to me and told me they were looking for a character to play an acid-casualty hippie in two or three episodes. So I went along to meet the producer, Beryl Vertue, and the writer, Simon Nye, at Thames Television. It was a hot summer day, and my train was late, so by the time I arrived I was sweating like a rapist in the dock and looked like shit. I think that is why I got the part. Sometimes when you go to a casting, they will say, "Can you come dressed like a hippy?" or "Can you come looking like a vicar?". I always say "yes" and arrive in my normal clothes anyway. I reckon that if they think you are almost right for the part, they will believe the costume will do the rest. But if you are already in costume when you arrive and they are still not sure, then the chances are you won't get the job. It is a method I have always followed, and I haven't changed it for anyone since I started.

They asked me to read the part of Neville, a sixties burn-out who runs the stall next to Tony's (Neil Morrissey's character) in the market. I read it once and they offered me the job. I suppose all that research I put in the sixties was starting to pay off. They told me that each episode had a four-day rehearsal period and was filmed in front of a live audience at Thames TV's studios in Teddington. It sounded great. I love working in front of a live audience, especially for comedy. There is nothing like that adrenalin rush that you get when you hear an audience laugh at a gag.

At the first rehearsal I met all the team. In addition to Beryl and Simon there were the director, Martin Dennis, and the regular characters, Martin Clunes, Neil Morrissey, Leslie Ash and Caroline Quentin. They were already a tight-knit group when I arrived, but they weren't exclusive or cliquey. Martin, in particular, has a fantastic sense of humour that is much more cerebral than his trademark rubber-face would suggest; he is one of these rare funny-men who also likes to laugh at other people's stories, not just at his own. The rehearsal period in a church hall in Twickenham (oh! the glamour of television) was a non-stop hoot. I say non-stop, but that's an exaggeration. We stopped often because we just got too hysterical. By the time we got to record the show in front of the live audience we were having so much fun with it that a half hour episode took three hours to record.

The funny thing about playing a sitcom in front of a live audience is that it doesn't matter how many times you mess up, the audience still laugh at the punchline, even when they have already heard it six times before. I think it is because they feel a complicity in the humour. They know what's coming but they love the anticipation of the actors actually getting there. And when it is in the can, they feel smug that they know something that the viewers at home don't know – that it took six takes to get a particular scene because Martin kept forgetting his lines, or that the scenery kept falling down when a door was slammed, or I had eaten a biscuit immediately before delivering a line which precipitated an almost fatal coughing fit.

I did two episodes of *Men Behaving Badly* in that series and another one later on. I had no idea what a sensational success the programme was going to be and nor, clearly, did Thames TV. They dropped the show after the second series and the BBC picked it up to make another five series, which enjoyed a fanatical following. The programme was a perfectly-judged observation of the prevailing social trend of the time: the depressing "lad" culture of lager, sex and football. They are the only themes in the entire series of 40-odd episodes, and even football doesn't get much of a look-in. Like all successes it spawned its knock-offs, and I happened to work on the worst of them, the dim-witted and crudely-drawn *Game On*. It seemed to me to exemplify all that was worst about the way British TV was heading. Generic TV for undiscriminating couch potatoes who couldn't tell good from bad. *Men Behaving Badly* wasn't exactly a masterpiece, but next to *Game On* it was *King Lear*.

* * *

In January 1993, Bill Clinton assumed the Presidency of the USA, having beaten the ncumbent, George Bush, in the previous November's election. His presidency promised a return to more liberal social and foreign policies than the presidencies of Bush or his predecessor Reagan had pursued, and I was relieved and hopeful at that prospect. Professionally the year started well for me, too, with a part in a new Richard Loncraine film called *Wide-eyed and Legless*, with Jim Broadbent and Julie Walters, and the offer of a part in a West End production of an Agatha Christie play called *Murder is Easy*.

Murder is Easy was a creaky old period piece, but the producers spent a lot of money on it and put it into the Duke of York's Theatre with a good cast and a very good design on a revolving stage. The characters were the usual *dramatis personae* of a 1930 pot-boiler set in a Cotswold village – the squire, the major, the vicar, the battleaxe, the flapper and the sleuth. I played Roger Ellsworthy, a gay art dealer "from London", referred to rather obliquely as "one of the purple-shirt brigade". The play starts with a murder, one of a series, and, of course, everyone in the village is a suspect. It then lumbers along pleasantly enough for a couple of hours with good humour and few pretensions.

The cast were mainly stalwarts of the London stage and TV, people such as Nigel Davenport, Peter Capaldi, Irene Sutcliffe and Charlotte Attenborough. We rehearsed for a month in a studio upstairs from the Old Vic, and it was very good experience for me. Working with someone such as Irene Sutcliffe, a totally consummate professional, with a sound technique and a wonderful method of working, was a real education, and I never tired of watching her· She has worked in every field of the profession, from playing Maggie Cook for six years in *Coronation Street* to Mrs. Blenehassit, the owner of the cake shop in *Withnail and I,* appearing in Loncraine's *Richard the Third,* and doing countless plays in the West End and at the National Theatre.

The Scot, Capaldi, was fresh from his success with his Caledonian road movie, *Soft Top Hard Shoulder,* a good if sentimental film, and an impressive debut as a director. I liked Peter but he never seemed totally at home as the love-interest sleuth "just back from Burma". He was using the role to broaden his popular appeal and to keep the money coming in to bankroll his next project, the short film, Franz Kafka*'s It's a Wonderful Life.* Once the play was up and running he spent most of his time locked away in his dressing room, working on script and direction ideas for the film, which starred Richard E. Grant. His impressive ability to focus and be single-minded paid off – the film won him the Oscar for Best Live Action Short Film in 1995.

The show was a breeze to do, even if Irene Sutcliffe is the worst giggler in the world onstage, and sometimes called me Richard instead of Roger in the course of a scene. When she realised what she had done, her shoulders would start to shake as she fought desperately with the giggles and she would have to avert her gaze so as not to get me going.

One night I made the terrible mistake of inviting Martin Clunes and Neil Morrissey to the play, and afterwards we went to one of those bizarre, after-hours drinking clubs for actors that seem to exist in the most unlikely places and behind the most tightly closed doors. We hit the booze hard and, with the aid of a South American friend, we were still carousing as dawn came up. We had with us Andy Powell, the wild-eyed, stick-thin actor who was playing the chauffeur in *Murder is Easy*, and a guy who was playing the lead in the musical, *Buddy*, who seemed determined to entertain us with the entire repertoire from the show. When we finally slipped away he was still singing *Peggy Sue* to anyone foolish enough to buy him a drink. Martin and Neil were in great form that night, and are famously generous *maîtres de plaisir*.

One Saturday we were told that the Prime Minister, John Major, and his wife, Norma, would be coming to watch the play that evening, and so the matinee had been cancelled to enable the security services to complete a thorough search of the auditorium to check for packages and devices. The curtain was supposed to go up at eight o'clock and at 8.20 we still had not had the "act one beginners" call, informing us that the play was about to start. Eventually we got a message from the front of house manager informing us that an old lady had died in the foyer, and arrangements were being made to get the Prime Minister and his wife in past the body without causing them undue distress. The curtain finally went up at 8.45, and by the time we finished we were very worried that we would not make it to a bar before last orders. Our fears were confirmed when the stage manager announced that all members of the cast were required onstage, as the Prime Minister and his wife wished to meet us.

We reluctantly traipsed down to the stage, resigned to the fact that it was to be a dry Saturday night, and as we mustered onstage the curtain was raised and John and Norma climbed up. They were charming and enthusiastic about the play and, after assuring us that they had enjoyed it enormously, John actually offered his opinion of our long-term prospects. With all the originality and wit we had come to expect from him, he confided, "We think it will run and run." They shook us warmly by the hand, congratulated us once more, and departed through the stage door and into a waiting car.

As we turned to disperse, there was another announcement, this time from the producers of the show. They announced, "Ladies and gentlemen of the cast, it is with deepest regret that we have to announce that due to poor advance bookings, we shall be closing the show in one week. We close next Saturday. We apologise for this and assure you that it is nothing to do with the efforts of the cast or crew, merely a sign of the straightened times the theatre is going through at present. Thank you and may we wish you a happy weekend." The curse of Major had struck again. Not only was the corpse of some poor pensioner slowly cooling in an ante-room to the foyer, but in a week we would all be signing on again. *Murder is Easy*, indeed, and who in their right mind would suspect the Prime Minister?

Just as I was losing my job at the theatre, Charlotte was changing hers and got a posting in London with a new employer. It was what we had been hoping for all along but never really dared think would happen. We closed down the flat in Berlin where we had been so happy, loaded all our stuff into a truck and had it driven over to London. We had found a house with a small garden to rent in Cleaver Square, a pretty Georgian square in Kennington. The house and the square, which had a real sense of "neighbourhood," was a joy to be in. To be able to have dinners and parties and re-establish friendships, and to forge new ones from scratch with Charlotte, was a constant source of happiness and fun.

As a great fan of Emile Zola, I was very happy when Michelle asked me if I would like to do another play so soon after *Murder is Easy*. The trouble with doing theatre is that the money is so bad. Not only that, but the commitment to a play is always much longer than the commitment to a film or a television programme. Consequently, not only is it bad money, but bad money for a long time. A rehearsal period of between four and six weeks is normal, followed immediately by the run. However, when she told me the play was an adaptation of Zola's *La Bête Humaine*, to be re-titled *Crimes of Passion*, I found it irresistible. The fact that the director would be Pip Broughton, one of the most interesting of the younger British directors, meant that I needed no more convincing. The only drawback was that the play was at the Nottingham Playhouse, and that rehearsals would also take place in Nottingham, thus removing the possibility of picking up the odd day's filming work or voice-over in London once the show was up and running. Charlotte was, as always, incredibly supportive, and urged me to do it because it was quality work of which I could be proud.

Rehearsals began in the middle of September. I found some acceptable digs to live in near the castle and moved in to my temporary home. Pip's way of working was very different from either Lyubimov's or Wyn Jones, who had directed *Murder is Easy*. She was a much more instinctive director, encouraging us to contribute to the psychological reading of the play, rather than her imposing a psychology from above. She likes to work in a very organic way, letting relationships develop out of rehearsal and improvisation, and has a wonderful gift for finding the sense behind the lines that the actors speak.

The rehearsals were a very intense period for me, learning this new way of working, which started every day with physical warm-ups, taken each day by a different member of the cast. Pip would say things like, "I want each of you to go to the stage and strike a pose that you think would be typical of a photograph of your character found in an old photo album. I want a snapshot." Or "Show me how your character played with another child when he was 10 years old." Or "Show me how your character, walking on the street, would greet each of the other characters in the play in turn."

It was a fascinating way to work, constantly challenging the actors to make their own decisions about their character, from which ultimately Pip would select the character traits that she wanted to accentuate. Often it was like a cross between role play and therapy, and on more than one occasion, as she took us deeper and deeper into our characters, I found myself unexpectedly and involuntarily reduced to tears. She engaged psychologists to come to talk to us about the psychology of murder, or railway engineers to come to educate us on the French railway system in the nineteenth century. I learned an enormous amount from Pip, both about acting and about all these other unrelated topics.

The cast contained one 24-four carat star, the great Sam Kelly, and one desperate wannabe, Greg Wise. The difference between the two was such that it was hard to imagine they had chosen the same profession to work in. Watching Sam, another old northern pro like Irene Sutcliffe, go about his rehearsal was a revelation. Watching him find his character, his ticks, the cadence of his voice and his body shape was like watching a masterclass. He is an actor who is as much at home in 'Ello 'Ello as in Pinter or panto. He was bemused by Pip's way of working, but went along with her and stole the show. He probably would have done anyway.

Hunky Greg Wise, on the other hand, had all the charm of a spoiled adolescent and, like many actors, his ego was in inverse proportion to his talent. I had never heard of him before we met in Nottingham although he was anxious that I should know that he had been a heart-throb in some or other television series, and considered himself to be the one "name" in Crimes of Passion. I always found him a tad wet but maybe that's just how our romantic heroes are these days. He didn't bother me much during the rehearsals or the run; indeed, he told me that he had a tantrum one afternoon, but I think I was doing a crossword and I must have missed it. But then again, he was an underwhelming sort of guy.

For the most part there was a good sense of company on that production and Nottingham is not the worst place on earth to be. The whole job lasted nine weeks from beginning to end, and I look back on that time with a certain fondness. I was left with something of an aversion to chicken dinners, however. Every night and two matinees a week, I had to eat a chicken dinner onstage. I was playing Camy-Lamotte, the Justice Minister, and Pip had this thing that she wanted all the characters of the play to be visible for the entire duration of the action, whether or not they were directly involved with playing the scene onstage. In the beginning the assistant stage manager who provided me with the dinner was quite careful that it had been well prepared, but inevitably, as the show went on, her interest in gastronomy declined, and eventually I was being served filth-on-a-plate.

One of my scenes was set in a cell of the prison where Sam's character, Roubaud, was being held for murder. As a justice minister involved in a potential scandal involving Roubaud's young wife, I had to visit the prisoner to ascertain his intentions. My opening line to him was, "And how are you today?" One matinee we had a party of mentally-handicapped children and adults from the local hospital in the audience as part of the "theatre in the community" initiative. Before Sam even had time to formulate his well-rehearsed reply, a voice from a wheelchair at the back of the auditorium, primed to respond to that same question whenever a doctor asked it, piped up with clarion clarity "I'm all right, thank you." It nearly brought the house down and Sam and I were like incontinent wrecks for the rest of the scene. The trouble is when something like that happens, not only does it corpse you at the time, but the next time you speak those lines in the following performance, you are half expecting the same thing to happen, and *that* makes you laugh too.

MOROCCO

We finished the run towards the end of November, and Charlotte and I immediately headed out for our first holiday of the year, 10 days in Morocco. At the airport, in the departure lounge, my heart sank slightly when I spied Jane Withers across the room, clearly heading for Morocco on the same plane as us. We chatted with her and her friend, Christoph Kicherer, until we were boarded. Jane had by now separated from Anthony Fawcett, and was a very established and respected journalist, specialising in design and architecture, and she explained that she and Christoph, a photographer, were heading for Essaouira on the Moroccan Atlantic coast to do a feature on a new hotel. The more we spoke, the more I regretted that I had demonised her so in the past, as she was a lively, interesting and easy-going travel companion, and not at all the monster that I remembered from a hundred private views in the eighties. We arranged to meet up a few days later in Essaouira.

Essaouira is a great coastal town, immortalised in the opening scene of Orson Welles's epic 1949 film of *Othello*. The procession of Iago, imprisoned in his cage, along the ramparts, gives a pretty good impression of the grandeur and the elegance of the city. Jane and Christoph had finished their work at the small but chic Villa Maroc, so after lunch we headed for the tiny ruined village of Diabat, a short drive out, which was once almost bought in its entirety by Jimi Hendrix, who wrote his song, *Castles Made Of Sand*, there. He was deported for drugs offences before the deal could be brokered, which may have saved both the village and Essaouira from the more extreme excesses of sixties rock star lifestyle.

The first half of 1994 was appalling for me, work-wise. You get used to the fact that, as an actor, your life is never going to be predictable. One year in which you seem to get nearly every job you go up for, is often followed by another in which even the jobs you are convinced you have got don't materialise. One month becomes two, and it can easily happen that six months go by without a sniff of a job. That is what makes it so hard to budget when you *do* get paid. You never know whether that fat cheque from a commercial or a film job has got to last you a month or the best part of a year, though I can't pretend that financial prudence has ever been a major part of my make-up, and as often as not I have splashed out the moment a big cheque is banked.

Many actors I know go into their shells when they are not working. They feel unfulfilled. I am lucky as I have always had music and writing to fall back on, to keep my mind off *me* and to avoid those horrible periods of self-loathing and insecurity when the phone doesn't ring. I admit that there have been times in the past when I have lifted my telephone to check that it is still working because it has rung so infrequently, but I have never felt that when I wasn't acting I was dying. Acting is an interpretive art, not a creative one. I don't really buy the tortured artist thing with actors. It's a strange job, spending your entire working life being paid for pretending to be someone else. A psychoanalyst would have a field day explaining that one to us. Yes, we are insecure, shallow, self-obsessed exhibitionists, indulged or ignored by the industry according to our position in the pecking order, but none of us are Beethoven, Bergman or Brel.

Slowly bits of work started to come in, a commercial here, a bit of TV there. I did an episode of *Crocodile Shoes*, another of *Surgical Spirit* and the money started to trickle in again. At no point did Charlotte ever utter a single word of complaint or disapproval at what I was doing, even though she was the sole breadwinner for the best part of two years while I tinkered away at new songs well into the night.

I decided I wanted to perform my new songs in public, and booked the Man in the Moon, a small theatre in the King's Road, for a couple of showcase gigs. I worked with David Coulter on getting the songs into a shape that we could perform together, and once again his extraordinary versatility brought the songs to life. Sarah-Jane Morris, by now his wife, and Steve Boltz also appeared with me, and the sell-out shows, which I entitled *Undrugged*, were a great success. I mixed some old songs in with the new, but principally I wanted to see how the new songs would sound in a live situation, and I was happy with the result.

The following year we moved again, still in Kennington, but this time into a 200-year-old house that had been almost ruined in the seventies. Charlotte spotted it, and although it didn't look especially promising from the outside, she has a great eye and could see that it had what estate agents call "potential". We met the guy who was selling it, a developer–architect called Mike Rundel (who went on to work on Damien Hirst's Pharmacy restaurant and Jay Jopling's Hoxton Gallery White Cube[2]) and agreed a price. Mike's path and mine should have crossed many times and in many different ways over the years, but we never actually met until we bought the house from him. It took the best part of three months to get the house into a state whereby we could move in, but since we were living just around the corner it was possible to keep a close eye on the builders and keep them on a fairly tight leash.

Among our first visitors after we moved in were Charlotte's parents, who were over to visit us from Germany. Charlotte's father has one great passion in life, almost comically for a German – "the War". I was determined to keep him off his pet subject for as long as I possibly could as it only ever led to disagreement and embarrassment. His love of the War was not limited solely to the Second World War, although obviously that was the one that he had first-hand experience of as he had been a Wehrmacht soldier in the Russian campaign. He was also very knowledgeable about all aspects of European conflict since the ancient Greeks, and was a fascinating man to listen to when he spoke about ancient history.

To keep him off the War we took him to Greenwich Maritime Museum for the Nelson exhibition, hoping that this would divert his interest for the day. He found the exhibition interesting and it fulfilled its desired function for the entire morning. Back at home for lunch afterwards, I had prepared a very good Cullen skink, the Scottish smoked haddock, cream and potato soup. As I set the tureen before him I had my strategy all planned out: I would use the soup to divert his conversation to things Scottish. In German I told him, "I hope you will enjoy this soup. It is made from a very traditional Scottish recipe. Were you ever, by any chance, in Scotland?" Quick as a flash the answer came back. "Nein. But in ze var I vas a prisoner of ze Cameroon Highlanders." All my strategy had come to nothing. With a deft side step he had thrown me, and we were on to his favourite subject for the rest of lunchtime. He was too smart for me.

GOTTSCHALKS HAUSPARTY

Needless to say, as soon as Charlotte and I headed off on holiday to Burgundy that summer, the weather changed so dramatically that our time at the house we were staying in was spent building fires and cooking warming soups and stews, rather than lunching in the shade of a chestnut tree. At the end of our tether, we closed up the house and headed for Paris where the weather was no better but at least there were sufficient diversions to keep us entertained.

The only bright spot during the stay in that house was a telephone call I got from a former boyfriend of Charlotte's, who was a TV producer in Germany. We had met a few times and had always got on, and he called me to tell me about a new show that he was about to start work on for German TV. It was to star Thomas Gottschalk, the biggest name in German TV, who is a sort of cross between Chris Evans, Chris Tarrant and Terry Wogan. He presents all the big gala shows in Germany as well as having his own occasional series that invariably tops the ratings. The plan was for him to present a weekly prime-time weekend show, which would be something between a game show and a chat show. It would be broadcast live from a studio in Munich that had been dressed up to look like a country house. To complete the tacky scenario, he wanted to have an actor to play his English butler, who would act as both his assistant and his fall guy. My friend asked if I would like to test for the part for the pilot, with a view to doing a dozen or so shows if it worked out. I agreed to do so at the end of our stay in Paris.

When I returned to London, I met him at the Dorchester and we chatted about some ideas that they had for the show. He then gave me a tape of Gottschalk to enable me to get some idea of his style. Gottschalk is a curly-haired, blonde guy with great teeth, who has developed a relaxed, wise-cracking, slightly naughty style, and who dresses in a self-consciously flamboyant manner, like a Bavarian Elton John on a tight budget. Like Evans, Tarrant and Wogan, he began his career in the less restrictive medium of radio and developed a huge following among young and old alike. His musical taste is very safe and conservative but he has a penchant for practical jokes and stunts that ensure that he is never out of the public eye. It was only a matter of time until he made the transition to television and for most of the eighties he was the highest paid entertainer in Germany.

The independent German television company, SAT 1, were keen to use Gottschalk in their weekend prime-time ratings battle with their great rivals, RTL, and *Gottschalks HausParty*, freely adapted from the abysmal, but highly successful, British format, *Noel Edmonds' House Party*, was reckoned to be the vehicle with which they could win over the big spending advertisers. I was offered the part as Gottschalk's butler, who would be required to speak bad German, something I did well. I was told that a pilot would be shot in November, but it was assumed by everyone involved that it was a forgone conclusion that the show would become weekly or fortnightly immediately after Christmas, and that I would be required for every show.

I accepted the contract they offered, told Michelle about it and went to Munich to shoot the pilot. A large part of the appeal of the show was the calibre of the guests that it would be able to attract because of the huge audience. Typically, they would be film stars, pop stars and sports stars, the great staples of all chat and family-type shows the world over. As often as not they would have a film or a book or a record to plug, but sometimes it was just enough to have them on the show. For the very first programme they booked Sophia Loren to chat while she gave a demonstration of Italian peasant cooking in the House's kitchen. This was part of the trouble with the show. Left to his own devices, Thomas Gottschalk is an amusing, likeable, instinctive performer who knows his audience and the limits of his own talent better than anyone. Sadly, though, there is a Thomas Gottschalk "industry", which includes a manager, a production company, the TV company SAT 1, a programme director, several producers, and a whole team of writers, all of whom are drawing sizeable pay cheques for their input to the show. The problem was that none of the writers were as funny as Thomas is when he is chatting off-the cuff but, being live TV, no one dared to leave so much to chance. Consequently, week after week we were hampered by a lumbering, puerile script that Thomas knew was substandard, but which he believed he could rescue on camera by sheer force of character.

In addition to the scripted parts of the show and the informal chats with the star guests, there was usually an audience participation spot where someone from the studio audience would, by completing some simple or embarrassing task, have the chance of winning a car or a holiday in Florida, (the prize provided, of course, with none-too-subtle product placement, by a local car manufacturer or travel agent). My role was fairly clearly defined: I was to assist Thomas during the games, look after the guests when they were not actually on camera by serving them with drinks or snacks and, every week, to open the show with a pre-recorded filmed episode which alerted the audience to the theme of that week's show – Christmas, Carnival, the World Cup, Disco, the Oktoberfest or whatever. It was a breeze for me and slowly my role in the show became more and more prominent, and I was frequently featured alone in a set-up, while Thomas went off to change costume or just to have a breather.

Richard the Butler started to become a nationally known figure, such that soon I couldn't go anywhere in Germany without being approached for an autograph or a request for a photo. I was so well known as an archetypal Englishman that, in 1998, when England was playing Germany in a crunch match for qualification in the *Europe '98* football competition, I was telephoned by a German radio station for a live breakfast-time interview about the match. They had warned me about the call the night before, so I ordered all the English news-papers to be delivered the next morning so that I would be fully briefed about the game. After a few minutes of general chat on the phone, they asked me what the British press were saying about the game. I told them verbatim: "One says, 'Achtung Fritz. For you the war is over!' and another leads with 'Twenty things you didn't know about the krauts. Number one – zey don't like it up zem!'" The interview came to a fairly prompt end soon afterwards.

The TV guests kept coming but as time went by it became clear that, while some of them were still megastars in their own right, others had only been famous once, and many were famous most recently for having been declared bankrupt. One such guest was Grace Jones. This was 1996 and I kept asking, "What does Grace Jones do now?" and everyone would say,

"She was in the James Bond film *A View to a Kill*," and I would say, "But that was 1985, and so was *Slave to the Rhythm*." This is the curious thing about celebrity – for some it is self-perpetuating. As long as there is an international chat-show, gossip-column circuit prepared to pay you $2000, a business class flight and a night in a nice hotel, you can go on forever.

Grace has a reputation for being difficult and unpredictable (they are more or less the same thing in the anodyne world of entertainment). It possibly dates back to the time she wrestled the English chat show-host, Russell Harty, to the floor on air; with that single manoeuvre she revitalised not one but two careers that were on the skids. When she arrived at the Bavaria Filmplatz Studios for the rehearsals of her appearance in *Gottschalks HausParty*, everyone was on tenterhooks as to how she would behave. My stock soared when, as soon as she arrived on set, she came over to me and announced to the entire studio, "Aaah, it's Richard Strange, my friend from New York," and planted a huge kiss full on my embarrassed lips. I hadn't imagined for a moment that she would have remembered our meeting 15 years earlier when I met her at the Psychedelic Furs gig at Hurrah on my first US tour, nor the show we did in Paris together. The warmth of her greeting seemed to put the entire crew at ease, and while she rehearsed that afternoon she was professionalism and charm personified.

Unfortunately, that's when the production people who were supposed to look after her for the period between rehearsal and the show itself took their eye off the ball. They left her alone in her dressing room for four hours, and when she actually made her live entrance it was clear to anyone with an eye for such things that she had been hitting the chemistry set very hard in her room for most of those four hours. She was wild-eyed and hyperactive, the carefully rehearsed moves had been forgotten, and when the time came for her exit, she stayed put, basking in the limelight, much to the consternation of our host. Finally, during one of the frequent commercial breaks (they had to pay our wages, after all), Grace was persuaded to leave the stage for some repairs to her make-up and was bundled back into her dressing room. There she stayed until long after everyone else had left the studio, when an astonished cleaner found her, with a very good-looking Belgian boy, apparently in a state of extreme contortion. The next day she headed for Milan to do a chat show, and was, by all accounts, rather lively there, too.

Not all the guests were as mischievous as Grace. Many were happy to come on, push the envelope and behave themselves. Omar Sharif, still dazzlingly good-looking, charmed the audience with his stories of *Dr Zhivago* and *Lawrence of Arabia*, but then rather spoiled things by trying to flog his new line of fragrances, called Omar. The suave Egyptian had the entire range set out on a table before him, aftershave in the pyramid-shaped bottle, *eau de toilette* in the sphinx. Or was it the other way round? It is part of the received wisdom that Sharif is a master bridge player, who has made a fortune from the game. I can only imagine that his backgammon is not so good.

The noisome Spice Girls performed their first hit *Wannabe* and ran riot in the studio, as vulgar as a seaside postcard. The toothsome Bee Gees played live and were clinically effective. The sixties troubadour, Peter Sarstedt, appeared and sang, well, guess what? Yep, that wretched song – *Where Do You Go To My Lovely?* Thirty years after he had his hit, he was still trailing that irritating song round with him, like a show pony that has turned into an old nag that he cannot bear to have put down. It made me truly glad that I had never had a hit record, because to have had just one hit, like Sarstedt and thousands like him, must be the most miserable existence imaginable. To have tasted it, the sweetness on the tongue, and to not be able to ever let it go. To have to feed that sugar addiction for the rest of your working life must be hell on earth. So much better to fail and move on.

Still, the falling stars kept coming through our doors, eating the tired-looking canapés, then out for dinner afterwards to the Italian restaurant, and bleary-eyed and sheepish over breakfast at the hotel the next morning, fearful that they may have been rumbled as only B or C list stars. The retouched Engelbert, the drunk James Belushi, the tetchy tennis-player, Gabriella Sabatini, German footballers with permed hair, smarmy Bavarian politicians sensing an election approaching, washed-up old TV stars still prepared to wear their costumes for a fee, all were happy to grin asininely for the cameras as Thomas massaged their egos and they his. Anthony Quinn, John Cleese, the pneumatic Anna Nicole Smith, before she won and then lost the jackpot, Creedence Clearwater Revival and a well-oiled Gerard Depardieu, I let them all into our little make-believe world through the rickety front door of our plywood mansion on the hill.

I was asked to do more and more ridiculous stunts to keep the audiences happy. On one embarrassing occasion I was obliged to get into the wrestling ring with a seven-foot, 22-stone brick shithouse called the Undertaker and taunt him for five minutes. I was wearing full butler garb and a Union Jack tie, while the Colossus and his *aide de camp*, the improbably named Paul Bearer, took increasingly unfocused swings at me before the WWF favourite finished me off by pile-driving me to the canvas and tying my legs in a figure-of-eight knot. As my personal popularity in the show grew, they indulged me more and more. They published a sort of pin-up calendar of me, in a different ludicrous costume or embarrassing situation for each month of the year – Easter bunny or Christmas snowman, you can imagine the sort of thing.

My German friend Uli, from the International Noise Orchestra, never one to miss a trick, suggested we make a techno record, *Ich bin der Butler*, to cash in on my popularity. It seemed a suitably ludicrous idea. He recorded a storming backing tracking and I went into the studio to add my repetitive, mesmerising vocal line *Ich bin der Butler, und hier im Haus, im Haus da kenn ich mich aus* ("I am the butler, and I know everything that goes on in this house"). I even convinced Thomas that it would be great for the show if the record was a hit and that he should add a few choice catch-phrases to it to increase its marketability. He agreed and we mixed these in, and it was irresistible.

But then suddenly there was a cooling off, as if there was a certain resentment or anxiety that I was getting too big for my patent shoes. They refused to let me release the record and gradually down-sized my role in the show so that, by the end, I was doing very little except opening and closing doors. In fairness, I don't think it was Thomas himself who was behind the change, but rather his paranoid management and the production company who feared the star was being hijacked by the sidekick. It is a story as old as show business itself.

I did *Gottschalks HausParty* on and off for two years. The routine was always the same. I travelled to Munich on a Friday morning, rehearsed with Thomas all day, shot the show's introductory clip and had dinner with friends. On Saturday we rehearsed with the guests, had a dress rehearsal and then did the live show. Afterwards, dinner with Thomas and guests, and first flight home on Sunday morning. Munich is a town I got to know very well. It is not really to my taste, being rather staid and too affluent and too predictable, but for two days a week it was an easy enough place to be, and some good people passed through.

Back in London, I was still able to work weekdays and immerse myself in my music, spending whole days in my studio, where winter days would start and end, writing countless new songs and trying out new ways of working.

One night, after a party in Notting Hill, I hailed a taxi to take me home. Exhausted and half-cut, my heart sank as I realised that the driver intended to engage me in conversation. As he spoke, though, I found him more and more intriguing. He asked me what I did and I told him I was an actor and a musician, and he told me that he was a playwright, driving a cab partly to make ends meet, partly to gather ideas for his writing. He went on to outline a play that he was working on called *Rubber*, in which the three central female characters were inflatable sex dolls, Cindy, Bendy and Snuff. Cindy was sort of dowdy and housewifely, Bendy was a naughty schoolgirl type and Snuff was a doll you could kill for your sexual gratification. The action took place in the apartment of the guy whose dolls they were, after he went out to work one day.

I was intrigued by the possibilities of the narrative, and when he told me he had written a play called *Whore*, which Ken Russell had filmed, I was even more interested. He spoke with such infectious enthusiasm about his work, and with such intelligence, that by the time he was dropping me off, I wanted to be involved in the project. He told me his name was David Hines. We exchanged telephone numbers and the next day he called me and said he had been thinking about our conversation, and had decided to make *Rubber* a musical, and wondered whether I would be interested in writing the music for it.

I was both flattered and excited. Although the play was not yet fully written, we met over the next few weeks and discussed musical styles and characterisation, and set to work on writing lyrics and music. Hines had written some lyrics himself, which required music, and he asked me to write the lyrics and the music for other plot points in the play. We decided that a short play, around 75 minutes, should be able to sustain seven or eight songs, which would then bring the whole play up to about an hour-and-three quarters, a good length for a play without an interval. I immersed myself into the project with great enthusiasm and energy, and found the writing very easy.

I had certain misgivings about the play itself, but felt that David would knock the edges off it as he went along. He managed to find a producer, a flashy man who sold taxicabs, to finance the play, and we booked ourselves a period at the Etcetera Theatre, above a pub in Camden Town, for a run in July. David Hines and I talked at length about the delicacy of the subject matter, how it could easily deteriorate into a voyeuristic travesty, and decided that it would be best to get a woman to direct it so that the inherent smuttiness of the subject matter would be held in check. David found a girl who seemed to have good credentials, and the four of us, David, the director, the producer and myself, set about casting the three girls to play the dolls.

I had never been the other side of the casting process before, watching the endless trail of young hopefuls passing through, singing a song, chatting for 10 minutes, doing an audition piece and leaving with our promise that we would "be in touch". The girls were of extremely mixed ability, some could act but not sing, some could sing but not act. Most, in all honesty, could do neither. Fringe theatre, traditionally, is the first job of a drama school graduate, and there was no shortage of applicants for these auditions. Gradually we whittled them down to a short list of half a dozen, and then selected our final three.

Throughout the rehearsals, which took place while I was still commuting between London and Munich, I tried to persuade Hines to cut the long monologue that makes up act one, as the girl couldn't carry it off, but he stuck with it and it stymied the rest of the play. Five of the eight songs I wrote for *Rubber* were pretty good, two were okay and one was a dog. Unfortunately, it was the first song that was the dog, sung by an actress with a shrill voice who couldn't really act, and it got the thing off to a bad start. I pleaded with Hines to cut the song but he loved it. When we went to the opening night with Louisa and Tom, Kathy Acker, David Johnson and Richard Durden, I wanted to crawl under my seat as she sang that song, *Mr Lonely*.

The play was gradually redeemed as it progressed, principally by the entrance of the other two actresses, but it was never quite ready or quite good enough. The girl playing Snuff, the doll you could kill, was an actress called Bridget Fry. She hadn't done much since leaving college, but was very charismatic, and attacked her part with such dynamism and energy that she totally eclipsed the other two girls. She was great to watch and could sing in tune and with power, but the effect was such that the other two looked hopelessly out of their depth and the play became lopsided. It was also a sweltering July, and no one wanted to sit in a dark, airless, cramped theatre above a pub for an hour and three quarters. It suffered accordingly. The one good thing that happened was that Michelle came to see the play. She shared my enthusiasm for Bridget Fry and signed her up. I spoke to Kathy and David Johnson afterwards, and I knew they had hated the play. I also knew why. It is always hard when you can't enthuse about your friends' work, so I didn't push them.

Kathy also had rather more serious matters on her mind. She had been diagnosed as suffering from breast cancer after a series of malignant tumours were discovered. Mistrusting conventional Western allopathic medicine, she chose to undergo a double mastectomy ("Hell, who wants to have only one tit?" she asked, when told that a single mastectomy was all that was required), but refused to undergo chemotherapy. In an interview she did that year, she said: "OK, so I have always been radical, but at some level I always believed the men in the white coats had all the answers. But they didn't. It was like they had taken all the meaning from my body. I thought: 'I will not die a meaningless death. I will find out the answers. I will make myself well or at least I will die in control of my body.'" She had recently returned to London and bought a terraced flat in Islington. For someone who had been through so much she looked fantastic, and she never lost her intelligence, curiosity or sense of humour.

With *Gottschalks HausParty* off the air for a summer break, Charlotte and I ran for cover to Ibiza as soon as the run was over. Brian Clarke and Micha Spierenburg had rented a beautiful house there and we had the most fantastic couple of weeks. I had never been before and was completely exhausted by the end. I needed a holiday. Tony Shafrazi, the New York art dealer who was the first to show the New York graffiti artists, and who, as a young man had infamously vandalised Picasso's *Guernica*, stayed with us, and three French girls seemed to be semi-permanent house guests. Micha and Brian are ludicrously generous people and they made sure we had the most amazing time. The house and garden were so beautiful that some days we never went further than the pool. Other times we took it in turns to prepare ever-more lavish dinners, with Tony, in particular, being an enthusiastic cook.

The nightclub scene in Ibiza was unlike anything I had ever seen before, with enormously ornate, purpose-built buildings standing alone in the middle of parched scrubland, thrusting towards the sky like opulent desert palaces. Clubs are not really my thing anymore, especially not the high-decibel, high-energy clubs of Ibiza, but they were fascinating places to go people-watching. There is something inherently odd about watching people at a discotheque or nightclub from the oasis of the VIP lounge, once removed from the action. Tony and Micha preferred the comfort that the lounges offered, and because Tony is well-known on that inter-national scene, we always had access. Tony loves to party, and has a terrific nose for sniffing out the hottest clubs and the coolest bars. Back in New York his fellow gallerista, Larry Gagosian, respectfully calls him "The Mayor of Midnight"

One night, in Pasha, or Amnesia, or whatever the club was called, a party of Saudis arrived in the lounge where we had settled. There was a vast retinue of bodyguards, drivers, helpers and hookers, and they pitched their camp in the middle of the lounge. One of the drivers manhandled a huge air-conditioning unit into the middle of the room, where the big cheese, a prince with the Middle East franchise for Pepsi Cola, sat on a sumptuous sofa, holding court, surrounded by curvaceous blondes, like some scene from *Scheherazade*. When the temperature was too hot, he would raise a finger and a gofer would increase the air-con work rate. When it was too cool, Prince Pepsi would turn his open palm to the ground, and the machine would be eased back. It was impossible to turn away, the spectacle was so ludicrous.

Although the time on Ibizia was fun, I wasn't sad to leave the place as it was starting to bore me, and I began to see the island as a hell-hole with a very seedy underbelly. There is nothing on Ibiza except hedonism and, even for an old hedonist like myself, that starts to wear thin quite quickly. I returned to London to play cricket and to visit Louisa and Tom in Dorset.

When I began with Gottschalk again in September, I decided to take advantage of being in Germany and do a German course at the Goethe Institute. I enrolled for a six-week inter-mediate class and, for the first in my life, at the ripe old age of 45, became a student. I stayed in Charlotte's empty flat and for six hours a day, surrounded by Russian, Japanese, Korean and American kids, I learned my verbs and nouns, my conjugations and declensions, and loved every single minute. I still emerged speaking bad German, but a much-improved bad German. I was even presented with a certificate at the end to vouch for my hard work and dedication.

Arriving back in London at the end of the course, Charlotte and I passed on the stairs as she was off to Kazakhstan on business. She apologised that the food cupboards were completely empty but explained that she had been practically living out of a suitcase herself since I had been away. I drove her to the airport, and on my way back I stopped off at Sainsbury's to stock up on food. The trolley was groaning as I pushed it through the checkout, paid and headed back to the car park.

Halfway back to the car I felt a hand on my shoulder, turned and saw that it belonged to a burly Sainsbury's security guard. "Excuse me, sir," he said in the way that they have learned from a hundred sitcoms, "would you mind coming back into the store with me for a few minutes?" I asked why and he said it would be best if we spoke in private. I started to worry that I had inadvertently walked through the checkout without paying for a newspaper or something, but once inside the office, it became clear that it was more serious than that.

"What is this all about?" I asked, attempting to sound as officious and authoritative as I could. "Well, sir," said the blue-serge, uniformed gorilla, "you have been identified on one of our screens as being the man who carried out a serious sexual assault on one of our female staff here last Tuesday. Not just any female member of staff, actually sir. In fact, she was my wife." He looked at me with venom in his eye. I knew the charge was ridiculous but in that Kafkaesque situation I asked pathetically, "What did I do?" "She was standing up a ladder sir, filling the shelves, when you walked past, put you hands on her buttocks and fondled her." He made the obscene hand movement you might use if you were squeezing two ripe melons in a particularly lascivious manner. "You asked her 'Are you alright up there or do you need a hand?' and slid your hand up her skirt."

I was dumbstruck. Despite the comic potential of the scenario he described, it was actually way beyond a joke. I began my defence. "I am afraid you wife is mistaken. Firstly, I would never assault a lady in such a grotesque manner, for fear of being brained by a tumbling pyramid of baked bean cans, and secondly, and rather more pertinently, although I would admit to having long arms, they would not stretch the 800 miles from Munich, which is where I was last Tuesday. Indeed not only last Tuesday, but also the Tuesday before that and the one before that, and most other Tuesdays in recent history. You see," I was warming to my defence, "I returned form a six-week stay in Munich just an hour and a half ago." Remembering the certificate in my pocket, I rummaged it out and presented it to him "And here is the proof." He looked crestfallen and gazed at it blankly. It was, after all, a slightly tatty, rather vulgar document, written in German Gothic script. But there, clearly on it, were my name and two dates, those of commencement and completion of the course. I wanted to point out the three stars too, but decided against it.

Sensing imminent defeat, and with a new-found politeness, he asked me to wait for a moment while he went to check with his wife. Minutes later he returned, red-faced, and apologised saying that his wife had studied the tapes again and decided that it wasn't me at all. (It should be said here that I do not exactly look like Everyman. A mistaken identity involving me would suggest the witness had all the powers of observation of a mole.) He opened the doors expansively and told me that I was free to go, and that he would get someone to help me take my trolley to the car.

Returning home, I managed to build up sufficient anger to telephone the manager of the supermarket and remonstrate with him as to what had happened. I used my best "Enraged of Cheltenham" telephone voice, and told him I was disgusted at the shabby treatment I had received at the hands of his employee. He was about to apologise and I told him, "Don't say anything to me now. I am too angry. Call me in a couple of days." I gave him my telephone number and hung up. A couple of days later he duly called, with more apologies on his lips. I told him I couldn't possibly shop at Sainsbury's again unless I had a letter of full apology absolving me of all suspicion in the matter. This he duly agreed to send. I could feel his hand hovering over the telephone, anxious to hang up and be done with the matter, so I blurted out "And if you feel like putting anything else in with the letter, by way of compensation, it would be no more than you ought to do." With that I hung up. The next day a grovelling letter of apology duly arrived together with vouchers to the value of £150. With Christmas coming I thought they would come in handy.

The following day I had lunch with Brian Clarke, Mick Jagger and Marie Helvin at San Lorenzo. I told them the story of what had happened and Mick chortled and said "The same thing 'appened to Jerry in L.A. It's 'cos they recognise you from the telly and can't separate that from reality. All these birds wanna be involved in a little drama." He spoke with the assured authority of one who had been involved in more than his fair share of dramas with "the birds".

I cashed in the vouchers just before Christmas and flew into a snowbound Prestwick airport from Munich after recording the Christmas show with Thomas. I drove through deep snow from the airport to spend another delightful New Year with Cecilia and Alexander McEwen at Bardrochat. Charlotte had already travelled up from London, and once again the other guests comprised the usual company – Bunter Somerset, Jools Holland and Christobel, and a gathering of The Clan.

No sooner had the New Year celebrations finished than I was back to regular commuting between London and Munich. The guests on the show were getting more and more bizarre, ranging from home-grown German favourites such as Claudia Schiffer and David Hasselhof from *Baywatch*, to porn stars, *schlager* singers and generic teenybop fare such as The Backstreet Boys and Ricky Martin. The show was ludicrous and crass, but I could do it with my eyes closed and it got me out of debt. Sometimes that is a good enough reason to do a job.

* * *

April 1997 was darkened by the death of my old friend and sparring partner Giovanni Dadomo. In March, complaining of general pains, he was admitted into hospital and diagnosed as suffering from cancer. Soon afterwards, he died. He was 48 years old. A truly wasted talent. At his funeral, a kindly Italian padre told the sniffling congregation of music hacks, minor rock stars and expatriate Italians, "Giovanni was not a bad man. He was a good man. A kind man." So true. The padre might also have said that he was a very funny man, too. I was reminded by a mutual friend recently of one of the songs Gio used to sing with the Snivelling Shits – an up-tempo, funk number called *James Brown Has Got Cancer*. The big C got you first, Gio. Ciao, my friend.

Brian Clarke and I sat next to each other in church for the funeral service, trying not to lose it on what was a desperately sad occasion. Outside the weather was appropriately bleak and the huddled masses drew furtively on cigarettes and discussed which pub to go to. We couldn't face it and we slipped away.

* * *

I needed to get away and as Charlotte had gone skiing with her family, I decided I would do something that I had intended to do for many years: to go to Seville for the annual *feria de Abril*, the fabulous festival of flamenco, horses and wine. Almost as an afterthought I asked Geno if he would like to come with me, little expecting him to say "Yes", (if my father had asked me to spend a whole week with him when I was 20, I think I would have rather died) but to my surprise he jumped at the offer and we spent a fabulous week together, talking non-stop as we drove from Malaga to Ronda, Seville, Cordoba and Granada, stopping wherever we wanted to eat or to stay or to explore. As there were just the two of us, we got to know each other again on that trip, and I was able to talk to him at length for the first time about my reasons for leaving Rene, and consequently leaving him. He is a very loyal boy, and I am, for the most part, very loyal to my friends, too, so I never sought to drive a wedge between him and Rene, nor did I expect him to take sides in a drama in which he was a wounded bystander, caught in the cross-fire. I only wanted him to properly understand what had happened, and if he was angry with me to talk it through so it wouldn't hobble us in years to come.

The *feria* itself was unforgettable, and Geno and I were totally won over by the irresistibly infectious family atmosphere of the whole celebration, and the elegance of the dancing, food and drink. Fortified by ice-cold Manzanilla sherry, we attempted to join the locals as they danced the Sevilliana, the folk-dance close cousin to flamenco. We were hopeless, unable to master the complex counting patterns which seemed second nature to both the eight-year-old girls with garlands of flowers in their hair and to their mahogany-faced grandfathers who stood an extra six inches taller as they danced the extravagant courtly dance with their wives. The parties in the tents got into full swing around 2–3 am, and we bounced from one to the other, grinning like lunatics as we were swept along by the pure vitality and exuberance of the event. Seeing the great cities of Andalusia in April was one of the greatest trips I have ever made. To have done the trip with my son, and for us to have loved each other so dearly, made the trip doubly important in my life.

* * *

With Britain being seen in the summer of 1997 as a beacon of modernism and media-friendly politics, thanks to the election victory of Tony Blair and the marketing triumph of New Labour, it was not surprising when the Polish Government got in touch with a past master of spin, Malcolm McLaren, and asked him to help them "sell" Poland as a similarly progressive and trendy place. He had made an album called *Paris*, which cobbled together a bit of old 1950s beat-nostalgia with some 1990s sampling techniques, added some glamour in the form of Catherine Deneuve and Françoise Hardy, and flogged it as a concept-album "homage".

The Poles flew Malcolm out to Warsaw and asked him for his observations, and what he could do with their city to make it hip. Now Malcolm is never one to pass up the opportunity to make a buck so he went out, all expenses paid, and cast his eye over the place. After a couple of days he had formed his opinion. "So what do you think of Warsaw, Mr. McLaren?" asked an official. "Not much," replied Malcolm, "It's boring. Paris has Arabs, London had Indians and Afro-Caribbeans, and New York has blacks and Hispanics. All you have here is Poles." It was a damning appraisal. "What should we do?" they asked him in desperation. "Get some Africans here. Have a hip-hop festival or something." Then, in a moment of brilliance, "No – even better. Change the national flag. It's boring. Re-design it and stick a pineapple in the middle of it. Put a bit of Africa in the flag, man! That will bring in the Africans." He pursued the idea, then, sensing a business opportunity for himself, suggested, "And open a lifestyle store in the middle of Warsaw. Selling fashion, music, art and food. I will tell you who to stock".

When Malcolm came back from Poland and told me this stuff it had me in stitches. He had already been grafted on to some sort of Millennium Committee in the UK to devise and advise on entertainment and spectacles to commemorate the upcoming millennium, so he had experience in dealing with government officials who wanted to appear trendy. When the establishment appointees on that committee suggested such lame ideas as shooting lasers across the Thames at midnight, Malcolm, now almost as camp as Quentin Crisp, with a bouffant to match, killed the idea. "They shoot lasers every time Joan Collins opens a fucking supermarket in L.A. We need to do something radical." Then, rehashing a theme suggested to Jocelyn Stephens or Lord Rogers or whoever was on the committee, "We need to change the national flag. It's boring. By the time the Millennium comes the Scots will be out on their own, so will the Welsh. All that leaves is a red cross on a white background. We look like a fucking charity organisation. Re-design it and stick a pineapple in the middle of it. Put a bit of Africa in the flag, man!" More interestingly, in a spirit of internationalism, he advocated that everyone under the age of 26 should be given a free ticket to anywhere in the world, "so they can get the hell out of this country for the Millennium celebrations." He didn't last on the committee much after that.

* * *

I had spoken many times to Duncan Ward about absurdism, surrealism and Dada, and I was delighted when he told me he wanted to blow the dust off an old play by the little-known, nineteenth-century German dramatist, Christian Dietrich Grabbe, called *Comedy, Satire, Irony and Deeper Meaning*, a proto-absurdist work written in 1827, nearly 70 years before the premiere of Alfred Jarry's seminal absurdist work, *Ubu Roi*. He had secured a spot at the prestigious Gate Theatre in Notting Hill, and wanted to put a company together to do a series of rehearsed readings of the play, with a view to staging it later. I had enjoyed working with Duncan on his film, *Dead Men Don't Remember*, and admired his energy and enjoyed his sense of humour. I consequently agreed. He assembled a cast of 10 or 12 very good actors and actresses, all working simply because they were drawn into the project by Duncan's louche charm and enthusiasm. We rehearsed for about a week. Although the project was essentially a rehearsed reading of the play, (no learning of lines necessary, no moves to remember, the entire cast seated onstage reading from their scripts), the play was to be semi-staged inasmuch as all the men wore black tie and the girls wore long dresses, and there was a certain amount of action and choreography, albeit undertaken from our seats.

The whole performance was "conducted" by a wonderful white-haired septuagenarian artist–actor–mask-maker named Roddy Maude-Roxby. Roddy is one of the most fascinating men I have ever met. He is a fearless and inspirational performer, most at home when improvising and using found objects as props, or making customised masks for a production. In the performances of *Comedy, Satire, Irony and Deeper Meaning*, Roddy stood at a lectern, away from the rest of the cast, and directed the action like a wild-haired maestro who had been plugged into the electric mains. He coaxed, cajoled and exhorted the cast to redouble their efforts, and he read the stage directions and descriptions of the characters to the audience in a manner of which Brecht would have been proud.

Duncan was buoyed up by the reception and re-iterated his desire to follow up this success with the same company putting on a fully-realised production somewhere at some point. Of course, we were all out of pocket after the performances, so it was with some relief that I got a call from Martin Clunes telling me that there was an episode of *Men Behaving Badly* coming up in which there was a wedding (his, I think), and they wanted all the actors who had appeared in earlier episodes to be in the wedding episode. That is one of the nice things about Martin and Neil; they have seen the down-side of the business as well as the up-side, and look after their mates whenever they are in a position to do so. I think we shot the episode in Acton or somewhere out that way, and while we were shooting the party scene, there was never any question about the drinks being anything except real.

May 31 was Geno's twenty-first birthday – twenty-one years since Rene was in the Royal Free Hospital and I was at Abbey Road recording *Figments of Emancipation*. It seemed like a lifetime ago, yet at the same time it seemed that the years had been blown away like dust. He had expressed a desire to go to Australia to play cricket through the coming winter and for his birthday I bought him his air-ticket. I was immensely proud of him for showing the guts and independence to do something so exciting. Even when your child is 21 you still feel a huge protective instinct, and as I bought the ticket I prayed that he would come to no harm.

The autumn began with Kathy Acker participating in a performance she had co-written called *Pussy, King of the Pirates*, in Freedom, a small basement theatre in Soho. I always thought that Kathy was at her best as a performance artist rather than as a writer pure and simple. She had an engaging character and she had that essential component for any great performer – charisma. Kathy once told me that Gertrude Stein was her favourite writer, but it was William Burroughs who proved to be her true mentor. "He was my model. For me, he was the first writer, the only one who was working politically in the field of language as power. He was questioning language. Everybody else was just thinking about it," she explained. I knew exactly what she meant. It chimed perfectly with the effect that Burroughs had on me, way back in the sixties, when Joe Gilbert and I scoured the shelves of Shakespeare and Co in

Paris. After the show we all had a couple of drinks, then tumbled up the road to the Groucho for dinner. Although she looked more frail than we had ever seen her, Kathy was flying on the sheer enjoyment of the evening, and she wasn't going to let anything as trivial as cancer get in the way.

As a result of my increasing celebrity in Germany (thanks to my Butler's costume and my shit-eating grin) I was flown out to Berlin to participate in a Unicef gala evening. It was a worthy, rather than an exciting evening and featured Peter Ustinov performing excerpts from his one-man show, which the Germans so love. Gottschalk and I did a few introductions, but otherwise looked a bit spare. As with all such charity events, they tried to pack the front few rows with stars for the TV cameras, and fill in the next few rows with Eurotrash with low-cut gowns, good teeth and improbable hair. Behind them are the ugly dignitaries, and the corporates who have paid a fortune for the opportunity to take their wives to drink cheap *sekt* with a TV weather girl or an underwear model. We all stayed the night at a good hotel and the following morning I flew back to London sandwiched between Roger Moore and Vanessa Redgrave. It was like sitting between Oswald Mosley and Leon Trotsky. As good show-business people, we all chatted amiably on neutral topics and breathed a collective sigh of relief when we landed at Heathrow and parted company.

* * *

After a poor night's sleep on 31 August, I was woken at the usual time around seven o'clock by the radio-alarm, which I had forgotten to disable the night before. Normally when I forget to do that it is of no major consequence, as listening to the price of barley or some whinging farmer droning on about how bad things are in the West Country on Radio 4's *Farming Today* is enough to send me straight back to sleep. But on the Sunday morning of 1 September there was not a word about the price of barley, nor a single whinging farmer. Indeed, the programme didn't seem to have any agricultural content whatever. Groggily coming to, I realised that the only topic of conversation was Princess Diana, and I didn't have to listen for very long to learn that she had been killed in a motor accident in Paris.

I woke Charlotte up and we listened, stunned, together. The fragments of the story filtered through: that the previous night she had left The Ritz Hotel with her boyfriend, Dodi Fayed; that as they left they seemed to have been pursued through the late night streets by a gaggle of paparazzi on motorcycles; and that, as the publicity-shy Princess' driver tried to accelerate away from them in the four lane underpass near Place de l'Alma, he lost control of the car and hit a supporting pillar in the tunnel. Braking had forced the front of the car down, so the impact threw the rear of the car upwards, crushing the front part of the roof. Fayed and the driver had been killed on impact. Diana, originally thought to be seriously injured, was taken to hospital where, despite all possible medical attempts to save her, she had died of her injuries at 4am, Paris time.

I recalled the indelible image of her dancing in that desperate, distracted fashion at Bunter's wedding, and it seemed obvious to me then that she would never grow old. What wasn't obvious was that she would end up as another banal road traffic accident victim. For the next hour or so Charlotte and I just lay there and felt numb. I had always remained totally unimpressed by Diana, but it was an indisputable fact that she was the most famous person in the world, and that's what gave the event its morbid fascination. She was young(ish), beautiful(ish) and tragic, and all the elements of a truly romantic filmstar death were there – Paris, The Ritz, the speeding car, the handsome suitor. It was awful. Perfectly awful.

By eight o'clock Charlotte's family had started to telephone from Germany to commiserate and offer us sympathy, as though Diana had been a close friend or relation. This was a common experience for many that day. People telephoned their friends or family, or stopped strangers on the street, to try to express their shock or grief. By the time dusk was falling, vigil-mentality had gripped London and thousands of people, clutching photographs, candles and posies, were travelling to locations associated with Diana or Dodi, like so many grim-faced medieval pilgrims. Kensington Palace, Buckingham Palace and Clarence House soon looked like ancient religious monuments at the far end of a sea of flowers, candles and cards. Unfortunately so did Harrod's, the Knightsbridge store owned by Dodi Fayed's controversial father, Mohammed, who had wasted no time in turning his prime retail outlet into a kitsch shrine to the two doomed lovers.

"A massive outpouring of public grief", "A nation grieves", "The People's Princess", "The Queen of all our hearts", the newspapers reiterated those words over and over like a mantra. Within a week, the lawns that stretched up to Kensington Palace, Diana's last London home, were smothered with so many flowers that they created a new ecosystem. It was a most un-British way to grieve. Perhaps it was just the supreme symbol of those caring, sharing, touchy-feely nineties that ordinary folks wanted to show that they had real feelings, too, or perhaps it was a surge of a millennial republicanism that wanted to teach the Royal Family a lesson for treating their Fairy Princess so shabbily.

Whatever the reason, the week between Diana's death and her funeral was the most kitsch week in British history. The British don't do the public grieving thing well. That is why we felt so uncomfortable when the earliest of those confessional TV shows such as *Oprah* and *Jerry Springer* first started to work their spell over here. We were both repelled and fascinated by the vulgarity of families tearing themselves apart for a voyeuristic public to enjoy, and to watch them weep, fight, gnash their teeth and tear their hair in a way that we would never do (at least, not for another three or four years).

On 6 September, the day of the funeral, I was back in Munich working with Gottschalk on the show. Once again, as the only Brit on the set, I was the centre of attention, receiving words of sympathy and regret from moist-eyed technicians and make-up girls alike. Between rehearsals we clustered around the TV set in the Green Room to watch the funeral beamed live from Westminster Abbey. It was both compulsive and repulsive. As with all occasions of State, the British establishment got the tone just about right, only to have it undermined by two of the most distasteful performances imaginable, both outrages being perpetrated in the Abbey itself.

First, the noble Sir Elton John, whose career, it might be noted, was not exactly at its zenith at that point, gallantly agreed to perform a funeral mix of his song, *Candle In The Wind*, to the largest global television audience of all time, donating the subsequent royalties for the song to charity. The song itself, the most mawkish, sickly claptrap imaginable, sounded like it had been thrown together using a Burroughsian cut-up technique that used Mother's Day greeting-card schmaltz and tombstone doggerel as its raw material. As too many syllables clumsily fought for space within the melody, we were introduced to a character of pure fiction, England's Rose, who called out to our country and now belonged to heaven. It was, of course, a smash. Why did they invite Elton to the ceremony anyway? Well, I guess they wanted to ensure that there was at least *one* emotional queen in the Abbey that day.

Diana's brother, Charles Althorp, the Earl of Spencer, in an ill-advised, inappropriate piece of populist score-settling, attempted to seize the moral high ground over the Royal Family. His famous speech seemed to me to be nothing more than an unseemly squabble over a still-warm corpse as to who should inherit a highly valued piece of furniture. Althorp, himself a member of a supremely dysfunctional family who had handled his own marriage with all the sensitivity of a hobnail-booted navvy attempting a *pas de deux*, fulminated none-too-cryptically against the Royal Family in general and Prince Charles in particular. For a man who, a mere six months after marrying Victoria Lockwood, had rekindled an affair with an old flame, he certainly showed some brass neck when, in his funeral address he confided, "Diana explained to me once that it was her innermost feelings of suffering that made it possible for her to connect with her constituency of the rejected." Oof! Take that Charles!

Speaking of the two young princes, William and Harry, he continued, "I pledge that we, your blood family, will do all we can to continue the imaginative and loving way in which you were steering these two exceptional young men, so that their souls are not simply immersed by duty and tradition but can sing openly as you planned" Get that, Your Majesty? "Blood family". This from a man whose best friend and best man, Darius Guppy, was already in prison for fraud. No wonder Her Majesty winced at that.

"We, like you, recognise the need for them to experience as many different aspects of life as possible, to arm them spiritually and emotionally for the years ahead." Asking the Althorps to "arm children spiritually and emotionally" would be like asking Dr Josef Mengele to teach your children about dentistry. It was a truly sickening, manipulative address, which was applauded all the way by a public who already saw Diana as a martyr-in-waiting. Inside the Abbey, the unlikeliest people rubbed shoulders. Half close your eyes and you could imagine that George Michael, Sting and Pavarotti were at a music-biz awards ceremony, while Tom Hanks, Tom Cruise, Nicole Kidman and Steven Spielberg all looked like they were waiting to hear those magic words, ". . . and the winner is . . ."

As the cortège left the Abbey and wound its way up through the London streets, silent and eerily empty of all traffic, towards Marble Arch and the MI, its path was strewn with a million flowers as the crowd warmed to the ritual. Tentatively at first, and then with the confidence that participation in mass public behaviour brings, people showered the hearse with flowers in scenes reminiscent of Christ's entry into Jerusalem. I felt oddly detached from the whole spectacle in my seat in the Green Room in Munich, even though I knew every inch of the journey that the procession took, all the way to Northamptonshire. I had made that journey myself so many times with The Doctors of Madness, albeit in rather less orderly fashion. That evening the show went on like any other and afterwards Gottschalk and I went for dinner.

Back in London the following week the grief-fest continued, and Kensington Gardens, with its carpet of flowers, became the number one tourist attraction in London, probably in the world. Like all those tourists I, too, went along to gawp. It impressed by virtue of its scale, but I didn't know what, if anything, it all meant.

THE BEELZEBUB SONATA

Two weeks after Diana's funeral, Kathy Acker announced that she had sold her flat in Islington and was leaving London to return to the States. She had become increasingly ill over the summer but had blamed her illness on drinking contaminated canal water. It somehow seemed unlikely to us but she was adamant and we thought that this was her way of dealing with her gradual physical deterioration. Relying on faith healers and other alternative medical treatments, she convinced herself that she was, indeed, cured of cancer, even after an Appalachian faith healer informed her the previous year that, "You have cancer all over your body . . . I see a huge black leech in the centre of your heart." Wanting to be free of cancer, Acker relied exclusively on advice from her healers and had discontinued any regular conventional medical check-ups.

A few of us arranged to meet her for a farewell drink at her Islington flat the night before she left. Charlotte and I, Rene, Louisa and the Turner Prize-nominated artist, Cathy de Monchaux (for whose catalogue Kathy had written an introduction), all arrived to find her sitting in an empty room, surrounded by towers of cardboard boxes into which she had packed her whole life, including her travelling library of four or five thousand books, waiting for repatriation. Somehow we all felt a desperate chill and sense of foreboding in that room, as we sipped wine from plastic cups and tried to keep each other's spirits up. Beneath the joshing and the reminiscing and the promises to stay in constant touch, we somehow all knew that Kathy was returning home to die, with the unfathomable instinct of a wounded animal needing to return to its birthplace.

She told us she was heading to California to drop off her things, then crossing the border into Tijuana, Mexico, where there was a radical new cancer treatment being practised, so new that it didn't even have clearance to be licensed in the USA yet. She was going to give it a shot. We hugged her and kissed her, and told her to try to get a lot of rest and promised we would all meet up again. In truth we knew that we would never see her again.

Autumn was a time of saying goodbyes as in October, Geno and his friend, Mark, headed out to Australia to play cricket and to seek their fortunes. Geno had taken his A levels in London and passed all three, and had worked for a while at a theatrical PR and marketing company in Soho, but now he wanted to test himself. For Rene it was especially hard as Geno was still living with her, and for all the conflict that their strong personalities provoked, they were intensely close and she knew she would miss him terribly. For me it was easier, sharing a different sort of bond with him, but the idea of him travelling across the world, albeit at the age of 21, still made me feel a pang of apprehension. I drove Rene and the boys to Gatwick and we hovered by the departure gate, making that small talk you make at those times. Eventually it was time for them to go, and all three of us embraced and wept as we parted, while Mark hovered at a discreet distance. All the way home Rene and I, alone in the car, could barely find a word to utter, but tried to exchange the occasional word of comfort and reassurance to each other.

I got a commercial job to do for Swedish TV, something about the Swedish football pools I think, and had to go to Leeds to shoot it with a Tomas Brolin, an overweight Swedish foot-baller with a great future behind him. While I was in Leeds I decided that I would try to track down my brother John, who I had not seen in twenty years. He had performed an amazing disappearing act after his divorce, before our father died. He showed none of my hypocrisy by attending the funeral, and was never subsequently in touch, even though the three of us brothers were the sole nominees on the trust that held the family house until Mum's death. I could understand perfectly his reasons for doing what he did. He had decided (I surmise) that he wanted to re-invent himself, to re-start his life, and it was not possible to do that effectively while staying in touch with those who had known you before year zero.

We knew that he had moved north, and while his disappearance was especially hurtful to Mum, who took it hard and personally, I could only sympathise with his course of action. I surprised him with a telephone call to his office, telling him that I was in Leeds, and that if he wanted to meet for a drink I would like that, and if he didn't I would fully understand and would never bother him again. I was surprised that he agreed to meet, and we arranged a rendezvous in the neutral surroundings of a bar of a large hotel. We recognised each other immediately, of course, with that uncanny radar that siblings have, which goes way beyond physical recognition, and I ordered a couple of stiff drinks and we sat down.

Inevitably, the meeting was, at first, a mix of forced joviality and guarded formality, but gradually the temperature rose and we started to talk more freely. He had changed the way all men change after they are 40, with more weight and less hair than when I had seen him last, but temperamentally he was still very much the same. Intelligent, serious but humorous. We moved from the bar to an Italian restaurant and over dinner exchanged a lot of reminiscences about our early lives. As I suspected, John was as damaged by Dad as I was, bewildered, angry and sad that we had been denied a "normal" father, but determined to get over it in a practical, rather than in a psychological–emotional way. Like me, he has compensated for our father's lack of sociability by developing a surfeit of it, but I suspect that, also like me, there is a part of him that is forever dark, forever black and forever dissatisfied. I felt glad to have seen him but drew no conclusions, and we made no promises to keep in touch. We exchanged telephone numbers, and I told him that I wouldn't tell Mum that we had met until and unless he wanted to see her again.

Louisa Buck launched her new book, an indispensable *Who's Who* of the British art world called *Moving Targets* at the House for Fallen Women, in Soho. Louisa is a great writer, erudite and opinionated, but with a peppy, slightly racy style. A resplendent George Melly, the singer and art historian, and an old flame of Louisa's, gave the book the thumbs up, and every major name in British art dropped by to pay her their respects. One person who would have loved the party was Kathy Acker, but we knew she wouldn't be making a surprise entry. We had heard that her health had deteriorated even further, but we were still devastated to hear on 29 November that she had died. The "huge black leech" that the medicine man had seen had proved too strong for her. I got an e-mail from a friend, the guitarist Lu Edmonds, who had been playing guitar with Kathy on the *Pussy* project. He had attached an e-mail he had received detailing Kathy's last hours. Somehow it was comforting to read it, and my fears that it would be too mawkish were unjustified. The Americans are actually rather good at this stuff sometimes. Notwithstanding Diana, generally the British are just too stiff-upper-lipped to get emotionally involved in death.

The e-mail was from Kathy's friend, Matias Viegener, the art historian and critic, to their mutual friend Lynne Tillmann, the feminist writer and New York art world luminary. The e-mail described with such aching beauty her parting that I include it here, with special thanks to Matias. It reads:

Dear Lynne,
Kathy really couldn't talk the last two days; she understood everything we said and was able to nod yes and no. She smiled often, beaming, an amazing joyful sight. I think she knew how much she was loved, able more than ever in her life to accept the love of others. Soon after they arrived we were all four gathered around her bed, and she had the most peaceful expression, really as though she were cradled by those who loved her, and for the first time stopped breathing, almost for 30 seconds; we were all frozen and thought it was happening then, but she gasped, pulling back, as though frightened, and began to breath again.

This happened a few more times during the day, as though she was testing, going away and coming back, seeing that it was safe. Connie Samaras came and I napped while she sat with Kathy; she woke me a few times when she thought it looked serious, and finally at one o'clock in the morning, it was serious. Kathy was very clear, looked both of us in the eyes – we were caressing her and telling her she was alright, that she was safe – and just stopped breathing. She gasped a few times and then just stopped. If there is any thing as a beautiful death, this was one. She knew exactly what was happening and all her fear seemed gone; she had a beaming, open look on her face. Connie and I just held her gaze, as though elevated with her. Then her whole body relaxed, her palms turned upward.

Only once she was gone did we begin to cry, and after that we went back to her, caressed and sat with her, telling her that we loved her, as she grew cold. The hospital left us alone with her for almost two hours, then came in to remove all the catheters and IV stuff, and we decided to take off the piercings together. I had decided with Amy, Ira and the Antins that she should be cremated (she had never told me what she wanted). The mortuary people arrived at four, and we wanted to stay with her until they took her away. They wrapped her in the clean white sheets of the bed, it was very beautiful to us, and laid her on a stretcher which they covered with a dark red velvet cloth. Then we walked with them to the hearse, and watched it drive away.

All of the spiritual work she had done in the last two years came alive to guide her; she had no fear in the end. She was on almost no painkillers, just some Valium for sedation. I must believe that a life of great tempest was finally at peace, that some profound wisdom eased her passage or calmed the storm.

After the body was taken away, we wanted to leave the hospital too and took a cab to the border, walked across and caught the 5:00 trolley to San Diego, which was full of drunken sailors and teenagers, scrambled lowlife headed home from Tijuana. K. would have liked that contrast, the men passed out on benches or rambling about Camp Pendleton, a few wild chicks even more zonked, and Connie and I huddled in corner with our tears. Then the 6:00 train to LA, which passes the most beautiful empty beaches. I'm missing her terribly and am pulled into remembering all her wounds, sadness and defeats, when I know that essentially it was an extraordinary life, explosively rich.

No more to say now.

Much love
Matias

It is one of the more unacceptable aspects of getting older that one loses ones friends with greater frequency. Robert Fraser, Philip Core, Michael Dempsey, Giovanni Dadomo and now Kathy Acker. All gone. I sat down, my eyes still wet with tears, and wrote a song for Kathy called *Sleep The Gentle Sleep*.

Well the last train has gone and snow has covered everything
The barman pours a drink so I guess we're staying on
And I just got the news so anyway I couldn't go
'Cos you lost that final showdown in Tijuana, Mexico
This year I swear the winter will be colder
And the air will freeze my tears 'cos you're not here.
Hey now now, Hey now now, Hey now now
Sleep the Gentle Sleep.

It is a song that, to this day, I find impossible to sing without seeing Kathy's face, with her huge eyes and delicate, almost elfin features. Her funeral and cremation were in California, organised by a few of her close friends. None of us could get across, which we regretted, but we felt she would have understood.

* * *

One afternoon in the eighties, at a noisy table in The Soho Brasserie, I had introduced my friend Duncan Ward to the work of two characters who would have a profound effect and influence on him: the Austrian-Ukrainian writer, Wilhelm Reich, and the Polish polymath, Stanislaw Ignacy Witkiewicz. I had just finished reading Reich's short book about mass control called *Listen Little Man*, in which he rails against the sentimental plague, the propaganda of his time, and calls to anyone who is willing to listen to stop being the little man who refuses to assume responsibility for his own life, and to become what he is meant to be, an aware, responsible individual. It is a short book that is long on ideas, and I raved about it to Duncan the way you do when you have just finished a book that has truly touched a nerve. Reich had good reason to rail against authoritarianism and the excesses of the state. His books, almost uniquely for a writer, were burned in both Nazi Germany and post-war USA, where he eventually died in prison.

Somehow or other I went from discussing Reich to ranting about the genius of Stanislaw Ignacy Witkiewicz, sometimes known as Witkacy, the great Polish philosopher, playwright, artist, essayist and one of the great creative talents of the early twentieth century. He was also a pioneer of absurdism, clearing the way for the later exponents such as Ionesco and Beckett. Throughout the twenties and thirties he wrote many plays and philosophical essays and was, at the same time, Poland's leading society portrait artist. In 1939, when, as a consequence of the Molotov/Ribbentrop treaty, the Russian army marched into Poland, he shot himself in a forest near Zakopane, guessing that whatever the outcome of the war, he would be unable to function freely, as neither the communists nor the Nazis were likely to allow his radical work much space. I had recently seen a collection of his portraits somewhere and was enthusing about them to Duncan, and recommending some of his proto-absurdist drama such as *The Locomotive* and *The Madman and the Nun*.

Years later, at the beginning of 1998, I was chatting to Duncan about how we should follow up the encouraging success of the Grabbe play that we did at the *Gate Theatre* the previous May, and we both started talking enthusiastically about Witkiewicz again. Duncan had the idea of presenting *The Beelzebub Sonata*, a lesser-known piece, but a very appropriate diatribe on the nature of art and how it can survive the homogeneity of a mechanised, soulless world. We read the play through and he asked me if I would play Beelzebub who, in a Mephistopholean pact, persuades Istvan, the young composer, to write *The Beelzebub Sonata*, a diabolically brilliant piece of music which will ensure his artistic reputation, but damn his mortal soul to hell. The play is about loss of innocence, and the greed, ambition and vanity of artists.

We got very excited about the play and agreed to co-produce it ourselves. We formed a company called the Found Theatre Company and got to work. Duncan got the company of actors together, including some of those from the Grabbe piece we had done at the Gate. We were a company of about 10 by the end, with Roddy Maude-Roxby, Rose Keegan and myself from the Grabbe piece being joined by a fabulous and exotic collection of individuals. Rupam Maxwell played the composer, Istvan, and Katrine Boorman played Hilda, the opera-singing tart. Working with Katrine is always hilarious and hugely enjoyable. She is one of those people who is so full of love and fun and generosity of spirit that you feel she does not have a bad bone in her fabulous body.

I set about looking for a venue for the play, and when Dominic Berning introduced me to a friend of his to whom he sold art, I knew we were in business. Lucy Morris had recently bought an old church hall in Notting Hill and was using it very occasionally as a bridge club. I told Lucy about *The Beelzebub Sonata* and she said she would be thrilled if we would do it in her church hall. We began work almost straight away, rehearsing in the hall through January and February in a near-Arctic chill, and devising the piece as we went. Duncan's directorial style was a mix of Tadeusz Kantor, the Théâtre de Complicité and anally-fixated boarding-school infantilism, but somehow the whole play started to take shape. There were endless fights and falling-outs, and the show, despite relying on a fairly simple set, was choreographically and dramatically quite complex.

Janusz Podrazic, the Polish avant-garde composer, wrote a wonderful score that somehow managed to be both ethereal and erotic. He also wrote a show-stopping humdinger of a song, set in a cabaret club. It was a delightfully bawdy number, which the entire company, led by Katrine, sang.

We rehearsed every day for a month or more for no money, and eventually decided to open on 13 March, the thirteenth being a suitably diabolical choice of date. Together with Katrine and her husband, Danny Moynihan, Duncan and I combined our address books and the four of us did a massive mail-out to all our friends, and invited the wealthiest to the opening night gala performance, which would be a fund-raiser for the rest of the run.

We had already built a stage and installed stage lighting, and we dressed the building out so that it looked like a fantastic Eastern European baronial banqueting hall, with tables, chairs, candles and food. We knew we had sold out the first night in advance and the cheques had all cleared, so we had a good feeling about the run, which would last for only eight performances. Our success was assured when, on that opening night, Katrine's dad, the film director, John Boorman, arrived from Paris with Gerard Depardieu and Carole Bouquet in tow. The press photographers outside our small theatre went ape. Those were only three of the faces who turned up, and the following day the London *Evening Standard* had a huge picture of Depardieu and Bouquet with a story saying "*The Beelzebub Sonata* is London's hottest theatre ticket." Every fringe production needs a bit of luck to get a buzz going, and that was ours. We sold out every night, and every night was like a fantastic cocktail party. We would peer through the curtains to see who was in that night, and saw Mick Jagger, Bryan Ferry, Malcolm McLaren or Tracey Emin.

One night, in a perfectly piquant coincidence, Damien Hirst had a table next to that of the collector, Charles Saatchi. There is a fabulous moment in the play when Beelzebub appeals to the greed and blind ambition of the innocent young composer, telling him to leave his scruples behind and collaborate with him on the Sonata. It seemed to so perfectly echo the relationship between Damien and Saatchi at that time that the audience was absolutely spellbound, almost embarrassed by the poignancy of the moment. Even the oafish Keith Allen, by now officially engaged as Damien's pet monkey and cheerleader, couldn't break the spell, despite a constant attempt to divert attention away from the stage and on to himself. It is both baffling and sad that an actor of Keith's undoubted talent feels the need to behave so boorishly every minute of the day. I am sure there is a deep-seated reason for his feeling of inadequacy, and having seen him perform nude, I can guess what it might be, but it is irksome, not to say unprofessional, nevertheless.

A more welcome face in the audience was Geno, who had completed his six-month journey through Australia, Indonesia and Thailand, and arrived home in great shape and with his confidence hugely bolstered by the fact that he had made the journey. It was an enormous relief for Rene and me to have him back, and he was immediately talking about wanting to try to get into the film business. I only gave him one piece of advice: write out a CV, knock on every door of every film company in Soho and be prepared for a lot of rejection. But if someone does offer you a chance, grab it with both hands and be reliable, punctual and conscientious. He did as I suggested and found work first as an unpaid runner, then as a production assistant and he is now a unit manager and location finder. When Rene and I think back over the chances we took with him, and the chaotic nature of his early years with us, he is a towering testament to the durability of the human spirit. He came and saw the play a couple of times, and was enthusiastic and supportive.

As we were performing just around the corner from his house, Brian Clarke, typically generously, came several times with several different parties. One night he told me, "I loved it, but I kept getting distracted by the gaze of a rather stern, pasty-faced woman on the next table who seemed to be constantly looking at me. It was only when the lights went up that I realised it was Malcolm McLaren."

Charlotte, together with Malcolm's girlfriend, Charlotte Skene Catling, ran the door and the bar, heroically coming straight from work and clocking on for the evening shift. They had to contend with liggers such as Bob Geldof who tried to gain free admittance, rather than cough up £15 for a ticket. There are none as cheap as the very rich.

The show had many great moments. Roddy carried off the lynchpin character of Rio Bamba, the plantation owner and narrator, with typical improvisational aplomb. Katrine always threatened to steal the show with her lewd dance routines and Demian Burger, a dashing-looking Swiss film producer and director with only one eye and one hand, who played the Spanish ambassador, triumphed in his first time ever on a stage. He looked perfect with his eye-patch and leather *el muffti*, velvet pantaloons and unwieldy sword, and in a minor deviation from Witkiewicz's original, he brought the house down as he handed round a tray of Ferrero Rocher chocolates piled into the trademark pyramid of that tacky confection, and was told "Ambassador, you are spoiling us with your extravagance." After the closing show we had a wonderful party and swore we would do it all again somewhere, sometime.

During the rehearsals and the run of the play I had become very good friends with Demian. He is an extraordinary guy who is interested in absolutely everything, and knows something about just about every topic, and those that he knows nothing about he is keen to learn. He is a guy who lives life to the full, and doesn't let anything as trivial as the loss of an eye and a hand prevent him from ski-ing, driving or rolling cigarettes. The bizarre details of his injuries are suitably South American to warrant the telling.

One afternoon in Montevideo (his wife, Helena, is a Uruguayan opera singer) he was lounging by the swimming pool, wondering how they could celebrate that evening's fiesta in high style. Having decided that the local fireworks were rather under-powered, he set about emptying the gunpowder out of several dozen fireworks on to a glass table by the poolside. As the mountain of powder got higher and higher, his enthusiasm for the task increased until there was a small Kilimanjaro on the glass. The midday sun was burning fiercely down and, inevitably, ignited the gunpowder, causing a massive explosion that shattered the table. The flying glass severed his left hand and blinded his right eye, and did such appalling damage to one of his legs that it was initially thought that it would have to be amputated. Fortunately, a local man with some knowledge of tribal medicine stopped the bleeding and wrapped the limb in a polythene bag with a variety of local herbs. His quick-wittedness saved the leg. Sadly, in the furore, no one had noticed that a shard of glass from the table had been blown across the pool, and had severed an artery of his best friend, who was sleeping on the other side. While everyone rallied around Demian, his friend slowly, silently bled to death. It was a tragedy so arbitrary, so absurdist, that it could have been invented by Jorg Luis Borges or Gabriel Garcia Marquez.

* * *

Mike Rundel, the architect from whom we had bought our house, had been involved in the design and building of Pharmacy, Damien Hirst's restaurant venture on Notting Hill. Before it even opened the restaurant was controversial, with local residents' groups asking that it be renamed as it might confuse people who wanted to buy an aspirin. Hirst merely re-arranged the letters so that one night it was called Army Chap, and the next Achy Ramp and so on, until the local council came down on the side of common sense and they re-arranged the letters once more and called it Pharmacy again.

When the restaurant finally opened in spring 1998, there was, of course, a massive and totally chaotic party. It was chaotic because they had dramatically under-estimated the number of guests who would turn up. Then, for some reason, the water supply ran out and then there was a fire in the kitchen. About 20 fire engines arrived and blocked the whole of Notting Hill Gate. It was sheer bedlam. We headed across the road and ate pizza instead. When we eventually got back into Pharmacy for dinner about a week later, I went to chat with Maia, Damien's girlfriend, who was having dinner at another table with Mariella Frostrup. She was in great form and invited Charlotte and me to visit the farmhouse that she and Damien had bought in Devon for a weekend. It was a part of Devon I remembered well from childhood holidays, a favourite place of mine.

Charlotte and I drove down and met Damien in the village pub, where he was already a great favourite and was probably single-handedly keeping them in business outside the tourist season. We played a few games of pool and chatted with Damien and Pam Blundell, the fashion designer, who was also staying at the house. By the early evening Danny Webb, who had played Hamlet, arrived, with his wife, Leila. Danny is a fanatical surfer, and he and Maia took advantage of some lively seas to indulge their sickness.

Damien was a little like a child with a new toy, proudly showing us the round, stone-built dairy – the outbuilding that he intended to convert into a library and snooker room. In the evening Damien cooked a delicious dinner, and the evening was relaxed and convivial.

Damien seemed to be able to be himself in his hideaway, leaving the bullshit and the image back in London. There had been a recent falling out between Damien and Marco Pierre White, the ill-tempered chef at Damien's first restaurant venture, Quo Vadis. The spat ended with Damien removing all his art from the restaurant, and White replacing it with his own versions. Having seen White's artworks and tasted Damien's cooking, I think on balance that Damien is the more multi-talented.

We spent the weekend in Devon walking, chatting, eating and drinking. It was great to spend some time with Danny again, and while we were in the house we relaxed and listened to a lot of music. Damien had just got the Beach Boys rarities and out-takes of the *Pet Sounds* CD, and we played it over and over. I told him about Nick Kent's excellent book, *The Dark Stuff*, his collected interviews with the more eccentric rock stars, of which the Beach Boys', Brian Wilson, is a contender for greatest fruitcake of all. He had never heard of it so on returning to London I sent him a copy.

Damien is a complex, erratic, infuriating character, sometimes seemingly hopelessly trapped in his "bad boy of British art" caricature, but possessing a rare and mercurial talent. He is responsible for some of the most memorable images of the last decade of the last millennium and will, without doubt, be one of the artists whose work endures long after the silliness and excesses of Brit Art are forgotten. Like many artists of his generation his work veers between the sublime, (the sheep, the shark, the horse's head, the medical cabinets) and the silly (the "spot" paintings, allegedly painted by his chums for 10 quid an hour and selling for in excess of £100,000, the spin paintings and the restaurants). But when it works it is impressive, monumental, emotionally and intellectually challenging art.

Incidentally, and importantly, he also has the wordsmith's gift, giving his works such enigmatic and resonant titles as "I want to spend the rest of my life everywhere, with every-one, one to one, always, forever, now" (the ping-pong ball on a column of air); "The physical impossibility of death in the mind of someone living" (the shark); and "Some comfort gained from the acceptance of the inherent lies in everything" (the sliced cows). He is not *just* a metaphysical taxidermist, but if he were only that, he would be unique, and that would almost be reason enough to cherish him. The self-obsessed art of the Britpack – of Tracey, or Webster and Noble – the mythologising of their little lives, will be seen as tiresome and irrelevant. They seem hell-bent on either being or meeting celebrities. They desperately want to make enough cash in their 15 minutes of fame to buy the Notting Hill townhouse or the cool Clerkenwell loft before the bubble bursts and people ask "Where's the beef?" Jake and Dinos Chapman are almost unique among the Brits of their generation in bringing an intellectual rigour to their work. And the high-concept work of Darren Almond, Richard Wilson, Connie Parker, Langlands and Bell, Rachel Whiteread, Mark Wallinger and Gavin Turk will always repay closer contemplation. But most of the others just bleat and whinge. You may disagree.

* * *

My summer cricket tour to Cornwall was truncated by a call from Michelle. I had been offered a part in a big budget, US television film of *Alice in Wonderland*. It was an offer of three weeks work for good money, shooting at Shepperton Studios and starting immediately. I said goodbye to my willow-wielding colleagues and drove straight to Shepperton, where I met Joyce Gallie, the first casting director I had ever encountered, 14 years earlier, when Carina Cooper had invited me to Shepperton to meet Franc. Joyce was the casting director on *Alice in Wonderland* and offered me the part of one of the playing cards. "It's not a huge part but it's a very nice part" she half-apologised, as casting directors invariably do. She didn't need to. I knew that the production company, Hallmark, were involved in making high quality, big budget adaptations of classic English books, and they did them well. They followed a simple formula. They adapted a much-loved book, hired actors who were not quite at the top of the Hollywood tree, spent a lot of money on lavish costumes and design, and got a good director in to ensure that the whole thing worked. Nick Willing directed *Alice*, and the formidable cast included Miranda Richardson, Whoopi Goldberg, Simon Russell Beale, Jason Flemyng and Robbie Coltrane.

The role of a playing card was not, as you might imagine, an over-taxing one; once the croquet game was finished, I was left with a lot of time on my hands in my dressing room. I started to think about how best to use my time at Shepperton and hit on the idea of making a short video film of my own. I decided to make a sort of Ed Wood-style, low budget sci-fi spoof, originally limiting myself to only filming in my dressing room, with two fellow actors, to see how creative and inventive we could be. I called the project *I, Morbius*; it seemed to have the appropriate fifties schlock ring to it. The intention was to film on a home-video camera a five-minute piece of nonsense, which we could show at the cast-and-crew party, the traditional get-together at the end of filming when the production company digs into what is left of the budget and hosts a party. Usually the stars are already off on another job, or heading to L.A. to berate their agents for *not* having another job lined up, but the supporting actors and the technical people will go almost anywhere for a free drink and a chicken drumstick.

Somewhere along the line, however, *I, Morbius* became an altogether different proposition. It became the reason I went in to work each day, far superseding *Alice in Wonderland* in importance. Indeed, whenever a second assistant director had the temerity to come to our dressing room to tell us we were required on set, it seemed like an unfortunate and unreasonable intrusion. Every night I wrote a script to shoot the following day and, gradually, the reputation of *I, Morbius* had spread throughout the entire cast and crew. To be offered a cameo part in it became something of a seal of approval. The story had expanded from a sci-fi spoof to a hard-boiled, absurdist *film noir*, complete with space ships, crazed intergalactic tyrants, a fifty-foot woman and the bloody body of a transvestite in the shower.

I coaxed Miranda Richardson into playing the shaven-headed Supreme Leader of the World, wrote her a speech and even directed the former Oscar-nominee in her performance in her dressing room. She didn't need much direction, it must be said. She is a supremely talented and instinctive actress. Probably the best of her generation. Not locked into any stylistic straitjacket, she can play glam or dowdy, comic or straight, and possesses an intensity rarely found in English actresses. Simon Russell Beale and the young American actress playing Alice, Tina Majorino, sat in a car and quaked with fear as the 50-foot woman rampaged through our set, and Jason Flemyng, hot from *Lock Stock and Two Smoking Barrels*, played Jackie Herz, our hard-nosed Pittsburgh cop. His performance was only slightly undermined by the fact that, since he was playing the Jack of Hearts in *Alice*, he was obliged to have his wig in curlers for most of his scenes.

As the project spiralled out of control, I started writing cameo parts for friends outside of *Alice*. Marie Helvin played an embittered, drunk supermodel fabulously. In October in New York, I filmed Tony Torn, the son of the American actor Rip Torn and a very good actor in his own right, as the Tourette's syndrome-afflicted husband of the Supreme Leader. We shot his improvised scene in a supermarket on Ninth Avenue and, typically for New York, no one batted an eye as he ranted and raved and pushed his trolley down the aisles, dressed only in a dressing gown and sneakers.

You will understand why the project collapsed under the weight of its ambition, and why there are now nine hours of rushes sitting accusingly in a cupboard, awaiting editing. I also wanted Cristina to play a bed-ridden, heavily-bandaged, cosmetic-surgery patient but, typically, she couldn't quite fit it in with her social calendar. It was especially galling, as I had already splashed out on the bandages at the Duane Read drugstore on Broadway. She did, however, tell me that Michael Zilkha, by now her former husband and the man who signed me to ZE Records, had recently sold his 12-year-old oil business, Zilkha Energy, for $1 billion.

The reason I was in New York for October was to attend the opening of an exhibition of mainly unseen paintings by Francis Bacon at Tony Shafrazi's Soho gallery. The private view for the show of these ghoulish slices of Bacon was held on Halloween, 31 October. Now, the Americans celebrate Halloween in a way that leaves the Brits open-mouthed. They love to get into devil costumes, witch costumes, skeleton costumes, ghost costumes, with a fervour rarely seen outside of Mexico. When they are not in the traditional costumes of the festival, they dress as rock stars, movie stars or pieces of furniture. In London, no self-respecting trendy would go to a high-profile cultural event in costume, for fear of *not* being recognised. In New York they don't give a damn. In fact, they relish it. This made star-spotting at the private view a hazardous affair. "Is that someone dressed as a dead Lou Reed over there, or does Lou Reed *really* look that bad?"

In a fabulous moment of absurdity, there was a call to the gallery from Leonardo diCaprio's publicist saying, "Leo will be coming to the show with three friends, and they will be dressed as the rock band, Kiss. Make sure the photographers know that is Leo, OK?" Tony's assistant took the call and duly alerted the paparazzi to the imminent arrival of the superstar. Sure enough, within 10 minutes a sleek limousine purred up alongside the gallery and four young men dressed as the rock band, Kiss, ran into the gallery. Flashbulbs popped, the costumed and masked quartet posed for the cameras, drank a glass of champagne and split.

The photographers were delighted – until, five minutes later, another limo drew up outside the gallery and another, visibly different version of Kiss sprinted, as best they could on eight-inch platforms, the five yards required to get them into the sanctuary of the gallery. Once again flashbulbs popped and the costumed and masked quartet posed for the cameras, drank a glass of champagne and split. Of course, ultimately, it didn't matter which version of the band were plastered across the gossip columns of the next day's newspapers, as they were all masked anyway, so long as the name Leonardo diCaprio appeared underneath the picture, but the nature of celebrity is such that, at that point in time, it was a matter of life and death.

UP AGAINST IT

At dinner at Malcolm McLaren's house in Fitzrovia one night, Malcolm was enthusing about *The Beelzebub Sonata*, and suggested the next play we should do was Joe Orton's *Up Against It*, the screenplay that he wrote for the Beatles to film, but which so scandalised Paul McCartney and Brian Epstein that it was shelved and all but forgotten. Malcolm suggested that he would like to co-produce it with Duncan and myself in the West End, which sounded a feasible idea at the time. The play was way long since out of print, but I managed to track down a copy of it by finding the office of Orton's former agent, Peggy Ramsay, who had died in 1991. The office still handled Orton's estate and they managed to find a scorched, xeroxed copy for me in a back room. I told that I was thinking of putting it on in London but I didn't mention Malcolm. His name closes as many doors as it opens. I had it copied and went through it with Duncan.

It was clear that a lot of re-writing would be necessary, as it had dated quite badly in places, although it had been scurrilous at the time it was written. It illustrated how far the barriers of taste and decency have been pushed back since the sixties, and how little respect there now is for any form of authority, whether it is for the Monarchy, the Church, politicians, teachers or the police. We all know too much about them, we have seen their feet of clay and we are unimpressed. The play would have needed a large injection of polemic to carry its lunatic narrative through, but we decided it was worth looking at.

Typically though, Malcolm had other ideas. He telephoned the agent for Orton's estate and bought the theatre rights of the book for one year for £1500, so preventing anyone else from staging the play for that period of time. He had had a few discussions with Duncan prior to that, suggesting that he had got Alan McGee, the owner of Creation Records and the man who discovered Oasis, interested in the project. Duncan and Malcolm were slowly edging me out of the picture, but Duncan didn't realise that he was expendable too. With Malcolm holding the theatre rights, (and, knowing Malcolm, I can't imagine it was *his* £1500 which secured them) he was free to take the play to anyone he chose to direct it. He saw the artistic director of one of the large West End theatres who asked, "Who is this Duncan Ward? Is he an integral part of the package?" To which Malcolm, of course, answered "No." Malcolm can't help it. He is like the scorpion in the story who just has to sting. It's in his nature. He is totally untainted by morality. He even explained to Duncan that it wasn't personal, just business.

I must admit he made Duncan and me look like we were sixth-form students trying to put on a show. He told us he had got Oasis, at that time the biggest rock band in Britain, interested in writing an original score for the play, and that it was "All systems go!" All systems went, the year expired and neither I nor Duncan, neither Malcolm nor Alan McGee, neither Oasis nor any large West End theatre put on Joe Orton's *Up Against It*. But for Duncan and me it was certainly a steep learning curve.

Malcolm is an interesting, engaging but very slippery guy. I think that he actually has very little genuine creative talent of his own, but possesses an incredible knack of finding and working with people who have. And he is an undisputed master of marketing and packaging. He pontificates on every social trend as it comes along and has almost become a brand name for youth punditry. For the last 25 years he has managed to carve out a lucrative career as the former manager of The Sex Pistols. *Manager*, mind you. He wasn't even Johnny Rotten. That is impressive. Did The Sex Pistols change the world of pop? Look at the charts today and you tell me.

In the space of about three months in 1999, I worked on three new films: a Scandinavian film called *Aberdeen*, a filmed version of the Martin Amis book, *Dead Babies*, and the embarrassing *Guest House Paradiso*, by television comedians Rik Mayall and Adrian Edmondson. I found it very depressing working on that film, as Rik and Ade had been around at the beginning of the eighties when I was running Cabaret Futura, and they had been at the vanguard of so-called alternative cabaret. Now they, and many of their colleagues from those days, are just part of a self-satisfied, self-congratulatory New Establishment, furnishing lucrative and untaxing advertising jobs for the boys (and girls).

Rik and Ade, Dawn French (what *would* her gag be if she wasn't fat?) and Jennifer Saunders (Mrs. Ade Edmondson), Lenny Henry (Mr. Dawn French) and the rest, all huddle around the trough of formulaic television light entertainment. On the rare occasions that they *do* have an amusing idea, like *Absolutely Fabulous* or *The Young Ones*, for example, they milk the idea till the poor beast can no longer stand, and their subsequent series totter and lurch like so many *milch*-cows in the latter stages of BSE. Most sickening of all this group, big head and shoulders above the rest, there is Ben Elton, that porky, smug, oily hypocrite, in a *mélange à trois* with those other great champions of the "alternative": Rupert Murdoch and Andrew Lloyd Webber. Is there anything he would not do for a pay cheque? It can only be a matter of time until he agrees to write the libretto for the album *A Birthday Tribute to Margaret Thatcher*. The legacy of this cartel is poisonous. Nowadays British comedy only ever seems to mean television comedy, and if it doesn't start there, that's what it aspires to and that's where it ends up.

We are the soft generation. Lippy, trippy and amoral. We invented the protest movement, environmentalism, feminism, drugs and the media (we think) but none of us ever had to get into a uniform. None of us ever had to carry a gun. Instead we became cynical, ironic and post-modern. And we will reap the whirlwind for that.

After filming the not-hilarious *Guest House Paradiso* I did a TV crime-thriller called *Breathtaking*, which starred the darkly beautiful Joanne Whalley, in which I played a pathologist. We shot the scenes in a real mortuary in Kingston that was rented out to TV and film companies for a fee to help make ends meet. It was a very macabre job. As we arrived at the start of every day, the mortuary technicians would be knocking off from the night shift, closing huge metal drawers, each of which contained a human cadaver under-going autopsy, into the chiller. These technicians, like their kinfolk, the undertakers, almost invariably have a morbid sense of humour, which they offset by wearing novelty waistcoats or flashy ties. There was a human brain, punctured by a neat bullet hole, in what looked like a goldfish bowl filled with oily formaldehyde. It stood on a shelf with a label attached, which said "Carole Taylor – 32 years female – Murder. Do not dispose of". Beneath it someone had written "Not tonight darling. I've got a terrible fucking headache" It was in my eye-line the whole time I was there.

THE OLD MAN OF STRATFORD-UPON-AVON

It is important for me to keep getting away from music, so that I can return to it afresh. You will have noticed throughout this story that I can never let music go completely. I can never draw a line under it and move on. It troubles me and eats away at me. I never leave home without a notebook in my pocket, and barely a day passes in which I don't scribble a couple of lines of a song into it, which I hope I will one day develop. Back in London again, David Coulter telephoned me from Stratford-upon-Avon, where he and Sarah-Jane now live. He asked me whether I would like to come and give a lecture at the college where he was now teaching music, and of course I agreed without a second thought.

David asked me to talk to the students for about an hour, illustrating my talk with some slides and video clips, and warned me to be prepared for lethargy and disinterest. I prepared a few bullet points, and started to remember a few stories that might amuse them. As one story triggered the memory of another, I felt the lecture starting to turn into something more ambitious – and here we are.

However, that Monday morning in September, armed with a few pages of notes and some videotapes and slides, I drove up to Stratford-upon-Avon, so terrified at the prospect of an embarrassing hour with a room full of 18- and 19-year-olds that my hands were actually trembling. David noticed the state I was in and was both amused and sympathetic. He said, "You have played gigs to thousands of people at a time, worked with Jack Nicholson, opened clubs, done a world tour of *Hamlet*, yet you are trembling like a leaf at the prospect of addressing 16 teenagers. Why?"

I didn't really know why but I suspected that it was something to do with the nature of pop being a young man's game. As I stood at the lectern as the first students filed in, looking hungover, bleary-eyed and scratching their arses, I felt, for the first time in my life, like an "old geezer" about to give a lecture. I was reminded about what Balzac said about Paris, and it seemed perfectly apposite to my relationship with pop in that room. He said [of Paris] "there are only two ages – youth and decay. A bloodless, pallid youth and a decay painted to seem youthful." I didn't need reminding which category *I* fell into.

David had asked me to combine my anecdotal material with information for students considering a career in music. (how about "Don't"?), and we discussed the possibility of doing some writing–recording–performing workshops. The format we hit upon was the following. The 16 students could all play instruments so we split them into three groups. I divided my new material into three generic styles, "weird", "dark" and "rock", and asked each group which style they would like to interpret. I was lucky. They each chose differently. I gave the three groups four of my new songs each, and told then to work on arrangements for the next week, with the only proviso being that the finished song must be in my vocal range so that I could sing it with them.

I rehearsed with each of the three groups separately and it was astonishing how much flair, invention and sheer technical expertise some of these students had brought to the songs. They were still half-formed, but were sounding so full of promise that David and I suggested we do a couple of concerts at the college a fortnight later to present the work to an audience. I put some visuals together and played with each of the three bands in turn, culminating with a massed band of 16 young men and women, plus David and Sarah-Jane Morris all on stage together for a raucous finale, full of righteous religious fervour, called *This Lifelong Sinner*. It rekindled all my love of live performance. I wanted to document the work we did for posterity so I took all the students into a 16-track studio outside Stratford; in the course of a week we recorded 11 songs and mixed them in two days. David and I co-produced, and it was one of the most enjoyable recording sessions I have ever been involved in. We called the band, unironically for once, "Happiness".

The Colony Room is a drinking club in Soho which had been frequented by all the Soho bohemians in the fifties and sixties when London's licensing laws made it impossible to get a drink legally for most of the hours of the day. The Colony was where Francis Bacon, Dylan Thomas, Jeffrey Bernard and countless other legendary London drinkers went to find out-of-hours succour, and it had been taken up again recently as a refuge from the nearby Groucho Club by the new London bohos. Damien, Tracey Emin and Sarah Lucas had all hosted evenings there, and now it was time for Ben Langlands and Nicki Bell to take their turn behind the hallowed bar in the cramped, green-painted first floor room. They asked me to sing a few songs, and I played a few of the bitchy topical songs I had recently written about the London art scene, and they went down predictably well. There was a regular clientele for those shows that crossed all age groups. I played alone or with Minnie Weisz, Rachel's sister, who is a natural cabaret chanteuse, Alex James, the bass player from Blur, was a permanent fixture, as was Luke Haines, premiering his new band Black Box Recorder, who I liked enormously, not least because they reminded me of how Cristina might sound if someone made a new record with her. The comedian and poet Phil Dirtbox acted as MC and Anita Pallenberg, part of the sixties Rolling Stones inner circle, held court in the corner of the club and occasionally played bass guitar with her own band. They were amusing, lively and very lubricious evenings. You never tried to drive home afterwards.

* * *

Every once in a while my musical career gets some attention or some approval from totally unsolicited source. Out of the blue one day I got an e-mail from Julian Cope, the former leader of the Liverpool band of funsters, The Teardrop Explodes. Cope is a man who, over the years, has made my attempts at self-sabotage look positively amateur. He is engaging, bright, erudite and original. But he hit the chemistry set very hard in the eighties and that smell of burning is Julian's brain. In the e-mail he asked me to give him a call so that we could have a chat. Although we had never actually met, our paths had crossed frequently over the years. He had toured the USA with The Teardrops at the same time that I was touring solo, and he also worked with Ruth Polsky as his agent. In addition he had been an occasional visitor to Cabaret Futura, enjoying its egalitarian atmosphere and its lack of a VIP lounge.

I called him one afternoon and we clicked immediately, as if we had known each other forever. Although I don't much enjoy the telephone, we talked for a couple of hours, hardly drawing breath. He explained to me that he and his chums from the band, Spiritualized, had been talking about me recently, and had been going over the top about what an influential and seminal band The Doctors of Madness were. He told me that he was curating a "mini-Meltdown" festival at the South Bank Centre the following April, and wanted to build an homage to The Doctors in the foyer of the Queen Elizabeth Hall. On asking him what sort of homage, he explained, "I want to call it The Doctors of Madness – the smallest disco on Earth".

He went on to describe how he intended to build a structure the size of a large telephone kiosk, with a glass floor lit from underneath, *à la Saturday Night Fever*. The disco would only be large enough to accommodate two people at a time, and there would be two suited bouncers permanently stationed outside to ensure that there was no over-crowding. The music being played inside, he went on, would comprise only one track – The Doctors of Madness song, *The Noises Of The Evening*, from our first album, on an endless loop. The other component to the installation would be, with my permission, my old, broken KID-shaped electric guitar, now sadly in many pieces after bit of stage business with it went badly wrong. The fragments of the guitar would be set into a glass cased, lined with pink fake fur. Once finished it would be displayed like a reliquary of St Kid of Tooting Bec.

As you might imagine, I found the idea totally delicious and agreed to co-operate. We talked further about our lives in general, and he told me of the books he had written: two volumes of autobiography and a lovingly researched and well-informed volume called *The Modern Antiquarian*, which contained Julian's photographs and descriptions of every megalithic site in Great Britain. He told me he would send the three books by the next post and was as good as his word – they arrived a few days later. The two autobiography volumes, called *Head On* and *Repossessed* were now twinned into a single book, and inside he had inscribed "For The Kid – With great love from one outsider to another. Love on Ya! Julian", which I found very touching.

He drew my attention to certain chapter headings, as if to demonstrate his sincerity – and I was intrigued that they included "Kid Strange", "Urban Blitz", "Peter di Lemma" and "Stoner", plus "Mainline trains could never find drivers to run a service out to here", the refrain from our song, *Mainlines*. I enjoyed his books a great deal. He has a lively style and writes with an energy and dynamism that carry the reader along on his bumpy, often hilarious, sometimes heart-breaking, ride. At the end of the telephone conversation we agreed to stay in touch. It was good to have made contact with him after so long, and he is one of those people whose energy and enthusiasm and individual take on things leaves you feeling inspired and high for hours after you hang up the phone.

As the millennium drew to a close, many of my friends were providing the artistic content for a structure by the river at Greenwich, which was to become one of the most vilified public buildings ever – the Millennium Dome. It seemed that everyone we knew was on the Dome gravy train, Langlands and Bell, Richard Wilson, the architects Nigel Coates and Philip Gumuchdjian, and every one of them had a horror story to tell of the management, the organisation or the lack of care. The most common public criticism of the Dome was its cost. And the objection was always the same – "They could have built 20 hospitals/schools/libraries (fill in the gaps yourself) for that money." The criticism was true but, I felt, invalid. No country can *ever* afford a one-off vanity building project like the Dome. There are always so many other things that need to be built. But every once in a while I think a nation has to say "Sod it! We can't afford it, but we'll do it anyway." Otherwise all that is left to architectural posterity are hospitals, libraries and schools.

I loved those caring, sensitive nineties. Who can forget the tears of the footballer Paul Gascoigne, the spoilt, cry-baby booked for a reckless foul in the World Cup, and realising he would be playing no further part in the competition? Or those of the ousted Margaret Thatcher, given the heave-ho by an ungrateful Tory party as she left Downing Street for the last time? The effect of their tears was only spoiled by the fact that they were both crying for themselves out of self-pity. To paraphrase Oscar Wilde, you would have needed a heart of stone not to laugh your head off at those two. And God, how we laughed.

The eighties had begun the cult of celebrity, which then snowballed down the hill of the nineties and crashed bloated and hideous into the millennium. The page three girls, the bingeing anorexic soapstars, the soccer player, obscenely rich and weeping for his lot, the corrupt politician, the serial killer, the victim, the dangerous dogs, the terrorists and the paedophiles, the dysfunctional minor royal, the Duchess of York, the coke sniffing, gun-toting rapper and the queer TV comedian. The vulgar prurience at the trough, all was tarted up by the press in the fancy-dress of public interest.

Charlotte and I saw out the old and saw in the new at Bardrochat, enjoying the company of friends and watching the celebrations as they were beamed in on TV from around the world as the new millennium dawned gradually on Earth, first in Australasia and then, like a creeping damp patch on a wall, across Asia, Europe and Africa, and finally the Americas. That night, Alexander McEwen and I took out our guitars and sang the same songs we sang every year, except that I added a millennial rant of my own, called *The Time Is Now*.

The time is now, the time is now. As the countdown on the clock begins
The seconds tick, the planet spins out of control
The time is now, the time is now, And the only things on the lifestyle page
Are therapy and urban rage and fake plastic soul.
And as we reach the last few hours will the streets be full of blood and flowers
Will flashy showbiz grief turn out the light?
Or will all the trash at last be gone, Mariah Carey and Celine Dion
Like garbage sacks left outside overnight?

The Millennium and Beyond

TRULY BLESSED

For Charlotte and I, the beginning of the New Year was taken up with making preparations for a month-long trip to India in February. Before we departed I got another call form Julian, asking how he could get hold of my broken guitar so that it could be entombed. As we were talking, I realised that his event sounded like so much fun that I wanted to be involved personally, rather than merely being commemorated by a monument. He was thrilled when I suggested that I do a short set of Doctors songs, which I would re-arrange for myself and David Coulter to perform. The date was set for 1 April at the Queen Elizabeth Hall and, when we left for India in February, it was good to know that I had that show to look forward to when I got back.

The trip to India exceeded all our expectations in terms of beauty, diversity, cultural richness and human suffering. I was astonished to see how much Charlotte loved the place, as it must have seemed much more foreign to her than it did to a Brit. We were cushioned from the most abject horrors of poverty and disease by our very circumstances, as relatively affluent tourists who, when everything got too much, could retire to a comfortable hotel with clean sheets and cool drinks.

We spent our first days in Bombay, slowly acclimatising to the scale, the bustle and the apparent chaos of India. We met up with Beezy Bailey, a South African painter, who was staying at the same hotel as us. "We are a tribe," he declared as soon as we met. "We are scattered all across the world but we will always find each other because we are destined to." Beezy was a very amusing, very personable man given to flamboyant dressing and intense conversation. He came from one of the wealthiest families in South Africa and, like all South African white liberals, carried a huge amount of guilt.

In Jaipur, we met up again with Beezy. By now, he was with his American friend, a larger-than-life goddess called Betsy de Lotbiniere, who was in India researching a book. We hit it off before we had even opened a bottle. She is a wise and perceptive woman, a refreshingly original poet, who turned out to be one of the greatest jewels we found in India. She is a woman with an enormously generous spirit and a sharp, New York wit, who enlivens every gathering and enriches any room by her sheer presence and *chutzpah*. She and Beezy were staying in a funky, faded palace, and on blood-warm evenings we sat on their roof, sipping whisky and listening to the desperately romantic sounds of an Indian wedding party wafting up from the gardens below.

Once back home, Coulter and I re-arranged four or five Doctors songs, using a variety of instruments and styles. I decided I would play *Mainlines, Waiting, Sons Of Survival, Mitzi's Cure* and *I Think We're Alone*. Coulter played violin, omnichord, musical saw and percussion, and the songs sounded fresh and crisp.

I still hadn't met Julian at this point, but when I went along to the South Bank to check out the space I knew that he would be there. He was. But as soon as he saw me he fled. I was puzzled. He sent a message of apology later, explaining that I am such a huge figure in his life that he was freaked-out when I arrived, and felt unprepared to meet me. I thought it was a little over dramatic, as I do not really subscribe to the "We are not worthy" ideal, but Julian is a fanatic. Indeed, he once compiled an album called *The God-like Genius of Scott Walker*, which gives some idea of how seriously he takes the idolatry thing. I expected to see him the following day at the gig and didn't take a great deal of notice. People react to pressure in different ways and I imagine that Julian was under a lot of pressure getting this particular gig into some sort of shape. In addition to the music, there were the installations and a commemorative double CD to organise.

The gig itself was a revelation for David and me. Doctors fans from all over Europe had come for this rare performance of old songs and, roaring their approval, they sang along, often remembering the words to the songs better than me. Rene and Geno were in the audience, as well as many friends. Afterwards everyone came back to our house for a small celebration.

In London, there was a political storm brewing at this time. As the deadline approached for the parties to announce their candidates for the mayoralty of London, it became clear that the Prime Minister, Tony Blair, was determined that his man, the dull, uncharismatic, gnome-like Frank Dobson, should stand as the Labour Party candidate, despite the far greater popular support for his rival, the London-born Ken Livingstone. Livingstone, a former leader of the defunct Greater London Council, was forced to declare himself an independent candidate and was expelled from the Labour Party.

To add extra spice to the contest, the Tories were going through similar dramas, though these were caused by the arrogance and mendacity of their prime candidate, the novelist, liar and adulterer Lord (Jeffrey) Archer, who was forced to withdraw from the fray when it was announced that he was to be tried for perjury in an earlier libel case he had brought against a British newspaper. (Archer is a dreadful man. Whichever of his many diaries you read will attest to the fact that he was at Lord's cricket ground for a game in the 1999 Cricket World Cup. I know this for sure because I was in a hospitality box with some friends, and could hear Archer's irritating, high-decibel bray from his box 100 yards away, above the noise of a packed house of 25,000 spectators. They say you can tell a lot about men from the company they keep, and if someone had bazooka-ed that self-satisfied box at that moment, we would have lost Archer, David Frost, Richard Branson, Melvyn Bragg and Michael Parkinson. Wouldn't that have been awful?)

To complete the mayoral election circus, none other than my old friend, Malcolm McLaren, announced that he, too, was standing as an independent candidate. Only a cynic would suggest that his entry into the race had anything remotely to do with the fact that he was also about to pitch his autobiography around the leading publishing houses of the world, and that he had been out of the public eye for some time. Shortly before polling day McLaren withdrew from the race. Again, only a cynic would suggest that his withdrawal from the race had anything remotely to do with the fact that he was registering only 2 per cent popular support in the most favourable opinion polls. Livingstone, my old school fellow from Tulse Hill, romped home by a huge margin, in a campaign distinguished only by the embarrassing ineptitude of the two major parties.

SAM TAYLOR-WOOD

Because of the scurrilous nature of some of the songs I was writing and performing about my art world chums, it was with some trepidation that I opened a letter from the artist Sam Taylor-Wood one Monday morning. The tone of the letter was delightful and cordial, and asked whether I would be gracious enough to pose for her for a huge piece of corporate art that she was producing for the Oxford Street department store, Selfridges's. As the store was undergoing a total facelift, Sam had been commissioned to create a massive photographic work that would cover the scaffolding, seven storeys high, and would stretch around the entire block that Selfridge's occupies. She explained that she wanted to take a panoramic interior shot, using some groupings and poses from art history, but updated into a contemporary setting. The project sounded fun and I agreed. We shot it at the Peacock House, in Holland Park, a sumptuous Arts and Crafts townhouse built, ironically, by the founder of another great Oxford Street store, Lord Debenham.

When I arrived at the house on the Saturday of the shoot, I was astonished to see the cast that she had assembled, and was rather touched that she had asked me to join in. She had invited about 50 actors, musicians, models and faces-about-town, including Elton John, Richard E. Grant, Ray Winstone, Timothy Spall, Jodie Kidd, Jane Horrocks and Alex James. A lavish banquet was laid on for us in lieu of payment, and rail after rail groaned under the weight of clothes, which had been brought from the store to dress us in. Sam arranged us in groupings in the hallway of that magnificent house and, with the camera on a slowly revolving tripod, she photographed us all together and then in smaller groupings, which she would manipulate on the computer later. All the while her husband, the art dealer, Jay Jopling, suave and unflappable amid the good-humoured chaos, chatted to the participants, sipped champagne and offered words of encouragement to his wife, whom he clearly adores. Despite their infuriating descents in to the vapid world of the *Hello*-fuelled fame-fests, I really like Sam and Jay. She is grounded, feisty and as brave as we all would like to be in the face of her appalling illness, and he is wry, witty and loyal.

The finished work looked down on Oxford Street for six months, much to the delight of my mother, who would go and stand beneath my panel two or three days a week until some poor hapless stranger gazed up at my leaning, towering figure. She would immediately leap upon them and engage them in conversation, asking them what they thought of the work, and whenever they offered a few positive words she would smirk and announce, "That's my son." Alex told me later that his mother had done exactly the same thing at the other end of the store, where *his* portrait was. We should, of course, have got the two proud mums together. It would have made the innocent passage along Oxford Street much quicker for those pedestrians who were forced to run the maternal gauntlet.

* * *

Considering the disappointment and sense of betrayal I felt when Duncan ditched me for McLaren after *The Beelzebub Sonata*, before he himself was ditched, I was surprised when he approached me to appear in his newest project, *Last Night,* a play based on the life and writings of the great French polemicist, writer and director, Antonin Artaud. Duncan and I had had our ups and downs over the years but I agreed to go to his first read-through of the play, at a disused sweatshop in Spitalfields. Once again many of the usual suspects were there – Roddy, Katrine, Demian and Janusz, plus a few new faces who Duncan had silver-tongued along. Marie Helvin looked as bewildered as the rest of us as we read through the play for the first time. She told me she didn't know whether she was supposed to be reading or helping Duncan to fund-raise. Sometimes you just don't know with Mr Ward. Personally, I found it a disjointed, rather insubstantial piece, which seemed to speak more about Ward's psychic trauma than Artaud's. After a second reading it still was not doing anything for me, and that week I told Duncan that I wished him well but would not be available to participate.

A couple of days later I was telephoned by Danny Moynihan, Katrine's husband, who had been asked by Duncan to mediate with me and persuade me to do it. He told me that I was an essential part of the company, that without me the play would still go ahead but it wouldn't be as much fun. Like most actors I am a sucker for flattery, so reluctantly and against my instincts agreed to do it, and committed myself to working as hard as I could to trying to get it right.

When we started rehearsals at the Chopra Factory, the sweatshop that would be our theatre, it was clear from the outset that some things had changed in the way Duncan worked and some hadn't. The play itself was the familiar concoction – two parts Artaud, one part Kantor, one part Complicité, one part Ward, but the vibes were bad from the start. Whereas on *Beelzebub* Duncan had swept the entire cast along with his enthusiasm and had made everyone feel integral and irreplaceable, in *Last Night* we all felt undervalued, like marionettes who were only engaged as a means to an end, and that end was the advancement of Duncan's career.

On *Last Night* Duncan's egomania was his undoing. Part of the problem was that Duncan, who had been a golden boy, full of potential, at the age of 30, was now much nearer 40 and his career had not been as meteoric as he had wished. I understand what it means to under-achieve. It is the only thing I have over-achieved at in my life. I know how easy it is to shrug it off at 30, with your whole life still ahead of you and the high octane mix of recklessness and optimism still very much coursing though your veins. During the entire rehearsal period, the prime motivating force for Duncan seemed to be desperation, which was not very attractive.

There is a strange inverted correlation between how much you pay an actor and how hard he works. In my experience the hardest I have ever worked on a play or film has been on those occasions when there has been least prospect of a financial return. It is a love of the piece and the pride in one's work that gets the best results. *Last Night* was unable to instil that love and pride, and consequently the actors, all of us, started to whinge and became resentful. When you have no confidence in the piece you are doing, it is impossible to sell it to an audience except in the most shallow way. The actor who was playing Artaud, Rupert Procter, was a sensationally gifted, totally committed actor of extraordinary intensity, and managed to overcome many of the problems that the text posed. The rest of us were like satellites around his performance, and because all the satellite parts were under-written, we all felt under-used and superfluous.

Duncan, writer, director, co-producer and even, by the end, performer, could not or would not take criticism or suggestions from his cast, even though the most successful sections of *Dead Men Don't Remember* and *Beelzebub*, as well as the Grabbe piece, had been devised through a collaborative, improvisational way of working, rather than the dictatorial methods Ward was employing here. Katrine, who had worked with me on Duncan's projects before and found them challenging and hard, but nevertheless fulfilling, was at the end of her tether. She no longer trusted Duncan's methods or his motives, and although we saw the piece through to performance, it was not a job I remember with any enjoyment or sense of satisfaction. Duncan felt that I was being disruptive or disloyal whenever I voiced misgivings, but I honestly felt that I had the best interests of the work at heart. It was never going to be a piece which launched a thousand careers, but I still wanted it to be as good as it could possibly be.

The action of the play was set in the asylum where Artaud died in 1948, having been a voluntary patient for two years following almost a decade of confinement at various sanatoriums. The haunted figure of Artaud was assailed in his imaginings by two distinct groupings. One group was of three versions of his own mother, all seemingly uncaring but beautifully groomed, dressed in black cocktail dresses. No wonder someone described it as like watching a Robert Palmer video directed by Bertolt Brecht. The other grouping was of three generals, seemingly fused at the hip into some diabolical military machine. Roddy played Artaud's doctor and I played his agent, whom Artaud frequently assaulted in an extremely violent way.

Visually it was occasionally stunning and the Chopra Factory contributed in no small part to the *mise en scène*, with its bare, whitewashed walls and huge institutional windows looking over the rooftops of the East End. While Artaud's impassioned plea is for "an end to the subjugation of the theatre to the text", it was the very inconsistency and scrappiness of the text that ultimately sabotaged the play. Duncan had taken chunks of Artaud's own writings and deconstructed them into an absurdist whole. The trouble with absurdism, of course, is a fairly crucial and unavoidable one: If everything is possible, nothing really matters.

Once again we were supported principally by our loyal friends who came along to fly the flag and we performed a dozen or so shows before closing. I said goodbye to Duncan and regretted that I had not trusted my instincts and stayed out of the play. It might have preserved our friendship.

* * *

That summer, Charlotte and I holidayed on the Monte Argentario, off the Italian coast, to relax and recuperate. We were joined by a whole contingent of friends from New York. Our house guests included Vicki Wickham, a great English lady who is slightly eccentric, but unselfconsciously so, given to sensible shoes and good advice, and one of the Great Women of Pop. Vicki had been the producer of the seminal British TV pop show, *Ready, Steady, Go!*, in the sixties, then she had gone on to produce live concerts at the Saville Theatre with artists like Jimi Hendrix. She went on to manage Dusty Springfield, and now manages Marc Almond and Morrissey.

Vicki arrived with her girlfriend, Nona Hendryx, the amazing black soul diva, who had been a part of the flamboyant R'n'B act, LaBelle, in the eighties, the girl group that first recorded the perennial *Lady Marmalade*. Nona is an enviably bright woman with a great sense of humour and an energy for work that is almost criminal. When she wasn't making a fiery salsa for some tuna fish, she was teaching an old LaBelle dance routine to half a dozen guests on the terrace under the shooting stars.

We also invited the Armenian architect, Philip Gumuchdjian, Jane Withers and Ilaria Benucci, Charlotte's fabulously leonine Italian girlfriend. Ilaria is like a Renaissance Bond girl, someone who can catch a deep-sea fish with a rod and line and then cook it to perfection, at the same time as mixing a perfect Martini and practising her dance-steps in the kitchen – all the while dressed in a white bikini. Later arrivals included Richard Branson's sister, Vanessa, an art dealer, who is the most powerful sea swimmer I have ever known, a veritable Captain Webb, and Howell James, who was John Major's former special adviser and a man of awesome intellectual clarity and charm.

The warm, lazy days were spent swimming, reading and planning the evening's menu, and the evenings were spent over long dinners at the outside table, delicious fish and vegetables all locally produced, pepped up by heated arguments about some or other artist's work. Later I would play the guitar or we would dance hysterically on the terrace to a dreadful seventies disco CD that Howell had brought with him. It was so third-rate we ribbed him that he must have nicked it from Downing Street while he was working for John Major. In fact, we dubbed it *The Norma Collection* or *Now That's What I Call Norma*. Exhausted and worse for wear, we would flop out on our backs with grappa and watch the shooting stars bisect the black sky, luxuriating in real darkness, or mutely gaze out at the cruise ships as they slid across an inky horizon. The next day we would do it all again.

* * *

No sooner was I home from Italy than my friend Bea de Visser, the Dutch artist, telephoned me and told me about a short film she wanted to make about a man falling apart or, as she so delicately and quaintly put it, "a man who has temporarily lost his tracks". She wanted me to play that man, who delivers a monologue in a God-forsaken landscape. The film was called *The Barren Land*. I flew to Rotterdam and we discussed the script, which was loosely constructed from fragments of existing texts, into which she wanted me to introduce an improvised personal element. We tried different things out over a two-day period, wrote and re-wrote and eventually agreed on what might work and what might not. I introduced some stuff that was very personal to me, the sort of unfathomable things my Dad would say when he was "on one". *Non-sequiturs*, doggerel, clouded ideas, too personal to convey meaning, all were grafted on to Bea's original text. I was excited by the project because I trusted her aesthetic approach and her integrity. I had never worked directly with her before but I had always admired her as an artist and as a person, and I knew that she was capable of making this film work.

In September, we shot it on a wind-ravaged stretch of sandy reclaimed land on the very edge of Holland. It was the perfect location – tufted grass growing out the sand dunes, the slate grey sea in the background and a towering phalanx of turning, groaning wind turbines, like some bizarre Calvary Hill. Most of my action centred on a hole I was digging in the sand, part grave, part refuge, part hunt for long-lost treasure. I was the only character in the film so I was able to dictate the pace and the dynamic. It is very exciting and challenging for an actor to have to work in isolation, for all the dynamic of the film to have to come from him. It wasn't something I had ever done before and I took it as seriously as any job I have ever done.

We worked with a small crew and, although the filming was sometimes fraught, not least because of the intensity the part demanded, and Bea and I were often both exhausted by it, we enjoyed working together enormously. There was something wonderful about actually working together after having known each other for so long. The finished film was premiered at the Rotterdam Film Festival, with full Dolby surround sound, to great acclaim. It has subsequently been shown in film festivals in France, Germany, Spain and Canada, and now has world distribution.

* * *

I went straight from Bea's low-budget labour of love to something right at the other end of the movie scale. Once again, it was a call from Michelle that set everything in motion. It was simple enough. Martin Scorsese was shooting his new film, *Gangs of New York*, in Rome, and once again much of the secondary casting was being done in London. I went along to the London offices of Miramax, the production company, met the casting director and chatted for a while about the film and the characters she was looking to cast. Finally she put me on video, all the while keeping up a commentary on film for Scorsese who would receive the tapes by courier the following day.

For most actors, indeed for most cinema-lovers of my generation, Scorsese is the Big One; not every film he makes is a masterpiece, but his strike rate is a hell of a lot better than most. His films are an integral part of my personal cultural iconography. It was impossible to watch *Mean Streets* (1973) and *Taxi Driver* (1976) in my early twenties and not want to head immediately for New York. And once there, it was equally impossible not to see the city filtered, to some extent, through the eyes of Johnny Boy Cervello or Travis Bickle. Those films defined a certain New York at a certain time, just as Godard did with Paris in *A Bout de Souffle* or Fellini did with Rome in *La Dolce Vita*. Scorsese distilled the essence down into heady concentrate, like an overwhelming perfume.

I knew that working with Scorsese was a fantastic opportunity for me to get moving again professionally, and so I travelled out to Rome with mixed emotions of excitement and trepidation. I don't get fazed by these things usually, but this job definitely felt different. By the time I arrived at my hotel, a kitsch, country house hotel in the middle of nowhere, it was 8pm. I decided to get something to eat from the restaurant a little way down the hill. It is almost impossible to eat badly in a small, family-run local restaurants in Italy, and this place was no exception. In the restaurant I realised that I needed spectacles, as I held a menu so close to the table candle to try to read the small print that it went up in flames.

It was a delicious dinner, but I have an extreme aversion to eating alone. Dinner, especially, is a meal to be shared with others, with conversation a mandatory condiment. Without it, a good book becomes an essential companion, and I took Simon Frith's splendidly provocative book about popular music, *Performing Rites,* with me that evening. It was interesting to read about the use of music in films and it occurred to me how integral music in film has become in recent times. This is partly due to financial reasons – a film production company can earn a lot of money from sales of the soundtrack album of a film, and if there is a hit single featured, the promotional video will usually feature scenes from the film and will thus act as a rolling marketing tool. (I know this at first hand. I appeared in the wretched video for Bryan Adams's massive hit, *Everything I do (I do for you)*, from *Robin Hood, Prince of Thieves*. It was number one in the UK charts for something like 15 weeks. Every time it was shown on *Top of The Pops* it plugged the movie. After much activity on the part of both my agent and Equity, I eventually got a derisory, one-off payment of about £700 from the film production company for my brief appearance in the video, flaming arrow in head and all. They insultingly referred to it as a "goodwill payment". (Ha, some goodwill.)

In addition to the marketing angle, the integral use of music in a movie means that the film's producers can sometimes persuade a record company to stump up some cash for the development or production of a film with the promise of a share of the rights for the sound-track album. All this goes some way to explaining why *Batman 2,* for example, has music playing through something like 93 per cent of the movie. Outside of a discotheque, you hear more music per hour at the cinema than anywhere else on Earth!

Obviously, not all film music comes from the world of pop. It is a curious fact that a lot of music that would not have a life in the concert hall is heard uncomplainingly by millions of cinemagoers worldwide every week. Music that is too "difficult" for radio, recordings or the auditorium goes down a treat when accompanying moving images on a screen, and no one ever heads for the exit at the cinema just because the music has gone 12-tone and weird. (Have you ever sat through the "difficult" music of Penderecki and Ligeti? If you've watched Kubrick's *The Shining* you have.) The Polish-born composer, Janusz Podrazic, scored the music for the two plays I did with Duncan. Janusz is a serious composer who works principally in the rarefied atmosphere of the *avant-garde*, as any good East European composer should. (Although recently, by way of a lucrative distraction, he has been working with the delightful *chanteuse*, Sade.) Janusz strongly believes that music should *never* be used in film as he feels it cheapens and vulgarises the action on screen.

While I don't have an axe to grind one way or the other in this particular debate, I would argue with him that music is just one element of the film-making process, and that he might just as easily criticise costume, cinematography and even script-writing for exactly the same reasons. Certainly, music is frequently used to fill in the emotional gaps in a scene from a film, but costume and lighting are just as frequently used to cover the historical or atmospheric shortcomings, or to provide psycho-dynamics. The point, surely, is that there is too much *bad* music, *badly* used.

I digress. This happens when I dine alone. A book like Frith's will send me off on some tangential reverie and the next thing I know I have eaten a three-course dinner, had coffee and a cognac, asked for the bill and not tasted a single mouthful! I made my way back up the hill to my hotel, went to bed and slept badly. Not a good sign.

Next morning a car was sent to take me to Cinecitta Studios for a costume fitting. Cinecitta has an extraordinarily illustrious history. It was built by Mussolini in 1937, primarily for the production of propaganda films for the Fascists. By 1942, directors such Visconti and Rossellini were already directing films that used Cinecitta as a base, but the high point of the studio's golden age was really the fifties and sixties, when great historical epics such as *Quo Vadis?*, *Ben Hur* and *Cleopatra* were all produced on this plot of land on the south-east edge of Rome. As a result of the massive influx of acting talent that these extraordinary large-scale films drew into the city, the shops, hotels and bars of Rome were like a *Who's Who* of Hollywood glamour. Elizabeth Taylor, Richard Burton, Charlton Heston and Kirk Douglas were routinely spotted on the Via Veneto, along with the great home-grown stars such as Sophia Loren and Marcello Mastroianni. It was this period that Fellini chronicled in his great masterpiece, *La Dolce Vita*, which also utilised Cinecitta as its studio.

Once at the studio I was told that I would be working the following night but I was rather disappointed to be told that the scenes I was in had no dialogue. This was the first that I had heard of it. I had assumed that my role was a speaking part, since I had been asked to do accents at the casting back at Miramax in London. I felt quite deflated as I got back to my hotel and phoned Charlotte for a fix of commiseration.

The following morning I was awoken by a call from the front desk telling me that there was a fax for me. The production office had faxed me a script for the scene I would shoot that evening. Suddenly it was a speaking part again, albeit only a dozen or so lines long. I spent the morning learning it with an Irish accent, since I had been asked to use an Irish accent at the casting back at the Miramax offices in London.

I arrived at Cinecitta around four in the afternoon, got into costume then went into make-up. The make-up artist was fantastic, and after two hours in the chair he had aged me 20 years, with latex wrinkles and a grey moustache. On arriving back at my trailer, there was a knock on the door and an American guy told me he was the dialogue coach and asked if I would like to go over the lines with him. I told him that this would be very helpful and I gave him my 12 lines of Irish brogue. He said, "That's great, but I'm pretty sure that Marty wants the undertaker to be an American gent. By 1860, the job of an undertaker is highly respectable. It's not something that an immigrant just off the boats would do. So the accent by 1860 is recognisably American. Can you do it American?"

I was rather shocked by this revelation, as it is much harder to unlearn an accent than to learn one. It's like learning a song and then being told that the lyrics are staying the same but the melody has been completely changed; it is hard to shake off the residue of the melody you have learned. It has become ingrained in the words. The Irish kept coming back. The coach was very helpful and gave some good pointers and tips; after 45 minutes the American accent was adequate.

I went to check the set, which had been built on the back lot, and it was astounding. They had built a whole neighbourhood of 1860 New York, complete with a waterfront, docks and two full-sized three-masted ships tied up. Rowing boats ferried pieces of lighting equipment between the two of them. A thousand extras were milling around, and on the quayside hundreds of wooden coffins were being offloaded from the ships, representing the casualties of the Civil War returning north from the battlefields. In my scene my character, the under-taker, is hard-selling a grieving mother the most expensive and luxurious coffin that he has. We rehearsed several times with the first assistant to the director, sketching out the shot according to the director's storyboard – telling people where to walk, what to do, where the cameras will be and so on. I walked through the scene, slightly disconcerted by the fact that the grieving mother was being played by an Italian extra who spoke no English, rather than by an actual actress.

When the first assistant director was happy with the look of everything, he sent a message to the director and within a few minutes Martin Scorsese arrived. He is a very short, power-fully compact guy, like a street fighter, with busy, beetling eyebrows and darting dark eyes. He walked purposefully on to the set and exuded an impressive calm authority. He greeted me warmly and to my astonishment remembered who I was, what I had put on tape and that I had recently arrived from London. I was impressed that he did his background stuff so thoroughly. After all, I think I was number 62 on the cast sheet. That's a lot of actors' names and details to remember. We walked through it four or five times and shot it a couple of times. Marty (I'm sorry, but *everybody* calls him Marty) came up and said, "Richard, that's just great. I'm just sorting out a couple of problems with the lighting and the background action [extras] and we'll shoot it again. What you're doing is great. Enjoy it."

The next time we went for it, for some inexplicable reason, panic set in and nothing would stick in my mind. No two lines would hang together and the accent kept going. The Irish kept insinuating its way back into the vowel sounds. The terror of not knowing how a line that you have started will end is indescribable. It is like crossing a motorway blind-folded. It is the actor's greatest nightmare. Every single person on set is just waiting for you to deliver your 12 lines in order. The panic is far worse because it is Marty, of course, and I am desperate to impress. Surprisingly sensitive and understanding, he says, "It's OK, it's not a problem, just relax." But it's a bit like going to bed with a beautiful woman you've been pursuing for ages and when you are finally in the sack together you can't keep an erection. It doesn't matter how often she says, "Don't worry, darling, it doesn't matter," it doesn't help. It feels terminal. Marty tried to relieve all the pressure by calling an early lunch, but I didn't want to eat. I was mortified and wound up. Instead I stayed in my room and just kept going over the lines.

Sometimes the memory was a complete blank and I was staring at the script as if for the first time. The lines seemed to be sliding off the page. I tried them again, slowly. Part of my brain knew, for example, that the word "sacrifice" was coming, but my mouth formed the word "sacrilege" or "sarcophagus" or "secrecy", any word but the right one. It didn't improve with repetition. You solve one problem but, like a leaking pipe, a new one appears further down. When you watch that scene in the film, if it survives the editor's cuts, you will see a man drowning. You will see a man who looks in the mirror and sees no reflection. It is like something from an Edgar Alan Poe story. In 25 years of singing and acting I had never once frozen, either on stage or in front of the camera. I discovered that the feeling is excruciating and terrifying. You feel disembodied. You feel like screaming to the crowd, "I can do this!" but the facts attest otherwise. You are consumed by a terrible combination of shame and embarrassment, and an overwhelming desire to hide under a stone. You nurture the desperate hope that any second you will wake up and that reality will right itself

Because of some technical problems the break for lunch was followed by a delay of another couple of hours to fix a piece of equipment. By now it was 3am and my brain was getting tired and wanted to shut down. I took a nap and woke with a start to try out the words again, fearing that they had slipped away again while I slept. Mercifully, they were still there, and when we shot the scene the nerve held and we got through. It had been the worst day of my professional life and I wanted it to be the best. Marty said, "Thank you, that was great" and I was left wondering if he had already planned on cutting the scene from the final edit. I was unnerved and despondent. We have no control. They are out there to get us! Needless to say, for the rest of my stay in Rome I couldn't *forget* the bloody lines! I phoned Charlotte and told her what had happened. "Forget it, honey," she said, fabulous as always, "Everyone has the occasional bad day at the office." Of course she's right, but you just don't want to have your bad day at the office when Martin Scorsese happens to be visiting.

According to news that emanated from the studio floor, I escaped quite lightly. The previous week the star of the movie, Leonardo diCaprio, incurred the full force of Scorsese's famously tempestuous wrath in a 10-minute tirade on the studio floor, in front of the entire cast and crew. It was reported that Scorsese had lost patience with diCaprio's irresponsible and disrespectful attitude to his fellow professionals, which had manifested itself in the actor constantly arriving on set late for filming and looking "like a pile of shit". The film was getting behind schedule and that usually means that the producers start to get on the director's back.

I was told that Leo, the star of the huge hit movies, *Titanic* and *Romeo and Juliet*, as well as the superior *What's Eating Gilbert Grape!*, had been hitting the Rome nightclubs every night till the small hours with his current girlfriend, the voluptuous Brazilian supermodel, Gisele Bundchen. Rome, of course, invented both *La Dolce Vita* and the paparazzi so there was no shortage of photographic evidence of the young star's transgressions. When he arrived late and bleary-eyed once too often, the director went ballistic and savaged the boyish superstar to such a degree that he was reported to have been on the verge of tears. An Italian extra, who played a rival gang member, said: "I couldn't understand it all because he was speaking so fast but he was very angry. We didn't know where to look." It was also reported that diCaprio's subsequent time-keeping was impeccable.

I never did get back to Rome to shoot my second scene. By the time I should have been called they had already over-run by two months and were looking to cut whatever scenes were not essential to the plot, to try to claw back some of the spiralling costs. I was never sure whether my scenes would have been cut anyway, or whether I made such a hash of them that they decided not to use them. I got a message from Marty saying the stuff we had filmed had looked great, but that they just had to trim the film and my scene was just one of many that was excised. I will never know, but *Gangs of New York* will always feel like a golden opportunity, which, stone-cold sober, I blew.

* * *

Throughout the late nineties there was a disturbing trend towards a style of TV that was prurient, voyeuristic and, above all, cheap. Fly-on the wall programmes, set in hotels, the Royal Opera House, a provincial airport or in the car of a driving examiner, became the prime-time norm. They not only served to satisfy the gargantuan public appetite for prurient voyeurism, but also meant that programme makers no longer had to deal with two of the more capricious and "difficult" elements of the industry: writers and actors.

By 2000, the voyeurism had been augmented by sadism and the pub quiz. The TV show, *The Weakest Link*, was an inspired idea, tapping in perfectly to the TV-viewing *Zeitgeist*. It is a programmer's dream come true, combining the sadism of elimination TV models such as *Big Brother* (where a group of 20-somethings are forced into the Sartrian hell of sharing a house under the prying eye of a hundred television cameras) or *Popstars* (where tearful young hopefuls audition for the chance to be a member of an anodyne pop band) with the get-rich-quick, pub-quiz tack of *Who Wants to be a Millionaire?* Fronted by the steely Anne Robinson, who had a licence to be as rude and insulting to her contestants as she chose, she had the added good fortune to be given a memorable catchphrase, which quickly entered the vernacular as a multi-purpose put-down – "You are The Weakest Link. Goodbye".

On the back of these fly-on-the-wall and elimination TV shows, the most unremarkable people are thrown up as celebrities for a few short minutes. The programmes demonstrate how powerful the desire for celebrity is among even the most mild-mannered and diffident members of society. A disagreeable traffic warden or a gay airline steward can, if they want it badly enough, be a star for a couple of weeks, open a supermarket or have a life-style magazine come and photograph them in "their beautiful home". And in our wannabe world, most of them *do* want it badly enough. In the millennial world, where we believe in nothing, five minutes of fame means a lot. In the millennial world we have no politics, only celebrities and sound-bites. No wars, only neuroses, and no concerns, save with our own self-image and our body-fat ratio.

* * *

Born in January 1951, I lived through all but 24 days of the entire second half of the twentieth century. Did the world ever change so dramatically in 50 short years as it has done in my lifetime? Was there ever a 50-year long period of history before in which a fit and healthy Englishman has not had to join an army and fight against some or other European neighbour? To have been born in this peaceful window of history was sheer good fortune, for which my entire generation should give daily thanks. Taken all in all, I have been incredibly fortunate, using the tiny gifts I have been allotted by nurture and nature to live a life that is so rich, so full of experiences and laughter, of love, friendship and excitement. I know I have squandered chance after chance, through poor judgement, laziness or lack of ambition, yet still I am given another bite. The countless opportunities I have had and wantonly wasted come to others but once in a lifetime. I am ashamed, but powerless to undo what is done. I have snatched failure from the jaws of success.

* * *

On my fiftieth birthday, at a party hosted jointly by Charlotte and Brian Clarke at Brian's house, I am surrounded by my family and a hundred friends. I am overwhelmed. I tell them that I hope they will forgive me that the constraints of time dictate that I can only spend three-and-a-half minutes with each of them that evening. They forgive me. Betsy reads a poem she has written for me. I sing a song with Sarah-Jane because it's my party and I'll sing if I want to. I toast absent friends, dead and living, and gaze into the sea of faces and see Charlotte and Geno, and they are both beaming up so much love to me. Rene is there and so is Sophie. I am encircled by all these people who have meant so much to me, and for a short moment I think of my father, who never had a single friend, and I know I am truly blessed.

Bibliography

Kathy Acker   *Blood and Guts in High School*
Lisa Appignanesi   *Cabaret*
Teodor Adorno   *Essay on Cultural Criticism and Society in Prisms*
Samuel Becket   *First Love*
Samuel Becket   *Worstward Ho!*
Louisa Buck   *Moving Targets*
Louisa Buck   *Relative Values*
William Burroughs   *Junkie*
William Burroughs   *The Naked Lunch*
Louis-Ferdinand Celine   *Journey to the End of the Night*
Caroline Coon   *Sex Pistols Diaries*
Julian Cope   *Head On* and *Repossessed*
Philip Core   *Camp – The Lie that tells the Truth*
Tom Dewe Mathews   *Censored*
T.S. Eliot   *The Wasteland*
F. Scott Fitzgerald   *All The Sad Young Men*
Simon Frith   *Performing Rites*
Allen Ginsberg   *Howl*
Allen Ginsberg   *Kaddish*
Allen Ginsberg   *Reality Sandwiches*
Malcolm Gladwell   *The Tipping Point*
William A. Gordon   *Four dead in Ohio. Was there a conspiracy at Kent State?*
Graham Greene   *The Quiet American*
Christopher Isherwood   *Farewell to Berlin*
C.L.R. James   *Beyond a Boundary*
Nick Kent   *The Dark Stuff*
Jack Kerouac   *On the Road*
Jack Kerouac   *The Subterraneans*
Naomi Klein   *No Logo*
Hans-Joachim Maaz   *Der Gefühlsstau (The Emotional Bottleneck)*
George Melly   *Owning Up*
Ian McDonald   *Revolution in the Head: The Beatles Records and The Sixties*
George Monbiot   *Captive State*

Flann O'Brien	*The Third Policeman*
Tony Parsons and Julie Burchill	*The Boy Looked at Johnny*
Gary Pulsifer	The Guardian *Obituary to Kathy Acker*
William Penn	*Some Fruits of Solitude*
Friedrich Nietzsche	*Twilight of the Idols*
Julie Salomon	*The Devil's Candy – The making of Bonfire of the Vanities*
William Shakespeare	*Hamlet*
Iain Sinclair	*Lights Out for The Territory*
Evelyn Waugh	*Brideshead Revisited*
Emile Zola	*La Bête Humaine*

Songs quoted

Lyrics by Richard "Kid" Strange; published by Bryan Morrison Music:
*I Won't Run Away, Mainlines, Network, The Phenomenal Rise Of Richard Strange,
The Road To The Room, Suicide City, Triple Vision, Wild Times*

Lyrics by Richard Strange:
Next!

Lyrics by Richard Strange; published by Ausfahrt Musikverlag, Germany:
Banco Celestial
Damascus
Pioneering Surgery

Lyrics by Richard Strange; published by EMI Music, London:
The Ghost Of Brian Jones
God Help The Wealthy Man
Wake Up America
Waterlilies

All used by kind permission of the publishers

Index

14-hour Technicolour Dream (happening) 24
Abbey Road Studios 74-5, 76
Aberdeen (film) 261
Acker, Kathy 165, 172, 184, 217, 239, 245-6, 249, 251-2
Action Syndicate 187, 207
Adam and the Ants 149
    see also Ant, Adam
Adams, Bryan 219, 273
Advert, Gaye 85
Adverts, The 78, 83, 85, 86
Afrodiziac 158
Afterglow (song) 55, 57-8
Al Fayed, Dodi 246, 247
Al Fayed,Mohammed 247
Albion 145
Alice in Wonderland (film) 257-9
Alksnis, Anita Mara 101
Allen, Dave 157-8, 160, 171
Allen, Keith 112, 115, 123, 144, 254-5
Almond, Marc 114,271
Althorp, Charles, the Earl of Spencer 248
Amsterdam 33
Amstrup, Birgitte 28, 202
And Son Music 52
Ant, Adam 60
    see also Adam and the Ants
Anzilotti, Münzing and Schmitt 171
Appignanesi, Lisa 112-13, 144
Archer, Jeffrey 267
Arista Records 150, 151, 155, 158, 160, 161-2, 166, 167-8
Artaud, Antonin 269, 270
Ash, Leslie 227
Australia 206-9
Aylwood, Fred 172

B2 Gallery 143-4
"Back From The Dead" (song) 86
Backstreet Boys, The 242
Bacon, Francis 28, 259
Bailey, Beezy 266
Bailey, David 145-6, 153
Ball, Dave 114
Ban The Bomb marches 17-18
Barren Land, The (film) 272
Barrett, Syd 25, 46
Basinger, Kim 182, 183
Batman (film) 179-85, 195, 225, 273
Bausch, Pina 172
Bazooka Joe 60
BBC 8, 113, 133, 227-8
Beadle, Laurence 148
Beale, Simon Russell 258-9
Bearer, Paul 237
beat music 8, 13
Beatles, The 8, 13, 14-15, 25, 26, 32, 36
BeBop Deluxe 63-6, 68, 98
Beckett, Samuel 90, 169
Bee Gees, The 45, 47, 236
Beelzebub Sonata, The (play) 249, 253-5, 260, 269
Belgium 71
Belushi, James 237

Bentley, Colin see Stoner
Bentley, Elaine see Stoner, Elaine
Benucci, Ilaria 271
Berlin 88, 203-6, 219-21, 222-3, 224, 246
Berning, Dominic 254
Bidmead, David 42
Billington, Michael 197
"Billy Watch Out!" (song) 55, 57, 69
Birch, James 165, 221
Blackhill Enterprises 30
Blair, Hugh 95
Blair, Tony 267
Blake, Ian 110
Blake, Peter 146
Blancmange 112
Blitz Kids 119-20
Blitz, Urban 42-3, 44, 55, 56, 58, 60, 63, 64, 67, 68, 69, 72, 74, 75, 86, 87
Blondie 85
Blundell, Pam 256
"B-Movie Bedtime" (song) 55, 56
Bohn, Chris 92
Boltz (Steve Bolton) 100, 103, 125, 128, 136, 158, 160, 233
Boorman, John 254
Boorman, Katrine 253, 254, 255, 269, 270
Bouquet, Carole 254
Bowie, David 36, 37, 41, 48, 55, 100, 119, 166
Braidman, Alan 153
Braidman, Michelle 153, 165, 168, 170, 179, 184, 185, 199, 221, 223, 227, 230, 234, 239, 257, 272
Branson, Richard 32, 84, 115, 125-7, 159, 267
Branson, Vanessa 271
Breathtaking (TV crime thriller) 261-2
Bright, Spencer 164
Broadbent, Jim 228
Brolin, Tomas 250
Brooklands Rise residence 41-2, 76
Brooks, Bob 165
"Brothers" (song) 74, 75
Broughton, Pip 230-1
Bryars, Gavin 193
Bubbles, Barney 77
Buck, Bienvenida 222, 224
Buck, Louisa 162, 164-5, 202, 217, 220, 221-2, 224, 239, 240, 249, 250-1
Buck, Sir Antony 221-2, 224
Buckley, William F 14-15
"Bulletin" (song) 87
Bundchen, Gisele 277
Burchill, Julie 79, 80
Burdon, Eric 26
Burger, Demian 255-6, 269
Burns, Ray (Captain Sensible) 77, 90
Burns, Robert 149, 174
Burroughs, William 56, 245-6
Burton, Tim 179-80, 183
Byrne, David 85

Cabaret Futura 108, 111-18, 117, 120-29, 133-37, 139-44, 186, 261, 264
Cabaret Voltaire 88-9